Harvard Historical Studies · *133*

Published under the auspices
of the Department of History
from the income of the
Paul Revere Frothingham Bequest
Robert Louis Stroock Fund
Henry Warren Torrey Fund

Migration and the Origins of the English Atlantic World

ALISON GAMES

HARVARD UNIVERSITY PRESS

Cambridge, Massachusetts, and London, England | 1999

4156437

Copyright © 1999 by the President and Fellows of Harvard College
Printed in the United States of America

Library of Congress Cataloging-in-Publication Data

Games, Alison, 1963–   .
    Migration and the origins of the English Atlantic world / Alison Games.
        p.   cm. — (Harvard historical studies ; v. 133)
    Includes index.
    ISBN 0-674-57381-1
    1. New England—History—Colonial period, ca. 1600–1775.
2. Great Britain—Colonies—America—History—17th century.
3. West Indies, British—History—17th century.   4. New
England—Emigration and immigration—History—17th century.
5. West Indies, British—Emigration and immigration—History—
17th century.   6. Great Britain—Emigration and immigration—
History—17th century.   7. Immigrants—New England—History—
17th century.   8. Immigrants—West Indies, British—History—17th century.
9. Immigrants—Great Britain—History—17th century.   10. Ships—
England—London—Passenger lists.   I. Title.   II. Series.
    F7.G215   1999   99-26018

For my parents and Tim

Acknowledgments

What a pleasure to thank people and institutions formally for all the assistance I have received in researching and writing this book. I used a great number of libraries and archives in the course of this project and was welcomed everywhere by helpful staff. Most of these libraries are mentioned in the notes and bibliography, but let me thank especially the librarians and staff members at those institutions where I planted myself for considerable periods of time, including the New England Historic Genealogical Society, Widener Library, the Historical Society of Pennsylvania, the Library Company of Philadelphia, the Van Pelt Library at the University of Pennsylvania, the Folger Shakespeare Library, the Huntington Library, the Massachusetts Historical Society, the Virginia Historical Society, and the Virginia State Library and Archives. Jon Kukla and other then-members of the publications staff at the Virginia State Library opened for me the files and indexes of both the Dictionary of Virginia Biography and the Virginia Colonial Records Project long before these indexes became publically accessible.

I would also like to thank the librarians in England and Scotland at the National Register of Archives, the Public Record Office, the British Library, the Royal Commonwealth Society, the Scottish Record Office, and the county record offices in East Suffolk, Essex (Colchester and Chelmsford), Hertfordshire, and Buckinghamshire. Particularly generous was Ann Wynfield of the Mercers' Company in London, who shared her office with me as I worked through the company records. The staff at the Barbados Archives in Lazaretto, St. Michael, was also helpful. John Adams and Sandra Rouja of the Bermuda Archives in Hamilton proved informative and friendly guides indeed.

Several people have turned a stern eye and a well-tempered ear to portions of this manuscript, and their editorial comments have been invaluable. I would like to thank especially Richard Blackett, Richard Dunn, Roderick McDonald, Simon Newman, Robert Paquette, Bill Pencak, and Karin Wulf. Other historians have made extended comments, both formal and informal, on different aspects of the project—James Banner, Trevor Burnard, David Devereaux, Stanley Engerman, Jack P. Greene, David Hancock, Gad Heuman, Wim Klooster, Allan Kulikoff, Jane Landers, Peter Mancall, Larry Poos, and Andrew O'Shaughnessy. James Horn offered critical assistance at a very early stage in my research and has been unfailingly supportive ever since. Richard Beeman and Bruce Mann read and commented thoughtfully on the original doctoral dissertation. Bernard Bailyn, Nicholas Canny, and two anonymous reviewers read earlier versions of the manuscript and have labored to save me from many a gaffe. I hope that the final version has profited somewhat from the efforts of so many generous historians.

I would like to thank others who have commented on portions of this project that have been presented at conferences and seminars, especially audiences at three different meetings of that most collegial of groups, the Association of Caribbean Historians; and seminars at the Folger Library, the Huntington Library, Northern Illinois University, the College Park Seminar in Early American History, the McNeil Center for Early American Studies, the Charles Warren Center, and the retirement conference for Richard S. Dunn. Richard merits special note here: he has been generous with his time not only during my years at Penn but ever since. He has opened his home, his research notes, and many a wine bottle to me, and his enthusiasm for my project has meant a great deal to me. My gratitude to Richard, both personally and professionally, is profound.

An educational summer with Philip Curtin and the participants in his NEH seminar helped me reconceptualize my project at a critical juncture. Bernard Bailyn's inaugural seminar on the history of the Atlantic World proved similarly stimulating. Professor Bailyn also invigorated my interest in early American history while I was an undergraduate, as did Fred Anderson, Drew McCoy, and my friends and tutors Betsy Fisher Gray and Russell Snapp.

When this project commenced as my doctoral dissertation, financial support was consistently and generously provided by various University of Pennsylvania fellowship programs. I would also like to thank the Mellon Foundation and the Daughters of the American Colonists for their support. Subsequent fellowships from the Folger Shakespeare Library, the Huntington Library, and the National Endowment for the Humanities, along with summer grants from Grinnell College and Georgetown University, permitted the revision of the dissertation into its current form. All of my former colleagues in the History Department at Grinnell College and my current students and colleagues at Georgetown University, especially Meredith McKittrick, John McNeill, and John Tutino, have stimulated my work and provided an environment where it could be completed. I especially thank Tommaso Astarita, my friend for twelve years and my colleague for four, for his steady encouragement and his delightful company. I am also grateful to Aida Donald, Elizabeth Suttell, and Gail Graves of the Harvard University Press for their patient stewardship. Carolyn Ingalls proved an attentive and thoughtful copy-editor. Robert Forget made the maps for the book.

Portions of this work have appeared elsewhere, and I am grateful to the editors of *Revista/Review Interamericana, Pennsylvania History,* the *Indiana Magazine of History;* to the University Press of Florida; and to Frank Cass for permission to use material here. British Crown copyright material in the Public Record Office is reproduced by permission of the Controller of Her Britannic Majesty's Stationery Office.

The patterns of migration detailed in this study have been echoed in my own life in the past several years. I thank those friends and relations who hosted, entertained, and otherwise distracted me during various research ventures around the United States, the Caribbean, and England, and in my homes in Philadelphia, Grinnell, and Washington—especially Allyson Booth, Katherine Penovich Clark, Tom Cohen, Julie Edwards, John Ferris, Katie Gibson, Nancy Granert, Margaret Harding, Tom and Heather Hietala, Cathy Keesling, Kristine Larson, Robin Lumsdaine, John Malloy, Anne Manson, Jenny Michael, Charlie Mingo, Anne Olcott, and Anita Tien. To friends from the University of Pennsylvania, especially Rose Beiler, Nan Dreher, Jim Heinzen, Ann Little, and Marion Winship; and through Richard Dunn's extraordinary creation, the McNeil Center for Early American Studies, in particular, Wayne Bodle, Susan Branson, Brendan McConville, Rosalind Remer, Cynthia Van Zandt, and Jim Williams, I offer thanks.

Above all, I'd like to thank those family members whose encouragement has been so unstinting—King and Penny, Lena and Bruce, an exaltation of cousins too numerous to name, my grandparents, Tim and Louise, and my parents. My brother remains my first friend and my first critic. As if it weren't enough that my parents serpentined through a poll tax riot to meet me during a research trip in London, my librarian mother helped out by locating errant books while my father shared his frequent flyer miles and inquired with increasing impatience and trepidation whether I could possibly still be working on the same book. Thanks especially to them, it is finally done.

Contents

Tables and Figures

Tables

Figures

Introduction

It was five years into the Personal Rule of Charles I and five years before the outbreak of war with Scotland, a conflict that heralded the disintegration of royal authority in England, when a young man named John Wise made his way to London in search of "better fortune." In these troubled times, however, Wise's plans went awry, and he found himself on board the *John and Catherine,* bound for Barbados. John's cousin William Hudson, sent to retrieve his wayward relative, argued that the voyage to Barbados "will not be only the heartbreaking of his parents, but utter ruin for the lad," and protested to the Commissioners for the Admiralty and Navy that Wise was but "a country lad" who "was deceived and most violently brought on board." Hudson's petition was successful, and Wise was removed from the *John and Catherine*. But this timely intervention did not keep Wise from England's Atlantic colonies for long: a year later, this time joined by his erstwhile protector William Hudson, Wise set sail for the distant shores of Virginia.[1]

Wise and Hudson were part of an exodus of almost 5,000 people who sailed for America from the port of London in 1635. They were joined at the port by over 1,000 other passengers and 1,500 soldiers, all bound for various destinations on the continent. The names and ages of these voyagers were recorded by clerks in the port register of 1635, the largest record of embarkation from one port for any single year in the colonial period.[2] The 7,507 voyagers together comprised the equivalent of somewhere between 2.1 and 2.5 percent of London's total population.[3] The colonial voyagers traveled on 53 ships to thirteen different Atlantic destinations, including the island colonies of Providence, Henrietta, Tortuga, Barbados, Bermuda, Nevis, Antigua, and St. Kitts; and the mainland colonies of Virginia, Maryland, Massachusetts, Connecticut, and Plymouth. Those who did not die or return to England moved on again. Within a decade some of their number had dispersed to New Haven, Rhode Island, Trinidad, the Bahamas, St. Lucia, and Long Island; and within three decades these migrants had scattered to Surinam, Jamaica, the Carolinas, and New Jersey. (See Figures 1 and 2.)

1

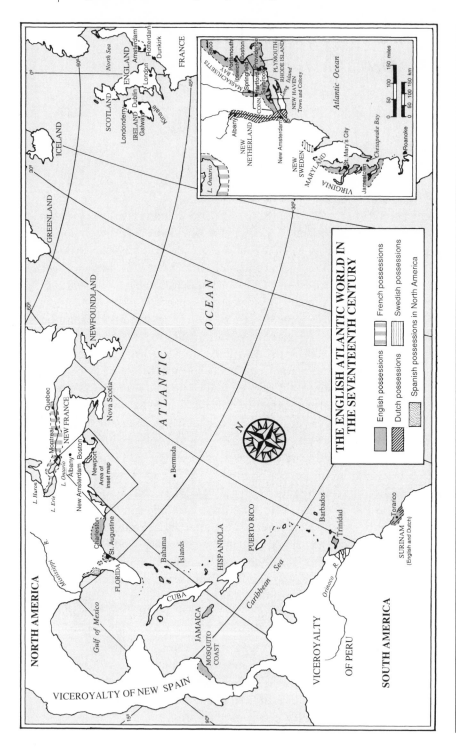

Figure 1. The English Atlantic World in the Seventeenth Century

This cohort of travelers included distinguished men such as the future regicides Henry Vane and Hugh Peter; fourteen ministers, most noncon-formists, whose religious enthusiasms defined and altered colonial worship; two men traveling in their capacity as colonial governors and five men who would become governors: all were individuals capable of exerting a profound impact on their new homes. Accompanying them were two colonial promot-ers and one boy of thirteen who would later become Massachusetts' most distinguished seventeenth-century historian. Members and progenitors of some prominent colonial dynasties traveled as well—the Belcher, Bennett, Eliot, Major, Saltonstall, Stiles, Thoroughgood, and Winthrop clans were all represented here. But mostly it was John Wise and the thousands like him who boarded ships for the colonies in 1635, having first reached London in search of adventure or employment and voyaging overseas only after their metropolitan ambitions had failed.

London, including the port of Gravesend, was only one of many possible ports of departure, and so the London port register does not contain the

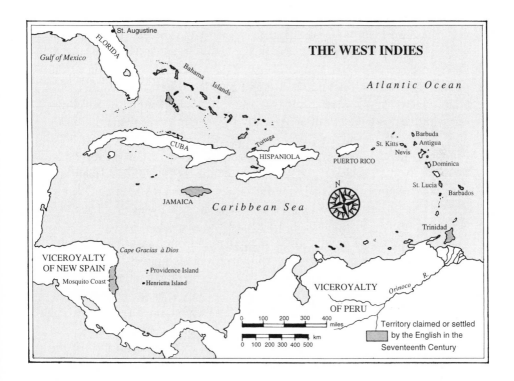

Figure 2. The West Indies

names of all voyagers to the colonies in 1635. Moreover, one important colonial destination, Ireland, appears not at all in the London register, despite the thousands of Scots and English who ventured to plantations there.[4] As for the American colonies, ships holding as many as five thousand more travelers sailed that year from several other English ports, such as Weymouth, Ipswich, Plymouth, Southampton, Harwich, Dover, Bristol, and Sandwich. The ten thousand or so men and women who left England in 1635 constituted a significant portion of the approximately eighty thousand who left during the troubled decade of the 1630s.[5]

These travelers participated in a crucial migration that secured England's precarious Atlantic empire in New England, the Chesapeake, and the Caribbean. This decade witnessed the largest growth rate in colonial populations for any single decade in the seventeenth century. In 1630 the colonial population was an estimated 9,500. Ten years later, despite the high mortality rates endemic to England's new colonial ventures, the population had grown more than five times, to 53,700. No other decade in the century came close to matching that rate of growth: the next largest leap transpired between 1640 and 1650, when the population grew by 55 percent.[6] Migration, not natural increase, was wholly responsible for this tremendous growth in the English population overseas. What we see in the single decade of the 1630s, then, is an originative moment: this westward migration, primarily composed of young male laborers, secured England's Atlantic world. By the end of the decade, colonies such as Virginia that had been incapable of sustaining themselves a mere ten years earlier were successful arenas beckoning the adventurous with the possibility of profit. And it was during this decade that Barbados and Massachusetts, far younger colonies than Virginia, received the solid economic foundation that enabled them to prosper later, as Barbados did so dramatically during the sugar revolution of the 1640s. English men and women were quick to respond to the allure of these remote developing lands. Thus during a disastrous decade for the English polity, which by 1635 was already riddled with political and ecclesiastical divisions and was soon to unravel in civil war, a rapid transfer of population from England to the colonies ironically heralded the growth of England's new empire.

This rapid population movement signals the centrality of migration for the continued existence and success of England's first overseas empire. Indeed, the English Atlantic world was a place created by migration. This new world emerged in three different stages: imagination, creation and elaboration, and integration. First came the age of imagination, in the last decades of the sixteenth century and the first decades of the seventeenth century. Expectations of England's global control and expansion had emerged by the reign of Elizabeth I. The circle of men around the two Richard Hakluyts, cousins who shared a passion for exploration and geography, most fully articulated the hope for commercial and colonial vitality that characterized the aggressive expansion of Elizabeth's reign. These men anticipated global trade opportunities, and England's merchant companies fulfilled many of these visions at the turn of the century in their trade with Russia, in the Mediterranean, and ultimately India. But accompanying these commercial ambitions were colonization schemes that centered on America—utopian visions to relieve England's poor and to enhance England's glory while filling the coffers of investors and planters. In short, the Hakluyts and their most illustrious successor, Samuel Purchas, saw a world encompassed by Britain's reach. These visions in the late sixteenth century proved chimerical. The Elizabethan conquest of Ireland signaled the success of colonization schemes close to home; but further afield, across the Atlantic, the English experienced violent and humiliating failures in North and South America, embodied in the lost colony of Roanoke and in the repeated debacles of plantation efforts in the region of the Amazon. Thus overseas colonization achieved its fullest form only in the imagination of men in England. Expectations far exceeded experience and ability.

It was in the second stage, the age of creation and elaboration, that the English Atlantic world emerged. This phase commenced in the 1620s and 1630s, when the painful accumulation of experience slowly began to temper the inflated aspirations of colonial promoters, proprietors, and investors. Ultimately, it was not the first tentative voyages of exploration to measure and chart the ocean's winds and currents that created the Atlantic world, nor was it England's long familiarity with the rich fishing banks off Newfoundland and the coast of North America that shaped that world. Even the frenzied and avaricious activities of colonial investors were not sufficient. People had to be cajoled and seduced overseas in order for colonies and a range of other enterprises to be viable. Beginning with the first ships carrying men to Virginia after the settlement of Jamestown, but picking up with a fresh intensity during the 1630s, transatlantic migration enabled England's colonies to survive. The quickening pace of this essential migration in the 1630s is captured for a moment in the London port register of 1635. The travelers who were recorded there, and the tens of thousands like them, made the Atlantic world. The process of creation and elaboration was simultaneous: the vast migrations across the Atlantic sustained new colonial enterprises, but each colonial undertaking proved different, like a quickly improvised variation on an unfamiliar theme. Thus in the span of a few years, vastly different colonies were planned and settled.

Analysis of the London port register affords a rare and valuable opportunity to investigate the English Atlantic world in these crucial first decades of its tangible creation, during this momentous shift from imagined colonies to real plantations. The register permits us to re-create individual careers, to construct a prosopographical portrait of an entire society in motion, and to explore the development of particular colonies at a time of emerging colonial viability. In tracing the careers of these passengers, we scrutinize England's Atlantic realm at its inception in the first half of the seventeenth century. But this migration signaled only the commencement, not the refinement, of the English Atlantic world. The third stage in the creation of the Atlantic world was integration, the tightening of the web that joined Europe and America, measured in part by cultural homogenization and economic congruence. Although migration ensured the vitality of overseas settlements and embodied an important and visible connection between the old and new worlds, the actual integration of these two hemispheres would be more properly a story of the eighteenth century. Even then, however, the imperial rupture in the final quarter of the century demonstrated how flawed that process of integration proved. Indeed, the intermittent organization of new Atlantic colonies throughout the eighteenth century, including Georgia and the many new territories acquired by Britain after 1763, ensured that the process of colonial creation and elaboration begun in the seventeenth century would accompany and challenge the complete integration of the English Atlantic world. The migration of the 1630s laid a foundation for the Atlantic world, but that world would be shifted and redefined at a number of critical junctures—by the commercial regulations of Oliver Cromwell and Charles II, in the aftermath of the colonial restructuring at the end of the seventeenth century, and by the wars and upheavals of the eighteenth century. The seventeenth-century English Atlantic world, created and sustained by migration, was as chaotic and disconnected as the distracted nation that spawned it.

Recognition of the centrality of migration to colonial viability and to the character of colonial societies has drawn many historians to the topic. Those interested in the formation of new world societies have justifiably concerned themselves with the confrontation between people of different polities and cultures that occurred when English settlers sought to establish themselves on the Atlantic periphery of Europe. Moreover, land and labor have a peculiar relationship in a colonial setting that renders the whole process of migration absolutely central to understanding colonial development in the seventeenth century, when heightened English mobility led to overseas migration. Peopling the new colonies with English laborers was of enormous importance to promoters and settlers alike, and it has similarly remained in the forefront of historical interest. Indeed, two historians who recognize this process have employed transatlantic migration to offer explanatory syntheses of the colonial period broadly defined.[7]

The attention accorded migration to different parts of the seventeenth-century colonies, however, has been uneven. Studies of migration to New England are abundant for the exodus still known as the Great Migration, and we have reached the point where we can identify and trace most travelers, especially men, by name.[8] The literature on the Chesapeake is much smaller: only one comprehensive study of migration to this region exists.[9] Migration to the Caribbean has been studied only in the most general terms, making it difficult to assess the structure and development of these island societies as individuals experienced and shaped them in the uncertain first decades of the islands' settlement. One goal of this book is to furnish a comparative study of early-seventeenth-century migration to the English colonies on the North American mainland and on the islands. The travelers of 1635 present an unusual opportunity to take English men and women who shared a single point and time of departure, and to make sense of their experiences on both sides of the Atlantic.

In tracing these travelers from London, I have replicated the method of other historians of migration who have used a port register or a ship's passenger list as a starting point for a closer examination of the experiences of travelers to America.[10] In a world in which local migration was normative, the gathering at London allowed me to reach out and grab these people as they assembled at the port and prepared for what was by English standards a particularly arduous and lengthy migration. And then I could chase them down. The database that informs this study derived from a straightforward research strategy: to read extant archival and printed sources for all the early-seventeenth-century English colonies in search of the travelers from London in 1635. Most of these travelers never appear in the idiosyncratic remnants of the colonial records: altogether some 1,360 colonial passengers could be found, or approximately 27 percent of the total cohort bound for America. And few lives could be re-created systematically or fully, especially for women and for the passengers to the non–New England colonies. More often, I could catch only a brief glimpse of a colonist during public moments: an appearance in court to settle a debt or to protest a master's harsh treatment; a public profession of faith to gain admission to a gathered church; the presentation of a will or an estate inventory to signal a traveler's death. And since colonists spent most of their time outside churches and courts, most of their experiences must remain, as they were then, private. Lives have been reconstructed from snippets and legal minutiae, hardly the stuff of which solid biography is made. This book tells the story of these travelers from London in 1635: any other individuals mentioned later either traveled as well in the 1630s or were prominent colonial figures. The passengers were not selected for their distinctiveness of experience or pedigree, but simply for their appearance at the port and their presence in colonial records. Whenever possible, I have permitted those few individuals who survived in the records to speak for themselves, thereby retaining all original spelling with the single exception of switching the letters *u* and *v*, and *i* and *j*, when necessary for greater clarity. All years are cited in the text in new style.

The consequences of limited and uneven biographical information will be apparent in the chapters that follow. The available data drive the analysis in ways that are not always ideal. Comparisons between colonial populations are difficult because sources vary, and although percentages can at times be sizable, the numbers themselves are often quite small. The population itself shifts, so that different men and women illustrate different chapters and arguments. At times the evidence can be, at best, suggestive of broader trends. Wherever possible, I draw on the colony records or other works to provide context and fill in holes, but the holes remain.

The focus on this single cohort of travelers, moreover, gives the study a static air. It is an investigation prodded by a single moment of migration: for many, a starting point; for far more, the route to an early grave. This study can offer, then, only a slice of society at one moment in time. But the varied aspirations of the travelers who gathered at the port of London in 1635 have made it possible occasionally to widen the frame of analysis. Several travelers were old colonial residents returning home in 1635, whereas others were only visiting the colonies on short business trips in that year. Considered together, the careers of the entire cohort span some seventy years, from the 1610s, when the first members of this cohort settled in Virginia and Bermuda, to the 1680s, when those who settled in New England began to disappear from the records. But the emphasis is on the 1630s and 1640s. For some colonies these were important and formative decades: these were the years of New England's greatest religious schism and its first major Anglo-Indian war, perhaps the twin symbols of the divergent strains that Europeans and indigenous Americans endured in new world settlements, and the era of Barbados's shift to sugar cultivation, an economic development that made the colony the single most valuable asset in England's array of colonies in the seventeenth century. My hope is to compensate in some way for the chronological narrowness of the project with a geographic breadth that spans the Atlantic and integrates even the most short-lived colonial experiments.

This study, then, engages a maturing literature on Atlantic history. Atlantic approaches to the study of British America are venerable, in their earlier forms embodied by the strenuous efforts of colonial historians to set their research in an Anglo-American context informed by research on early modern England. Some historians have built on this broad Anglo-American context with a close scrutiny of the varied ways—economic, material, commercial, cultural, or political—in which the different parts of the Atlantic world were integrated by the eighteenth century. Indeed, the historian Ian Steele has recently referred to Atlantic history as "an alternative integration model."[11] Other historians have complicated the possibility of integration. They have reframed the Atlantic world altogether by offering different (non-Anglo) perspectives on its varied populations—European, indigenous, and African. They remind us of the challenges that contemporaries faced inhabiting, much less integrating, a world shaped so profoundly by the ethnic, cultural, religious, and linguistic diversity of its inhabitants. This fractured ocean community was a new world for all its inhabitants, especially in the late sixteenth and early seventeenth centuries when Dutch, French, and English ships plied the Atlantic and the Caribbean with enthusiasm and forcibly joined North America and Europe into new, uncertain, and volatile unions. Even in the small portion of the Atlantic world ostensibly controlled by the English in the 1630s, there was little to be integrated and much to be created. This project therefore seeks to measure the scope of the emerging English Atlantic world in the seventeenth century by tracing the people who inhabited it. Inspired and integrated by trade networks, this Atlantic world was embodied in the migration of men and women from England to new colonies and the return migration of new world products from the colonies back to England and then on to the continent. Central to this process was regular movement and shipping between Europe and the new world, a process already established in the 1630s when English ships and mariners made regular visits to colonial ports.[12] To people this world was not only to create it by conquest and settlement but also to define it, and the movement of people throughout England's first empire redefined England and its outposts in ways that knit together this new and unfamiliar world.

This new Atlantic world was shaped by a web of interactions—maritime, cultural, commercial, diplomatic, military, and epidemiological—that drew a series of disparate events and adventures together under a common rubric. But arguing for the primacy of the Atlantic world does not necessitate that that culture was either singular, uniform, or harmonious. The real empire that England created was marked by what J. H. Elliott has called the "element of disjunction" between new and old worlds.[13] To talk of a new Atlantic world is not to claim that England and its colonies, or that England, Spain, France, Portugal, and the Netherlands, shared a single common culture after 1492. The Atlantic world was rich and varied. But although the particulars of conquest and contact varied greatly, the process did not, and it was that process that transformed, in different degrees and fashions, Europe, the Americas, and Africa. The process of creating this oceanic basin of conquest and discovery recurred across time and space throughout the age of European expansion, lending commonality to a range of events that overrode marked dissimilarities.

To illustrate these commonalities, the chapters that follow consider the migrating population in its entirety. Four areas of the British Atlantic world in particular—the West Indies (illustrated by the colonies of Providence and Barbados), Bermuda, the Chesapeake (most fully illustrated by the experiences of travelers to Virginia), and New England—lie at the center of this study, which integrates the reconstructed experiences of real individuals who lived in precarious colonial communities into the larger story of the Atlantic world.[14] In so doing, this study is rooted in the minutiae of daily life of even the most impecunious colonial resident without permitting any one person or place to speak for the experience of the whole. Although attention is paid to individual town polities in New England or to distinctions dictated by labor practices and staple crops, my emphasis here is on convergences and on the primacy of the Atlantic world over the localism of individual colonial communities.[15]

The book's approach is topical. Chapters 1, 2, 6, and 7 draw on the particular experiences of the travelers of 1635 to focus on different aspects of migration within and out of England and within the Atlantic world. The three central chapters focus more narrowly on the experiences of these people in the colonies as they labored to create new homes for themselves. Here the chapters echo the building blocks of colonial societies—laborers, the family, the church—and investigate the ways in which men (and a few women) secured the trappings of success overseas, as measured in ownership of land, servants, and other capital goods. These chapters emphasize the necessity of considering different regions together because colonial creation accompanied elaboration in this phase of English expansion across the Atlantic. A spectrum of experience characterized early colonial settlements, and the intent of my approach is to delineate both the variety of colonial societies and the common processes by which they were formed. Such a thematic approach runs the obvious risk of obscuring important differences within the experiences of the travelers of 1635. My strategy has been twofold in order to address this problem: where differences shaped by destination are significant, I have offered a discussion shaped by each colony, as in Chapters 4 and 5. Where commonalities overrode regional distinctions, I have tried to pull the experiences of all the travelers together, as in Chapters 3 and 7. And where available evidence permits the discussion of only one region, I have focused on that place, as in Chapter 6. Even within topical explorations, however, I always make it clear where a traveler lived. The point is not to ignore or dismiss particular colonial settings but to explore ways in which there were experiences or processes common to this new Atlantic world that were not themselves shaped solely by the particular place of settlement. The varied ways in which newcomers both navigated and created colonial homes not only attest to the enormous heterogeneity of England's colonies but also reinforce the commonality of the processes by which men and women strived to render familiar the exotic.

Although the voyagers' aspirations in the colonies and their pursuits of distinctive strategies in gaining land, forming families, and seeking office reflected a broad range of responses to conditions in England and overseas, the travelers of 1635 all shared certain fundamental expectations about social organization that they carried to the colonies, filtered through individual lenses of gender, age, piety, and wealth. Whether in struggling to form alternative family life or by moving on, the colonists who left London in 1635 displayed the symbols of a shared culture that provided unity to a series of seemingly incompatible colonial adventures. But however they endeavored to replicate elements of the lives they had left behind, the new colonial residents were unable to re-create England in their overseas outposts. The most fundamental features of parish and domestic life were altered in the colonies: the ecclesiastical oddity of gathered churches in New England, Bermuda, and Providence, and the variant forms of colonial families, dictated as they were on Bermuda and Providence by number and race, demonstrated that aspirations to make "New" and "Little" Englands—as two places were optimistically called—were ultimately unsuccessful. English people abroad in this era dwelled in a chaotic and uncertain world where new world exigencies overpowered the force and weight of custom. Only by ignoring the particularities of different colonial societies, which were defined and altered by the presence of Indian or African populations, by the proximity of Spanish colonies, or even by the presence of tobacco, can one see these colonial societies as English at all. The consequence everywhere was a truncated institutional life that bore at best the veneer of English practices.

At the same time, however, the colonies contained a cultural breadth and vitality unknown in England. In their migration from small parishes and provincial towns, and even from the great metropolis of London, most of the passengers of 1635 unwittingly created and joined societies far more culturally, linguistically, and ethnically complex than anything in their previous experience. The most obvious indication of departure from English patterns was the presence of Indians and Africans in colonial homes, men and women who brought with them languages and cultural practices that elaborated and, in some cases, sustained colonial life at the same time that indigenous Americans offered unrelenting reminders of the uncertainties and novelties of overseas settlement. Moreover, the colonies were peopled by Britons. English, Scottish, and Welsh inhabitants dwelled in close proximity to each other and were joined in the colonies by the Irish as well, especially in the wake of the Irish uprising of 1641. In some instances people from different parts of Britain and Ireland settled apart. But elsewhere they were jumbled together, bringing their local customs with them to a new hybrid world. The peopling of England's colonies by inhabitants of four continents produced a heterogeneity that most fully signaled what it meant to live in an Atlantic world.

What linked these markedly varied colonial societies with their diverse inhabitants was both the common, albeit chaotic, process that created them and the migration that sustained them. Although the colonies were inhabited by Britons, this was, in the first part of the seventeenth century, an *English* Atlantic world, settled largely by English colonists, governed by English officers, and controlled from London for the most part by English investors and proprietors. The westward flow of passengers from London that is the centerpiece of this project delineates the origins of England's Atlantic world. But what connected and secured that world were patterns of repeat and return migration demonstrated by colonists everywhere. This was a world built both on the ground and over the water, not in the dreams of proprietors, investors, or schemers in England. Not until real experience in the Atlantic world permeated all ranks of English society, a process that began in the 1620s and 1630s, could an English Atlantic world be created. In their voyages to other regions of the colonial world and in their financial and political investments in colonies far different from their own, colonial residents and visitors demonstrated in measurable ways the extent to which the Atlantic world was knit together not only by the common experiences echoed again and again in different American locations but also by the real experiences people had with different parts of the Atlantic. Migration secured, created, and ultimately defined the English Atlantic world.

1 | *Clearinghouse and Countinghouse: London and Overseas Expansion*

William Booth occupied an unfortunate status in the land of primogeniture and the entailed estate. A younger son from a Cheshire family, he journeyed to London in May of 1628 "to get any servis worth haveinge." His letters from there to his oldest brother, John, who had inherited the bulk of their father's estate, and John's responses, drafted carefully on the back of William's original missives, describe the circumstances that enticed men to London in search of work and the misfortunes that subsequently ushered them overseas. Unable to find suitable employment in the metropolis, William Booth implored his brother to procure a letter of introduction on his behalf from their cousin Morton. Plaintively reminding John "how chargeable a place London is to live in," William also requested funds for a suit of clothes in order to make himself more presentable in his quest for palatable employment. In a time-honored strategy of impatient and petulant young men, William threatened his older brother with military service on the continent, preferring to "goe into the lowcuntries or eles wth some man of warre" if he could find no position in London. John Booth, dismayed by his sibling's martial inclination, offered William money from his own portion of their father's estate rather than permit William to squander his own smaller share; and in what proved to be a gross misreading of William's personality but perhaps a sound assessment of his desire for the status becoming his ambitions, John urged William to seek a position with a bishop.

The eleven surviving letters between the Booth brothers convey William's growing impatience with his failure to secure a position in London, his canny ability to manipulate his brother with threats of military service, and John's helpless concern from distant Cheshire. William's humiliation at his repeated failures in London reached its pinnacle when his tenacious pursuit of an unpaid debt led the purported debtor, Sir Edward Whitton, to refuse to receive him. Finally, after less than five months in London, William decided he had had enough. London had answered his hopes with disappointment. "I will stay noe lounger," he wrote John in July, "but a weay with the first that

13

doth goe let what will follow[.] it is better to indure slaverie where a man is not knowne then in his owne cuntry[.] I have spente more in seekeinge for a servis then I shall gaine in 2 yeares servis and am sorie I had not resolved upon this course souner." William traveled to Gravesend in September. From there he chose to sail not, as we might expect, to the new American colonies where an ambitious and fortunate young man might anticipate economic advancement and adventure; instead, scorning the degrading labor that such destinations promised, he sailed straight across the English Channel toward North Holland, to serve as a soldier with English forces on the continent.[1]

William Booth's travails in the metropolis and his journey to the continent embody the processes of internal and overseas migration that together generated the London port register of 1635. He was one of the thousands of men and women who journeyed to London in the seventeenth century in numbers sufficient to double the size of the city between 1600 and 1670. By the middle of the century, these migrants equaled one-sixth the population of England.[2] Unlike most of the people who traveled to London in search of work, profit, or adventure, William Booth recorded his struggles there and the reasons behind his departure. But like most of these men, Booth's venture failed.

William Booth's quest for adventure and position in the great metropolis was so common that it had already become embedded in popular culture. The most celebrated person to make his fortune after a journey to the city was young Dick Whittington, later the Lord Mayor of London: the Whittington legend established a pattern for future fictitious adventurers, although most subsequent aspirants for success in London found their plots revised as they met with disappointment, dissipation, and despair in the city. The first part of the formulaic saga described the adventures of a young man who migrated to London. So commenced the story of one Leonard of Lincoln, a character whose ambitions were recorded in a ballad, "The Cheating Age: Or Leonard of Lincolnes Journey to London to Buy Wit," which was printed only three years before William Booth made his own way to London from Cheshire. We learn from this experience that nothing could have prepared a provincial man for London. This city, with a population of between 301,000 and 351,000 in 1635, was the largest in Europe, and was congested, busy, loud, and rank.[3] A new arrival would not know what to make of the noises and sights of the metropolis. Even the tuneful cries of London's many competing vendors hawking their wares would baffle the newcomer with their babble. Leonard of Lincoln did not stand a chance. As soon as he "entered Bishops wide gate," he fell among bad company who enticed him into a tavern. Over the course of his adventures, Leonard squandered "most part of (his) state" and was reduced to selling his cloak and sword in order to pay his debts. Rather than finding the wit he had envisioned, Leonard to London "with griefe bid adiew." "My journey to London long time I shall rue," he lamented. "I ne're in my life met with villaines so wilde, / To send a man home like the Prodigall Childe."[4]

With the advent of viable colonial ventures in the early seventeenth century, authors of ballads like "The Cheating Age" found new endings to their London stories as secondary migrations out of the capital offered alternatives to humiliation or penury at home. These fictitious models echoed the real experiences of men for whom London was a destination ultimately replaced over the course of the seventeenth century by more promising and more remote ones. Richard Norwood, the great Bermuda surveyor, made his home on Bermuda only after a series of adventures on the continent and in the Mediterranean. His family's frequent moves within England disrupted Norwood's childhood education; and finally, having failed to win a scholarship that he coveted, Norwood went to London at the age of fifteen as an apprentice to a fishmonger, "a stern man." In London Norwood was captivated by passions other than for fish. His master's house was frequented by mariners who excited Norwood with talk of their travels. Norwood developed an interest in navigation, "wherewith," he recalled, "I was so much affected that I was most earnestly bent both to understand the art which seemed to me to reach as it were to heaven," and he resolved to go to the East Indies. Breaking his apprenticeship, he went to sea and visited many European ports: at one point he even considered a pilgrimage to Jerusalem. He finally returned to England but set out yet again, this time for Turkey and other places, learning navigation as he traveled. Once back in London, Norwood was recruited by the Somers Islands Company because of another skill that he had acquired during his travels, that of diving; and Richard Norwood finally voyaged to the colony that was, after more fits and starts, to become his adult home. Norwood's Atlantic career, then, followed the taste for adventure that was first sparked in London, next succeeded by long travels around the world, and then developed after he had cultivated skills that made him valuable to colonial investors.[5]

This pattern was replicated by thousands of Norwood's contemporaries, who ventured to London for fortune, advancement, and adventure. Metropolitan culture, however, was hardly a pleasure trove. Norwood and Booth proved luckier than most—in the charnel house of the metropolis, they survived to move on. Plague was endemic in London, producing mortality rates as high as 24 percent in the worst outbreaks, as in the year 1563. And the diseases that feed on poverty, poor sanitation, and malnutrition had free reign in London.[6] Many destitute migrants who were ensnared in the legal apparati of the poor laws found themselves eventually boarding ships, like William

Booth or Richard Norwood—whether reluctantly or enthusiastically—for a range of overseas ventures.[7] Such was the case in 1635 for five boys sent by the Bridewell Hospital, an institution for indigents, to Bermuda, after they had been brought in by a London constable. And another traveler in 1635, Thomas Reynolds, was taken in by the night watch and described as "an old prisoner." Reynolds was shipped to Virginia.[8] Joining Reynolds that year on voyages from London to Virginia were fourteen prisoners from Newgate.[9] Thus a number of people unable or unwilling to support themselves legally in London were shipped overseas along with those men like Norwood or Booth who had skills and expectations but thirsted for advancement. London functioned as a filter for a population moving into the city from all over England and leaving the city on ships for the continent or for any one of a range of English commercial or colonial ventures.[10]

Migration to London in the early seventeenth century was embedded in broader patterns of migration that were themselves responses to a particular set of domestic circumstances. Migration within England was a part of the life cycle for most young men and women. Young boys moved to commence apprenticeships, whereas both men and women moved annually in search of agricultural or domestic service.[11] Migration, moreover, was not constrained to one age group alone: young adults moved to new communities when they married, and families picked up their stakes for better opportunities elsewhere. As the examples of William Booth and Richard Norwood suggest, migration also enhanced imperial development as men blundered their way onto ships to serve in the army that secured England's sovereignty or to explore, invade, and settle the colonies that promised wealth and power. Both migration and commercial ventures similarly shaped the character of London.[12] Thus migration played a role in the life cycle of individuals and in the life cycle of the nation. As part of the life cycle of the nation, the increased migration of the early Stuart period provided able manpower for a variety of new commercial enterprises that ultimately transformed England into an empire.

Historians of seventeenth-century England have identified various causes of these enhanced rates of migration. But surely the single most important demographic change in the early seventeenth century occurred in the growth of the English population, which rose by 40 percent between 1580 and 1640.[13] The commensurate strains on rents and food prices were exacerbated in local regions by the collapse of England's textile industry.[14] The consequences of these intertwined demographic and economic pressures were many and varied. One important consequence was the redistribution of population throughout England and ultimately to the colonies, a redistribution that occurred in several stages. Migrants desperate for ways to keep body and soul together trekked long distances from town to town, "overshadowed by the tramping curse of necessity." Betterment migrants like Richard Norwood, often apprentices, moved short distances in search of social mobility and respectability.[15] With declining—or nonexistent—opportunities, men like William Booth from gentry families in search of jobs better suited to their frequently inflated expectations joined the peripatetic destitute on England's major thoroughfares. Subsistence migrants tended to be young and male, menacing in their poverty and freedom from masters and parents, and the presence of so many wandering poor prompted great anxiety on the part of those in authority, who devised laws and institutions to remedy the problem of vagrancy. Migrants became vagrants when they could find neither food nor shelter nor work.[16]

Vagrants moved to urban centers, motivated in part by traditional expectations of prosperity and opportunity there. The larger the town, the farther migrants traveled to reach it. The immense city of London, then, attracted people from all over the kingdom.[17] The startling growth of the metropolis in light of its high mortality rates reflected that fact: east London, for example, grew from a population of 21,000 in 1600 to 91,000 by 1700.[18] In that same section of London, only 14 to 22 percent of deponents had been born in the city.[19] In direct response to the growth of the metropolis, Charles I in 1634 ordered an inquiry into the population of the city and outparishes.[20]

As Charles I's metropolitan survey indicates, the Stuart kings viewed this abundant internal mobility with considerable alarm, not only because of the local instability vagrants provoked and heralded but also in light of the political and economic instability that distinguished the reigns of James I and Charles I. If not completely at odds, Parliament and the Crown were, at best, struggling to find an amicable and practicable middle ground in this period, and the fiscally beleaguered government ultimately collapsed entirely when faced with invasion from Scotland.

One manifestation of this confluence of political and economic strains that disordered the kingdom was an increased rate of migration and travel overseas. This process prompted in turn an enhanced effort on the part of the Crown to regulate the physical movement of English men and women out of the country. With the growth of England's commercial empire and with the rise of London as the center of that empire, new forms of control developed as part of a preexisting practice of restricting movement. Especially during the years of the so-called Personal Rule, Charles I found it necessary to refine and expand on proclamations passed originally by his father in order to curtail the movements of his subjects.

Although colonization and trade were for the most part organized by private ventures, the Crown played an important role in supporting these ventures by providing monopolies both to individuals and to corporations, or joint-stock companies. The Crown also regulated the departures of ships and people. In an era of sensitive and transitory diplomatic alliances, the king had trouble controlling men eager to plant their own fiefdoms overseas. It was obviously difficult for the king to enforce his will on foreign soil, and some proclamations reflected his frustration. A 1618 proclamation outlined James I's efforts to curtail the movements of Sir Walter Raleigh, who had flouted his original license for his South American expedition by fighting with the Spanish. Two years later, a similar broadside sought to discipline Roger North, who had sailed off to the Amazon without permission and so was stripped of his powers from across the ocean.[21] These futile efforts—and the harsh punishments awaiting North and Raleigh on their returns to England—symbolized James I's growing understanding of the complexity of controlling a far-flung trade network. But North and Raleigh carried small crews to an infant and ultimately unsuccessful colony. More dangerous were the successful colonies because of the movement of people that they prompted.

As colonization increased, then, the pace of monarchical regulation increased as well. A series of broadside decrees by Charles I visibly demonstrated invigorated royal attention to the population of England's overseas outposts, symbolic of a troubled Stuart government struggling to assert its authority over a restless land. In May of 1630 Charles reaffirmed an earlier decree of his father, James I, forbidding people to leave England freely for any foreign port—including "Souldiers, Marchants, Marryners, and their factors and Apprentices"—and appointed commissioners of various English ports to administer an oath to all people, including women and children, who left for anywhere. Particular instructions enjoined these commissioners to record the names of passengers, their place of birth, "state, degree, vocation, trade, mysterie or occupation, and the true cause or causes of their going over."[22]

After 1633 Charles I was joined in his regulatory efforts by the Archbishop of Canterbury, William Laud, whose policies produced a population disposed to migration. Under the helm of Archbishop Laud, the Church of England underwent a variety of liturgical and doctrinal transformations that marked a departure from the policies of Charles I's predecessors and threatened the puritans' culture of discipline.[23] Laud's reforms, stressing hierarchy in the church and valuing ritual over preaching,[24] were interpreted by his detractors less as an innocuous emendation of Anglicanism than as a deliberate rapprochement with Rome. This perceived movement toward Rome fueled contemporary anxiety about Catholicism.[25] Laud's control over church practice permeated England and resonated in local parishes, where nonconforming clerics were deprived of pulpits while recalcitrant churchwardens were admonished for the inaccurate placement of communion tables and altars. Ministers were required to have licenses to preach: those who did not found themselves summoned before the ecclesiastical courts.[26]

Sensitive puritans interpreted Laud's ecclesiastical policies as calamitous.[27] Perhaps Laud's greatest achievement lay in creating a party of opposition among puritans, whom he pushed into an extreme defensive position. Laud recognized this opposition without crediting himself as its source. In a letter to Thomas Wentworth, the future earl of Strafford, Laud remarked that he was surprised that Wentworth was unable to procure men to settle the Munster plantation, "and that the while, there should be here such an universal running to New England, and God knows whither, but this it is, when men think nothing is their advantage, but to run from government."[28] What these men ran from in the 1630s was Laud, and as the Archbishop noted, many of these men moved either literally or economically in the 1630s into colonizing ventures: at the upper echelon of society, a veritable who's who of future puritan parliamentarians organized the Providence Island Company, while other men of less exalted stature moved themselves and their families overseas. As Richard Saltonstall, Jr., wrote ominously to John Winthrop, Jr., "Bishop Laude . . . hath the very sperit of Elimas; and doth daly more and more, both plott and practis to bring into the Church, downe right poperie."[29]

Engaged in a bitter struggle with his puritan critics, Archbishop Laud sought to ensure the conformity of these dissenting church members, and an important 1634 decree reflected that commitment. By an order of the Commission for Foreign Plantations in December of 1634 that was directed to "our loving Freinds the officers of the Port of London," all subjects bound for the plantations from the port of London were to present proof that they did not owe taxes. This order superseded an earlier decree by the Privy Council in February of 1634, which required the restraint of ten ships waiting to sail to New England in order that the passengers might be interrogated. According to the December decree, passengers below the rank of subsidy men were required to provide letters both from the justices of their parish certifying that they had taken the oath of allegiance and supremacy and from their local clergyman, who would certify that they were members of the church in good standing. These parish certificates were intended to ensure that nonconformists could not depart. Subsidy men, those assessed in the annual lay taxes, required licenses from the king's commissioners themselves. The order was initially enforced, however, only for passengers to New England. The Commission for Foreign Plantations thereby hoped to prevent the departure of those of "idle and refractory humors, whose only end is to live as much as they can without the reach of authority." In order to arrest the "promiscuous and disorderly parting out of the Realme," the clerks were to provide the commissioners every six months with a "particular and perfect list of the names and qualities of all those that have in the meane time imbarqued in that port." Lest the clerks misunderstand the urgency of their task, the commissioners reminded them that "in the performance of all which you are in no sort to faile, as you will answer the neglect thereof at your perills."[30]

The clerks at the port of London in 1635 attended to their duties with the prescribed care. On the very day of the December 1634 proclamation, they commenced a record of travel that encapsulates the movement of some 7,500 men, women, and children through London, the largest city in Europe, to the American colonies and to cities on the continent. The record for travelers to the continent commenced December 24, 1634. The first soldiers were listed on December 31, 1634; the first passengers to America, on January 2, 1635. Dutifully recording the names, ages, and occasionally occupation, place of origin, and purpose of travel for those people who passed through their port, these clerks created an invaluable historical document. The register's comprehensive inclusion of men and women involved in a range of imperial efforts sets the different overseas migrations in context. The port register, recording as it does the activities of merchants, ministers, planters, servants, artisans, soldiers, and mariners, reminds us that London may have been a clearinghouse for young men like William Booth or Richard Norwood in search of fortune and adventure; but London was also a countinghouse, the commercial heart of a fragile empire.

The London port clerks recorded the names and ages of almost 5,000 men and women who sailed to the colonies; they enumerated 1,595 soldiers bound for the continent; and they listed 1,034 individual men, women, and children who voyaged to different continental ports such as Amsterdam, Delft, and Rotterdam, "on their own affayres" (Table 1.1). The largest cohort, over 2,000 people, sailed to the colony of Virginia. A few people in this contingent also settled in the newly established colony of Maryland, but the port clerks did not record Maryland as a destination for any ship, perhaps because travelers were reluctant to admit to a Catholic destination. Hundreds of servants were in the Chesapeake contingent, bound for labor in the tobacco fields. Over 1,400 people sailed south from London, then west across the Atlantic, to the eastern fringes of the Caribbean, to Barbados and St. Kitts. A small group made a still longer voyage, pushing farther west into the Caribbean to reach the island of Providence, England's remote and precariously perched colony in the heart of Spanish-dominated territory off the coast of central America. Two ships carrying over 200 people sailed to the Caribbean before tacking north on a long and difficult voyage, to reach the elusive island of Bermuda. And a lesser migration, compared with the large flows to the Chesapeake and the West Indies, contained more than 1,100 people who made a northern crossing of the Atlantic, bound for New England.

Table 1.1. 1635 London port register: travelers and destinations

Destinations	No. of Travelers
American Colonies[a]	4,878
Virginia	2,009
New England	1,169
Barbados	983
St. Kitts	423
Bermuda	218
Providence	76
Various continental posts (soldiers)	1,595
Continent	1,034
Destination blank	30
Rotterdam	158
Amsterdam	111
Dunkirk	107
Middelburg	63
Flanders	59
Flushing	58
The Hague	58
Bergen op zoom	43
Dort	34
Low Countries	21
Leiden	20
Hamburg	17
Guttenberg	16
Utrecht	16
Other[b]	223
Total travelers from London	7,507

Source for Table 1.1 and subsequent tables in this chapter: E 157/20 1-e, PRO.

a. The destinations indicated here are listed as they were recorded in the port register and are not entirely accurate. Passengers bound for New England could land in Massachusetts, Plymouth, or Connecticut; those bound for Virginia could land in Maryland; ships bound for Barbados and St. Kitts also visited Nevis and Antigua; and the ship bound for Providence called at Henrietta and Tortuga. See Appendix A for a discussion of my corrections to the London register.

b. This category includes destinations where fewer than 15 people traveled, including such places as Paris, Constantinople, Russia, Prussia, Antwerp, Brussels, Bruges, Spain, Ostend, Newport, Cleveland, Ghent, Dieppe, Haarlem, Nijmegen, and 23 other cities.

These transatlantic travelers were joined by over 2,500 soldiers and passengers bound across the English Channel to the continent. The presence of these other voyagers signifies the essential component parts of England's embryonic empire and offers an important perspective on the value of the register itself. Although the few times that historians have employed this record of migration have been to delineate migration to the colonies, the register was not simply about colonization or about travel to America. In fulfilling Charles I's order to regulate the traffic of people through London, the clerks delineated the push factors of poverty and despair and the lure of a trade empire and overseas opportunity. That these names were united in a single register, interspersed with each other on a single page, symbolizes the connections between these important migration patterns, and sets overseas migration in a context of English military activity and financial expansion and investment. Thus the register in its entirety depicts a three-pronged, interconnected process of movement out of London, the great staging ground for a range of overseas enterprises. Indeed, because of the complex web of motives and expectations shaping overseas travel, I have eschewed the word *immigrant* in this study in favor of *traveler, passenger, voyager,* or *migrant. Immigrant* presupposes two attributes: first, a movement from one national entity to another; and second, a permanent migration. *Immigrant* ascribes a sense of purpose or mission that may in fact be absent from an episode of travel. Indeed, migration, whether temporary, for work, for marriage, or for pleasure, whether to the next parish, the nearby provincial market town, London, Rotterdam, Constantinople, or even the colonies, was not necessarily a disruption of the life cycle but a necessary and appropriate interlude. *Traveler* restores the uncertainty of mission experienced by each passenger and embraces a terminology employed by contemporaries.[31]

The ordered departures suggested in the 1635 port register should not be confused with a sense of permanence, clarity of purpose, or single-minded investment of purse or person. London was only one of many ports of departure for America, and America was only one of many possible destinations. In this same period thousands of men and women also ventured to other colonial and continental destinations, especially Ireland, which continued to attract people during these decades of high migration to America. Altogether some 100,000 people from England and Scotland are estimated to have ventured to Ireland before the rebellion of 1641. So successful, indeed, was the English plantation in Munster that Nicholas Canny has determined from a study of inventory records that it "was probably the wealthiest English overseas settlement that had developed anywhere by the middle of the seventeenth century."[32] Even those individuals most indelibly associated with New England flirted with the possibility of Irish settlement. John Winthrop, Sr., wrote to his son John while he was studying at Trinity College, Dublin, and remarked, "I wish oft God would open a waye to settle me in Ireland, if it might be for his glorye."[33] God apparently opened the way to Ireland for thousands of other Britons, if not for John Winthrop. In fact, 1635 marked the peak of Scottish emigration to Ulster.[34] Migration, moreover, as the port register suggests, did not necessarily entail colonial aspirations: cloth workers from the Weald of Kent settled in the Palatinate in the 1630s even as hundreds of their neighbors set their sights on New England and the Chesapeake.[35] In 1635 more men ventured to the continent as soldiers than went to Barbados and St. Kitts combined, and more men served on the continent than traveled altogether to New England from London.

This record of migration and travel is contained in a single folio volume. The first portion of the volume enumerates the colonial travelers and the soldiers bound for the continent. These voyagers were recorded by name, by general destination, and frequently by age in the order they appeared at the port. Thus a single date might accommodate passengers bound for New England, travelers for Barbados, and soldiers destined for Flanders. They gathered at England's busiest single port.[36] The summer months in particular were a frantic season for the port clerks, who struggled to assign children to the proper families, servants to the correct master, and people to the correct ships and destinations. Multiple listings and scrawled corrections in the register reflected the clerks' confusion. This business at the port coincided significantly with the period of peak internal migration of subsistence migrants, which was between the months of June and October.[37]

The passengers bound for the West Indies and the Chesapeake appeared en masse, grouped by vessel, before ministers at Gravesend to take the required oath of allegiance. Most of the soldiers were brought before the clerk in the hands of a sergeant or other officer who had recruited them, as when Captain Prichard brought twenty men with him to the port in December of 1634: William Booth suggested this process when he wrote to his brother John that a sergeant in his company was voyaging to London for "a supplie of men."[38] The New England passengers apparently presented passes (although none seem to have survived) from their ministers and the justices of the peace in their home parishes in order to demonstrate their conformity to the Church of England, and in many cases the clerks carefully recorded this information in the port register.

The second portion of the register, comprising some thirty folio pages, delineates the passengers destined for cities on the continent. These people encompassed a remarkable array of individuals, including English families already resident in foreign cities; merchants; Irish travelers on their way to visit friends; and three young men intent on studying languages. It was this section of the register that is the most complete, with the traveler's purpose detailed more often than not—a feature uniformly absent from the listings for travelers to the colonies. This discrepancy between the different portions of the port register might suggest which flow of travelers most concerned the crown. Particularly because so many of these continent-bound travelers were expatriates and likely dissenters, who were involved in international trade and

Table 1.2. Sex ratios by destination

Sex	Colonies		Soldiers		Continent	
	N	%	N	%	N	%
Male	4,008	82.4	1,595	100	752	73
Female	856	17.6	0	0	281	27
Total	4,864	100	1,595	100	1,033	100

thus closely connected with foreign merchants and monarchs, the king might have wanted to reassure himself of their whereabouts, loyalty, and adequate tax payments.

Who were these 7,500 passengers, and how did they differ one from another? A survey of some of the most basic demographic features of these travelers details some measurable distinctions between the three different flows: travelers to America, travelers to the continent, and soldiers. This chapter will consider the American passengers as a whole: the following chapter will break down this cohort into categories by colonial destination. Although it is easy to conjecture that the indentured laborers and soldiers profiled in the port register would be drawn from similar pools of young men, this in fact proves not to be true. The different groups of passengers were hardly identical.

Sex ratios offer an immediate way to assess significant differences between migrating populations (Table 1.2). The soldiers, of course, were entirely male, or at least appeared so to the clerks. Both of the other groups of travelers were predominantly male as well, between 73 and 83 percent, although the cohort bound for the continent more closely approximated the sex ratio of England itself. Still, travel was clearly a man's affair.

Alone, sex ratios mean little, but when combined with the age structure of the different migrating populations, a profile emerges of the varied characteristics of these three cohorts. Average age, for example, although not a very complicated demographic measure, offers an immediate point of comparison between the different streams of travelers (Table 1.3). The soldiers and the travelers to the continent were on average more mature, by four and five years, than the people bound for the American colonies. A division of the three cohorts into standard life cycle divisions appropriate for this time period offers a more subtle glimpse at the composition of the travelers and puts important differences into stark relief. Ages 0 through 4 were infancy; 5 through 14 were the ages of childhood; and those between the ages of 15 and 24 were young adults, primarily engaged in service outside their childhood

Table 1.3. Age structure by destination

Age	Colonies N = 4,870	Soldiers N = 1,406	Continent N = 972	England[a]
0–4	3.1%	—	5.8%	12.40%
5–14	7.5%	.1%	6.4%	19.73%
15–24	59.2%	55.6%	31.9%	17.72%
25–59	30.0%	44.1%	54.8%	42.03%
60+	.2%	.2%	1.1%	8.12%
Average age	22.3	26.0	27.2	

a. E. A. Wrigley and R. S. Schofield, *The Population History of England, 1541–1871*
(Cambridge, Mass.: Harvard University Press, 1981), p. 528. Figures given for the year 1636.

homes. Ages 25 through 59 encompass the adult years of marriage and family construction, and 60+ is considered old age.[39] When regarded through these divisions, the 1635 travelers have distinctive characteristics that set them apart from each other and from the English population as a whole as it looked in 1636.

Dramatic differences distinguish these populations. The merchants and the soldiers were significantly older than all the travelers to America. The continental travelers, while obviously differing from England as a whole in the percentages of people in each age category, did manage to replicate England's overall age distribution and sex ratios, with the preponderance of people falling between the ages of 25 and 59.

Like the travelers to the continent, the soldiers were older than the American-bound travelers. Men in their forties and fifties traveled as soldiers. The age difference suggests that experience was important in the recruitment of soldiers. Men who hesitated to expose themselves to the ravages of colonial life or to the lengthy Atlantic voyage were, for whatever reasons, more willing to partake of England's military excursions, and a middle-aged man who might not thrive or even survive in the colonies could still possess valuable experience that made military service a recurring opportunity. In contrast to the young child-servants who were sent to the colonies, only one young boy, fourteen-year-old Robert Sanders, went to serve as a soldier, and he was differentiated by the London port clerks from the other soldiers as a page.[40] That there were so many soldiers reflected not only the supply but also the demand: the exodus in 1635 coincided with the high point of the Thirty Years War on the continent.

Other immeasurable factors might have selected soldiers. William Booth preferred to become a soldier and to fight overseas than to accept a position inferior to his expectations at home. Moreover, men who fought for England were celebrated in popular culture. A 1632 ballad, "Gallants, to Bohemia," called on "ye noble Britaines" to go to war (Figure 3). The ballad drew a comparison between soldiers and adventurers. Toiling like "bees" with unglamorous diligence, soldiers sought no glory for themselves. "Faint and cold," they fought only to preserve true religion. This verse offered a pointed comparison between these soldiers nestled in their defensive burrows, sacrificing "riches, Pearle and Gold" for their own unassuming obligations. Yet the comparison should not be drawn too sharply. Noble adventurer-warriors provided stirring examples to entice men to war.

> Gilbert, Hawkins, Forbisher,
> and golden Candish, Englands starre:
> With many a knight of noble worth,

The fecond Part.   To the fame tune.

Figure 3. Illustration from "Gallants, to Bohemia" [1632]. Reproduced with permission of the Pepys Library, Magdalene College, Cambridge University.

that compass'd round the circled earth:
Have left examples here behinde,
the like adventures forth to finde:
The which to follow and maintaine,
Come, let us to those warres againe.

In looking to the examples of these English explorers, the soldiers demonstrated that their own efforts were part of the same process of exploration: the soldiers secured the explorers' successes. Those who followed the explorers' lead and joined the effort on the continent would show themselves "true Englishmen."[41] But although there were demographic differences between soldiers and travelers to the colonies, it would be dangerous to draw too many distinctions between the two flows. After all, former military men did take part in colonial ventures, most illustriously in the case of Captain John Smith and the colonial governors Nathaniel Butler and Philip Bell.[42] In fact, the qualitative evidence of colonists with previous military experience would suggest that the age structures should be reversed, with colonists the older of the two.[43]

What the data for the colonial voyagers attest to above all are youth. The most distinctive feature of these travelers is their concentration between the ages of 15 and 24, with 59 percent of the passengers in this age category denoting the time when youths tended to be in service. This was also an age cohort that was likely to be roaming England in search of employment. And, indeed, the people identified in the register came from all over the kingdom. The Commission for Foreign Plantations recognized this geographic mobility and ordered in 1634 that a traveler receive certification from the Justices of the Peace in "the place where he dwelt last or where he dwelt before, if he hath dwelt but a while there."[44] Despite the confusion engendered by frequent migrations and inaccurate listings, the most recent residence can be determined for some 1,200 of the 7,507 travelers of 1635. Table 1.4 displays the range of counties, countries, or colonies of residence: where possible, the last place of residence indicated in the port register has been verified with a variety of genealogical and archival sources, and some corrections made.[45]

Three major trends emerge in Table 1.4. First, the people who embarked at the port of London came from all over Britain. Some travelers, indeed, were obviously Welsh, Scottish, and Irish, as in the case of Thomas Ap-Thomas, Hugh Evans, Griffith Hughes, and Evan Ap-Evan; or that of Dennis Mortagh, Dennis McBrian, Dermond O'Bryan, Teague Quillin, Donough Gorhie, and Brian McGawyn. Few origins are known for the travelers to the Chesapeake, the West Indies, and Bermuda: this fact attests to the mobile nature of England's population and the likelihood of young vagrants whose

Table 1.4. County and country of residence for travelers from London in 1635

County	To New England N	%	To other colonies N	%	To continent N	%	All passengers N	%
London/Middlesex	147	22.0	34	45.9	106	20.2	287	22.6
Essex	78	11.7	2	2.7	4	1	84	6.6
Suffolk	71	10.6	2	2.7	1	.2	74	5.8
Kent	59	8.8			6	1.1	65	5.1
Hertford	60	8.9			2	.4	62	4.9
Buckingham	45	6.7			2	.4	47	3.7
Northampton	39	5.8	3	4.0	1	.2	43	3.4
Surrey	26	3.9			14	2.7	40	3.2
Bedford	22	3.3					22	1.7
York	21	3.1					21	1.7
Cambridge	19	2.8					19	1.5
Sussex	18	2.7			1	.2	19	1.5
Huntingdon	8	1.2					8	.6
Devon	7	1.0					7	.6
Oxford	1	.1			6	1.1	7	.6
Berkshire	6	.9					6	.5
Northumberland	5	.7			1	.2	6	.5
Stafford			1	1.4	5	1	6	.5
Cheshire					4	.8	4	.3
Glamorgan					4	.4	4	.3
Leicester	3	.4			1	.2	4	.3
Lincoln	3	.4			1	.2	4	.3
Wiltshire	3	.4			1	.2	4	.3

Table 1.4. (continued)

County	To New England N	To New England %	To other colonies N	To other colonies %	To continent N	To continent %	All passengers N	All passengers %
Cornwall					3	.6	3	.2
Hereford	3	.4					3	.2
Warwick	1	.1			2	.4	3	.2
Worcester	3	.4					3	.2
Derby	2	.3					2	.2
Dorset	1	.1			1	.2	2	.2
Lancashire	1	.1	1	1.4			2	.2
Norfolk	2	.3					2	.2
Bristol			1	1.4			1	.1
Gloucester	1	.1					1	.1
Monmouth					1	.2	1	.1
Somerset	1	.1					1	.1
Elsewhere in England	3	.4					3	.2
Ireland					42	8	42	3.3
Scotland					7	1.3	7	.6
Continent	3	.4	3	4.0	308	58.6	314	24.7
Bermuda			11	14.9			11	.9
Virginia			10	13.5	1	.4	11	.9
West Indies			6	8.1			6	.5
New England	7	1.0					7	.6
Total	669	99.2	74	100.0	525	101	1,268	100.2

Source: Drawn from London Port Register (E157/20 1-e) and supplementary genealogical and archival sources.

origins little concerned the clerks ending up on board ship. Many of the Providence-bound passengers, for example, were probably from Essex, although no certain evidence exists on this point: the Providence Island Company depended on the personal recruitment by Company members of potential settlers, and the bulk of the Company members were Essex gentry, including Sir Nathaniel Rich, Robert Rich, the Earl of Warwick, and Sir Thomas Barrington.

But not all counties in England were represented equally by the passengers from London. The west, southwest, and west midland counties are significantly underrepresented in the London sample, which most likely reflects the proximity of local west country ports, such as Bristol and Plymouth, from which these travelers could depart. Men and women from northwest England and southwest Scotland also emigrated to colonies, but as Nicholas Canny has demonstrated, their destination was more likely to be Ireland.[46] Another region poorly represented, the north of England, is again consistent with convenience: these travelers could depart from Harwich or Ipswich, both of which ports were closer to travelers coming by coast from the north. The breadth of counties represented here for the New England-bound passengers is particularly important in light of the important role customarily afforded East Anglia in explaining the peculiarities of New England culture.

A second significant feature of this table is the predominance of London itself as a place of origin (22.6 percent). These 287 people were actually residents of the city, not people who just passed through. Thus this table has corrected some of the clerks' listings for passengers to New England certified from London but in fact clearly not residents there. The family of Robert Titus, for example, was certified by the parish minister of St. Katharine by the Tower in London. Robert Titus was listed as a husbandman, which agrarian occupation suggests that he was not a Londoner, and his children's baptisms do not in fact appear in the published parish records.[47] Presumably Titus journeyed to London without a license and procured one precipitously before his departure from an obliging cleric.

The London origins of passengers suggest that the port city was not just a clearinghouse for migrants from other parts of the kingdom. Colonial merchants who traveled in 1635 to Virginia or Barbados, including Thomas Armitage, Nathaniel Wright, Nathaniel Braddock, George Grace, John Chappell, Abraham Johnson, and John Butler, were based in London.[48] Doctor Edward Abbs and the planter Bartholomew Hoskins were Londoners, as was the planter Walter Jenkins. The Bermuda-bound travelers William Alberie, John Glassington, Samson Meverill, and Isaiah Vincent were also denizens of the metropolis.[49]

A final feature of Table 1.4 is the large group of people (25 percent) who were residents abroad when they embarked at the port of London. Thirty six people were already colonial residents and were returning home. Six colonial-bound voyagers—three men, two women, and one child—traveled from the Netherlands. They included the minister Hugh Peter; the engineer Lion Gardiner and his wife, Mary; and the Van Heck family, Oliver, Catherine, and Peter.[50] But the travelers bound for the continent were primarily responsible for the international flavor of the register, with 30 percent of this cohort living abroad. Fortunately, we know why they traveled. These men and women were of particular interest to the clerks at the port: only for this population was the purpose for travel scrupulously recorded (Table 1.5).

The majority of travelers to the continent (308) left London in 1635 in order to return to foreign dwellings. Some of these men were tradesmen who had established themselves abroad; many were probably merchants or factors, and many probably returned home in that year to cities that were members of the Hanseatic League. In an age of shifting diplomatic alliances, the prudent merchant had ships that sailed under different flags. For merchants with Dutch ships, which had to sail in and out of Dutch ports, it was essential to have reliable factors permanently in residence. The Rich family, for example, maintained an agent in either Middelburg or Amsterdam after 1600.[51] More-

Table 1.5. Stated purpose for travel to the continent (excluding soldiers)

Purpose	N	%
To return to residence abroad	308	30.0
On affairs or business	242	23.0
With master or parents	111	11.0
Unknown	104	10.0
To join family	88	9.0
To fetch ship	87	8.0
To visit friends or relatives	22	2.0
To work	11	1.0
To live	10	1.0
To learn language	3	.3
Other [a]	49	4.6
Total	1,034	99.9

a. "Other" includes people retrieving debts, settling family estates, and running a number of other errands.

over, Middelburg served as an important port for English ships: the accounts of the *Abraham* noted that much of the tobacco loaded on board the ship at Barbados in 1637 was destined for Middelburg.[52] Indeed, the expansion of Dutch trade in the seventeenth century attracted many to the region's major ports and cities. Antwerp and Amsterdam were major trading centers, while Leiden and Haarlem were industrial centers. Middelburg and Flushing, which attracted a total of 121 people in 1635, were the major ports of the province of Zeeland. The presence of so many expatriates on these London ships attests to the expectation by men engaged in mercantile activities of temporary sojourn abroad, perhaps a stint in service to family trade interests.[53]

Another 88 people were traveling to join relatives on the continent: these individuals may already have lived abroad themselves, but the register is not entirely clear on this question. These were not only men traveling alone, but entire families, and couples traveling together. The nuclear family of John Whalley, for example, returned to its dwelling in Amsterdam on January 17. The evidence from the register suggests that women accompanied their husbands on their trips across the channel, as in the case of William and Joan Stare, who boarded a ship in July to return to their dwelling in Husenden. Some women returned to England to deliver babies, subsequently boarding ships in London with infants to return to their foreign dwelling. Such was the case for Elizabeth Yard, age 20, who on June 27 registered at the port with her 11-week-old daughter, Elizabeth, and her 2 maidservants. The Yards were bound for Rotterdam, where Elizabeth's husband, a merchant, lived. Likewise, Grace Bowemann and 7-month-old Sarra Bowemann traveled in December of 1634 to Middelburg to join husband and father Symon. Perhaps the danger of childbirth prompted young mothers, especially those facing their perilous first confinement, to delay joining their husbands on the continent until after the child's birth or to rejoin their own families in England at this life-threatening moment.

That some families had lived abroad for a while is indicated not only by the children's foreign places of birth, diligently noted by port clerks, but also in their names. Marie Harris, for example, dwelled in Rotterdam with her husband Francis. She boarded a ship in May with her five children, the middle of whom was named Cornelius. Either Marie herself was Dutch, or residence in Rotterdam had encouraged the Harrises to bestow a distinctly Dutch name on their son. The reverse policy was true for the family of Jane Deboyes, described as the "french wife of Peter Deboyes frenchman." She boarded a ship to Calais in April with her four children, Edward, Susan, Jane, and Judith, French names that had been easily Anglicized and were perhaps selected for that purpose.[54] What this portion of the register reveals, then, is the cosmopolitan nature of life not only in London with its clusters of well-traveled merchants and resident aliens but also in cities abroad that contained sizable populations of expatriate and assimilated English residents.[55]

Residence abroad did not sever people from their friends and family, as the steady stream of visitors attested (110 in this London register alone). Visits to parents, siblings, and grandparents drew London residents overseas. Hugh Davyers of Wigmore went to Flanders to visit his brother Robert, a merchant in Ghent, in December. Likewise, Elizabeth Powell and her infant son, John, traveled in April from London to Leiden to visit her mother. The cosmopolitan nature of these visitors is signaled most dramatically in the case of 3 young men who traveled to the continent solely to study languages. These men were presumably pursuing economic advantage in their studies—their language study was not exactly a junior year abroad. Their youth suggests their status as dependents whose fathers or masters needed their facility in the languages of international trade.[56]

The detail of some of the entries suggests the acute interest the clerks had in these cosmopolitan continental travelers. The register records errands overseas with great care: on February 9, John Rundy was permitted to pass to Rotterdam to recover a debt and was to return within two months. The accuracy could take us to a particular dwelling: when William Best, age 23, presented himself at the port on January 20, the clerk reported that Best lived in the house of one William Loughlyn, a resident in St. Brides Churchyard, and Best was to pass to Amsterdam "to worke on his affayres."

The appeal of opportunities on the continent drew 21 people to the port who planned permanent departures. Of the 11 men who stated their purpose "to work" overseas, occupations were recorded for each one—an indication of the state's interest in these migrants and temporary workers. Three were brick-makers, 4 were shoemakers, and 1 each was a tobacco-pipe maker, a picture maker, a tailor, and a bitmaker. The tobacco pipe maker traveled to Amsterdam in March: his destination was the center of the Dutch Republic's tobacco industry, where Chesapeake leaf was processed before it was exported.[57] The record distinguished these workers from those who were going "to live" on the continent. This category was dominated by women and children, including Samuell (age 8) and Elizabeth (age 5) Vanderpost, 2 recent orphans of Dutch parents who were sent to live, or so the clerks carefully and optimistically stipulated, with "friends" in Middelburg, "their parents being dead."

One motive for travel to the continent that is omitted in the register but that was certainly present in the minds of some travelers who were returning to continental homes or were relocating permanently was religious freedom. The same impulses that led to the Privy Council's heightened concern for travel overseas to England's colonies here pushed some English men and women to the continent: the Netherlands was the first and most convenient refuge for nonconformists eager to leave England.[58] Clusters of nonconformists lived in Amsterdam, the Hague, Leider, and Rotterdam, among other cities. Hugh Peter, who voyaged in 1635 from London to New England, lived first on the continent with other English divines and their congregations: in 1633, 21 English ministers lived in the Netherlands. Most of these served military regiments, but 6 served towns: Hugh Peter served Amsterdam. Seven of these men were members of the English classis, whose unpopular regulation inspired relocation to the colonies.[59]

The exodus of Hugh Peter and other continental ministers to the American colonies signaled important Atlantic connections that are suggested only faintly in the London register. One passenger, Lawrence Fassett, ventured to Ostend in November, as the register put it, "about his merchandizing affairs having carried goods in the Elizabeth of Lo [London]," which that year made a trip to New England in April with 79 passengers. Presumably Fassett intended to sell goods that the *Elizabeth* had brought back from America. As the *Elizabeth* voyaged on from New England to Virginia, she probably returned laden with tobacco.[60] And Richard Wright ventured to Middelburg to receive money due him for a West India voyage. One busy woman precisely embodied this American connection. Jane Gibbs appeared at the port on July 21. She was a resident of Virginia and was to pass to Flushing "about certen her affares."

George Grace reversed Gibbs's travel pattern. Like several other travelers to the colonies, Grace was a merchant. Many merchants were seasoned colonial traders, like John Redman, John Chappell, Nathaniel Wright, Nathaniel Braddock, and Thomas Bradford.[61] Grace traveled to Virginia in 1635 on the *Globe*. In 1638 Grace's wife Agnes petitioned the House of Commons for relief, and in so doing provided a brief, sympathetic, and informed history of her husband's career. Agnes Grace described the London merchant's declining fortunes that took him to Virginia. Before his American voyage, Grace exported cloth to Holland and owned a house in Delft where he kept his goods. Unfortunately, George Grace's servants in Delft died during an outbreak of plague, and when Grace went there himself to examine his affairs, he discovered that his servants had accepted, in lieu of debts owed Grace, "a great number of English bibles," which Grace shipped to London. Because it was illegal to import Bibles, however, the books were seized at the customs house. The Bibles, claimed Agnes Grace, were worth £300, and their loss destroyed her husband's business. George "was constrayned . . . to forsake the kingdome & to goe to Virginia."[62] The travels of George Grace, Jane

Gibbs, and Lawrence Fassett demonstrate the ways in which the single trips of individuals could together enhance the integration of the Atlantic economy.

Grace's enterprises in Virginia and Delft mirrored on an intimate scale the numerous investment opportunities available in this period, especially for men based in London. The city functioned not just as a clearinghouse for travelers but also as a place for overseas investors to gather. David Hancock has noted in his study of a cluster of eighteenth-century merchants called the Associates that these men "could have fully integrated their diverse collection of businesses only from London—the center of world commerce in the eighteenth century."[63] In the seventeenth century, London played a similarly vital role in organizing and financing the colonial and trade ventures that together formed the haphazard and precarious origins of England's empire. The varied activities undertaken in London articulated the overlapping interests of men involved in different colonial adventures and investments. As men such as the Bermuda surveyor Richard Norwood undertook journeys to the east and to the west, so did these investors who gathered in London consider opportunities throughout the world. London facilitated these enterprises. Companies met there, enjoying both the advantages and inconveniences of the metropolis. Companies containing gentry whose estates were scattered throughout England were particularly dependent on London as a central meeting place because these men could gather only seasonally.

London merchants seized opportunities to invest in different overseas ventures. Even as merchants scrambled in the 1610s and 1620s to profit from colonial ventures in America, the London guilds organized their own colonial investment in Ireland starting in 1610, the Londonderry Plantation. The London guilds and companies that controlled the city contributed individually to this effort in the same years that the Virginia Company enthusiastically published broadside after broadside begging skilled artisans to venture to Virginia.[64]

With all these simultaneously tempting opportunities, it is hardly surprising that men involved in one trade opportunity eagerly seized on a second or third. T. K. Rabb has painstakingly demonstrated the overlapping nature of company membership and the role of single proprietors and investors in a range of experiments: men such as George Calvert, Lord Baltimore, who had invested in three different companies (East India, Irish, and Virginia) before setting his sights on founding colonies (Newfoundland and Maryland) as religious sanctuaries.[65] Men of such distinctive wealth, however, were outnumbered by men capable only of modest investments who risked their money in joint-stock ventures such as the East India or Virginia companies.

The overlap in company membership at times could be striking: all the men in the Gosnold Company also belonged to the Virginia Company. Of those members of the Bermuda Company who joined another company (88.8 percent), 94 percent were members of the Virginia Company. And 63.5 percent of the New England Company members who belonged to another company also belonged to the Virginia Company. Many merchants who made their careers in this period used the colonies as their springboard: these were the "new-merchants," men outside the established great London Companies who plunged directly into colonial trade, building their own plantations and, with the profits, establishing themselves as merchants. Once they had secured their careers in London, they turned their attention to other colonies and formed networks with men like themselves.[66] Such men functioned outside charters and companies: hundreds of others invested in colonial companies and joined together to make their interests formal and legal.

But overlapping interests were not dictated by investments in only one kind of enterprise in the Atlantic. That is, men did not put all of their money only into American colonization schemes or into trade with the east or into support for voyages of discovery. These entrepreneurs speculated in a diverse range of activities. Over half of the members of the East India Company invested in other companies, especially the Virginia and Levant companies. Exactly half the Providence Island Company members invested elsewhere: their interests lay in the East India and Virginia companies. Members of the Massachusetts Bay Company were less inclined to invest elsewhere than their counterparts (only 35.2 percent did so), but their investments reflected a cosmopolitan range, with emphasis on the East India, Levant, and Virginia companies. So the disparities in colonial cultures and in mercantile enterprises were not dictated by investors alone, who happily speculated on enterprises from Massachusetts to Africa, from settled plantations to risky trade ventures.[67]

This overlapping membership of investors meant that men in London had experience in a range of enterprises and could bring this experience to bear when they funded and planned new ventures. The planters of Providence Island, for example, complained about the amount of their produce that they were required to give to the company. They protested "that to work by halves is too hard a condcon, alleadging that it is the practice onely of this compa and the Sumr [Somers] Islands." But the members of the Providence Island Company, knowledgeable about colonial affairs, deflected their complaint, answering "that it hath beene the practice of other plantacons."[68]

The knowledge that investors and proprietors brought to their varied overseas investments was echoed by that of the men actually sent to colonies who themselves had experience in other plantations. The result was a population of men with cosmopolitan exposure to a range of military and mercantile efforts. Several travelers from London in 1635 were themselves men experienced in one colony venturing to another. Proprietors competed for such people, wooing them to stay on colonies. Richard Lane, for example, returned home to Providence Island in 1635 aboard the *Expectation,* having been a Providence Island Company employee for almost four years. Lane was loathe at first to return to Providence, as the Company hoped he would do, because of "some Miscariages in the Govermt there." The Company concurred with his assessment of island affairs, and he returned to Providence armed with the Company's support, "he being reputed honest and industrious leaving him at libty to make choice of any ground in the Island." To encourage his return, the Company granted Lane permission to bring his wife and three children with him.[69] Accompanying Lane was another triumph for the Providence Island Company, one William Thorpe, who had previously worked in Bermuda, newly appointed to serve as a lieutenant.[70]

Numerous men crucial to the success of colonial enterprises, like these skilled planters and officers, were sought by different colonies. Governors were in especially high demand. Philip Bell served as governor of Providence, Bermuda, and Barbados. Nathaniel Butler was governor of Providence and Bermuda. John Winthrop, Jr., probably the most cosmopolitan man to grace New England's shores in the middle decades of the seventeenth century, returned to New England in 1635 with the charter for the Saybrook colony, which he was to govern.[71] In a recurring pattern, incentives were offered to those already in the Atlantic world to move from one colony to another. In the planting of Tobago, for example, the Earl of Warwick depended on precisely this willingness to plant new colonies and sought to recruit men from Bermuda and St. Lucia for the new colony. These men were to be offered free transportation, arms, and "great freedomes" to "incourage them to stay and perfect that plantacon."[72]

Thus the American exodus from London, the largest metropolis in Europe, was a product of a time when the adventurous and the desperate faced a plethora of options. Even the ships listed in the 1635 port register reflected these fluid and competing interests. Information about the ships and their sailing patterns demonstrates the important connections between different commercial ventures. Consider, for example, when ships set sail. Attention to health intermingled with trade interests, which together dictated sailing patterns. It was this conflict between what was beneficial for the passengers and the safe passage of the ship and what was advantageous for international trading schemes that increased mortality rates for many new arrivals to the colonies.

Experienced planters advised newcomers about when to reach new colonies. The Virginia Company's secretary, John Rolfe, noted that travelers should leave England in June and arrive in Virginia in September, at harvest time. Newcomers were urged to arrive before winter in order to get their clothes ready in time in a country with few tailors. These practical considerations of what was good for newcomers and what was good for the colony also tied into the benefits for English trade. In this vein Rolfe continued that the ships could then leave Virginia after the harvest and be back in England by Candlemas before the East India ships set out, "wch will help ye speedy venting ye [tobacco]."[73] The ships that the Virginia company sent in 1621 more or less complied with Rolfe's advice. They were concentrated in the spring and summer, but three ships sailed in November, and the four ships that left England in August must have landed their new arrivals late in the harvest season, therefore requiring the ships to return to London in a second uncomfortable trip during the long and dangerous hurricane season.[74]

Table 1.6 displays the sailing patterns of ships for all the colonial destinations delineated in the 1635 register. Of the twenty ships leaving for Virginia

Table 1.6. Sailing patterns of ships from London to America, 1635

	Destination					
Month sailed	New England	Virginia	St. Kitts	Barbados	Bermuda	Providence Island	Total ships
January		1		1			2
February				1			1
March	1						1
April	5		1	3		1	10
May	2	2	1	1			6
June	1	3			1		5
July	5	6					11
August	1	5					6
September	2	1	1		1		5
October		2	2				4
November				1			1
December				1			1
Total ships							53

from London in 1635, most tried to plan arrivals in Virginia for the late summer or early fall: fourteen of the ships left London between July and October. One ship braved a winter crossing, whereas five others left in May and June. The ships to the Caribbean did not display a comparable commitment to arrival times that would spare newcomers the unpleasant summer months. Eight ships out of fifteen left between September and February, but the remaining seven ships left London in April and May, thus depositing travelers during the hottest times of the year.

Some of these ships and masters already maintained regular schedules, which was a critical process in the economic integration of the Atlantic world. When the *James* reached New England in June of 1635, John Winthrop noted that Mr. Graves, the master, "had come everye yeare for these 7: years."[75] The *Hopewell* of London specialized in New England voyages, making two such trips in 1635. The *Merchant's Hope* of London left on July 31 for Virginia in 1635. Almost precisely a year earlier, the same ship embarked on August 8 for Virginia.[76] Planters on Bermuda knew when to expect ships from London to collect their crops: a Spaniard there noted that the ships came every year at the same time to load tobacco.[77]

The register provides only the barest information about the ships that sailed from London. Ship, home port, master and destination were all the clerks thought necessary. Although clerks presumably did not intend to be inaccurate, the information they provided was incomplete. The *Expectation*, for example, was the one ship sent to Providence Island by the Providence Island Company in 1635. In fact, the Company's records indicate that the ship went first to St. Christopher, and after she called there, the Company rented the use of her for £110 a month from Mr. Woodcock, a member of the Company and the owner of the ship.[78] All ships leaving London for the southern mainland colonies were simply described as bound for Virginia. With the settlement of Maryland in 1634, many of these ships deposited passengers there as well, most notably the very first ship of the year, the *Bonaventure*.[79] Other omitted destinations, however, suggest that Atlantic voyages ranged widely over the colonial world. The *Hopewell*, for example, on her second voyage of the year to New England appeared in the port register with New England as her sole destination. But the ship carried goods which were to be delivered not only to New England, but also to Virginia. Unfortunately for the ship and its passengers alike, the pilot acquired by the ship in the Plymouth colony ran her aground, and the master, Richard French, abandoned the ship and sent the eleven or twelve Virginia passengers, which included a Mr. Bentley and his ten servants, south in other boats. The *Hopewell* limped back to London, which voyage was easier to make than the one down the coast to Virginia because of westerly winds.[80]

The voyage of the *Hopewell* to both Virginia and New England and that of the *Expectation* to St. Christopher and Providence reflect the practicalities of Atlantic travel and the need for mariners and merchants to man ships with full holds. Rare was a ship like the *Thomas and John,* which sailed to Virginia in 1635 and came directly back to London.[81] Ship's masters needed to be flexible, as the captain of the *Hope of Ipswich* demonstrated. Bound for New England in 1635, the ship was supposed to sail from there to the Isle of May. But "contrary winds" sent her to Barbados, where the accommodating captain loaded his vessel with cotton and tobacco and returned to London.[82] Few mariners received such detailed instructions as Thomas Punt, the master of the *Charity,* which was sent by the Providence Island Company to the Indies in 1632. After he left London, Punt was to call at Plymouth to collect a minister and other passengers. Then it was on to St. Kitts, Nevis, or Barbados to load water, cotton seed, and pomegranate slips, as well as salt from St. Martin. From St. Martin, Punt was bound for Association to deposit seven passengers and to load tobacco seed and guinea pepper. Then, finally, it was on to Providence to deliver passengers, goods, and letters. From Providence, the captain was ordered to sail back to Association and deliver fig slips acquired on Providence. There the captain was to take in wood and tobacco. Finally, if it were safe, the captain was to travel to Bermuda and deposit there the passengers from Providence.[83]

These multifaceted voyages also indicate that the transportation of passengers was only one aspect of commercial enterprises and ocean voyages. While passengers waited for ships to embark, filled with trepidation about the hazards of the voyage and the colonial conditions awaiting them, shipmasters were preoccupied with concerns about fair winds, safe seas, and ballast. These westward voyages were part of larger mercantile endeavors. The case of the *Love* reinforces this point. The *Love,* a small ship with only 8 registered passengers bound for New England in 1635, ultimately canceled her voyage because of insufficient time. John Thierry, who owned the *Love,* had hired her to William Woodcock and Joseph Yonge for a voyage to New England. Thierry allotted Woodcock and Yonge only ten months for the voyage, however, and the 2 men ran out of time after they had loaded on the ship 30 people in England, 450 sheep in Denmark, and 40 goats in Ireland. After these projects, Woodcock and Yonge concluded that the ship could not sail to New England and then return to England within the ten months stipulated, and the voyage was abandoned.[84]

The voyage of the *Love,* thwarted by the inflated commercial ambitions of its owners, highlights the place of London as a staging ground for a variety of commercial activities. For these merchants, transporting passengers to New England was simply part of a larger entrepreneurial venture. These merchants hoped to profit by selling a variety of goods in New England during a decade of high inflation, and peopling the colony was one small part of that endeavor. But although the transportation of people was for many an afterthought as ships were prepared for profitable ocean voyages, the migration embodied in this secondary economic interest would prove to be essential in securing colonies and their future profits.

The London register captures individuals and families only in snapshots, but the information in the register enables us to fill in other parts of their individual narratives: to fathom the trepidation with which expectant mothers greeted childbirth, a fear so immense that it sent them across the English Channel to their families and friends at home; and to share the grief and isolation of the newly orphaned Vanderpost children, who were traveling alone to a country that was no longer theirs, but indeed now foreign. What distinguishes this particular migration is the certainty with which we can measure its scope.[85] It is essential to see the westward movement that is the centerpiece of this book and that was the source of England's colonial success as part of a much larger range of mercantile and migratory adventures. It was precisely this migration that ensured the viability of England's new colonies and that slowly and uncertainly knit England and its colonies together into a new Atlantic world.

2 | *The Colonial Travelers of 1635*

The presence of 4,878 men, women, and children in a single port register groups together individuals of diverse experiences and expectations. Though sharing a common port of departure and the discomforts of a transatlantic voyage, the passengers who embarked from London in 1635 varied substantially according to their colonial destinations. Historians emphasizing the different nature of England's new colonies have rightly attested to the divergent character of their settlers. These interpretations have depended heavily on English temperament or geographic origin as main explanations for the varied nature of colonial societies. But the men and women who ventured to the American colonies in 1635 varied in other important features, especially demographic attributes captured in age structures and sex ratios, which were equally significant in constraining overseas travel and colonial settlements.

The consequence of these variations was skewed shipboard societies, measured by English standards, dominated occupationally by servants and demographically by young men, whose preponderance overturned age hierarchies in place in English society. These fundamental features shaped conditions of travel and the whole enterprise of removal overseas for the travelers of 1635. Moreover, demographic distinctions had lingering repercussions. For those colonies only recently established—Barbados (1627), Massachusetts (1630), Providence (1630), and especially Maryland (1634) and Connecticut (1635)—the age structures and sex ratios of the traveling passengers would echo those of the resident populations newly arrived, and distorted arriving populations would continue to distort existent colonial populations. Thus the obvious demographic distinctions between different traveling cohorts point to profound variations in each colony and epitomize some of the difficulty that new residents had in constructing cultural practices that resembled those they had been familiar with in England. Two vignettes from July of 1635 illustrate the varied experiences of men who embarked from the port of London.

On July 10, 1635, Nathaniel Braddock sat down to compose his will. A citizen and mercer of London, Braddock had lived in the metropolis for some fourteen years, since 1621 when he had first journeyed from his childhood home in Wyneton, Northamptonshire, to commence his eight-year apprenticeship with Edward Burrish. His new master was a member of the Mercers' Company, one of London's great companies, which, along with the city's guilds, directed London's political and economic life. After eight years Braddock had completed his apprenticeship, and he garnered the freedom of the Company in 1629.

The commencement of his membership in the Company, however, coincided with the growth of new family obligations. In the years since Nathaniel had left Northampton, his father had died. Nathaniel took his family responsibilities seriously, remembering in his will his two nephews by two different sisters, his brother, and a third sister, still unmarried, who would be particularly dependent on the good will of her elder brother if she were to gain a portion sufficient to ease her marriage. Braddock's two servants, William Salesbury and Bernard Osler, witnessed their master's will, by their presence silently attesting to Braddock's success in his trade.[1]

Nathaniel Braddock was a young man when he publicly and legally documented his solicitous attention to his brother, sisters, and nephews through the legacies he bequeathed them. These legacies were possible because of Braddock's lucrative profession. Braddock's father had wisely selected a trade for his son that would be distinguished by potentially enormous wealth: indeed, a company apprenticeship itself could cost hundreds of pounds. Mercers were merchants who specialized in importing and exporting textiles, England's largest nonagricultural product. The possibility of gaining a sizable fortune was very real, especially with the import of luxury fabrics from the Low Countries. And once a man became a trader of one commodity, he could easily shift his interests to other goods, including those from the new world. As for Braddock the temptation to venture into other marketable goods must have been strengthened by the demise of English textile production in the face of overseas competition. It is clear from his will that America had attracted his attention, as it had that of so many other London mercers. Fellow members of the Mercers' Company who traveled in 1635 from London included Robert Jeofferies, who ventured to New England with his family, and Lawrence Brimley, Rowland Sadler, and John Duncombe.[2] Many other men, small-scale traders who were not members of the most powerful London companies, launched their trading careers by venturing to America alongside these trained and well-connected merchants.[3]

What prompted Braddock's summoning of the scrivener was an anticipated journey, announced in his will as the precipitating cause for ordering his affairs. Three weeks after he wrote his will, Braddock left his home in the city and traveled to the port. There he was examined by the minister of Gravesend, who attested to his conformity with the Church of England, all the passengers having first taken the oath of allegiance and supremacy. Nathaniel Braddock then boarded the *Merchant's Hope,* bound for Virginia with seventy-five passengers under Captain Hugh Weston (Figure 4).

Braddock might have traveled to Virginia on his own behalf on a new speculative venture or as a representative of a private London merchant firm. Not until the middle of the seventeenth century did merchants turn to resident factors, and thus numerous men traveling were, like Braddock, individual merchants probably transacting business for a number of people.[4]

Figure 4. Nathaniel Braddock's name (bottom right) entered in the port register for his voyage to Virginia aboard the *Merchant's Hope* (E 157/20 1-e, PRO). Courtesy of the Public Record Office.

For all that his voyage was commonplace, however, Braddock traveled alone, leaving behind even his servants. And within less than a year, he was dead: in ten months Braddock's will was proved in court, and his brother-in-law assumed the tedious task of administering Braddock's estate. In his solitary travel and in his early death, Braddock typified the experience of hundreds of other travelers who left London for Virginia in 1635. In marked contrast was the experience of a group of travelers who had reached Gravesend earlier in the month, just as Nathaniel Braddock pondered the disposition of his London affairs. On July 4, the port clerks dutifully inscribed the names of a group of eleven men and women who traveled together, bound for New England aboard the *Defence* (Figure 5). This collection of neighbors, relations, master, servants, and patron sharply contrasted with Braddock's solitary departure from his home in London.

This group of eleven people was headed by Roger Harlakenden, a 23-year-old gentleman and a second son from Earls Colne, Essex. The Harlakenden family was a distinguished one in Essex. As noted patrons of puritan divines, the Harlakendens had offered protection to the nonconformist cleric Thomas

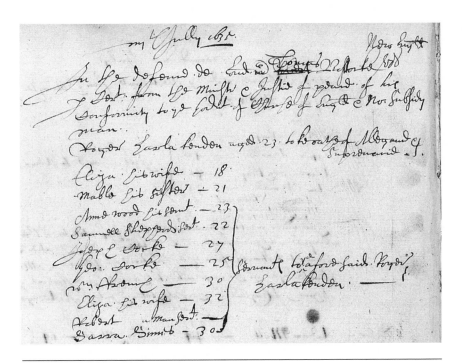

Figure 5. Roger Harlakenden and his ten companions, entered into the port register for their voyage aboard the *Defence,* bound for New England (E 157/20 1-e, PRO). Courtesy of the Public Record Office.

Shepard after he fell foul of the Laudian regime.[5] With Roger Harlakenden was his wife, Elizabeth, and his younger sister, Mabel. Accompanying the privileged Harlakendens were eight other people: five men and three women identified as their servants. And three of them, Anne Wood, Sarra Simes, and one Robert (with no reported last name), probably were servants.[6] But the other five were not. They included the brothers Joseph and George Cooke, the yeoman sons of an Essex neighbor; William French and his wife Elizabeth; and one Samuel Shepard. This Samuel Shepard was, in fact, the brother of the former Earls Colne minister Thomas Shepard.[7] Disguised as servants and protected by a gentleman, Shepard, French, and the Cooke brothers, all nonconformists, were able to secure permission to depart England, permission they could not obtain on their own behalf. Journeying with friends, neighbors, and a wealthy protector, these men and women made their way to London from Earls Colne with some trepidation about their experiences at the port, but buffered by their kin. In marked contrast to Nathaniel Braddock's solitary voyage, Roger Harlakenden took with him his wife and his sister, three servants to ease his travels, old neighbors and friends to help him in the plantation of New England, and the conviction that his flight served needs more pressing than his own.

The contrasts between these planned relocations were stark. Braddock undertook an onerous business venture that ended quickly in his death. Harlakenden and his companions, all hoping to be vessels of glory and journeying in large part "for the quiet of their own minds," together would seek to establish God's kingdom in New England.[8] Of their particular group, three would return to England, as Braddock had intended to do. Two would die within a few years of their arrival in New England. Harlakenden, like Braddock, died soon after his arrival in New England: within three years, he fell victim to smallpox, leaving behind his wife and daughters. But even his death transpired in the company of friends, with Thomas Shepard present, presumably on Harlakenden's deathbed, to witness the will and to salve the spirit of his former Essex benefactor's younger son.[9]

Braddock and the Harlakenden company enacted on an intimate scale the experiences of the thousands of other travelers in that year. Profiles of the migrating cohorts suggest that the important demographic features of these two relocations were shared by other passengers. Characteristics ranging from age structure to sex ratios to the number of passengers on each ship attest to the profoundly different populations in motion. Sex ratios provide a stark measure of these differences (Table 2.1). The passengers bound for the West Indian colonies of Barbados and St. Kitts were distinctly male-dominated, as were those bound for Bermuda and Virginia. The traveling population, moreover, was not unlike the resident populations. The most contemporaneous

Table 2.1. Sex ratios by colonial destination (%)

Sex[a]	New England N = 1,161	Providence Island N = 75	Virginia N = 2,005	Bermuda N = 218	Barbados N = 982	St. Kitts N = 423	Total N = 4,864
Male	60.9	62.7	86.4	90.8	94	94.8	82.4
Female	39.1	37.3	13.6	9.2	6	5.2	17.6

Source: E 157/20 1-e, PRO.

a. In some cases sex is not clear from some names, including particularly Constant, Christian (at least one New Englander and one Bermudian were female Christians) and Francis (again, with no deviation in spelling, both men and women were Francis), so the totals here are in some cases less than the total number of passengers.

demographic information for Virginia, the Muster of 1624/5, showed a population only slightly more balanced than that described in Table 2.1 for new arrivals, with 76.7 percent of the residents male a decade before.[10] While the sex ratios of the New England–bound and Providence-bound travelers more closely approximated English society as a whole, travel overseas remained overwhelmingly a man's business.

A close study of the age characteristics of the different populations reveals similar disparities between each cohort (Table 2.2). In each category the distribution of the travelers, regardless of destination, is a distortion of contemporaneous English society, and except for the New England–bound travelers, the distortion was as pronounced as it was in the case of sex ratios. The category of most important value, at least from the perspective of colonial

Table 2.2. Age structure by colonial destination (%)

Age	New England N = 1,169	Providence Island N = 72	Virginia N = 2,005	Bermuda N = 218	Barbados N = 983	St. Kitts N = 423	England[a]
0–4	11.2	4.2	.7	.9	0	.5	12.40
5–14	20.7	4.2	3.1	13.3	2.0	2.1	19.73
15–24	30.1	54.2	68.3	64.7	69.9	69.0	17.72
25–59	37.4	37.5	27.8	21.1	28.1	28.4	42.03
60+	.6	0	.1	0	0	0	8.12
Average age	22.2	23.8	22.7	20.5	22.7	22.8	

a. E. A. Wrigley and R. S. Schofield, *The Population History of England, 1541–1871* (Cambridge, Mass.: Harvard University Press, 1981), p. 528. Figures given for year 1636.

investors, was that of youths between the ages of 15 and 24. This was the age during which young men and women in England were likely to be engaged outside their parents' homes in agricultural or domestic service. The migrations to Virginia, St. Kitts, and Barbados were virtually identical in the percentage of individuals in this category. For all three colonies, the vast preponderance of passengers fell in the category of young adulthood with only tiny percentages of children, and virtually no infants, revealing the extent to which the Caribbean and Chesapeake migrations were not family affairs.[11] The absence of age differentiation between the Caribbean and Chesapeake migrations suggests that at this very early stage of settlement, there was little difference in the extent to which one colony received more skilled labor than another, as was later the case.[12] In that age of rising population and underemployment, I suspect that the majority of servants had few skills.

Those voyaging to Bermuda were also heavily in the servant category, but what distinguished Bermuda servants was their youth. In a pronounced departure from the English pattern, the majority of children in the 5 to 14 age category were indentured servants. The average age of these children was 12.5 years, and except for two possible sibling sets who may have been traveling with kin with different surnames or joining family in Bermuda, each one of the other twenty-seven children in this age group was traveling alone. There were, for example, five 10-year-old boys who traveled to Bermuda with no apparent relatives on board their ships. These children and the others who traveled with them were likely servants whose status had been secured by their poverty. They had been rounded up from almshouses and institutions such as London's Bridewell Hospital.[13] The Bridewell, created to deal with vagrant youths, provided lists of young people to be sent to the colonies: in 1635, five boys were registered with such a fate.[14]

Bermuda's willingness to accept these young vagrants was not new. The minister Lewis Hughes, in a 1625 account of island affairs, reported "that many poore boyes and girls, (taken up, out of the streetes, out of Newgate and Bridewell and the Hospitals) were sent to the Sommers Ilands." Their treatment there was shoddy, Hughes continued, for they were not instructed in the basic tenets of faith, and their children, when these young vagrants subsequently married, could not be baptized because of their parents' great ignorance.[15] By 1639 a Spaniard shipwrecked on the island noted the colony's continuing use of these young servants when he observed that the island's field-workers were "boys, who are either orphans or have been abandoned."[16]

As for individuals bound for the plantation colonies of Virginia, Barbados, St. Kitts, and Bermuda who fell between the ages of 25 and 59, they encompassed a range of occupations—some older servants, some first-time planters, some merchants. People who were already residents of the colonies but were returning home from London in 1635 also fell into this age cohort: a profile of these returners yields average ages between 37 and 42 for these colonies (see Appendix B, Table B.8).

The Providence Island passengers more closely approximated English society: there were at least some small children traveling with their parents, and the 37.5 percent of adults aged 25 through 59 more closely mirrored the 42.03 percent of the English population in this category. The presence of families, however, was a recent departure for the Providence Island Company. As a matter of policy, the Company had discouraged planters from bringing their wives with them. Only valued officers, such as Governor Philip Bell, who threatened to quit over a salary dispute and had to be placated, were allowed their wives. Not until 1635 did this policy prohibiting families relax, and that is why the sex ratio of this particular group of travelers was as balanced as it was for the New England travelers. The most vivid symbol of the Company's change of heart was the presence of a midwife aboard the *Expectation* in 1635.[17] In this year Providence Island still received many servants, with over half the population arriving in 1635 likely to be servants.[18]

Of the travelers bound for New England, many comprised families who brought small children with them. Thus the comparative youth of New England's population is explained not as in the Bermuda case by child-servants but rather by the presence of many children—363 of them altogether—who traveled with relatives or friends: Robert Long brought 10 children with him to New England, and Richard Hollingsworth traveled with 4 children, all under the age of 7 years. Of all the migrant streams, the New England cohort most closely resembled English society, but even there significant differences emerge. Most striking is the high percentage of passengers in the age category during which youths were likely to be in service. Some of these youths, certainly, were dependent children, yet of the 350 people in this age category, 216 were single travelers not with family members and not listed with occupations. Thus it is possible that as much as 61 percent of this age group were servants.[19]

In light of the segments of the English population most likely to be in motion in search of employment, the predominance of young men is completely consistent with patterns of internal migration, particularly in a period of population growth. The youth and overwhelming male majority of the non–New England travelers suggest that this desperate population found an answer to unemployment and hardship at home in secondary migrations overseas. Demographic information based on age structure intimates that the majority of travelers to the colonies were servants: qualitative contemporary evidence supports this view. Occupations can be re-created for one-fifth of the New England travelers and for two ships that sailed in 1635, the *Expectation,* bound for Providence Island, and the *Constance,* bound for Virginia. Thus the following three examples together demonstrate servant ratios for a variety of colonies: New England, with its family-centered economy; Virginia, with its labor-intensive tobacco plantations; and Providence, with its fitful plantation production, its mixed population of Indian, English, and African laborers, and its emerging commitment by 1635 to an economy centered on privateering.

The Providence Island Company, unlike some of the larger colonial ventures, was able to keep close track of the individuals sent out to the colony. Because the Company sent only one ship to Providence Island, Association, and Henrietta in 1635, provisioning that ship with both people and goods merited the vigilant attention of investors. Meetings held from February to May of 1635 recorded the different individuals destined for the colony and provide a fairly complete portrait of the occupational structure of the passengers.[20] By the time the *Expectation* set sail for the Caribbean, her passengers numbered 76, 48 of whom can be identified with certainty by occupation: 22 were servants.[21]

Travel to Virginia, too, was dominated numerically by servants. Depositions by the passengers in the failed voyage of the *Constance* mention 45 different individuals who intended to sail to Virginia (the port register itself lists a total of 85 people on board the Constance). Of these 45 people, 31 were explicitly referred to as servants, while another four men had their passage paid by other people. If the proportions of occupations on the *Constance* are any indication of trends for voyagers to Virginia as a whole, then approximately 77 percent of passengers were servants, while another 15 percent were planters who were either returning home to the colony or were first-time settlers of independent means.[22] Virginia ships had large numbers of single men over the age of 35 who do not appear in the colony records but were probably London merchants on business. Indeed, several of these men, including Nathaniel Braddock, John Redman, John Butler, and George Grace, appear in various London port books as importers of tobacco and other colonial products.

Evidence for the occupation of New England passengers is much more detailed than for passengers to other destinations although, unlike the examples of the *Expectation* and the *Constance,* it is unfortunately impossible to re-create completely the occupational composition of any single ship. The port clerks recorded occupations for 192 individuals, but supplemental information yields occupation for 254 passengers to New England from London in 1635.[23] Of these, 84 were servants.[24]

With this occupational information, it is possible to compare Providence, Virginia, and New England and to demonstrate with certainty what logic

Table 2.3. Servants to the colonies in 1635 (sample)

Destination	Virginia (aboard the *Constance*) N = 45	New England (all known) N = 254	Providence (aboard the *Expectation*) N = 48
No. servants	35	84	22
% servants	77%	33.8%	46%
% travelers ages 15–24[a]	68.3%	30.1%	54.2%

a. For the whole population bound for each colony.

dictates, that there is a close correlation between the percentage of travelers between the ages of 15 and 24 and the percentage of travelers engaged as servants (Table 2.3). The correlation is not exact, but the proximity of the two measurements—the percentage of servants and the percentage of people between the ages of 15 and 24—is clear. The variation was as small as 3.7 percent and as great as 8.7 percent. Thus the data presented here suggest that historians can draw certain conclusions about the occupational profile of travelers if they know the age structure of a population, at least for the first half of the seventeenth century. In this case we find that the great majority of travelers to America as a whole were servants in these early decades of colonial development, and that what immediately defined sea travel and colonial societies was the predominance of male servants.

The large numbers of servants, especially male servants, in an age of high internal migration and vagrancy, attest, moreover, to the ways in which this port register was particular to London, the great magnet for underemployed and unemployed English men. We see this feature most fully in the occupational composition of the passengers to New England (Table 2.4).

The population that sailed from London differed in two measures from New England passengers described elsewhere. Other studies have been uniformly consistent in their range of 20 to 25 percent of individuals in the cloth trade, whereas the London figures demonstrate that only 12 percent were in the trade. One explanation for this discrepancy is that of convenience: people in cloth-producing areas (East Anglia, Kent, and the West Country) lived closer to other ports, including Harwich, Ipswich, and Dover, than to London, and may have elected to leave from a nearer port. The dearth of people in the London cohort in maritime trades, too, is consistent with the possibility that fishermen and others who lived in coastal areas chose to depart from nearby ports. But the most distinctive variation lies in the percentage of travelers who were servants. Although only one other study measured this

Table 2.4. Occupational distribution of travelers to New England (%)

Occupation	Games N=254	Anderson N=139	Tyack N=147	Salerno N=124	Breen-Foster N=42	Cressy N=242
Professional	3.2	3.6	27.2	2.4	4.8	2.1
Agricultural	18.5	33.8	16.3	28.2	26.2	22.3
Cloth trades	*10.2*	25.2	23.1	24.2	23.8	20.7
Other trades	31.5	35.3	29.9	45.2	40.5	28.9
Maritime	.8	2.2	3.4	0.0	4.8	1.2
Laborers	.8	n.a.	n.a.	n.a.	n.a.	4.1
Servants	*33.8*	n.a.	n.a.	n.a.	n.a.	*20.7*
Other	2.3	n.a.	n.a.	n.a.	n.a.	n.a.

Source (except col. 1): David Hackett Fischer, *Albion's Seed: Four British Folkways in America* (New York: Oxford University Press, 1989), p. 30.

population of laborers, the rates are markedly higher for the population from London. Almost 34 percent of the travelers from London with known occupations were servants, compared with almost 21 percent in David Cressy's study of migration. The occupational evidence above for New England points to the ways in which this New England-bound population that departed London in 1635 differed not only from other populations bound for England's colonies but also from New England–bound passengers who traveled from other ports and in other years.

These differences between the cohort depicted in the London port register and those profiled by other historians, however, do not diminish the value of the register nor the representativeness of the population that it enumerated. London accounted for probably half, if not the majority, of all travelers to the colonies in this and other years. Historians of New England can no more dismiss people who traveled from London than they can dismiss populations venturing forth from East Anglian ports—the populations that have received such close scrutiny.

These characteristics of the passengers for the colonies in 1635 illustrate a single and familiar argument: that travelers varied greatly depending on their destination. The travelers to New England and Providence achieved a fairly even sex ratio, unlike their counterparts to the Chesapeake and to the other island colonies. All traveling populations were young, with few children traveling anywhere other than New England. Above all, the migrations were dominated by men traveling in conditions of servitude. But other features of the migratory flows shaped the experience of travel. The accumulated demographic features profiled here indicate that most passengers to New England voyaged with family members, whereas most travelers to other colonies traveled alone, or, at best, with siblings. Indeed, at least 60 percent of travelers to New England enjoyed the company of family members. No other migrating cohort enjoyed this luxury. Only 35 possible family groups, for example, went to Virginia, and that figure includes siblings who probably traveled as servants. Only 14 of those groups were nuclear families.[25] Among the Barbados-bound travelers only 30 people, or 3 percent of the traveling population, journeyed with relatives. Of the travelers to Bermuda, 18 percent enjoyed the company of relatives.

The traveling cohorts to New England, or "companies," could at times be huge. One of the largest family groups traveling together in 1635 was the Tuttle clan from St. Albans, Hertfordshire, who journeyed on the *Planter* to Ipswich, Massachusetts. St. Albans is an abbey town about 20 miles from London. In the seventeenth century, St. Albans was also a provincial market town. Benjamin Hare's plan of St. Albans, drawn in 1634, reveals the dense concentration of houses along the Watling road and around the abbey (Figure 6). For all its provincial importance, the town had only one main street, but it was a crucial thoroughfare whose existence ensured the economic viability of the community as the first major stopping point on the Watling road out of London. For the Tuttle family, the disjunction between life in bustling St. Albans, a city physically dominated by an immense stone abbey, and colonial life in Ipswich must have been stunning.

This disjunction between a "thronged place" and the "wide wildernesse" was softened for the Tuttles by the presence of family and neighbors in their new home.[26] The center of the family group contained Joan Antrobus Lawrence Tuttle, born in St. Albans to Walter and Joan Antrobus, and her second husband, John Tuttle. With Joan Tuttle traveled her four children from her first marriage to Thomas Lawrence. Three were underage—John, Marie, and William Lawrence, and the fourth was her daughter Jane, who had married George Giddings, a yeoman of Clapham, Bedfordshire, in 1634.[27] Joan Tuttle also brought her mother, Joan Antrobus, who had been widowed in 1614, and the four children from her second marriage, Abigail, John, Sara, and Symon. This family of twelve was rounded out by three servants transported by George Giddings, and one by John Tuttle.

The Tuttles had achieved in St. Albans a significant degree of local status. Joan Tuttle's father, Walter Antrobus, had been one of the twenty-four assistants of the borough of St. Albans.[28] Her first husband, Thomas Lawrence, was a constable of the borough in 1614, and at his death left a sizable estate of £823.1.8.[29] John Tuttle, Joan Antrobus's second husband, was a draper

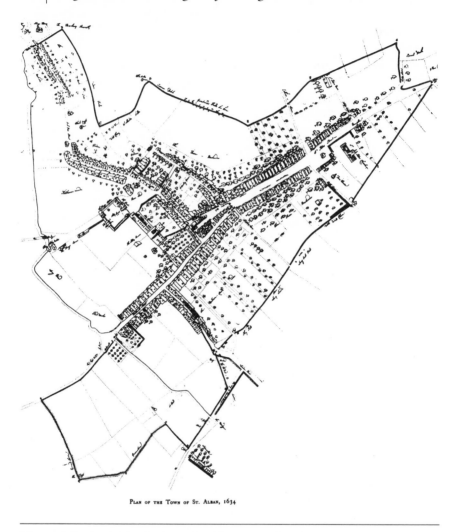

PLAN OF THE TOWN OF ST. ALBAN, 1634

Figure 6. Benjamin Hare's plan of St. Albans, Hertfordshire, 1634. Reproduced courtesy of the Hertfordshire Archives and Local Studies (ST ALB 380).

who paid £6 freedom money to the borough and merited the honorific of "Mr" in the court record of this transaction.[30] By 1630 he had served as constable of the borough.[31] Also accompanying the St. Albans Tuttles were Richard and William Tuttle, with their six children, two wives, and mother, relatives of John from Bedfordshire, John Tuttle's original home.[32] Thus, altogether twenty-seven members of the extended Tuttle clan journeyed together, after their rendezvous at the port of London, to New England. Their gathering at the port suggests the convenience that a central location like

London could offer these relatives who had lived scattered from each other in England.

Those New Englanders who did not travel with their entire families often achieved a family reunion on the other side of the Atlantic. As an early promotional tract acknowledged, "One brother may draw over another, a sonne the father, and perhaps some man his inward acquaintance."[33] The hazards of colonial life encouraged many men to delay their reunions with their families. The passenger lists in 1635 contained both men who went on ahead and families awaiting reunions. Ann Gillam and her toddler son Benjamin, who traveled from Stepney to join her husband, Benjamin, a carpenter in Boston, were among the ten women with twenty-three children who left from London in 1635 to meet husbands in New England. Elizabeth Eliot found an especially warm welcome in Roxbury, where she and her five children were reunited with her husband, Philip Eliot, and her brothers-in-law, John and Francis Eliot, and their families and other neighbors from Nazing, Essex, and the nearby parishes of Ware and Amwell, Hertfordshire. Some families left behind children who traveled later: Thomas Ewer, of Strood, Kent, traveled with his wife and two children, aged $1\frac{1}{2}$ and 4, but his son John, age 7 when the family migrated, remained in England, and later joined the family.[34] Young children who traveled in 1635, such as the brothers Daniel and John Prior, who joined their father in Scituate, or 13-year-old Elizabeth Epps, who traveled in the custody of her kinsman John Winthrop, Jr., demonstrated the gradual process through which family migrations were completed. But not only New England–bound passengers achieved reunion with relatives on their arrival in the colonies. Twelve-year-old Cornelius Maye traveled on the *Safety* to Virginia, where his father was a planter.[35] Katherine Wilson journeyed to the same colony with her young sons, Richard and Robert, to join her husband, Richard. In all, five mothers with children joined Virginia planter husbands, and six men without their wives traveled with their children to Virginia.

In other cases, children, especially adults, preceded their parents, as the brothers Philip and Nathaniel Kirtland did when they left their parents in Buckinghamshire for Lynn, Massachusetts, to establish a home for their family. But the Kirtland brothers hardly traveled alone. Accompanying them on the *Hopewell* were twenty-two neighbors and relatives from their home parish and adjacent parishes in Buckinghamshire. This cluster of Buckinghamshire neighbors and relatives typifies the organization behind New England voyages.

The New Englanders were distinguished from their fellow travelers in this important and measurable way—they traveled with purpose to London to board ships for the colonies. There, like the three branches of the Tuttle clan,

Table 2.5. Five sample ships bound for New England from London, 1635

Ship	Total no. registered passengers	Residence known		Month sailed
		N	%	
Planter	118	94	79.7	April
Hopewell[a]	68	53	77.9	April
Susan and Ellen	91	38	41.8	May
Defence	114	82	71.9	June
Abigail	180	101	56.1	July

a. The *Hopewell* made two voyages in 1635. The passenger list for the first voyage is used here.

they often joined kin from other parts of England to travel overseas. In the absence of extant sources documenting their organization, the invisible process of mobilization is suggested in the regional biases of individual ships in 1635: no single ship provided a microcosm of the New England-bound population as a whole in terms of the geographic origins of the travelers. The accompanying tables demonstrate the extent to which particular counties were overrepresented on five selected ships. For each of five selected ships, Table 2.5 indicates the percentage of passengers for whom the most recent county of residence is known.

By comparing the origins of travelers on particular ships with the geographic origins of the New England sample as a whole, Table 2.6 suggests the extent to which travelers organized themselves so as to brave the uncertainty of an Atlantic crossing with relatives and neighbors. The overrepresentation of any one county, marked in bold on the table, reveals the organization of passengers to New England. Of the 180 listed passengers on the *Abigail*, for example, county of residence is known for 101, or 56.1 percent of the total. Of those 101 people, fully 37.6 percent were from London or Middlesex, compared with 22.0 percent of the whole migrating population, while an additional 14.9 percent were from Sussex, compared with 2.7 percent for the whole migrating population. The *Defence*, by comparison, with 82 passengers for whom county of residence is known, represented a radically different set of counties, with 35.4 percent of its passengers from Essex, 15.9 percent from Bedfordshire, and 13.4 percent from Cambridge. The most exaggerated representation of any one county was that of York as the county of residence for those passengers traveling on the *Susan and Ellen*. County of residence is known for only 41.8 percent of the passengers on the *Susan and Ellen*, but of

Table 2.6. English county representation of New England passengers in 1635 by selected ship (%)

| | Ship[a] | | | | | |
County	Abigail (N = 101)	Defence (N = 82)	Susan and Ellen (N = 38)	Hopewell (1) (N = 53)	Planter (N = 94)	All known (N = 669)[b]
London/Middlesex	37.6	7.3	2.6	9.9	9.6	22.0
Essex	9.9	35.4	5.3	22.6	0	11.7
Sussex	14.9	0	0	0	0	2.7
Surrey	9.9	0	5.3	0	4.3	3.9
York	0	0	55.3	0	0	3.1
Bedford	1.0	15.9	10.5	0	0	3.3
Cambridge	0	13.4	0	1.9	0	2.8
Hertford	0	0	0	11.3	40.4	8.9
Buckingham	0	0	0	49.1	0	6.7
Northampton	6.9	12.2	0	0	12.8	5.8
Suffolk	3.0	0	5.3	1.9	22.3	10.6
Other	16.8	15.9	15.8	3.8	10.6	18.2
Total	100	100.1	100.1	100	100	100.3

a. N includes only known origins.
b. See Table 1.4.

those, 55.3 percent came from York. The *Susan and Ellen* was also the most diverse ship of this sample: passengers on this vessel came from areas as distant as York, Wiltshire, and Dorset.

These concentrations of neighbors and families demonstrate the invisible process of organization and recruitment that directed population movement to New England via London. Migrants bound to New England did not simply arrive in London and sign on to the next ship; instead, they planned to travel with family and friends on specific ships across the Atlantic. The *Planter* and *Hopewell* illustrate this organization because they sailed at the same time, in April of 1635, and passengers on the two ships made clear decisions about which ship to take. A single page in the register included people boarding both the *Hopewell* and the *Planter* (Figure 7). Over the course of several days, men, women, and children gathered at the port of London to register with the clerks for their overseas trip. Yet for all the bedlam of the port, there was no disorder in the minds of these travelers about which ship to board. The *Planter* carried a large group of family and friends from Hertfordshire and another from Suffolk, whereas the *Hopewell* carried another large contingent from adjacent hundreds and parishes in Buckinghamshire. Figure 8

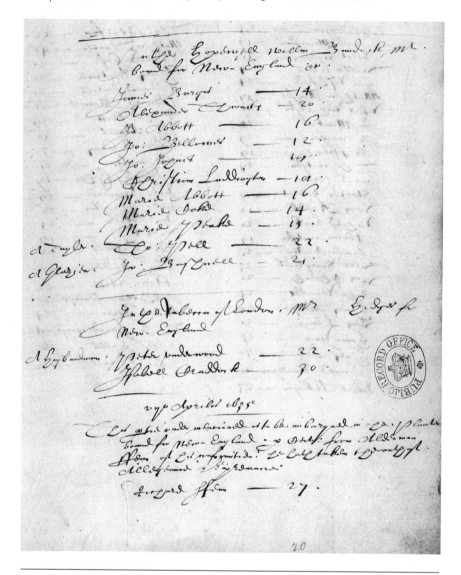

Figure 7. Page from the London Port Register showing registration of passengers on the *Planter* and the *Hopewell*, April 1635 (E 157/20 1-e, PRO). Courtesy of the Public Record Office.

Figure 8. Regional origins of passengers on the *Planter* and the *Hopewell*, April 1635. The different regional origins of the passengers on each ship demonstrate the organization that underscored overseas travel for the New England–bound passengers in general.

illustrates the marked divergence in regional origins of the passengers on the two ships.

Because no comparable evidence exists for other travelers to America, it is impossible to determine whether the majority of travelers to other regions voyaged with such purpose, but the demographic profile of the other travelers of 1635—young, single, and indentured—and the economic and social circumstances in which they traveled, suggests that such was not the case. Although Atlantic migrations allowed the reunion of some families and the re-creation of parishes in the new world, far more commonly they separated others when the 1635 migrants are considered in their entirety. Each solitary voyage of a single hopeful servant, planter, or merchant represented the destruction of family ties. Family separation was normative for people voyaging to the Chesapeake and the Caribbean. Many of these young travelers had long since bid farewell to friends and relatives when they first embarked on the road to London. Those traveling alone faced their voyages with the same trepidation as their fellow travelers who voyaged with kith and kin, but without the mediating influence of these friends. Like Nathaniel Braddock some of these travelers made their wills with care before they embarked, lest they die with no friends present to adjudicate the disposition of their estates. Wealth was no protector: all were vulnerable to the possibility of death at sea. Before Tom Verney sailed for Virginia in 1634 with his casks, barrels, servants, shot, and muskets, he signed over authority to a Mr. William Webster, who "in case of mortallity of the asaid Mr. Thomas Verney" was "to sell and dispose of his goods, provisions, and servants."[36] Ocean separations, indeed, were as permanent as deaths, or so one grieving father of a New England–bound passenger believed. A contemporary observed of Henry Vane's father that "Sir Henry Vane has as good as lost his eldest son."[37]

While Henry Vane's father mourned his loss, however, Vane himself traveled to New England in the company of friends. The presence of large New England companies meant that even the difficult ocean voyage proved no leveling experience for the passengers overseas. Although all voyagers shared the dangers and discomforts of an Atlantic voyage, they experienced their travels in different ways. For some travelers, family and friends provided mighty bulwarks against the hazards of colonial voyages. For single, young travelers, bonds of affinity to provide support in new and frightening circumstances had to be formed quickly aboard ship and reconstructed on arrival in the colonies.

The demographic differences between colony-bound populations that were recorded in the register shaped important aspects of Atlantic travel. Simple information from the register about ship size and the number of passengers suggests the important physical, spatial, and dietary differences that shaped travelers' lives at sea, as well as the colony-specific variations that circumscribed the crowding aboard ships. Vessels bound for different destinations ranged greatly in the number of people they carried (Table 2.7). The ships bound for New England carried an average of 69 passengers, whereas those bound for Virginia carried 100, and ships for Barbados carried 123. A variety of explanations present themselves for these differences. Ship size was most obviously a factor in the number of passengers a ship could accommodate. Unfortunately, the port clerks did not record the size of ships, but other sources occasionally provide this information. Ships ranged greatly in size, from the 25-ton *Bachelor* to 300-ton ships.[38] Those bound for New England seem to have varied more in size than those bound for Virginia. Four New England ships sailing from London in 1635 carried only 32 passengers combined, whereas the smallest number of people on any one Virginia ship was 32, and this was a marked exception to much higher average numbers. It seems likely that many small ships bound for New England, which were carrying primarily goods to take advantage of the inflationary decade of the 1630s, transported a few passengers as room permitted.

A second explanation for the relatively smaller number of passengers officially enumerated in the port register on New England–bound ships might lie in the number of men who were unable to secure legal passage because of their nonconformity. The obvious advantage New Englanders enjoyed by traveling with their friends, neighbors, and relatives did not mean that their voyages were easier in every respect. As the disguised status of Roger Harlakenden's travel companions suggests, some New England passengers had great difficulty leaving England. After all, the London port register had been created largely to document and control their movements. Thus some of the men best suited to puritan polities found it difficult to leave England. Status alone did not ease departure. Henry Vane, the oldest son of

Table 2.7. Average number of travelers from London in 1635 on ships for the colonies

Colony	No. Ships	No. Travelers	People/ship
Virginia	20	2,009	100
New England	17	1,169	69
Barbados	8	983	123
St. Kitts	5	423	85
Bermuda	2	218	109
Providence	1	76	76

Sir Henry Vane, a favored and privileged courtier, left England in 1635. Before he sailed, he wrote his father a letter describing his plans. Vane related that he had to prepare to leave quickly, as Mr. Craddock, the ship's master, told him that the ships in the Thames were ready to sail. Vane requested his father's assistance in procuring a pass for his voyage. As a member of the Commission for Foreign Plantations, Sir Henry Vane was singularly well qualified to ease his son's departure: men of young Vane's rank were required to obtain licenses from commissioners. Sir Henry condemned his dissenting son's interest in New England, but his son affirmed his own sense of the justice of his beliefs, and assured his father "that I will never do any thing (by Gods good grace) which both wth honour and good conscience I may not justify or bee content most willingly to suffer for. And were it not that I am very confident that as surely as there is truth in God: so Surely shall my inocency and integrity bee cleared to you before you dye. I protest to you ingenuously that the jealousy you have of mee would break my heart."

Vane found in his religious commitment the strength to confront his father and cherished "the sweete peace I enjoy wth my God amidst these many and heavy trialls wch now fall upon me and attend me."[39] He could not have pursued that "sweete peace," however, had his well-placed father not set aside his hostility toward the New England venture and procured his son's license to travel. In fact, according to John Winthrop, Sir Henry Vane did not support his son's ambitions, "but that acquaintinge the kinge with his sones disposition & desire he comanded him to send him hither, & gave him license for 3: yeares staye heere."[40]

Vane was not alone in his anxiety about departure. The most vivid description of efforts to leave England was provided by Thomas Shepard. Educated at the nonconformist bastion of Emmanuel College, Cambridge, Shepard had been the minister of Earls Colne, Essex, before he was deprived of his pulpit in 1630. Shepard then traveled north to Yorkshire and Northumberland, where he considered the wisdom of heeding his friends' advice to emigrate. He recalled that one reason for the timing of his departure from England, after friends had implored him to join them in Massachusetts for many years, was the impending birth of his second child. Shepard was reluctant to stay and have the child's birth discovered, because he would then have to baptize him in accordance with the rites of the Church of England. Shepard was also frustrated with the many moves around England necessitated by his beliefs. "And so," he explained, "seeing I had been tossed from the south to the north of England and now could go no farther, I then began to listen to a call to New England." Shepard listed several reasons why he should leave. Foremost was his inability to maintain himself and his family "in peace and comfort." Shepard then went on to point to the attractive letters written by

friends in New England, his distress over the "evil of ceremonies," his yearn-
ing to follow God's laws, the encouragement of his wife, and his desire to live
among God's people. Shepard thought it might have been his duty to stay in
England, to "suffer for Christ," yet despite his dread of the "sea storms" that
he endured in his first effort to leave, he did not see a reason to stay "now the
Lord had opened a door of escape."[41] Shepard finally decided to migrate, and
in the winter of 1634, he boarded the coal-laden *Hope of Ipswich* in New-
castle, whose trip was then aborted because of a terrible storm. Shepard next
journeyed to London, where he, his wife, and their newborn son remained in
hiding until they boarded a ship in August of 1635. Shepard noted in his
journal that accompanying him were Mr. Jones (the minister John Jones),
Mr. Champney (Richard Champney, later an elder in Cambridge), and Mr.
Wilson (the Boston minister John Wilson, returning from a trip to Suffolk to
attend to his brother's estate).[42] None of these men was recorded in the
passenger list for the *Defence,* although Jones's wife and six children were.

Other individuals of political or religious persuasions that were unpopular
with Laud appeared in disguise on the list. The brothers George and Joseph
Cooke, who achieved on their arrival in New England instant prominence in
Massachusetts politics, were registered as servants to the Essex gentleman
Roger Harlakenden. Thomas Shepard himself was disguised as a husbandman
named John Shepard in the port register. Thomas Carter was also recorded as
a servant but was in fact a graduate of St. John's College, Cambridge, and in
Massachusetts he served as a minister first at Dedham, and then at Woburn.
Clearly, then, for some individuals, escape from Laud's England was not easy,
and the resulting undercounting of the register results in the omission of
some prominent puritan leaders.[43]

It was not only the passage of ministers and prominent puritan sympathizers that was deterred or impeded by regulations: New England had difficulty
even in securing the servants whom it needed. In 1635 Philip Nye apologized
to John Winthrop, Jr., for not sending him as many servants as he had hoped.
"Some of the Gentlemen of the North," he wrote, "who lay som 3 or 4
Monthes in London transacting these affaires did thinke that their would
have been no notice of their purposes and thereupon assumed to send us up
servants but when they came down found the Countrie full of the reports of
their going now those two (being Dep leuetenants of the shire) did not care
to move any further in sending up of men for feare of increasing the reports."
So serious was the problem, Nye explained, that Lord Brooke, who had
promised to send twenty servants, sent not even one.[44]

The anecdotal evidence, then, abundantly suggests the difficulty that men
had escaping Laud's England. Extant evidence intimates that the number of
hidden passengers could be great. The *Abigail,* for example, left London with

180 registered passengers on board. In his *Journal,* however, John Winthrop recorded that the ship had arrived with 220 people "& many Cattle." The *Batchelor* left London with 4 registered passengers but reached New England with 14; moreover, the *Love,* with 8 named passengers, according to subsequent court depositions had 30 on board.[45] Thus the lower number of passengers on ships to New England might be a reflection only of the legal passengers who traveled, not the total number.

A third explanation for the discrepancy among colony-bound ships depicted in Table 2.7 may lie in the percentage of space on board occupied by family possessions and supplies. The large companies of neighbors and friends who voyaged overseas together possessed emotional resources denied solo travelers. Moreover, those who could assemble such large cohorts had a range of other advantages. English records attest to a certain economic comfort, if not outright wealth, for some of these New England–bound voyagers. Unlike the young, single indentured servants bound for the colonies, the household heads of the New England cohort had, over the years, accumulated skills, land, and goods. Some, like Robert Keayne and William Vassall, were cosmopolitan, affluent merchants who brought their wealth and acumen with them in their journeys to New England in 1635. Even men of more modest means were able to equip themselves with the necessities to improve the physical circumstances of their long voyages.[46] This English wealth translated itself into clothing, food, and equipment that altered every aspect of travel.

New Englanders made heavy investments in their new lives. Simon Eires and his wife, like many others, liquidated their assets for £80 in England before departing for the colonies. Philip and Anne Kirtland, who followed their sons Philip and Nathaniel to New England, in July of 1635 entered five separate land transfers in the Sherington Manor court rolls, presumably in anticipation of their subsequent travels.[47] With the money they acquired in these property transactions, the Kirtlands and the Eires could procure the provisions recommended for planters. According to one broadside, the poor could get by on £10.3.1 worth of goods per person, whereas those with more money could spend £17.07.4. Stipulated goods included food for one year, clothes, tools, munitions, and fishing equipment.[48] Additional items were also welcome. John Winthrop suggested that his family join him with bedding, woolen, linen, brass, pewter, leather bottles, drinking horns, axes, augers, candles, soap, beef, and suet.[49]

Records attest to the quantity of goods crammed aboard ships. One of the smallest ships to ply the Atlantic trade, the *Batchelor* was heavily laden with goods. In addition to 14 passengers and eight seamen were goods including iron and lead, 20 hogsheads of meal, 14 barrels of pease, barrels of oatmeal, butter, and iron ware, scythes, shovels and spades, linen, canvas, eight flock beds, 25 rugs, 40 blankets, 6 grindstones, 3 barrels of pitch and 2 of tar, cables, cordage, chains, hooks, and other miscellaneous items. Some of these goods had to be removed from the little *Batchelor* and placed aboard the *Truelove,* which was to sail after her, because the ship was overburdened.[50] No mention is made of livestock on the *Batchelor,* but New England ships also carried large numbers of domestic animals that required not only space for themselves but also the much larger space occupied by their fodder. The *Love,* whose New England voyage was ultimately canceled, had aboard 450 sheep from Denmark and 40 goats from Ireland.[51] It is small wonder, given the great number of animals, that the *Love* carried only thirty people.

Whereas a family might have endeavored to provide beds and blankets for all family members, tools for a colonial life, and food and other supplies to last a year, an indentured servant would have little more than the clothes on his or her back to care for on the voyage. The foresight of a generous master might alter that situation. Those planning to transport many servants, as indeed were most planters to Virginia or the islands, were warned to be prepared to provide for them. Tom Verney, bound for Virginia with servants in 1634, was urged to bring clothes for the servants and bedding for himself. He also had a gun, flour, food, and a supply of alcohol, but no reference was made to the sizable investment in household, farm, and crafts equipment found on New England ships.[52] Providing for his own servants, Thomas Moore traveled to Virginia in 1635 with cheese, butter, cloth, staves, shirts, stockings, and other goods.[53]

Supplies and funds, however, could be dangerously depleted as passengers waited for their ships to sail. The Virginia-bound travelers on the *Constance* in 1635 complained that even before the ship had left the coast of England, the supply of beer was so short that passengers drank salt water to slake their thirst. Food as well ran short during the vessel's two-week sojourn in the Downs waiting for fair winds.[54] Delayed departures imposed great financial hardship on passengers biding time in ports waiting for favorable winds or full ships. The Providence Island Company explicitly hoped to avoid these "unnecessary charges" caused by "too long attendance for the Ships."[55] Some delays in sailing were caused by official actions. Ships bound for New England, for example, were inspected in order to ensure that all passengers had licenses to depart the country. Richard Mather recalled the "searchers" who came aboard "and viewed a list of all or names, ministered the oath of allegiance to all at full age, viewed or certificates from the ministers in the parishes from whence wee came, approved well thereof, and gave us tickes."[56]

Once the ships had left port, the journey was occasionally lengthened intolerably by poor weather off the coast of England. Richard Mather recorded that his ship, the *James,* left Bristol on June 4 after waiting in the harbor for twelve days. Even as the passengers waited at anchor, they got seasick. When the wind seemed to blow in a favorable direction to depart, the captain and seamen were never available to sail the ship. When the *James* finally sailed, the wind turned, and the small convoy of New England–bound ships tacked and sailed around in the Channel, while everyone on board got violently ill. The passengers went on shore at Lundy and Milford, and again at Nangle, where Mather and his family took walks on the shore. The *James* anchored off Nantasket on August 16, over two months after attempting to leave Bristol, and Mather noted with relief that no one had died.[57] Francis Higginson's shipmates were able to go ashore at Cowcastle in England to do their laundry. Unfortunately for Higginson and his companions, the wind turned while they were on shore, and the ship sailed on to Yarmouth without them. Although a shallop was sent for the shore contingent, the sea was so rough that the women preferred to walk much of the way toward Yarmouth to join their vessel: that these women who were already daunted by coastal navigation then braved the Atlantic is indeed admirable.[58]

However many supplies a traveler transported, no one could control the passage of the ship. Foul weather was shared by all. After the goods were laded and ships were out of sight of the English coast, voyages varied greatly in length. As *A Relation of Maryland* noted, the voyage to the Chesapeake could be as short as five to six weeks but more typically required two months.[59] Whereas Francis Higginson reached New England in six weeks and three days (and the accuracy of his count suggests the eagerness with which he welcomed the sight of land and the conclusion of his voyage), a year later it took the *Handmaid* a grueling twelve weeks to reach the Plymouth colony from England.[60] One ship bound for New England in 1636 took twenty-six weeks altogether to reach the region's shores, eighteen of those weeks at sea.[61] The length of the voyage clearly contributed to hardship on board. John Dutton reported painfully to the Earl of Warwick in 1620 that his ship reached Bermuda after ten weeks and two days, whereas the *Garland*, which had left England in the same convoy, arrived two weeks later, "haveing made a hard voyage, many of her people dead at sea, allmost all sicke."[62] Accidents could strike ships at any time, even as they approached the coast of their new world destinations. As Henry Colt sailed through the Caribbean, his ship was struck by lightning, which killed five men.[63]

Even on the most sturdy and best-supplied of ships, little could be done to ameliorate the discomfort created by poor weather and Atlantic gales. A single storm could destroy a ship. The *Angel Gabriel* herself weathered a terrible storm in August of 1635 but lost most of her cattle and goods, the essential equipment newcomers needed to survive their first year in New England.[64] And disease was equally pervasive. Mortality rates on transatlantic voyages were great for both people and livestock. John Winthrop reported to his wife that twelve out of eighteen goats died on one voyage.[65] The death of passengers was, of course, more distressing. Those who made crossings in which all survived celebrated that fact, as when Richard Mather rejoiced that no one died in the passage of the *James* of Bristol in 1635. A second ship that arrived at the same time as the *James,* however, lost twenty-one passengers, and the *James* herself, although she arrived safely, lost three anchors.[66] The *Abigail,* which sailed from London in the summer of 1635, arrived in New England with smallpox.[67] A few deaths, however, seem to have been more the rule than the exception. One child who traveled to New England in 1635, Thomas Jones, died during his family's voyage. The death of relatives and friends—however newly acquired—was tragic: the loss of servants to shipboard diseases, a financial inconvenience. Those who valued servants as commodities accepted the risk of their death in transit. One promoter cheerfully reassured adventurers whose servants had died in the crossing that their financial loss would not be great, because they could easily and profitably sell the provisions purchased for the deceased servants on arrival.[68]

Thomas Rous described in a letter to Archibald Hay in 1638 one particularly gruesome voyage to Barbados. Rous's letter captured the many problems in overseas travel: unscrupulous merchants who shortchanged their passengers, poor weather, lack of adequate clothing, contamination by passengers, and the initial disease of the migrating population. Over 350 people set off to Barbados, a number originally thought viable because of the "great bulk" of the ship, "but such a sort of people and soe many of them togeather with noe shift would soone grow nastye and infect one another having alsoe noe clothes must keep below in cold weather and soe taint themselves and the ship." Two hundred people were sick at one time, Rous lamented, and the crew "have thrown overboard two and three in a day for many dayes togeather that in all we lost fourescoare of our people." Even the wealthy were not protected: of the 10 men in the "great cabin," who had thought themselves better off, 6 had died after only three weeks at sea.[69] In fact, the privileged men in the cabin died at a greater rate than did the people crowded together below deck.

Although Rous blamed the "great losse" on the "unreasonable covetousness of our marchant," it is apparent that conditions were poor from the outset. The experience of the poorly equipped passengers, with so few garments to clothe themselves that they were forced to stay below in the fetid hold of the ship, coronated poverty as a reigning attribute of shipboard life even as most travelers undertook their Atlantic journeys to escape despair and penury in England. Even those captains who sought to provide sufficient food could not ensure that the voyage would end before supplies were depleted. A full three weeks before the *James* anchored at Nantasket in New England in 1635, Richard Mather noted in his journal that hay and water were running low.[70] Particularly depleted were supplies on the *Constance*, which left Gravesend in 1635 with eighty-five passengers on board, bound for Virginia. But the ship was so "pestered with passengers" that food ran short within two weeks, during which time the ship had not even departed the Downs, and the people on board were forced to sleep on deck. The uncomfortable and impatient passengers threatened to go on shore, and agreed that they would not proceed with the voyage if there were any way to reach shore. Fortunately for the passengers, the *Constance* sprang a leak while she was still off the Downs waiting for favorable winds, and the seamen enthusiastically joined the passengers in their threats to abandon the ship. Several passengers, especially servants, escaped when the ship put in to Dover for repairs, and by the time the ship managed to reach Ilfracombe in Devon, all the passengers were put ashore, where, according to one deponent, they waited for three months before going on to Virginia.[71]

Even though the preceding descriptions of voyages suggest unmitigated hardship, it was the most spectacularly miserable voyages for which records, both private and legal, survive. Many travelers attested to the pleasant nature of their trip, although those who heralded their Atlantic travels as enjoyable experiences were invariably those struggling to persuade others to follow them. Daniel Tucker, the governor of Bermuda, thus encouraged Nathaniel and Sir Robert Rich to visit Bermuda and assured them that "it is a very pleasant voyage."[72] Thomas Weld, eager to entice his parishioners in Terling, Essex, to follow him to New England, called attention to the safe arrival of all the passengers. He asserted that his children actually boarded the ship in poor health but "came forth well as ever"; moreover, his wife was "all ye voyage on ye Sea better then at land." Another woman recovered from consumption, and Weld himself experienced no seasickness on this miraculous health cruise.[73] Francis Higginson dismissed the death of two children on his voyage, claiming that they were sickly children to begin with, and instead emphasized the delights of his passage.

It is tempting to accept the view of colonial promoters such as Higginson. As he recalled, those whom he had traveled with found the trip "pleasurable and profitable, for we received instruction and delight in beholding the wonders of the Lord in the deep waters and sometimes seeing the sea round us appearing with a terrible countenance."[74] But in fact, Higginson's journey was not as halcyon as he recalled: his own daughter died of smallpox on the voyage. It has become a virtual commonplace to assert the formative and collective experience of ocean travel, especially to New England.[75] New Englanders did, indeed, voyage with an extraordinary sense of mission. And for servants who were bound to the colonies, the experience of life aboard ship could have been very important. Many of these servants were displaced victims of transformations in England that had deprived them of both their livelihood and the privilege of remaining near their family and friends. Already accustomed to a vagrant existence on the road, the time aboard ship with other servants may have provided an opportunity to create a community, albeit born of a shared fear, whereas before there had been only chronic dislocation.

For better or for worse, travelers to all colonial destinations got to know each other very well and very quickly. At least three couples on seventeenth-century Love Boats to New England subsequently married: Marie Clifford and Jeremy Belcher, on the *Susan and Ellen*, Judith Phippin and James Hayward, on the *Planter*, and Marie Bates and Hopestill Foster, on the *Elizabeth*. The role of the ship in their matches, however, is not clear. Phippin and Hayward were indentured to the same family, whereas Bates and Foster were cousins.

The evidence—admittedly sparse—for the qualitative experience of seagoing voyages can be only suggestive. But there is evidence to point to a different kind of passage. All travelers to the colonies endured ocean voyages fraught with such danger and discomfort that the miracle was surviving with one's sanity intact. New Englanders did not undergo any unique hardship. Buffered by kin, friends, adequate supplies, and a profound sense of purpose, they probably suffered less than did passengers to other regions. Moreover, travelers did not land in the new world with shared, orthodox puritan ideas. Indeed, shipboard debates between those of divergent views exacerbated the differences between them. Recognition of the problem of maintaining order spurred the Providence Island Company to preempt conflict by dictating the hierarchy aboard ship. When the *Robert* sailed from London to Providence in 1634, two men on board, Edward Gates, who was noted in the records as a gentleman, and Samuell Symonds, who was a planter, were placed in charge of all passengers.[76] A similar injunction was made by Lord Baltimore that the governor and commissioners of his new Maryland colony "be very carefull to preserve unity & peace amongst all the passengers on Shipp-board" during the voyage to the new world.[77] Colonial investors thus endeavored to assert hierarchies aboard ships that were all too absent in the age distribution of their passengers.

These efforts to mitigate shipboard tensions, however, often proved unsuccessful. When Richard Norwood traveled on one of his many trips from Bermuda to London, he journeyed in the company of Nathaniel White, a minister who would soon lead the Independent faction on the island, and White's family. When the two men later found themselves at odds in the island's deeply divisive religious disputes, they traced their hostility back to their experience on board. According to White, Mrs. Norwood had insisted on putting the Norwood children into White's cabin. The captain of the ship argued that the children should not be there, but Mrs. Norwood was adamant. The children stayed put, and in the overcrowded cabin with White's own child and wife and the Norwood children, the Whites ended up battered and bruised when tossed around in the ship. White believed that it was because of that ordeal that Norwood disliked him.[78] Even a storm at sea could not forge a temporary community or peace in this instance.

Another minister had comparable difficulty demonstrating a spirit of charity during the long voyage across the Atlantic. The Providence Island Company, which had trouble finding suitable ministers who were willing to stay on the island, sent one Arthur Rous to the island in 1634. Rous did not last long. Complaints by another minister, Mr. Ditloffe, brought the Company's attention to Rous's purported abuse of his servants. Rous, Ditloffe reported insultingly, "was more fitt to weare a Buff Jerkin then to be a Minister." But what was particularly damning was Rous's behavior on board ship during his voyage to Providence. Mr. Rous insisted on teaching his fellow travelers rounds and catches, even on the Sabbath.[79] And a woman who journeyed to New England in 1635, Barbara Rolfe, was so unpleasant that no one on board ship was willing to take her in as a servant on her arrival in Massachusetts. Indeed, she was driven out of the colony itself.[80]

These examples, derived not from promotional works or seductive letters but from sources generated for purposes other than cajoling people overseas, point to the enormous emotional, physical, and psychological strain that long Atlantic voyages put on passengers. Petty differences were exaggerated. Mr. Ditloffe seethed over Mr. Rous's seagoing singing lessons until he could complain in person to the Providence Island Company in London. White's and Norwood's enmity, born of the terror and discomfort of an Atlantic storm, intruded on the political and ecclesiastical order of Bermuda a decade later. Passions fomented at sea festered on land. By the end of these long and arduous voyages, some passengers were only too glad to see the last of each other. And, indeed, that was precisely the experience of most of the servants who traveled to the colonies. The account book of the *Tristram and Jeane* details this process. In 1637 the ship transported seventy-four servants to be sold in Virginia, sixty-nine of whose names were recorded in the ship's accounts. These seventeen women and fifty-two men had endured several weeks together in close quarters at sea, with miseries and compassion unrecorded. Whether on their arrival in Virginia they were thrilled to see the last of each other or terrified at losing the painfully constructed temporary community of their seaboard life, we can only speculate. But we do know that they were, for the most part, separated. The servants were sold to forty-four different planters. Some of the servants were bought by one planter: John Davis purchased seven, and John Howe took six. Twenty-eight, however, were distributed individually.[81]

The shipboard community that was forged was at best a temporary one, and those travelers bent on staying in the colonies were compelled to start over again on arrival at their destinations, where they accommodated themselves to colonial communities both eerily familiar and frighteningly foreign to English norms. Lured to the new world by acquisitive merchants, planters, and profit seekers, armed at best with information that optimistically distorted new world realities or painted horrors too bleak to comprehend, young travelers in conditions of servitude braved their ocean voyage in solitary ways that were not suffered by the fortunate New England–bound migrants who traveled with their families and neighbors. Thus the demographic differences at the port—differences reflecting preparation, wealth, and a host of other variables—shaped the experiences of Atlantic travel. But the demographic and occupational features that shaped ocean voyages—families traveled on ships with fewer fellow passengers and more equipment, whereas single passengers, mostly servants, were crowded below deck in dark and dismal quarters with only a ship's rations and a captain's charity to sustain them—also shaped colonial life.

Once ashore, all would turn to the task of re-creating community life. The largest constraints on these new communities were the demographic differences between traveling populations detailed here: the majority of new arrivals to the colonies were servants, but the vast majority, as high as 94 percent in the West Indian colonies, were single men. They lived together in a world made by migration and inhabited by male migrants. The societies that these men joined and shaped were peculiar by English standards, as new colonists evolved Atlantic institutions to mediate between the structures they had known at home and the limitations they faced overseas.

3 | *Life, Death, and Labor in an Unsettled Land*

When prominent Puritans wished to travel to New England without coming to the attention of the searchers who inspected outbound ships for nonconformists, they disguised themselves as servants and thus safely embarked for the new world.[1] Within the traveling household of a friend or neighbor, these men passed undetected out of London. The repeated success of their disguises demonstrates the lack of interest that port clerks had in servants. Although they were essential to the viability of colonial enterprises, servants, with their dependence defined by their youth and their poverty, were legally and socially invisible at the port, as indeed they were politically invisible in England. Yet these servants, who comprised the preponderance of travelers to the colonies in 1635, shaped colonial societies in important ways.

Most of these servants were men. Moreover, the overwhelming majority of all travelers were young, single men, either free or indentured. The circumstances that dictated two fundamental features of colonial life (household composition and family structure) were determined not by place of origin in England nor by political persuasion, nor, indeed, by personal preferences, but rather by these basic demographic and occupational features: that colonies were overwhelmingly inhabited by servants (from 33 percent to 75 percent), that colonies were still more overwhelmingly inhabited by men (from 60 percent to 94 percent), and that colonial populations were characterized by youth. Thus customary patterns of authority were turned upside down in the colonies.[2] The young men recruited in London to cultivate new world crops, moreover, were among the most destitute migrants of the kingdom in an age when the miserable and the desperate jostled for space on England's thoroughfares and in cities such as London. They reached the new world at a final stage in a difficult journey to keep body and soul together. Dislodged from their homes and families by the strains of population growth and unemployment, they trekked to London in search of work. Unable to find it, they finally boarded ships for the colonies. They were members of no existing community and were long released from the social and familial constraints of parish life. Their masters had to discipline them to the rhythms of agricultural production in the new world while also erecting mechanisms to regulate and control a population recently accustomed to relative autonomy.

Thus not only was it the demographic constraints of a young male population that lay at the center of most new colonies, but it was also the added difficulty of regulating a population of unattached migrants, young men and women who were parceled out on their arrival in the colonies to serve strangers. Although migration was normative within England for all age groups, it was not customary to live in a society composed almost entirely of migrants so densely clustered in one age cohort. Such was the case in the colonies. High mortality and the continued demand for labor together determined that these demographic features and social constraints would endure throughout the seventeenth century. In its colonial forms, moreover, labor varied fundamentally from the different traditions at play in England. So the pervasiveness of labor, combined with the distorted sex ratios and age hierarchies, resulted in local societies at marked variance from English parishes. These pressures were particularly intense in the first decades of colonial settlement. The organization of colonial parochial and legal institutions was undertaken in the most disadvantageous circumstances, as colonies were beset by disease and failures. But the skewed demographic balance and the necessity of regulating the young servants who represented such a preponderance of the population required these new institutions to focus particularly on one segment of the population. Thus colonial institutions were formed not only amid the chaos and uncertainty of any new colonial enterprise but also among a distorted population. Replicating English institutions was not sufficient: these institutions had to be modified and altered because of the peculiar set of demographic and social constraints present in the first half of the seventeenth century. The success of a colony, from an investor's or a planter's point of view, depended on the mobilization of labor, but the health of a colony, measured from within by its inhabitants, depended as well on the control and socialization of the laboring majority.

A successful colony required a steady infusion of laborers, but that dependence on young servants had important consequences for the character of colonial legal and familial structures. Labor in its new world setting necessitated subtle but significant alterations in English mechanisms for housing, controlling, and educating young men and women. In England some 13.4 percent of the population were agricultural servants, and 60 percent of the population between the ages of 15 and 24 were servants. The majority of these servants—one third to one half—were servants in husbandry, that is, agricultural servants who served annual contracts and lived within the family of their master.[3] In the colonies, especially in the Chesapeake and the West

Indies, the bulk of the population between the ages of 15 and 24 were servants (primarily agricultural laborers, but also apprenticed to tradesmen): because few families traveled to these colonies, there were virtually no dependent children in this age bracket, and the independent young man under the age of 24 was the exception. The colonies that most required these infusions of agricultural labor were plantation colonies—witness the 2,009 travelers to Virginia and the 1,406 to Barbados and St. Kitts. Thus as the example of the *Constance* demonstrated, some 77 percent of the travelers were likely to reach Virginia, and probably Barbados as well, in conditions of indentured servitude, primarily bound for agricultural service, compared with 13.4 percent of the population in England. And whereas 60 percent of the population between the ages of 15 and 24 in England were servants, in the plantation colonies, it was more likely that some 90 percent of the population in this particular age cohort labored in some form of indenture. Even New England, which did attract hundreds of families in the 1630s and which achieved a demographic stability that improved on English expectations, contained in the 1635 cohort servants who comprised 33 percent of the population, 2.5 times the English norm.[4] These striking differences direct attention to the implications of a servant-dominated population, young and male, for the formation of colonial institutions.

In England the prevalence of service in husbandry shaped family formation and agricultural patterns in the early modern period: servants saved money during their terms of service; they married late, thus controlling the growth of the population and ensuring that family formation would accompany and symbolize economic self-sufficiency; and they maintained a steady demand for small farms.[5] Because hired labor was a normal part of the life cycle, servants did not identify themselves as a separate class outside the larger society.[6] Rather, their labor provided them with the means to join that society as full participants. Thus service in husbandry, and the commensurate family life that accompanied and sustained it, proved essential socializing mechanisms in early modern parishes. Historians of colonial labor have long since observed the transformation of servants into commodities. But colonial servitude not only transformed the experiences of laborers and their masters; because of the dominance and composition of the laboring population, servitude also shaped colonial societies that were themselves young and fragile.

The colonies were worthless without labor to cultivate the lucrative luxury crops eagerly anticipated by colonial promoters and investors. In Latin America, Spanish settlers had benefited in New Spain and Peru from the presence of densely settled agrarian populations long accustomed to coerced labor exacted by local leaders under the command of Aztec and Incan imperial officials. Moreover, Iberian colonists found vast stores of precious metals. To the great distress of the British invaders who were acutely aware of the earlier examples of conquest, subjugation, and enslavement, North American indigenous people proved virtually impossible to constrain and regulate for purposes of labor. Regardless of how expensive land was, without labor it was worthless, as the Barbados resident and proprietor's agent Peter Hay repeatedly reminded his cousins in Scotland when he characteristically, albeit accurately, whined that "a plantation in this place is worth nothing unless they be good store of hands upon it."[7] Without able hands, "there is no way to live."[8] It was English indentured servants who would cultivate the soil in order to produce the luxury export crops (as yet undetermined at first settlement) that would, in turn, render colonies profitable and their investors rich.

Central to the economic viability of colonial enterprises, then, was the mobilization of labor. What information has survived suggests that the recruitment process in the 1630s was flexible, accommodating of individual financial constraints, and possessed of an internal order that has been obscured by the absence of records. Few formal mechanisms existed for recruiting English men and women for overseas enterprises at this early stage. Rather, it was the responsibility of those investing in the colonies to people their own land, and, in this age when private enterprise dominated colonization efforts, a private affair.

From their distant plantations, colonists wrote letters, sent emissaries, and transported themselves to England, all in the pursuit of more servants. These pleas were often directed to large colonial investors based in England, men capable of equipping whole ships, such as the Earl of Carlisle, who personally funded, staffed, and sent one ship, the *Mathew*, with 132 passengers on board, from London to St. Christopher in May of 1635. Two companies in particular, the Providence and Somers Islands Companies, relied on the efforts of individual company members to recruit men for their colonial ventures. Early organizational meetings of the Providence Island Company recorded that each adventurer was to procure as many men and boys as possible to send to the colony.[9] Thus Lord Say and Sele promised in 1634 to send servants to some men certified from Oxfordshire by the next ship bound for Providence.[10] The Bermuda agent Thomas Durham implored Sir Nathaniel Rich to provide him with "3 men able to woorke, out of England, or lett me have 4 negroes: 3 men 1 woman."[11] Servants who traveled because of the organization of a prominent company investor, moreover, sometimes brought with them special protection. Robert Barrington wrote John Winthrop, Jr., in 1635 about the supply of servants he sent that year to the new Saybrook colony. "The bearer heerof," he directed, "being sent over among other servants for the use of the common stock, I shall entreate you for my sake to shew him what favour you may. I hop you shall finde he will deserve no less . . . I pray," he adjured Winthrop, "have a speciall Care of his spirituall good."[12]

Planters in need of servants traveled to England to acquire their own, as one contingent of Bermuda planters did in 1620.[13] Rising tobacco prices in Virginia also encouraged planters there to seek out their own laborers. By 1633 and 1634 tobacco prices had recovered from an earlier decline, making the desire for servants particularly acute.[14] In response to their expectations of the greater fortune that their crops would secure in these times of high prices, two Virginia planters, Christopher Boyes and Richard Rutherford, journeyed to London personally in 1635 to obtain servants. Their failed voyage on the *Constance* produced pages of depositions that described in some detail the organization and preparation of a vessel composed primarily of servants. The depositions describe flexibility in the payment of passage overseas and suggest that obtaining servants was a small-time operation. These planters made their own arrangements to transport servants. The shipmaster, John Thierry, collected money both at his house in Turnwheel Lane and at the Christopher Inn, Gravesend. Indeed, the Christopher Inn seems to have functioned as Thierry's place of business. Christopher Boyes made his arrangements at Hartle Row in Hampshire, where he paid Jeffrey Gough, the purser of the *Constance,* for the passage of his four servants and the servants of two other men, who had presumably commissioned Boyes to act on their behalf. Alternative payment in goods was also accepted, both in England and in Virginia. A second planter arranged to pay Gough tobacco in Virginia for the passage of his six servants, and Margery Jackson paid £18 worth of "strong waters," probably ale, to the ship's captain, Clement Champion, for her cousin and his two servants.[15] The average number of servants transported on the *Constance* by individual planters or merchants was small, with Richard Rutherford's seven the highest number. No single merchant monopolized the shipful of servants.[16]

The journey of these Virginia planters to London, moreover, suggests that it was difficult to obtain servants in the 1630s, despite the claims of colonial promoters. John Sadler, a colonial agent, assured the Verney family that they should provide their son Thomas on his voyage to Virginia with at least three servants "which may bee had heare at a dayes warninge," and continued confidently, "if I were to send 40 servants I could have them heere at a dayes warninge."[17] But although a man such as Sadler who made his living advocating colonial settlement invariably claimed that it was easy to procure servants, such was not always the case. Abundant letters between colonists and their English friends and employers conveyed apologies for failures to procure sufficient numbers of servants. Henry Hawley regretted that he was unable to repay the debt of £30 he owed Sir James Hay but explained that he had been unable to obtain the thirty men he thought would have permitted him to repay the debt and that he had to settle for only twenty-five men.[18] The Providence Island Company's secretary William Jessop maintained a vigorous correspondence with island planters and repeatedly explained to them his difficulties providing the servants they required.[19]

As a result, some deceit and misrepresentation played a role in seducing servants overseas. In attracting servants in Kinsale in 1636, the ship captain Thomas Anthony arranged for "the drume to be Beaten, and gave warninge to all those that disposed to goe servants for Virginea [to] repare to Kinsale." Anthony resorted to illegal means when he found it hard to raise a sufficient crew, and for his pains he spent two days in jail for kidnapping.[20] So common was this practice of kidnapping servants for American destinations that a new verb was coined, to be Barbadosed, to describe this misfortune. Less obviously illegal but still duplicitous was the practice of "spiriting," or seducing would-be servants on board ships with dishonest representations of what would happen to them on the other end. John Wise, who ventured in 1635 to Virginia, was apparently duped on board a ship a year earlier by someone such as Captain Anthony.[21]

These problems of recruitment transpired in an age of high population growth because simply finding bodies to fill a ship was not in itself adequate: colonies also required skilled labor. People in building trades, experienced farmers, and craftsmen were in great demand, especially in newly organized colonies.[22] Young Tom Verney, sent by his family to Barbados in 1638, asked his father to send him twenty men, of which he wanted two carpenters, two sawyers, one weaver, and one tailor.[23] Of the travelers to Virginia in 1635, several were tradesmen: Edward Leene was a tanner, Oliver Gibbons a shoemaker, William Berry and John Godfrey boat wrights. Edward Lilly was a joiner, and Henry Maddin, whose estate inventory included sewing silks, yards of cloth, and buttons, was presumably a tailor.[24] Such men, free or indentured, were coveted.

Benefiting from the example of unsuccessful predecessors, those embarking on a new colony were particularly eager to obtain reputable and skilled personnel. The Saybrook experiment, launched in 1635, illustrates this preoccupation with skilled labor. John Winthrop, Jr., experienced in the settlement of Massachusetts Bay, was appointed the governor of the new plantation. Having returned to England to seek a new wife and to obtain supplies for Massachusetts, Winthrop, patent in hand, traveled back to New England from London in 1635 to lead the new colony. Arrangements had been made in London to procure skilled assistants for the new project, men such as Lion Gardiner, an engineer, who traveled to New England from Holland. Recruited by Hugh Peter and John Davenport, then ministering to puritan flocks in the Low Countries, Gardiner accepted his New England post for the immense sum, by the standard of other colonial officers and employees, of £100 a year. Gardiner reminisced, "I was to serve them only in the drawing, ordering and making of a city, towns or forts of defence. And so I came from Holland to London, and from thence to New England."[25]

For its part, the Providence Island Company courted men with desperately needed military prowess. These islands were perilously close to Spanish holdings, and this location spawned a military culture. What brought the islands to Spanish attention was the role of Providence as a base for privateering, an enterprise successful enough to pose a real threat to Spanish shipping. In 1637 a Spanish ship laden with pearls from the Island of Margarita was pursued by a ship from Providence. The Spanish ship was spared only by the presence of two Dutch ships, which maintained that the United Provinces possessed a right to the Spanish treasure. The English and Dutch ships fought it out, while the Spanish captain wisely steered his vessel to safety.[26] Leaders of English forays into the Caribbean were qualified by cautions to "putt into Harbour" if there were any Spanish ships in the vicinity.[27] And the Spanish were equally careful. In 1637 Spanish frigates were ordered not to leave from Guatemala because of news of English and Dutch ships hovering near St. John and Providence.[28]

The Spanish took seriously the menace of predatory English ships that were based on Providence, and they launched retaliatory strikes. Protection from Spanish threats at sea and fortifications sufficient to deter invasion required a constant infusion of money, men, and munitions, and spawned an all-encompassing martial culture. When the island's minister, Hope Sherrard, wrote his patron, Sir Thomas Barrington, to report on spiritual conditions on the island, he unconsciously reflected the colony's preoccupation with safety by commenting first on the paucity of shot available on the island—not enough to last a day if the island were attacked. And he observed that the island had recently lost some fifty of its "ablest men" to the mainland and to England. Reminding Barrington of the peril of Providence, he noted that St Martin's had only recently been taken by the Spanish.[29]

Justifiably concerned with the island's safety, the Company sent the majority of its servants to work on the public defenses and to erect the many forts that decorated the island. By 1635 there were three forts around the harbor, and thirteen or fourteen fortified places throughout the island. Large guns dotted these fortifications, and one of the Company's first difficulties was to retain a gunner, who threatened to quit when the Company balked at the salary that the governor had offered him.[30] Experienced military men were courted with care.[31] They in turn taught island residents the skills required for their survival. John Coke wrote in his 1635 report on the island that all the planters there were trained and armed. A captain and "divers experienced sarjants" provided this essential instruction.[32] Newcomers to the island, according to orders given to Governor Robert Hunt when he went to Providence in 1636, were to "be very regmentlie excercised, especially upon the first comeing of psons to the Island till they be brought to a pfect knowledge of the use of Armes."[33] The pressure that the Spanish created, however, was unrelenting, and in 1638 the Company received word of a possible Spanish attack and so resolved "to have a new supply of able men."[34]

To obtain men with the engineering talent of Lion Gardiner or the martial training of William Thorpe or with other attributes desired by colonial investors, companies offered special incentives. The headright system was one common mechanism employed in Virginia and Maryland to entice independent men of any ability or interest overseas.[35] The Providence Island Company devised a graduated system of rewards to distinguish between different types of colonists: laborers with no special skill, who were to receive half the profits of their land; artificers, to work at their trades for either half profit of their land or else for wages of £5 per year and food and drink; and apprentices, who were bound for a number of years. Artificers and laborers were to be encouraged by receiving apprentices, while the Company assumed all costs for the voyage.[36] The Company furthermore agreed that "for incouragement of honest and able Artificers to goe over," those who went over as free men could bring servants that they could then hire out to other planters.[37] The Somers Islands Company planned in 1622 to offer two acres of public land at a yearly rent of two shillings to craftsmen, including shipwrights, carpenters, joiners, masons, brick makers, bricklayers, smiths, coopers, and sawyers, as long as they continued at their trades and did not plant tobacco, thus both enticing artisans and keeping the tobacco supply small (and thereby, they hoped, the price high).[38]

Some sought to attract skilled workers and planters not only by appealing to their quest for gain but also by challenging their sense of duty. Sir Richard Saltonstall exhorted Emmanuel Downing to encourage people to venture to New England. "If gentlemen of ability would transport themselves," Saltonstall wrote enthusiastically, "they might advance their own estates, and might improve their talents and times in being worthy instruments of propagating the Gospel to these poor barbarous people."[39] But as Saltonstall's plea for "gentlemen of ability" suggests, it was difficult to secure qualified people for colonial enterprises. For all the rhetoric about the ideal planter, those who settled overseas admitted the discrepancy between ideal and reality. Henry Adis, who settled in Surinam, wrote the colony's governor, Lord Willoughby of Parham, of his disappointment in the quality of the people there. "All new colonies you know of what sort of People generally they are made up of, so that, what we in probability can expect from them, must be from length of time, and the good example of those who have been more civilly bred, and God hath wrought upon, and better principled." Newcomers, fretted Adis, were poorly suited to the demands of colonial life.[40]

Both temperament and training could conspire to make a newcomer ill-equipped for the demands to be placed on him or her. Transportation to the colonies offered some families an outlet both for recalcitrant offspring and for those whose expectations exceeded their families' resources. Adventurers believed the Chesapeake and the Caribbean to be prime venues for quick profit: the youthful planters Tom Verney and James Dering traveled to Barbados in the 1630s to make their fortunes. In Verney's case Barbados promised a fresh start. Verney anticipated that his stint in Barbados would "be an engagement for mee for my new lead-life." His expectations were also financial: Tom Verney hoped to earn back his principal investment in a year's time.[41]

One family believed that New England offered a solution to the strains of a difficult daughter. Barbara Rolfe, who traveled at age 20 on the *Hopewell's* second trip to New England in the fall of 1635, was forced out of England by her parents. Rolfe's experiences remind us that although men were the majority of servants, women traveled as servants as well. The widow Bristow, for example, reached New England in 1635 with the hearty recommendation of Philip Nye in England. He wrote John Winthrop, Jr., that she was "a godlye woman an excellent huswife fitt for all domestike imployment and a great paynes taker."[42] Barbara Rolfe would never have garnered such commendation. According to Thomas Babb, the master of the *Hopewell*, Barbara's father, George Rolfe, approached Babb about his daughter, "whoo the said complt by noe fare meanes that hee could use could possiblie pswade to live in a civill and orderely course of lyfe, but contrary to his fatherly admonitions and persuasions did runne on in a coarse of disobedience both to the extreame griefe and discreditt of him the said complt; and hee the said complt said hee much feared if shee should continue heere in this kingdome that shee the said Barbara would come to some further mischeife." Mr. Rolfe persuaded Captain Babb to take Barbara to New England with him and to hire her out once he got there, for which service Rolfe agreed to provide Barbara with all necessities for the voyage and to pay Babb the same sum for her passage that other travelers paid. George Rolfe's wife, furthermore, agreed that the Rolfes would compensate Babb for all other expenses he incurred in transporting Barbara. George Rolfe gave Babb 20s. in partial payment for the passage, with £4 more due to Babb within a month.

Babb promised Barbara he would find her "some good place" upon her arrival in New England. Apparently the attributes that had spurred Mr. Rolfe to exile his daughter to the colonies, however, distinguished Barbara also on board ship: Babb reported that "her carriage in her passage to Newe England, and att her furst arivall there was soe eivell" that Babb was forced to provide for her himself for two months, because no one else would have her. Finally, Babb left Barbara with a Mr. Trelawney (a merchant of Plymouth, England, who was active in settling Maine), whom the people of Massachusetts, "seeing the loose behavior of the said Barbara inforced . . . to carry the said Barbara out of their pattent." Trelawney took Barbara 30 leagues away and found her a position. Babb later heard that Barbara married, but with her journey to Maine, Barbara Rolfe disappeared from sight.[43]

The tale of Barbara Rolfe, a troubled daughter sent off to the new world by her vexed parents, would seem extraordinary, indeed, bizarre, were it not for the appearance in ballad form of stories along the same line. Published in the 1650s, "A Net for a Night-Raven, Or, A Trap for a Scold," recounted the story of a weaver's wife, who was "witty, fair, and proud, but yet her wite deceiv'd her." Her torment of her husband led him to threaten to go to Virginia: he turned the tables, however, and presented himself to a shipmaster bound for Virginia, saying "I know of women you are lacking, I now have one that I can spare." For £10 the captain purchased the weaver's wife, whom the weaver duped on board. The captain sold her in Virginia for £50, and she found another husband. A second version of this story was published in 1709 as "The Woman Outwitted."[44] These ballads would appear to be only mechanisms for misogynist entertainment were it not for the fate of Barbara Rolfe, a daughter whose price for an uncooperative spirit was exile across the Atlantic.

Like Barbara Rolfe, another New Englander, John Mansfield, was temperamentally ill-suited to life in New England. His passage to Massachusetts was paid by his brother-in-law Robert Keayne, who followed Mansfield to the colony that same year. Mansfield's "distempered carriages and unworthy behavior" had brought grief in England in the guise of prison, debt, and "many quarrelsome businesses of dangerous consequence which he in his distempered fits had plunged himself into."[45] Less a victim of poor temperament than of ill health, eighteen-year-old Edmund Gurdon, the brother-in-law of Richard Saltonstall, Jr., and the son of the Suffolk sheriff Brampton Gurdon, traveled on the *Susan and Ellen* with his sister, brother-in-law, and niece. Family correspondence suggests he was sent for his health and general improvement to stay with the exemplary Winthrop family, yet it appeared that neither the Winthrops nor Edmund benefited from the arrangement. His mother wrote with chagrin to Margaret Winthrop in 1636, "I give Mr. Wintrup and your selfe many thanks for your care of my sonne Edmound. I did hope he would have bin of mor euse to have ben imployed by you then it seeme he was. The weaknes in his hands grew upon him not long befor he went from us. We ded hope the Sea would have been a good meanes to helpe it; but I rathar fear he is worse: my husband is desirous to give satisfaction for the charge he hath put you unto."[46] Gurdon soon returned home to England.

Like Barbara Rolfe or Edmund Gurdon, many of the people recruited for the colonies were poorly prepared for their arduous labors: indeed, what experience *could* prepare them? Where could English men gain familiarity with such crops as cotton, tobacco, indigo, or corn? Complaints about the inadequacy of labor recurred in different colonies. These complaints were brought not by colonial critics nor by apologists, both of whom might dwell on the poor nature of laborers there to attack the colonies or to explain away their deficiencies. Such a critic, for example, was George Donne, who wrote of Virginia that the policy of transporting there "the ragges and scumme of the people" harmed the colony.[47] More persuasive complaints came from men dependent for their lives and livelihoods on this labor. The inconvenience and menace of unskilled or unmotivated labor were lamented by John Dutton, the Earl of Warwick's agent in Bermuda, who complained in 1620 that the last three ships had brought in men who were "ill chousen, who, it may be feared, will prove unprofitable searvants."[48] Inadequate preparation spanned the social hierarchy. Gentlemen in particular often lacked necessary skills to wrest a living out of their colonial homes. Young Tom Verney adventured to Virginia despite the grave misgivings of his mother, who believed that men with experience "beyond the seas" might find a "prosperous journey" abroad, but "my sonne," she conceded with some trepidation, "hath neither beene bread abroad nor used to any bartering at home, but only bredd at schoole, and so I doubt wilbe to seeke in the employment that he is now goeing to undertake." She implored the colonial agent John Sadler to ask his acquaintances to "direct [her son] in his coarses" in Virginia.[49]

As ill-suited as gentlemen to the rigors of their colonial destinations were those vagrants seeking work in London who through misfortune or chance ended up bound for the colonies. The conditions that created vagrancy created a sizable pool of desperate men with few skills. As the agent John Sadler explained to the Verney family, Tom Verney should bring a cooper with him from the countryside, for in the city of London "wee cannot get soe redily heare" one of such ability.[50] Vagrants reached London and England's other ports in ill health and with few possessions and arrived in the new world weaker still, with not even a strong back to offer new employers, after months of searching for work in England and between six to fourteen weeks in the fetid hold of a ship, subsisting on meager ship's rations. These men were accompanied by prisoners. Fourteen Newgate prisoners were ordered transported to Virginia in 1635.[51] They proved unpopular colonists. "Newe-Gaitiers," as the Bermuda Governor Nathaniel Butler called them, had previously been sent to his island and aroused strenuous objections. He complained vociferously to Sir Nathaniel Rich about these prisoners who were "thrust upon me." "It is verely thought they infected the shyp," he wrote angrily, "and so have bin the occasion of the losse of many an honest mans life . . . As for the benefitt acrueinge to me by them, it is rather a Burthen, for noe man will hire them." Butler had no place to put these workers, and even if he had open land available, "they knowe not howe to worck."[52] John Dutton lamented that such "ill chousen" men had been brought to Bermuda, "who, it may be feared, will prove unprofitable searvants."[53] Young children could find themselves shipped overseas as well. Five boys brought in by London constables, from jurisdictions in Bishopsgate, the Tower, Farrington Within, and Fleet Street, were sent to Bermuda. The clerk's note that one of these boys, Edward Alden, was "willing to goe to Virginia" perhaps misrepresented the child's options.[54]

Rolfe, Gurden, the Newgate prisoners, the Bridewell vagrants—these were just 21 of an estimated 3,500 servants who traveled to the colonies from London in 1635. Most of these servants went to Virginia, which attracted over 2,000 people from London in 1635, and if the *Constance* is representative of ships to Virginia, some 77 percent of these people were servants. It would be easy to dismiss the large number of servants and the large number of men (two related but not identical figures) in colonies as a temporary demographic anomaly: after all, with the notable exception of New England in the 1630s, new colonies and immigrant communities typically contain far more men, who are generally the vanguard of migration, than women. But, as many historians have observed, what is striking about the seventeenth-century English colonies is the difficulties they had in rectifying this imbalance. Virginia, after all, had been settled for some thirty years by the time the ships reached the colony in 1635 with so many men on board, yet Virginia in that year received a new population that was 84 percent male.[55] And Bermuda was some twenty years old when it received a population that was 91 percent male. These skewed arrivals were not easily overcome. Barbados and St. Kitts, relatively new colonies by 1635, received populations that were 94 percent male, and it took each colony decades to recover from the demographic imbalance of the first few years of settlement. With few families traveling to the island, family life emerged slowly and painfully. Even as late as 1673, after almost fifty years of English settlement, 60.4 percent of the Barbados population was male, the ratio of the New England cohort in 1635.[56]

Disease, starvation, attacks by Native Americans, plague—all varied depending on place of settlement, but no settlers, indentured or free, were immune to the devastations of new world settings. Richard Dunn examined one parish on Barbados and found that between 1648 and 1694 the death rate for whites was four times the birth rate.[57] Although the London passengers of 1635 reached the island before the first yellow fever epidemics launched their deadly assaults, conditions were hardly salubrious for undernourished English laborers unaccustomed to tropical conditions, and the endemic diseases of the tropics plagued newcomers. A German mercenary, who had fought on the Royalist side in the Civil War and for his pains was shipped to Barbados after the Battle of Worcester as an indentured servant, complained about the unhealthy climate. "If one lies down on the ground for even one hour," he marveled, "one soon begins to bloat and swell up."[58] Dysentery, dropsy, and malaria weakened resistance to more deadly diseases when they did not themselves kill their hosts, and they increased the precarious nature of life in the Caribbean for European newcomers. High mortality dictated that what family life was constructed was short-lived. For those men who could find marriage partners in Barbados, then, the chances of the marriage being truncated by a partner's death were high. According to information available for 122 of the London travelers to Barbados, only 34 (28 percent) of the men in the migrant cohort married, and 31 (25 percent) had children.[59]

Virginia's population suffered similarly. Not until the late-seventeenth-century did the colony's population begin to reproduce itself. For most new arrivals, the likelihood of establishing family life was less than in England, given the sex and age ratios of servants and the disease environment awaiting them in the new world. Promises of land and opportunity were empty indeed for those who could not even survive the first year of settlement, the lethal seasoning period. In Virginia from 1625 to 1634, the colony received 9,000 arrivals, while half the population died in this nine-year period—and this rate was an improvement over earlier rates of mortality, thanks to a more widely dispersed population and improved diet. The Maryland population, likewise, was incapable of reproducing itself until the 1680s or 1690s.[60]

A glance at the existing Virginia population in 1634 clarifies the havoc that high mortality wreaked. In 1634 Virginia contained an estimated 4,914 people. A year later, 2,009 people arrived in 1635 from London alone, not counting ships that brought probably almost as many people from other English ports.[61] It would have been very difficult for a colony to absorb a new population at least 40 percent its size (counting the London passengers alone) were it not for the heavy toll exacted by the seasoning process. While conditions had improved since the disastrous early years at Jamestown, mortality rates in the first year of arrival remained high, possibly as high as 40 percent. What did that mean for this newly arrived population in 1635? In 1636 Samuel Maverick reported that 1,800 people had died in Virginia in the preceding year. As the newest arrivals, the passengers of 1635 would be hardest hit by disease. Assuming that another 2,000 people reached Virginia in 1635 from other sources, what should have been a virtual doubling of Virginia's population would have yielded a net increase of only 2,200 people.[62] Only residence in London during a plague year could possibly prepare a man for the demographic disaster awaiting him in Virginia, and even that experience would prove a modest dress rehearsal. The mercer Nathaniel Braddock's rapid death ten months after he embarked from London symbolized the failure of even wealthy men to thrive in this inhospitable place where death loomed as a silent and impatient partner.[63]

Even when disease did not weaken a colony's population, scarcity could. For most colonies, times of great scarcity occurred in the early years, when settlers were ill-equipped and poorly trained to plant or obtain foodstuffs. Such had been the case for Plymouth in its first winter and for Jamestown in its early years. Bermuda, in its first few years, similarly endured scarcity of food. The island's governor, with so little stored meal that the supply would not last a month, sent men who were "harlesse and lazie" to the main to feed themselves on berries. Lewis Hughes, the island's minister, joined these unfortunate exiles so that at least their souls would not starve as their bodies promised to do: when Hughes became weak from hunger, the exiled men propped him up against a pile of rocks so that he could continue to preach.[64] Richard Norwood, who was in Bermuda at the same time, described the colonists' plight with equal drama as they suffered the debilitating effects of starvation. "Being destitute of foode, many dyed," he recalled, "and we all became very feeble and weake, whereof some being so, would not; others could not stirre abroad to seeke reliefe, but died in their houses: such as went abroad were subject, through weaknesse, to be suddenly surprized with a disease we called the Feages, which was neither paine nor sicknesse, but as it were the highest degree of weaknesse, depriving us of power and abilitie for the execution of any bodilie exercise, whether it were working, walking, or what else."[65]

But even after a number of years and the presence of experienced governors, colonies could continue to endure debilitating food shortages. Providence suffered from such a scarcity in 1638, which resulted in a paucity of foodstuffs for island residents.[66] The remarkable reality to historians is the colonists' persistent inability to equip themselves properly for their new colonial adventures. In Richard Pares's distinctive words, "Over and over again, the pioneers who ought to have arrived healthy landed at the point of death; they brought with them four months' provisions where they ought to have brought ten (in some degree, of course, these two misfortunes cancelled each other out)."[67] Scarcity of clothing rivaled that of food. In 1645, over thirty years after its first settlement, Bermuda suffered such a shortage of cloth that were it not for all the children of the island set to spinning, the people would have gone naked.[68] Even experienced colonists behaved cavalierly. In 1638 some 130 Bermuda planters "transplanted" themselves to the island of St. Lucia. They neglected to bring the provisions or munitions necessary to supply such an undertaking, "where they have been assaulted by the savages, and suffered very much sickness, so that not one was in health."[69]

The very successes of colonies could cause scarcity. Edward Trelawney wrote from New England in 1636 that "the country at present is sick in a general want of provisions, by reason of the multiplicity of people that came this year and relying wholly on it."[70] In New England the scarcity of goods due to overpopulation was compounded by the poor quality of the soil. In contrast to the "affection, not judgment" that caused people to write of New England's rich soil, an unknown correspondent in 1637 ruefully observed that the soil "grows barren beyond belief" after five or six years planting.[71]

Material conditions in New England over the course of the seventeenth century were vastly better than in other regions of the Atlantic world. Life expectancies were as high as seventy years, and, because of largely younger ages of first marriage for colonial women, families were large.[72] These indications of demographic success, however, mask the reality of the dangers of first settlement. Newcomers did not know that they or their children would enjoy lifespans of Old Testament proportions: had they suspected this prospect, it would only have confirmed their sense of the divine justice of their errand. For new arrivals life was precarious indeed. Half the settlers at Plymouth died the first year. Massachusetts settlers suffered as well. Thomas Dudley reported in 1631 that when the Winthrop fleet arrived, people were sick and dying. Between April and December of 1630, 200 people died. Over 100 people, including the 1635 traveler William Vassall, returned to England, probably with great relief, when the Winthrop fleet set sail for England from Massachusetts.[73] It took Vassall five years to gird up his courage for a second effort at colonial life. The demographic imbalances wrought by catastrophic mortality rates in the first years of settlement had lingering consequences symbolized vividly by broken families and orphaned children. Even when the pressures of new settlement eased, the strains of colonial life continued. In his *Journal* for the year 1635, John Winthrop noted a range of catastrophes that beset the people of New England—over 25 people drowned, and some starved to death when their ship had to unload its goods between Connecticut and Massachusetts.[74]

The experiences of one traveler capture the many factors that contributed to precarious life and premature death in England's colonies. Few travelers in 1635 could have greeted their journey with greater trepidation than Joan Filby, who voyaged in the *Expectation* to Association Island, one of the smaller holdings in the Providence patent, now called Tortuga, off the coast of Hispaniola, or Haiti. She was a longtime island resident, one who had endured the difficulties endemic to this tropical island setting. Joan Filby had first journeyed to Association with her husband, child, and four servants in 1632.[75] She joined a small population there of only some 150 people. Life was not easy for the Filbies on Association. In 1634 her husband Samuel had written to the Providence Island Company member Sir Thomas Barrington from the island, describing conditions there. Filby was so weak he could barely control his pen. A man who could not hold his pen could hardly undertake the more crucial tasks necessary for his survival—clearing land, cultivating crops, directing his servants, or procuring game and fish. Poor health could literally ruin a man's fortunes in a colony by rendering him unable to support himself or to meet his financial obligations.[76] Mr. Filby reported bleakly on affairs on the island where a "great mortalitie amongst us my sarvants ar all dead . . . and my wifee is and hath bin sick a long tayme so that I am in a merserable case." Filby implored Barrington to intercede on his behalf with the Company, for he was "very sicke and ell at this toyme wherfoar I pray bear with me."[77] Filby was in the Company's debt, although he reported to Barrington that he had sent 1,000 pounds of tobacco in the same ship that carried his letter. He imagined that affairs could only deteriorate further, as his one remaining servant, John Lucke, would finish his indenture the following May, and without assistance Filby thought he would never recover financially. Help did not come in time: the order of events is not clear, but between August of 1634 and January of 1635, when the Spanish attacked the island, Mr. Filby and the child died. Joan Filby fled and returned alone to London, where she reported to the Company in April on "ye surprize of Association." The Company agreed to pay her passage back to the island and to ensure that she would gain possession of "her plantacon" when she returned. Moreover, the council there was ordered to restore to Filby her servants and goods.[78]

Joan Filby's solitary return to Association, clouded as it was by the unknown status of her home, represented an extraordinary commitment to colonial life. Indeed, when the *Expectation* left London in 1635, the Company recognized the possibility that the island of Association could have been either "deserted by ye English or possessed by the Enimy" and it also dictated contingency plans for Association's new governor, Nicholas Riskinner.[79] Mrs. Filby was to be put on shore wherever she wanted, on any island, if Association were no longer in English hands or if she no longer wanted to stay there.[80]

Filby's seventy-five fellow travelers on the *Expectation* could surely find little comfort in her presence. She embodied what newcomers to the colonies had to fear most: failure, invasion, and death, although her tenacity might have inspired some even as her husband's failure scared others. Filby would have been empty-handed indeed were it not for the munificence of the Providence Island Company. Her plantation lost; her husband, child, and servants dead; the island besieged by the Spanish: what could Filby offer to her fellow travelers except a cautionary tale? Her fellow passenger Nicholas Riskinner was soon to suffer the fate of Filby's husband. He died of disease within a few months of his arrival on Association; by 1636 there were only eighty English people living on the island.[81]

The Filby family's misfortunes attest to the potential disasters awaiting English residents in the colonies and illuminate the challenges of family formation and survival. And that these misfortunes took their toll on the morale of island residents is evident from a letter that the Providence Island Company's secretary, William Jessop, wrote to a Providence resident, wherein he sympathized "that hard fare and sickness should discourage the planters."[82] Servants, moreover, shared their masters' fates. Although all individuals in the colonies suffered from disease and Indian attack, none suffered more from the uncertainties and strains of new world conditions than did servants. They shared the dangers of new settlements, often joining with their masters to defend themselves against invasion and attack. They labored in the fields to produce both an export crop for their masters' profit and food for themselves. But servants also had to defend themselves against the demands of the strangers who were now their new masters, and their masters, in turn, had to structure their world to regulate young laborers. The fortuitous combination in the first half of the seventeenth century of a growing population in England producing abundant unemployed young men and of growing colonies desperate for agricultural labor meant that thousands of ill-equipped young men and women found themselves bound for the colonies to perform unfamiliar tasks in an unforgiving land. The servitude they experienced there was vastly different from the annual contracts that agricultural servants labored under in England. Despite the New England promoter and 1635 passenger William Wood's encouragement to servants to go to New England, where they would find "as much freedome and liberty for servants as in *England*" and where a wronged servant would be sheltered by "*volens nolens,*" servants in the new world were unprotected by the customary restraints on a master's conduct: family and neighbors were not present in the new world to enforce traditional standards of treatment.[83] In England agricultural servants toiled under renewable annual contracts. These contracts were arranged at annual hiring fairs: servants could interrogate future masters and other servants in order to secure the most palatable positions.[84] Indentured servants in the colonies possessed contracts that were a mixture of these annual contracts and the long-term apprenticeships of young boys and girls whose parents paid masters for educating and supporting the children.[85] Absent from these colonial indentures, however, were the informed negotiations undertaken by English servants in husbandry.

It is a commonplace among historians of slavery that slave majorities or significant minorities produced draconian slave codes that gave wide-ranging punitive powers to masters in slave societies.[86] In fact, one contemporary observer in Barbados noted in the 1640s that slave rebellion was far less of a risk than servant rebellion, because slaves who spoke different languages had greater difficulty understanding each other.[87] In English America in the 1630s and 1640s, it was a servant majority that characterized most colonies. And it was the servants who were targeted by their masters, fearful of servant rebellion, for treatment that would inculcate submission. Through the forum of the county and local courts in different colonial jurisdictions, where servants witnessed the exoneration of masters who brutalized their servants, servants were forcefully reminded of their dependence on the unpredictable goodwill of an arbitrary master.

Servants were just another commodity, bartered freely by their masters for goods and land. John Stotter of Barbados was still in service in 1640, five years after he had left London on the *Falcon*'s second voyage of that year, when he was sold, along with a pig and some farm implements.[88] As capital investments for planters eager to make quick fortunes off cash crops, servants were painfully vulnerable to the whims of masters who found it easy to regard their servants as replaceable goods rather than individuals to be incorporated into families as they were in England. Although English servants on both sides of the Atlantic were vulnerable to physical abuse, evidence suggests that new world masters at times ran amok. In all the plantation colonies, the hard toil that servants performed shortened their laboring lives, while planters' cupidity fueled their need for able-bodied laborers. Distance from the constraints of a densely settled parish, a community where a servant had kin, and distance from the normal context in which agricultural servants labored under one-year contracts, not long-term indentures that could be bought or sold, together contributed to new world excesses. Masters disciplined servants with little regard for traditional modes of control, which, though physically violent, were kept in check by mitigating forces.[89]

In the colonies as in England, laws and indentures dictated what servants should receive for their service.[90] Servants contracted themselves for a certain number of years, and during that time were to receive room, board, the training appropriate for their trade, and, on their freedom, a specified sum of money or goods. *A Relation of Maryland,* published in 1635, included a copy of the "forme of binding a servant." According to this boilerplate, a servant promised to serve for a specified number of years in return for his passage,

"Meat, Drinke, Apparell and Lodging, with other necessaries during the said terme," and on his freedom was to receive one year's supply of corn and 50 acres of land "according to the order of the countrey."[91] Servants who traveled to Providence were assured "meate drink and Apparrell dureing their Terme of service" and would on their freedom "receive all convenient Assistance and encouragement from the company."[92]

Freedom dues varied depending on the colony, but in all locations a servant remained dependent on the good faith of his master to provide the stipulated goods. A servant on Barbados, for example, by 1650 was to receive £10 or its equivalent in goods "if," as an observer commented frankly, "his Master bee soe honest as to pay it."[93] In Virginia a servant expected clothes when freed: Humphrey Belt, free from his service in 1641 after six years in the colony, went to court to petition for his share. John Gater, a Virginia planter long resident in the colony who in 1635 returned to Virginia from London, neglected to pay his servant Thomas Hall his freedom dues of one bed, one bolster, a rug, and a pot.[94] Not only did masters withhold freedom dues, the deprivation itself a source of injury and hardship; but they also connived to prolong their servants' terms of indenture. Mary Soanes's master, John Sibsey, forced her to serve seven extra weeks. He was ordered to pay her 40 pounds of tobacco in compensation.[95]

The difficulty with which some servants procured their contractually stipulated goods and freedom signals the vulnerability of colonial laborers. Servants, for example, had the right to make formal complaints against their masters but could risk severe retaliation by doing so. By 1624 Bermuda had drafted a law that decreed that on complaint or on suspicion of harsh usage of a servant, tribe (the early Bermuda parish) officers were to investigate the charge and to check provisions for food, accommodation, clothing, and "necissaries convenient for them." If appropriate, the governor would intervene between a master and his servant, "whereby they may proceed more comfortably in their affairs both in serving god, and following their lawfull employment in this plantation."[96] The Bermuda council was sensitive to English custom, ordering that idle children whose parents were loathe to put them out to work be put into service "according to the Law and coustomes of the parrishes in England."[97]

A Spaniard inadvertently waylaid in Bermuda in 1639, however, had a less favorable impression of servitude on the island than the law decreed. He was struck by the youth of the servants there and recorded that labor in Bermuda was "performed by boys, who are either orphans or have been abandoned . . . they serve for ten years at a very miserable wage . . . They are clothed on the same mean scale, and thus live poorly and practically in a state of slavery."[98] His sense of long terms was not at all inaccurate. Indeed, Edward Chaplin reached Bermuda at the age of 20 to serve for seven years, and Thomas Sharpe, who was 17 years old, had eight years to serve.[99] For those many servants who were younger, especially the orphan vagrants from Bridewell Hospital, terms of service would have been even longer.

As the Spaniard's view suggests, there was often a disjunction between legal requirements and compliance. While servants could be used harshly, there were apparently lines one could not cross. This line was not clearly defined: only in its breach was attention drawn to the unspoken mores that governed the treatment of English servants. When one Providence Island minister made complaints against another before the Company in London, he searched his foe's conduct for accusations that would have resonance before the court: this minister was accused of inappropriate conduct in teaching songs aboard the ship on his voyage to Providence, even on the Sabbath, and of abusing his servant once he reached the island.[100] The abuses of colonial servants were certainly not unknown in England. A fictitious account of a young man shipped to Virginia as an indentured servant by his despairing relatives recorded his time among Virginia's planters. The protagonist styled his masters as "those wild Barbarians, who had so often made his heart bleed by their Turkish usages."[101]

Particularly brave or dissatisfied servants could eschew legal action by negotiating directly with their masters. Twiford West traveled from London in 1635 and first appeared in the New England records as a servant in Plymouth in 1636. He was apprenticed to Edward Winslow for six years, but Winslow assigned West to Nicholas Snow. West "(after some triall) disliking to be with ye said Nicolas Snow," implored Winslow to let him serve Winslow himself. In order to acquire this new position, however, West had to agree to serve one extra year in his indenture.[102] Good servants in particular achieved strong bargaining positions. Anthony Hoskins, who reached Virginia from London in 1635, had a servant he could not hang on to. Hoskins's servant, Edward Farrell, was courted by John Jenkins, who promised Farrell higher wages if he left Hoskins and went to work for Mr. Angood.[103]

The requirements of indentures often permitted servants legal redress if they could demonstrate breach of the indenture.[104] Some servants had difficulty forcing their master to comply with his own responsibilities to train them in their trade. The courts proved particularly sympathetic to servants who placed this charge against their masters: it was, after all, in a colony's best interest to acquire skilled laborers through the mechanism of indenture. When the three Stiles brothers, carpenters by trade, reached Connecticut in 1635 aboard the *Christian,* they brought with them many servants.[105] Francis Stiles apparently did not embrace his responsibilities as a master. He was chastised for neglecting his duties and was ordered by the Connecticut court to teach three of his servants, George Chappell, Thomas Cooper, and Thomas Barber, the skill of carpentry.[106] Similar complaints occurred in Virginia. Richard Townshend, a Virginia planter who in 1635 returned from London to his home in the colony, was apprenticed to the occasional Council member John Pott, a doctor, in 1622. Pott was to instruct Townshend in "the art of an Apothecarye." Four years later, however, Townshend complained that his master had neglected his instruction. The court ordered Doctor Pott to "from time to time endeavor to teach & instruct" Townshend, in order that he would end his service as "a sufficient Apothecarye."[107]

But when grievances were more severe, when a servant found himself at real risk to his or her safety, the courts could be slow to respond. By the time conflicts between masters and servants reached the courts, matters had often degenerated to the point of permanent disfigurement or even death. It is clear that for many, the time of service comprised a reign of terror. Servants endured great hardship in large part because England's rising population kept the price of servants low. In Barbados, for example, a 1635 inventory appraised a servant with $2\frac{1}{2}$ years to serve at 225 pounds of tobacco, while a second servant, a boy with 3 years to serve, was worth only 350 pounds.[108] The servants who reached Virginia on the *Tristram and Jeane* were sold for between 500 and 600 pounds of tobacco apiece, for indentures that were not recorded but that probably would have ranged from 5 to 8 years.[109] Thus a servant could be had for less than 100 pounds of tobacco a year. Cheaply and easily replaced, servants found little charity at the hands of their masters. Richard Ligon described in some detail the circumstances of the English servants he observed in Barbados, where he deplored their treatment. "Truly," he wrote, "I have seen such cruelty there done to Servants, as I did not think one Christian could have done to another."[110] One Barbados servant, John Thomas, brought his two masters to trial in 1640 for their "inhumanly and unchristian like" treatment. He had been suspended by his hands while burning matches were put between his fingers. Having "lost the use of several joints," the servant was freed and compensated for damages.[111] Another visitor to Barbados noted that when servants became free after their four years service, they had "dearly earned" their freedom and the £10 freedom dues.[112]

In Virginia, servants were found hanged with chains; also in Virginia, servants drowned themselves; one especially angry servant murdered his master and mistress with a hammer as they lay in bed.[113] William Allinson deposed in 1643, after eight years in the colony, about the abuse of a servant girl, Elizabeth Bibby, who was thrown into a creek, shaken over an open fire, and suspended on a tackle employed for hanging deer by Allinson's and Bibby's mistress, Mrs. Burdett.[114] Another traveler of 1635, Arthur Raymond, also served the violent Mrs. Burdett in Accomack County. In 1642 he testified before the county court about an incident that had transpired three years earlier, while he was still in service. At Christmastime, while Raymond was at work in the quartering house, Mrs. Burdett walked in and asked him, "Art thou a true Man?" To this Raymond said he was: Mrs Burdett then grabbed his pestle and threatened to give him "a spell." Mrs. Burdett believed that some of her servants had stolen a hog, and she summarily threatened to hang them all. She was not without sensibility of the possible financial loss, blithely asserting she did not care if it cost her £40. Yet Mrs. Burdett paid a price for her cavalier treatment of her servants. She was forced to call the undersheriff of the county to observe her servants, saying to him, "I am affrayd they will overrun me."[115] For all the brutality of such treatment of servants, women like Mrs. Burdett without their husbands clearly were vulnerable to servants who took advantage of their masters' absences. Silvester Thatcher's wife came to the Lancaster County court in 1655 to complain that while her husband was away, two servants ran off for two months.[116] John Sibsey, a Justice of Norfolk County, proved such an unpopular master that his servants mutinied in his absence in 1638.[117]

As the mutiny of Sibsey's servants indicates, servants occasionally resisted their service in overt ways. Running away in the colonies posed a far greater danger than it did in England. Servants who fled their masters in England risked punishment but not usually their lives. However, servants who escaped in the colonies did risk their lives, fleeing by boat from islands such as Providence to brave the hazards of Caribbean winds and currents, or by land on the mainland to confront hazards ranging from the snakes, insects, and animals of the forests, the discomfort and danger of inclement weather, and the potential threat (or hospitality) of native inhabitants. As George Percy noted in Virginia, men who ran away to the Indians, in this instance in search of food, were never heard of again.[118] Yet evidence is abundant that, for all the risks, servants tried to escape. Francis Jarvis, a 1635 traveler to Virginia, ran away from his master, Thomas Ward, because, he told Daniel Pighles, "hee could not beate att the Morter."[119] In 1635 Clement Cole, George Wilby, and Simon Bird, who had only just reached Massachusetts from London as servants, were punished by the General Court of Massachusetts for stealing a boat and attempting to run away from their masters.[120]

Island laborers also resorted to running away from their service obligations. In an instance of large-scale escape, Henry Colt remarked during his stay in Barbados in 1631 that forty servants had fled in a Dutch pinnace.[121] Providence Island was similarly plagued by runaways who took to the seas. Governor Nathaniel Butler recorded regularly the efforts of the Providence minister Hope Sherrard's servants to flee their master. One Sunday while

Sherrard was engaged in leading services on the island, two of his black slaves "came away in a bote." The following Sunday, perhaps encouraged by this example of timing and audacity, two of Sherrard's English servants likewise fled in a boat, along with another English servant belonging to the island planter and councillor Richard Lane.[122] It was shrewd planning on the part of the English and African laborers to flee on a day when the island's English population was distracted by religious obligations.

The most extreme form of servant resistance was rebellion. Servants' "mischief" could lead to fires, which easily happened in quickly constructed wooden shelters or dry fields. And masters who provoked their servants "by extream ill usage, and often and cruel beating them," drove them to collective violence. Indeed, just before Richard Ligon reached the island of Barbados, there was such a conspiracy of servants, which resulted in the execution of eighteen and the torture of others.[123] Ligon's experience echoed that of Father White, who over a decade earlier reported a servant uprising on Barbados when he visited the island on his way to Maryland in 1634. "The very day we arrived," he wrote, "we found the Iland all in armes to the number of about 800 men. The servants of the Iland had conspired to kill their masters and make themselves free, and then handsomely to take the first ship that came, and soe goe to sea." One servant who, according to White, was "affraid to joine in the plott," revealed its plan, and the ringleaders, a pair of brothers, were punished. One brother was put to death.[124]

Service in the colonies thus varied substantially from service in England. The commodification of laborers, longer terms, harsh punitive masters, and the desperate resort to rebellion distinguished colonial servitude. It is obvious that the regulation of colonial servants demanded the attention of courts and planters, both in the colonies and in England. Two further examples suggest the ways in which male servant majorities had lasting impacts in different colonies. Household composition in the colonies bore little resemblance to that in England, and the youthful male cultures asserted themselves in the violence and belligerence that contemporaries noted.

The exuberant recreations of young colonists were themselves a product of societies that were primarily male.[125] It was not simply that the majority of colonial residents were young single men, but rather that so many of these young men had preceded their service in the colonies with periods of vagrancy in England. They had already been dislodged from the regulating structures of family and parish when they commenced their treks through England in search of work. One observer, Captain Henry Ashton, the governor of Antigua, explained the disorder of St. Kitts in terms of the prevalence of single men. Nevis fared better, he noted: that colony, thanks in part to "the honesty & Pyety of ye Gent there Governing," attracted married men and "the better sort."[126] Colonies like Barbados, St. Kitts, and Virginia, with their male majorities, resembled military encampments without the rigorous discipline and clear hierarchies of army life.

Visitors to the West Indian colonies consistently commented on the violence of the planters there. Henry Colt was particularly put off by the men he encountered. Of Barbados, Colt reported, "You are all younge men, & of good desert, if you would but bridle ye excesse of drinkinge, together wth ye quarelsome conditions of your fyery spiritts." This consumption of "hott waters" was particularly alarming to Colt, who maintained that they acted as oil to "encrease ye flame" of "your younge and hott bloods," which were better salved with cold water. The "manifold quarrells" of the young planters surpassed even their drunkenness. It took little to set off these young tempers, Colt observed, and he found little comfort in the ability of the governor, himself "but a young man," to restrain the planters. Distracted by their drunken revelries, the planters neglected their servants and plantations, allowing the one to shirk their duties and allowing the other to degenerate into disheveled reflections of the besotted planters themselves.[127]

The ensuing years failed to moderate these young planters: indeed, with regular infusions of more young men, little maturity reached the island for several decades. In 1639 Thomas Verney wrote to his father in England, perhaps to insist on his own newfound propriety, that drunkenness was the worst evil on the island. People were so drunk, Verney claimed, that in their stupors they did not even realize that they were being bitten by the little land crabs that rivaled drunkenness as the bane of island existence.[128] Drunkenness on the island continued to impress visitors in the 1650s, when Father Antoine Biet remarked that "drunkeness is great, especially among the lower classes." The upper classes hosted extravagant feasts at which guests were often too intoxicated to return home, whereas merchants who did business in Bridgetown transacted their affairs in taverns and inns.[129] Another visitor, mustering a contemporary ethnic slur, called the typical inhabitant a "German for his drinking."[130] The casual violence of these young societies resulted in the death of at least one of the new arrivals in 1635. John Brombie was "mortally wounded" by Thomas Scott in 1651, sixteen years after he had reached Barbados, and died at the age of 43.[131]

Inebriation was hardly limited to Barbados, although all visitors there seemed thoroughly impressed by the island residents' commitment to drink. Alcohol consumption in general was common in England and the colonies, for men and women, young and old alike, and young people elsewhere were equally seduced by the temptations of strong liquor. Even the worthy John Winthrop remarked crossly during his voyage to New England, after one maid servant had passed out from drink, that he found "a Common fault in our yonge people, that they gave themselves to drinke hott waters verye imoderately."[132] Winthrop at least could muster up the authority to quell these young, intemperate travelers. Hierarchy was clearly defined among these New England-bound voyagers, who in this period replicated as closely as was possible the age and gender structures that were in place in England. But elsewhere, where masters were little older than their servants and where the intense pressures of colonial survival encouraged equally extreme forms of relaxation and escape, drunken exuberance reigned and thereby encouraged violence.

This rowdy behavior, on the part of both masters and servants, and the real possibility of servant resistance made it important to find mechanisms for controlling servants on a more systematic basis than was provided by a master's discipline or intermittent court appearances. One simple way was to dictate their living conditions, and the institution employed was the family. In many colonies, servants and other single people were required to live in families that were created and defined for the constraints and peculiarities of colonial environments. Where nuclear families did not exist, colonial governments dictated alternate configurations. The Providence Island Company ordered Governor Philip Bell to "distribute all the Inhabitants into several ffamilies whereof one shalbe the Chiefe," who was not only to ensure that his family of laborers perform public duties, but also to pray with his family twice daily, "that [God's] blessing may be upon themselves and the whole Island." In some cases the precise configurations of these families were rigidly defined. The Somers Islands Company dictated the number of people in each family, ordering in 1622 that the inhabitants live "five in a family."[133]

These families were to provide mechanisms for order. With a vigilant chief, a household on Providence could be regulated as the Company hoped. Popular pastimes that were not in accordance with the Company's puritan vision could be monitored: no swearing, drunkenness, or profaning the Sabbath were to be permitted. "And take care," the Company admonished, "that Idelness as the Nurse of all Vice be carefullie exchewed."[134] When the Company heard that people on Providence had sent for "cards and Dice and Tables," it instructed Governor Bell to confiscate and destroy these items.[135] Thus a colonial "family" was defined by the quantity of its inhabitants, not by the different social and economic roles each performed nor by the degrees of relation; and living in a family meant living with a male householder.[136]

A family contained servants: the early modern use of the term automatically included servants as part of families. So it is no surprise to find English servants living in households as family members. But in the colonies two alterations to the English family transpired. First, the family that a servant lived in, not the family that he or she grew up in, became the primary mechanism for controlling and socializing laborers, who were required to dwell in families. The deviation from similar English practices, in which youths were customarily raised and trained in households other than those of their parents, is subtle but important. In those circumstances in which English parents deposited their children with family friends or patrons, the new guardian's responsibility to that child was clear. English youths in agricultural service often worked near their birth families, and contact could be maintained through oral messages or the occasional letter. Also, these English servants lived in households similar to those of their childhood, with parents and children surrounded by servants and laborers. Yet in the colonies these same servants lived in households that varied from the English model. Peculiar sex and age ratios in most of the colonies and the legal requirements ordering single people to form households provided a different socializing mechanism—one that often required the support of courts and other judicial bodies. The colonial family that was created and encountered by the travelers of 1635 was only a crude approximation of the English families long since left behind, and servants became unusually dependent on the sole authority of their master or mistress.

Regulations that required single men and women to dwell with families also contributed to the heterogeneity of family life, and this feature points to the second anomaly of colonial families: the diversity of people contained in them.[137] Requirements that single people dwell with families meant that colonial families boarded strangers. But the diversity of family life went well beyond the accommodation of unfamiliar English migrants. On Providence in 1636, African slaves were ordered to be settled in families and were divided among officers and planters. By 1638 the Company ordered that the ratio should be two English to one African in a family.[138] A family on Providence could also contain Native American children from the mainland, who were to be raised as English children.[139] On Barbados, Indians labored with Africans, both in conditions of slavery. Although the number of Native Americans, one Barbados visitor noted in 1650, was "but few," their presence was measurable.[140] The presence of Africans in significant numbers altered housing arrangements not merely by prompting colony governors to dictate ratios within the household but also by altering the domestic landscape with new outbuildings. Men of sufficient wealth, like Richard Norwood of Bermuda, were able to build a separate "Negroes Cabbine" for slaves.[141] On Barbados as well, at least according to a 1650 report, slaves lived in separate cottages.[142]

What these examples of household composition in the colonies suggest is that for all that a newcomer to a colony could build a house precisely on an English model, whether an East Anglian or New England saltbox or a West Country or Virginia great house, the grouping of who slept in that house at the end of the day bore little resemblance to that of the inhabitants of an old English counterpart.[143] Indeed, homes on English models were the exception in the colonial world in the first part of the seventeenth century. Whereas some great planters on Barbados constructed English edifices, complete with fireplaces that would be employed only at the great discomfort of the inhabitants, the Barbados planter Thomas Love detailed in his inventory his "boarded house."[144] Tom Verney constructed a "sorry cottage" in anticipation of servants to inhabit it.[145] Homes were equally simple on Bermuda. Although a few Bermudians lived in stone houses, for the most part in the 1630s modest cabins made of wooden posts, with palm branch roofs, dominated the island's landscape.[146]

Inside these little houses containing male laborers of three different races, the anomalies continued. Sleeping arrangements themselves were modified in the colonies, where in the tropics men slept not on beds but, as observers in Barbados noted, on hammocks strung between two poles.[147] The Barbados planter Philip Cartwright, who died with possessions such as horses, silk stockings, silver buttons, and twenty slaves that attested to his measurable wealth, had himself embraced this local practice by the time he wrote his will in 1672. He left to his son Philip "one cotten hamacco in ye parlor."[148] Whereas English people slept several to a bed, a hammock was designed for only one person. Even when beds were available, the heat of the tropics transformed customary practice: John Nicholl, whose misadventures earlier in the century took him to South America, reported that in Cartagena each member of his party was given a separate bed, "for the country is so hot, wee cannot lye but one in a bed."[149]

The new sleeping arrangements of the tropics symbolized the differences from domestic life in England. Instead of families of relations, colonists dwelled in families decreed by number and occasionally race. Demographic exigencies, combined in some cases with catastrophic mortality rates, dictated that family formation (as families were formed in England, by marriage and procreation) would become an extraordinary luxury for many new arrivals in the colonies. Yet a family shaped by affection, not just a dictated living arrangement, was a luxury greatly desired. Unable to re-create the households they had known in England, colonial residents settled instead for extended networks of friends and endowed these networks with familial significance.[150] Men in the West Indies, the region most defined by skewed demographic conditions, labored mightily amid their struggle for economic survival to define their relationships with neighbors and business partners in meaningful ways.

For travelers to Barbados the prospect of family formation as they knew it in England was obviously remote. Because fortune clearly favored families, those men who had brought kin or had found a wife were in luck. Some travelers, such as the brothers Edmund and James Montgomery, quickly acquired land and probably arrived with wealth. Philip and Elizabeth Lovell reached Barbados as a married couple in their early thirties. Philip Lovell amassed land quickly on his arrival and then bought and sold parcels of land with regularity. In five separate transactions between 1640 and 1643, Lovell sold one hundred acres of land and five servants. Elizabeth Lovell, too, made an appearance in Barbados records when she deposed in 1653 on the estate of Hugh Jones, who had traveled on the same ship as the Lovells.[151] A second unusual pair were John Bromby, aged 27, and his father Thomas, aged 59. Thomas Bromby purchased half of a plantation in 1640 and was still alive in 1652 when his son John died. At his death, John still had not married or had children but instead left all his property to his father.[152]

John Bromby's single status at his death reveals the difficulty Barbadians found in marrying. Probably 75 percent of travelers to Barbados in 1635 had reached the island as young, single servants. Rare was the traveler who arrived in the company of family. Only thirty people, or 3 percent of the traveling population, journeyed with relatives.[153] Given the reality of unsettled family life and early death, Barbadians constructed alternative ways of exercising familial care for each other.

What Barbadians devised was the extensive use of partnership, both as a means of funding land acquisition and as a mechanism for family living.[154] Men combined to buy tiny parcels of land. Partnership in Barbados had importance beyond economic expediency and prudence. The extensive use of partnership for small parcels of land suggests that there was not always a financial need for men to share ownership of estates or to choose to share one house on their property. Rather, the frequency of collective ownership suggests that young men derived personal satisfaction from cooperative ventures with friends in a setting void of familiar family life. Ralph Harwood purchased ten acres of land with Thomas Ferrier in 1640, as did Felix Line and his partner in 1642.[155] These men, as their deeds make apparent, shared small homes with each other. Thomas Brazie and Samuell Terrent, for example, covenanted with the 1635 traveler Richard Richardson and his partner Middleton Cooper to build *one* house.[156]

Partnership thus filled a need for companionship that transcended financial exigency. Planters found other ways as well to cement ties with their friends. A survey of extant wills for the 1635 voyagers to Barbados permits the reconstruction of the general configurations of some of these familial and affective networks. Whether or not planters had children of their own, they tended to remember their godchildren in their wills. In his will of 1651, Edward Bankes bequeathed £10 each to his two godchildren.[157] William Huckle, who died in

1672 with six children of his own, remembered his godchild Susan Coly with 200 pounds of sugar.[158] Dorothy Symonds had a son and a daughter in England to whom she left her estate to be divided equally. She also requested that each of her godchildren be provided with 100 pounds of sugar.[159]

Planters left money, land, and goods to the children of friends regardless of any formal definition of that relationship. Orphans received special attention.[160] George Norton left 5,000 pounds of sugar to John Clark, "a poor fatherless boy in his charge."[161] Anthony Skooler, who had married, died in 1665 with no surviving children or relatives. He remembered the daughter of his friend John Harrison in his will, however, with 300 pounds of sugar.[162] Alexander Smith, who had traveled to Barbados at the age of 18, married and soon had children. Smith apparently died in the 1640s, possibly in the yellow fever epidemic of 1647, and two different men, James Martin and Thomas Nelson, remembered his children in their wills.[163] Both Martin's and Nelson's wills were witnessed by Thomas Prosser, a shipmate of Smith. Prosser, Smith, and two other men, John Key and Arthur Winde, composed an unusual network of friends in the West Indies. All four men had traveled together on the *Hopewell* in 1635. In his will in 1657, Arthur Winde mentioned Katherine Key, the daughter of John Key, and the two sons of Thomas Prosser, to whom he gave ten acres. He appointed Thomas Prosser as his executor and called him his brother-in-law.[164] This evidence of continuing affectionate connections conveys efforts to construct, within the disorder of white Barbadian society, lateral ties of friendship and protection.

The strenuous efforts of Barbadian men to employ the legal and spiritual devices at their disposal—bequests, godparentage, cotenancy—to devise familial structures in an environment that deprived them of doing so in a fashion like that in England point to the anomalies of this new world setting. For men in Barbados and Virginia, family formation was obviously difficult, but it was passionately desired, and not in the form dictated by their colonial circumstances, but in the affectionate form they might have known at home. Thus they struggled to combat the destiny that demography promised with a destiny that affection composed.

The example of Barbados and its squadrons of single men, asleep in their hammocks in their boarded houses, offers a potent reminder that the communities that the travelers to the colonies joined, and in turn re-created, were by any standard in England, peculiar. The skewed sex ratios on the West Indian islands made these male societies resemble nothing so much as monasteries, albeit ones committed to bacchanalian revelry. In the Chesapeake, isolated plantations with their freshly built but quickly disintegrating homesteads replicated the work rhythms of English agricultural society, but without the sure certainty of manorial life, with its parish church, its manor house, its clusters of houses and outbuildings defined by longevity, where all disputes rested on the memory of man.[165] The cheapness and precariousness of life lent a tone of macabre lunacy to colonial undertakings. Any new arrival to the Chesapeake colonies could assume with grim certainty that as many as half the people whom he or she traveled with from England would be dead in a year. And as for New England, the remarkable replication of familial and community life gave these settlers an advantage over all elsewhere. But the rule of the saints made New England as out of place in an English context as did the reign of illiterate planters in Virginia. Men might have looked wistfully back to England for models of domestic life, but everything in their colonial world dictated against family construction. Servants and young men dominated colonial societies, ensuring their success with their backbreaking toil and contributing to the proliferation of domestic and institutional forms that the English created overseas.

4 | *The Trappings of Success in Three Plantation Colonies*

In their first few decades, new colonies were characterized by nothing so much as a chaotic scramble. A range of factors circumscribed these scrambles, including the patience and financial support of colonial proprietors and investors, the natural resources of a colony, the skills of planters and servants, and the demand for and the price of colonial staples in a world market. This scramble, moreover, took different forms—in Barbados, a frenzied and avaricious search for a successful export crop; in Virginia, a similar quest for a viable staple compounded by the struggle to stay alive amidst a series of Anglo-Indian wars and the assault of diseases; in Bermuda, a scramble nowhere in a colony that afforded only modest attainment; in New England, the gradual clarification of new ecclesiastical forms accompanied and defined by the fracturing of churches and towns. In 1635 the travelers from London reached their colonial destinations when each colony was at a different point in this slow and uncertain process of colonial creation. In the broader scheme of imperial expansion, the English colonies considered here were all young, and their success was unsure by any number of measures. Yet these new societies afforded starkly varied opportunities for newcomers. These newcomers arrived both as servants and as free men. A lucky few came as independent planters with wealth or credit to prime their colonial aspirations. They were accompanied by older colonial residents returning home in 1635. All of these people negotiated the hazards and uncertainties of colonial life as best they could to secure their share of the colonial spoils.

The presence of these different populations widens temporarily the single episode of travel detailed in the 1635 register. It is possible to track these passengers' efforts over a range of some forty years, from the time that the first members of the London cohort reached Bermuda in 1615 and Virginia in 1616 to the 1660s, when the majority of the cohort vanishes from extant records. Three colonies serve here, Virginia, Bermuda, and Barbados, to scrutinize the collective and individual strategies that colonial residents pursued in their quest for success overseas. Separate treatment of each colony delineates the peculiar strategies devised in different economic, geographic, and agricultural settings to secure land and position as servants and other newcomers struggled to gain each colony's measure of success. Although it was mere chance that put many an indentured servant on a ship to one colony as opposed to another, that choice at the port, whether accidental or deliberate, had enormous consequences for newcomers to England's plantation colonies.

All English colonies in the seventeenth century, whether in Munster or Nevis, were called plantations, and all male landholders were planters; but these three colonies were plantations in a more restricted sense: in each, bound laborers comprised the majority of the population, and the economic success of each colony was believed by proprietors and investors to lie in the cultivation of an export crop. Similar in their dependence on bound labor, the three colonies share enough features to permit reasonable comparisons. Virginia was the oldest at almost thirty years when 2,009 men and women reached its shores from London in 1635. Part of this colony's scramble had already been resolved by the planters' commitment to tobacco cultivation. Bermuda was the second oldest colony, just a few years younger than Virginia, and Barbados the most recently settled of the group, only eight years under English cultivation when eight ships sailed there from London in 1635.

There were obviously many significant measures of success in the seventeenth-century colonies: good health, proximity to friends and kin, the ability to return home, family formation, and church membership and organization (which was so fundamental to colonial aspirations that it will be the single subject of the subsequent chapter). But the emphasis here reflects the nature of each colony's surviving sources by focusing on the public and measurable accomplishments of the 1635 cohort, especially the acquisition of land and other capital goods, and officeholding. Fortunately, the acquisition of land and goods was a benchmark that mattered to colonial residents. Securing such possessions was precisely the reason so many young, single men ventured to the colonies in the first place. But the following interpretation is admittedly shaped nonetheless by the surviving records. The early seventeenth-century records for all three colonies are notoriously uneven. Thus in Barbados, only deeds and wills, and many recopied at that, have survived three centuries in their tropical setting.[1] As for Virginia, only three out of the eight counties organized in 1634 have surviving records for this first decade, a crucial period both for the counties themselves and for the passengers of 1635. Bermuda's colonial records are idiosyncratic: they are startlingly rich and revealing for the short periods that they exist, but the lacunae are tremendous. Because of these reticent records, the strategy employed of tracing passengers through the different sets of extant colonial records has not been pursued by other historians. Although the general configurations of Virginia's economic development might be familiar, then, the story told here for the travelers to Bermuda and Barbados is less well known. The starkly different experiences of the passengers to these three different colonies, moreover, illustrate the momentous results of the smallest decisions, both at the port of London and in the colonies.

Altogether 409 men and women appear in the extant colonial sources: 241 in Virginia and Maryland (12 percent of the Chesapeake cohort), 50 in Bermuda (23 percent), and 118 in Barbados (12 percent). The evidence is occasionally composed of mere snippets of biographical information. Especially because the information available for individuals is sketchy and uneven, it is impossible to offer a rigorous quantitative comparison of the different regions. Indeed, no systematic sampling method has underpinned this exploration of survival strategies. Any traveler who survived to appear in the colonial records has been investigated. But however fragmentary and frustrating the reconstructed lives of these travelers of 1635 might be, together these 409 men and women usher us through the ordeal of survival in three strange and inhospitable environments.

For the many servants who reached England's colonies in 1635, the first struggle, shared throughout the colonies, was to extricate themselves permanently from bound labor. Long indentures delayed this process: William Lowder was released from service in February of 1644, almost nine years after he had arrived in Virginia on the *Safety* at the age of 24.[2] Once free, many servants could not provide for themselves and thus were obligated to sign new short-term indentures. Two former Barbados servants, freed in 1640, were unable to take immediate advantage of their new status. They promptly acknowledged their continuing dependency by signing deeds agreeing to serve another year: Thomas Hubbard would receive payment of 120 pounds of cotton, one hammock, and one pig, whereas William Seere agreed to serve Francis Hall for a year in return for 100 pounds of cotton and a shirt.[3] A similar pattern of annual labor following the completion of indenture emerges in Virginia. In 1643 Rowland Vaughan had apprenticed himself for another year to one Philip Taylor of Accomack, whereas John Branch hired himself in 1644 to serve William Stone for another year for 500 barrels of tobacco and five barrels of corn.[4]

Others—likely the undocumented majority—who became free or arrived as free men died before they had acquired any land. Michael Victor, a free traveler in 1635, died twelve years later in 1647, leaving an estate valued at a mere 156 pounds of tobacco. His inventory included a hoe distinguished as the only item characterized as new in his inventory, an old ax, an old bag, an old blanket, an old pillow, an old shirt, and some other goods.[5] A second free traveler, John Parry, established himself as a wage laborer on his arrival in the colony. Parry and his brother William journeyed together on the *Primrose* in 1635. Parry made his oral will before he died in Virginia, only three years after the brothers reached their colonial destination. Parry, a cooper, had acquired no land and had only his clothes, bedding, tools of his trade, and wages due to leave to his friends.[6]

Of those men who survived to become free, how did they fare? Destinations played an important role, as did timing. By 1635 it was already too late for a servant or a free newcomer to make much of a mark in Bermuda or Virginia. The chaotic scramble had ended for these two colonies, making apparent at least for a few decades the basic configurations of each colony's social structure and the important sources of wealth and power. The increasingly restricted upper echelons of Virginia society could not accommodate newcomers of humble means by offering them important colony offices, although land remained available until the 1650s. Those who reached Virginia in 1635, then, were able to benefit from the colony's temporary tobacco boom without shaping it themselves. In comparison, those travelers who reached Barbados joined the erratic economy of the island at a time when they could have a crucial impact, if they were able to survive. For the colony's first sixteen years, planters tried several different crops, tobacco, corn, cotton, and indigo, in their quest for a lucrative export commodity. Servants and newcomers were able to take advantage of these economic uncertainties. But overall, the majority of travelers, especially those who found an early grave in America, would have been better served staying in England. As Nicholas Canny has observed, not until the mid-eighteenth century did America become a real land of opportunity—at least for its white inhabitants.[7]

The Chesapeake

The bulk of the evidence available for the Chesapeake in the 1630s describes the careers of travelers to Virginia. Only a few travelers ventured to Maryland from London in 1635, just a few scant months after the colony's planting, but evidence from that colony offers a useful comparative perspective for these two neighboring colonies that afforded very different opportunities for newcomers in this decade. These differences in opportunity masked important topographical and geographic similarities. Colonists there, especially in Virginia, lived in a world laced with rivers, streams, runs, and swampy waterways that stood as a strange alternative to the ancient footpaths and thoroughfares that these men and women would have known in England. They cultivated a crop foreign to English husbandmen, laboriously tending tobacco seedlings and removing insects by hand. The passengers of 1635 arrived twelve years after the Powhatan attack that killed one-third of the English colonists in Virginia, producing a grim accounting of the survivors but also constraining English settlement and Indian aggression sufficiently to provide two decades of peace. Another Powhatan assault on unwelcome English settlers would occur nine years later, but during the 1620s and 1630s white Virginians were able to settle down to tobacco cultivation, and those fortunes that the region promised were largely those derived from tobacco cultivation. Land, then, was the key to success.

Land proffered wealth and status in this agrarian society, and its acquisition was the first struggle that occupied newcomers and newly freed servants. Newcomers of various economic backgrounds did find it possible to gain modest holdings of land and livestock. Altogether, 115 people in this cohort acquired land in Virginia or Maryland.[8] Although the date of acquisition and the exact amount of land owned is not known for all these individuals, the ways in which people insinuated themselves into the tobacco planting community is apparent from the extant records.

Some of the largest landowners of the 1635 cohort were old planters who were returning to their holdings in Virginia in that year. Bartholomew Hoskins was such a large landholder: by 1653 he owned 2,250 acres. Hoskins first acquired land in Elizabeth City County in 1624, when he received a grant of 100 acres. In 1635, Hoskins was returning home from a visit in London, where he maintained a residence, and he brought with him then at least two servants, Robert Boddy and Richard Harwood, who served him for the first years of their residence in the colony.[9] Another large landowner was the planter Christopher Boyes, who lived in Warwick County but owned land elsewhere as well: in 1653, he claimed 602 acres in Northumberland.[10]

People who acquired land did so through a variety of routes. The easiest way, of course, was to reach the colonies with credit or specie in hand. Some people demonstrated in their rapid acquisition of land that they had reached the colony well-positioned to gain a footing in the colonial world. Eighteen of the new arrivals in 1635 acquired land within five years. Maudlin Jones, who braved her voyage at the age of 60, claimed 100 acres soon after her arrival for her own transportation and that of a servant, Robert Brian, who traveled with her on the *Assurance*.[11] Others made larger investments at their first arrival. Oliver Sprye had 350 acres within two years of reaching the colony.[12] Humphrey Higginson had several hundred acres by 1637 as well.

Another sound strategy was to find kin who could fund the efforts of their relatives. Bennett Freeman followed this path when he joined his planter brother, Bridges Freeman, in 1635. Within three years Bennett Freeman patented 450 acres in James City.[13] Dead kin proved as useful as the living:

inheritance was another way to gain land through the largesse of relations or other benefactors. Francis Townshend, the wife of the former Burgess and Councilor Captain Richard Townshend, gained significant wealth after her husband's death and during her remarriage. She retained control over her property, and in 1658 she deeded 500 acres of land to her son Francis, a toddler of two in 1635 when he traveled with his parents to Virginia. She included in the deed five servants and one child, two mares, seven cows, and other livestock.[14]

Those without wealthy kin could borrow from friends to start their new careers in Virginia. Such was the strategy of Thomas Whaplett, who traveled on the *Globe* in 1635 at the age of 21. His friend John Redman had paid 1,300 pounds of tobacco for Whaplett's plantation. Redman, who had also traveled on the *Globe,* was a London merchant who spent a considerable amount of time in the colony, enough, in fact, to serve as Whaplett's executor in Virginia when his friend died after less than a year there.[15]

Servants in Virginia had a tougher route than free travelers had to follow in their efforts to gain land. Lacking wealthy relatives or specie themselves, they depended on credit and the easy availability of land in order to start their scramble up Virginia's economic ladder.[16] One servant's career is fully developed in the Norfolk County records. Savill Gaskins, who traveled on the *Merchant's Hope* at the age of 29, enjoyed a career in Virginia marked by the gradual acquisition of the trappings available in early Virginia—livestock, servants, a slave, and local office.[17] In 1637 William [———] appeared in the Norfolk County Court to receive certification for transporting Savill Gaskins. This was not the same man who was Gaskins's subsequent master, nor, indeed, the man who patented land on Gaskins's headright.[18] It is not clear from the surviving records whether Gaskins traveled to Virginia as a servant, but sometime between 1635 and 1640 Gaskins bound himself as a servant to John Gooch on the condition that Gooch would pay Gaskins's debts. By 1640, however, Gooch had died before the debts could be paid and Gaskins was freed according to Gooch's will. But Gaskins remained saddled with his earlier debts, and the Norfolk court ordered him to pay Thomas Master 8,000 pounds of tobacco.[19]

Gaskins continued to accumulate debt, as indeed did most other planters throughout England's colonies, and was frequently ordered in court to repay debts ranging from £5 to 120 pounds of cotton. Gaskins's acquaintance with the court soon became more intimate. In November of 1643 Gaskins received permission to keep an ordinary, diversifying his economic interests and thereby protecting himself from the uncertainties of an income derived entirely from farming, and by 1643, court records refer to meetings held at his house. Gaskins and his wife, Anne, had children by 1645, when Gaskins gave his son Robert a cow named Primrose. One year later the Gaskins owned a slave (they already owned servants), and in 1647 Gaskins received his first county office when he was appointed constable.[20] Gaskins continued to run his ordinary, and to do so with perhaps an excessive eye on profit: he was presented before the court for selling sack at 100 pounds per gallon and brandy at the same price.[21] Gaskins's success revealed a modest ascent typical of the opportunity that lay in store for servants who arrived in Virginia in 1635 and who survived their terms of indenture. Although Gaskins could not hope for high colony office, he could earn a local respectability. Gaskins's career also stands out in the records as one that embodied many of the concerns of early Virginians at all levels of society—those who labored for profits, struggled to find mates and then had to mourn their premature deaths, and acquired and learned how to control their bound laborers.

Land was not the only measure of wealth and status in early Virginia, although its acquisition was the starting point to economic sufficiency in an economy based on tobacco. As Gaskins's array of capital goods attests, ownership of servants, slaves, and livestock also provided ways of storing capital and accruing wealth. Tithable lists provide one measure of the acquisition of servants. Seven of the 1635 passengers appear on the Northampton tithable list for 1662. Some of these men were clearly single planters struggling to stay solvent: Richard Ast, William Starling, and Richard Hanby were the only tithables in their households. But other men had larger households, a reflection of the presence of adult dependents and indentured servants. Richard Kellum's household contained six tithables, whereas William Satchell and Anthony Hodgkins had four each, and the former servant Christopher Dixon had two.[22] As a way of comparing these accomplishments against the county as a whole, in 1664 only 3 households (out of 150) in Northampton had six tithables, and only 14 had four tithables.[23] The Northampton men do not seem to have fared better or worse than their neighbors in other counties. In Surrey in 1668 Thomas Busby's household had three tithables, and Thomas Foxcraft's had two.[24] In Lancaster in 1655 William Neesam had six tithables, and Silvester Thatcher had three.[25]

With land, livestock, and servants came political responsibilities. There were important gradations in political power in the colony. The most coveted positions were those on the Council: appointed by the king, men on the Council had power to wield and enjoyed many financial advantages derived from their positions. The other distinguished colony office, although on a smaller scale, was that of burgess. Beneath these positions were responsibilities as justice of the county court and sundry county positions. According to the experiences of the passengers of 1635, men who had reached the colony in the 1610s and 1620s as servants or as free planters of modest means were able to gain Virginia's highest offices. By 1635, however, the access to political office that had characterized Virginia society a decade earlier, at least in this one respect, was beginning to disappear. This fact both prevented many diligent and industrious newcomers from gaining colony offices and signaled the increasingly restricted nature of upward mobility in the colony. Newcomers who gained office in Virginia after their arrival in 1635 were people possessed of dramatically more advantaged backgrounds, measured by wealth, status, or kin, than were those who had previously gained office in the colony. Despite the obvious problems of tenure caused by high mortality rates, Virginians selected officers by the 1630s using higher standards than they had been able to indulge earlier. The result was that the society was far less open than it had been earlier, and the servant-to-Council ascents of earlier residents were no longer possible.[26] Even the political opportunities seemingly presented by the 1635 coup that exiled Governor Harvy or the subsequent upheavals of the Civil War and Protectorate provided few openings for those unqualified by status or long tenure in the colony to gain office. The situation in Maryland was dramatically different: this new colony in its early years promised greater opportunity than did Virginia in the same decade after almost thirty years of settlement.[27]

Table 4.1 profiles the twelve men who traveled to Virginia in 1635 and achieved the highest offices possible in the colony by serving in the House of Burgesses or on the Council in order to compare the fortunes of early and later arrivals. Five of these men had been in Virginia by 1625. The social differences between the oldtimers and the newcomers of 1635 were pronounced. An examination of a range of features—honorifics or titles, age in Virginia, and age of first office—clarifies the divergent nature of office acquisition over a thirty-year span for this particular group of Virginia residents and officeholders.

Men who reached the colony in the 1620s or, in the case of Bartholomew Hoskins, even earlier in 1616, fared better than did their counterparts later on. The earlier residents lacked honorifics beyond "Mr." One councilor, indeed, had even been a servant in his early years in the colony. In contrast, three of the newcomers in 1635 who acquired offices were called "gentleman." Those seven men who were new arrivals to the colony in 1635 had to demonstrate tangible qualities of wealth, position, or familial connection in order to gain major colonial offices. Those who had been in the colony previously had often worked their way up the social and economic ladder "by brute labor and shrewd manipulation" to merit the offices they held.[28] Age was not a prerequisite for office in this society where death claimed men at young ages: Virginians achieved the colony's highest offices while still in their twenties and thirties.

Table 4.1. Profile of major Virginia officeholders (1635 cohort)

Name	Office	Year in office	Age in 1635	First year in Virginia	Age in office	Status or honorific
Robert Baldry	Burgess (Y)	1660	18	1635	43	Mr., Gent.
Robert Evelin	Councilor	1637	?	1634 or 1635		Gent.
Humphrey Higginson	Councilor	1641+	28	1635	34	Gent.
Anthony Hoskins	Burgess (NH)	1652	22	1635	39	Mr.
Bartholomew Hoskins	Burgess (LN)	1649+	34	1616	48	Mr.
Rice Hooe	Burgess (CC)	1633+	36	1624	34	Mr.
Edward Major	Burgess (NA) Speaker	1645+ 1652	19	1635	29	
Robert Sabin	Burgess (W)	1629	40	1622	34	
Rowland Sadler	Burgess (JC)	1643+	19	1635	27	
Robert Scotchmore	Burgess	1630+	39	1623	34	
Richard Townshend[a]	Burgess (JC,Y) Councilor	1629 1637+	28	1620	22	Capt.
Abraham Watson	Burgess (JC)	1653+	17	1635	35	

Sources: J. P. Kennedy and H. R. McIlwaine, eds., *Journal of the House of Burgesses* (Richmond, Va: 1905–1915), H. R. McIlwaine, ed., *Minutes of the Council and General Court of Colonial Virginia* (Richmond, Va.: The Colonial Press, 1924); Virginia Muster, Court Records of Northampton, York, and Norfolk, VCRP, *Dictionary of Virginia Biography* indexes and files at VSL. County abbreviations: York (Y); Charles City (CC); James City (JC); Warwick (W); Upper Norfolk (UN); Lower Norfolk (LN); Northampton (NH); Nansemond (NA).
a. Former servant.

Richard Townshend made the kind of ascent from servitude that ambitious newcomers in 1635 coveted. Townshend's rise to political office was typical of other men who had also been servants or small farmers when they started their careers in Virginia in the 1620s.[29] His journey in 1635 brought him home to the colony he had inhabited for fifteen years. Townshend had reached Virginia in 1620 on the *Abigail*, and in 1625 at the age of 19 he was recorded in the Virginia Muster as a servant of the Virginia councilman and doctor John Pott of James City, who was to instruct Townshend in "the art of an Apothecarye."[30] Townshend's service apparently concluded sometime after 1626, and by 1628 he had secured a position on the House of Burgesses. Two years later he moved with his wife to Kiskyacke, in York County. Although previously a servant, Townshend not only attracted a wife (no mean feat in and of itself in this skewed demographic environment) but, shrewdly and prudently, also acquired one of solid social standing: Frances Townshend's brother Robert Baldwin of London was called a gentleman. Townshend's ascent continued. By 1630 Townshend already possessed two white servants and three black slaves. He served the county as he had the colony, as Justice in 1633. By 1637 he had garnered a seat on the Council, Virginia's highest office apart from governor. Townshend was appointed by the King as an "able [man] . . . in respect of [his] knowledge of the affayres of that Countrey."[31]

Another successful early arrival was Rice Hooe of Shirley Hundred, who was in Virginia as early as 1624.[32] When Hooe testified in court in 1625, he was given no honorific by the clerk, neither Mr. nor planter nor gentleman, yet he served as a burgess in addition to filling other important local roles: in 1639 he was appointed to view the tobacco crop, and he served as a county commissioner.[33]

Hooe was typical of pre-1635 residents who garnered offices: no evidence has survived to suggest that he had status proffered by gentle birth. Those who arrived in Virginia a mere decade later in the 1630s, however, needed rather different characteristics to achieve high colonial offices. For newcomers in 1635 who acquired colonial offices later, wealth and privilege were crucial prerequisites. Robert Evelin, for example, was described as a gentleman in 1634, and by 1637 he had been appointed to the Council at the request of the King.[34] Humphrey Higginson was another well-placed young man who was called gentleman in his first land patent in 1637. His first known office was an appointment to inspect tobacco in James City County in 1639. Only six years after his arrival, he was appointed by the king to the Council, and he served on the Council intermittently through 1655, after which he apparently returned to England.[35]

Edward Major had traveled to Virginia as a young man in 1635 on the *Merchant Bonaventure,* but like Higginson and Evelin, he was not of humble background. A friend of Richard Bennett, Edward Major was claimed as a headright by Robert Bennett in June of 1653, but not because he had arrived as Bennett's indentured servant. Major's marriage within months of his arrival to a woman named Martha was indicative of his financial independence. Although he lived first in Charles River County in 1635, he soon moved with the Bennetts and other puritan sympathizers to Nansemond. Within two years of his arrival, Major patented 450 acres on the Nansemond River. Within nine years he had patented 350 more acres and owned land in Warwick, Nansemond, and York counties. By 1646 he represented Upper Norfolk and then Nansemond in the House of Burgesses. His friendship with the Bennett family may have secured his position as speaker in 1652, when Richard Bennett was governor and puritans dominated the Burgesses.[36]

Perhaps one of the last officeholders who reached Virginia as a newcomer in 1635 and who had nonelite origins was Anthony Hoskins. Even he, however, did not start as a servant. Hoskins arrived with sufficient wealth to acquire a servant soon after his arrival and was referred to as "Mr." in the county court records by 1640. He nonetheless did not yet have a great amount of personal wealth. In 1642, in order to satisfy a debt to George Minifye, Hoskins bound his goods to another man, and the inventory of his goods contained his servant Daniel Pighles, two beds, one steel mill, two kettles, eight pewter dishes, one pewter basin, ten hogs, some tobacco, and other items.[37] By 1647 he had acquired more possessions. He bound himself to Edward Gibbons of New England (a relationship indicating the likelihood that Hoskins was heavily involved in trading enterprises) for one maidservant, five cows, a bull, a bed and bedding, six pewter dishes (perhaps he had lost two of the original eight in the intervening years), and other items.[38]

Higginson, Major, Evelin, and Hoskins were free adults with wealth or important family connections when they reached Virginia in 1635 and were rewarded for their standing and, in some cases, accomplishments, by these important colony offices. For those new arrivals of more modest origins, county office provided an arena for public service. Offices were not, however, necessarily sought after. Bartholomew Hoskins asked to be excused from public responsibilities in 1647 "in respect of the said Hoskins is aged and infirme, and allsoe did belong unto the collony in Sr Thomas Dales Tyme."[39] Peter Starkey became constable for New Poquoson Parish in York only because Mr. Anthony Rooksby, who had received the office, complained that he had already been constable, "& been neare 20 yeare of the vestrey in the said Parish." Starkey was then appointed in his stead.[40]

But however reluctantly some planters held colonial offices, for many of the passengers in 1635, small local offices were the only recognition of their colonial accomplishments. The men who held local positions differed from those who gained colony office in their relative youth and in their lack of social distinction (Appendix B, Table B.11). Thirty-seven men were elected or appointed to local positions, including constable, sheriff, vestryman, justice of the peace, viewer of the tobacco crop, or juror. Except for those men who also held positions on the Council, none were called gentlemen. They were all younger by an average of three to five years when they reached the colony than were the successful men profiled in Table 4.1. Eight of these men had reached the colony as servants in 1635. Freed from service sometime after 1640, they could not hope to replicate the political success of Captain Richard Townshend. Instead, they turned their energy toward acquiring land and cultivating tobacco. The small local positions they held reflected that their political universe rested in the county.

Whereas substantial position or long tenure in the colony was an essential prerequisite for colonial office in Virginia, those who settled in Maryland found it much easier to acquire political positions.[41] Men who sat on the Maryland Assembly were planters of modest, but not extravagant, wealth. In fact, the three men who reached Maryland in 1635 whose position was significant enough to warrant their mention among the seventeen prominent planters of the colony in *A Relation of Maryland* all died or left the colony within a few years.[42] If the colony had relied on its privileged few for leadership, it would have found itself in a political vacuum. Instead, in the small population of the fragile plantation, some men were rewarded not for their English status but for other traits of diligence and leadership recognized by their contemporaries.

Table 4.2 profiles the 1635 passengers who held colony and county offices in Maryland. In contrast to the Virginia officeholders, these men were of more varied and humble backgrounds. With the exception of Robert Evelin, and possibly John Hill, who was one of the original planters of the colony listed in *A Relation of Maryland,* none of these men were distinguished by anything other than their success at surviving their first years in the colony. Robert Percy had traveled to the colony as a free adult and claimed land soon after his arrival. Philip Conner had also reached the colony independently,

Table 4.2. Profile of major maryland officeholders (1635 cohort)

Name	Office	Year in office	Age in 1635	Age in office	First year in Md.
Handgate Baker[a]	Assembly	1642	22	29	1642
Thomas Besson	Assembly	1657	24	46	1648
Christopher Carnoll[a]	Assembly	1642	23	30	1635
Philip Conner	Assembly	1641 etc.	21	27	1635
Robert Evelin	Assembly	1638	?		1638
Nicholas Hervy	Assembly	1642	30	37	1635
John Hill	Assembly	1638	50	53	1635
Robert Percy	Assembly	1638	40	43	1635
John Price	Assembly Council	1638+ 1648–60	34	37	1635
Richard Woolman	Parl.Com.	1654–58	22	42	1648

Sources: Edward C. Papenfuse et al., eds., *A Biographical Dictionary of the Maryland Legislature, 1635–1789,* 2 volumes (Baltimore: The Johns Hopkins University Press, 1979–1985); *Md. Archives* I, IV.
a. Former servant.

and the former Virginians Thomas Besson and Richard Woolman arrived in
Maryland with sufficient money to start new plantations. Christopher Carnoll
and John Price, on the other hand, emerged from humble backgrounds.
Carnoll was a servant when he reached the colony. John Price, an illiterate
planter, had reached Maryland as a free adult and worked his way up to the
Assembly in 1638 and to the Council by 1648.[43] The experiences of these
two men more closely resembled those of Virginians in the 1620s than they
did the careers of their counterparts in Virginia in the 1630s.

In Virginia, then, the pattern in place by the late 1630s suggests that servants
who reached the colony in 1635 and survived to their freedom would find it
difficult, if not impossible, to secure the major colonial offices that had been
available to humble newcomers a decade or two earlier. The ascent was harder
in Virginia by the 1640s. Even in a decade marked by demographic uncertainty, indigenous attack, and political upheaval, it was not easy for newcomers to have a significant political impact on the colony. The experiences of the
241 travelers of 1635, both old residents and newcomers, both servants and
gentlemen, suggest a trend in Virginia toward greater restriction in the availability of offices. Only a decade earlier former servants could gain important
colony offices: by the 1630s, these opportunities were negligible, at least for
the men in this sample.

In Bermuda, circumstances proved quite similar. On this small Atlantic
island, however, it was not status alone that denied advancement. It was,
instead, the congestion of the island and the modest maintenance that the soil
afforded that prevented gross disparities of wealth from distinguishing island
residents. To succeed in Bermuda, men had to be prepared to move on. To
stay on the island, men had to be willing to accept small shares of company
land.

Bermuda

If one had the temerity to aspire to survival, family life, and a relative freedom
from intrusive local or company authority in the new world, Bermuda was a
good place to go in 1635. The climate was salubrious, political and religious
institutions were firmly in place, and the proprietors were attentive to island
conditions, both economic and spiritual. Yet in the 1630s the island held little
hope for new arrivals who lacked wealth and status.[44] Bermuda, approximately 600 miles off the coast of the Carolinas, offered what contemporaries
understood to be a pleasant climate but what historians would consider a
congenial disease environment. In a 1615 publication, the Bermuda minister
Lewis Hughes celebrated the temperate island. Children were healthy, he

observed, because the climate was so "agreeable to our English constitutions."[45] Even in the heat of summer there was always a breeze to cool the air,[46] although in the late summer and early fall, the cooling breeze of the hurricane season would certainly prove daunting. Yet the island held little opportunity for economic advancement: social and economic distances on the island were narrow. Little land was available, and the ownership of servants and slaves proved the best avenue for displaying and securing wealth. Those who arrived in 1635 with position and credit fared marginally better than those who arrived as servants, but the overall impression derived from the experiences of fifty of the travelers of 1635 (23 percent of the total) is of modest attainment by almost any measure.

These narrow economic opportunities stand at odds with the institutional vitality of the island. The island's institutional fortunes can be seen through the career of the 1635 traveler Judith Bagley, who in that year returned home to Bermuda. Unlike passengers to most of England's colonies, Bagley had little to worry about in terms of the survival of her family and the tenure of England's hold on the island. Indeed, as one of ten Bermudian residents returning to the island in that year, she traveled on board the *Dorset* with two other longtime neighbors, the island's minister George Stirk and a woman of her own age, Christian Wellman.

Judith Bagley had first reached Bermuda by 1617, a few short years after the accidental discovery of the island by the shipwrecked *Sea Venture*. During her years on the island, she witnessed its transformation. The Somers Islands Company, which contained a large number of puritans, was strongly committed to constructing a complete cultural life for the colony. By 1640 the Company had built nine churches, one chapel, five houses for ministers, nine castles and forts, houses of justice, and other public works.[47] As early as 1634, the island organized a free school, whose existence reflected both the commitment of island residents to religious education and the expectations of a society sufficiently forward-looking to erect a school for children.

Bermuda's officers were quick to erect mechanisms for maintaining order, and Judith Bagley was caught in them. In 1618 Bagley was presented by the grand jury at the October assizes for her persistent disruption of church services in Pembroke Tribe with her "raylinge miscalling all other uncivill speeches."[48] Ten years later Bagley distinguished herself again in church, when the Grand Inquest presented her "for unreverent behaviour in the church." Few would disagree with their assessment: one John Stamers had made the mistake of asking Bagley to quiet her child, at which she "(swore) gods-blood shee would stabbe John Stamers . . . having her knife drawn in the church, insomuch that the said John Stamers was faine for to fly to the farthest part of his pew, when hee was reading of divine service."[49] Her traveling companion Christian Wellman, another longtime resident of the island, had herself been presented in 1630 on suspicion of incontinence, as, indeed, Wellman's husband Martin had been three years earlier.[50] Bermuda, then, as Bagley experienced it, offered a society with church and civil bodies prepared to define community behavior even in this isolated outpost. Their task was made easier by the presence of men and women with families to attend to and by the easy access residents had to England and thus to the ears of the proprietors, whether via letter or in person. And when first-time travelers ventured to Bermuda in 1635, not only did they enjoy the advantage of joining a colonial society prepared to offer the essential and familiar component parts of civil and ecclesiastical government, but they also journeyed with several longtime residents of the island who could alleviate their fears about the voyage and their destination.

The very qualities that made Bermuda so appealing and attracted new residents made opportunities for economic advancement rare for many of those who arrived as servants in 1635, over twenty years after the colony was first settled. Initial optimistic expectations that men who planted in Bermuda "may in time live very comfortably heere, and grow rich if they will provide seedes of Indico, &c. and plants of curants, figges, raisons, mulberry-trees for the silk worms, & vines" had proved unrealistic.[51] Bermuda's first years brought little wealth.

After years of hardship during which settlers endured political instability with a rotating governor and what Richard Norwood called the "wonderfull annoyance by silly rats," when the colony was literally besieged by rats that devoured crops and swam across channels from island to island, it was possible for those settlers who had reached Bermuda in the 1610s and 1620s to plant crops and live modestly.[52] Tobacco was the island's main export crop. Dependence on tobacco of a poor quality in a glutted world market, however, dictated only humble estates. Indeed, Bermudian tobacco planters often endured great hardship. Planters in 1628 were sufficiently disgruntled by their failure to turn a profit that they petitioned the Privy Council. A total of sixty-eight planters, who claimed to have been on the island since the colony's infancy, complained that they had made no profit in six years. These planters journeyed to London where their tobacco sat in a London warehouse under duty of 9d. per pound, but the price of tobacco had fallen below 9d. per pound. Some petitioners were in debt, some arrested, and others evicted from their residences.[53]

The poverty of tobacco encouraged planters to diversify their holdings. In the 1630s most people had at best a modest maintenance, with small plots of tobacco, corn, and potatoes, and cattle and chickens in abundance. They inhabited simple houses made of wooden posts with palm branch roofs. In their pursuit of greater wealth, some Bermudians were delighted when a ship foundered off the coast. The island's scavengers exploited this misfortune with an avidity that dismayed one shipwrecked mariner. "Their rapacity knows no limit," he complained, "and is indulged even at the cost of the shipwrecked men."[54] Indeed, the 1635 traveler Bernard Coleman was incarcerated in 1648 for pilfering Spanish goods, and in 1626 Coleman's fellow traveler Christian Wellman and her husband Martin were fined fifty pounds of tobacco and imprisoned for twenty-four hours for taking ambergris that had washed ashore from a wrecked vesel.[55]

The majority of the new arrivals in 1635 acquired only modest comfort, in accordance with the island's offerings (see Appendix B, Table B.1). Of the twenty-two Bermudians who are known to have leased land, or to have owned land, goods, or servants, eight had already been on the island before 1635, four were ministers, and only two reached the island as servants in 1635. To get land as a freed servant, as in Virginia, one had to have been resident in the colony in the 1620s. One successful man, for example, was Hugh Wentworth, who had reached Bermuda at least as early as 1618 when he lived on the land of the Rich family in Southampton tribe. Wentworth, "a very true labouringe man," had been a servant to the Riches but bought out his time with one-half year left to serve, and by 1627 he was a councilor.[56] Later arrivals to Bermuda could not hope for such rapid ascents unless, like travelers to Virginia, they arrived with wealth. Such men, like the island's governor, Josias Forster, fared quite well. Josias Forster traveled to Bermuda with his cousin John Oxenbridge in 1635. He mentioned in his will "negros and mulattoes" of unspecified number.[57] Wealth in land, however, remained on a modest scale. Land was held by the proprietors and normally only leased, not sold, to island residents. John Casson the elder of Paget tribe owned one mulatto man, Diego, who was to be given his freedom after the death of Casson's wife, but he held only seven acres of land, to be shared by his four sons. His estate inventory totaled only £30.18.11 of goods and stock.[58]

This cohort of landowners, compared with their Virginia counterparts, held only small shares of land. But they were the fortunate few on Bermuda. Six servants who had traveled to the island in 1635 left no record of their presence there except for their names affixed to a petition in 1644. They did not serve on juries nor did they appear in court to settle debts. It is unlikely that they owned the goods or land sufficient to gain local responsibility. Instead, they dwelled on the island, probably as laborers, their freedom from servitude marked by lingering dependence on their more fortunate neighbors and masters.[59]

The lack of opportunity on Bermuda stemmed from overcrowding. The island was measurably congested from an early period. Richard Norwood's survey of the island, made between 1613 and 1617, detailed the carefully divided island, with narrow strips of land soon allocated to individual tenants by the island's proprietors (Figure 9). These shares of land filled rapidly with English settlers.

In 1622 with a population of 1,500, Bermuda had 85.2 people to the square mile. By 1640 the population density on Bermuda had risen to 142 people per square mile.[60] Indeed, a year earlier a Spaniard who was shipwrecked on the island had counted about 290 households altogether and observed that "the inhabitants . . . have settled the whole of it."[61] As a point of comparison, Barbados, with richer arable land, contained only 7.4 people per square mile in 1635, and only 60.2 by 1641.[62]

In response to these crowded conditions, Bermudians quickly made repeated efforts to acquire land elsewhere. In 1622, a mere seven years after the island was first settled, the Virginia Company granted to the Somers Islands Company land in Virginia, "for the better support of the said Company, and of the Inhabitants of the said Islands."[63] In that same year the surveyor Richard Norwood warned that "the countrie is now almost fullie planted and inhabited" and commented that a man could own four times as much land in Virginia as he could in Bermuda.[64] Indeed, Virginia remained a popular destination for Bermuda residents, who repeatedly petitioned for land there.[65] Yet newcomers continued to reach the island in search of their own uncertain opportunities, as did the 208 newcomers in 1635. Their arrival exacerbated the island's congestion: within four years, the Governor and Company of the Somers Islands petitioned the Commissioners for Foreign Plantations and requested land promised them in Virginia between the Rappahannock and Potomac Rivers. Bermuda's overcrowding played an important role in new colonial schemes. By 1639 some Bermudians had migrated to St. Lucia, and the petitioners noted that there were 400 to 500 more prepared to depart.[66] A year later the planting of Tobago was planned with the conviction that men could easily be obtained from Bermuda for the new colony, and a subsequent exodus was planned two years later for Trinidad.[67] Bermudians had early learned the lesson that moving on was the best option for those who wished to move up. For residents of Bermuda, Atlantic and Caribbean voyages were fundamental survival strategies, as, indeed, were those economies such as whaling derived from the sea.

Barbados

On Bermuda and Virginia, planters and their indentured servants labored in tobacco fields, and success throughout the century would be measured in pounds of tobacco. Fortune on Barbados followed a different path. For over

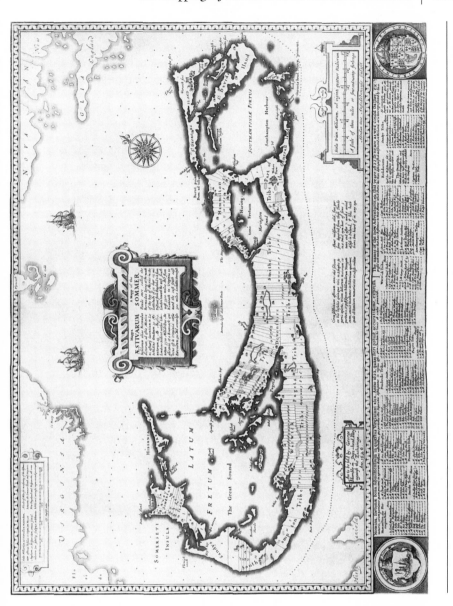

Figure 9. Richard Norwood's survey of Bermuda, first published circa 1622. From John Speed, *A Prospect of the Most Famous Parts of the World* (London, 1627). Courtesy of the Library of Congress.

a decade, English laborers on the island cultivated tobacco, cotton, and indigo before Barbados and other islands transferred their production to sugar. With the transfer to sugar, Barbados also turned from white indentured labor to chattel slavery and acquired the social and economic configurations common to many other islands of the Caribbean.

Before sugar and slaves defined the island, however, Barbados offered a surprising number of economic opportunities in the 1630s and early 1640s, both for those who arrived with wealth and for those who came as servants. Social, economic, and political conditions in Barbados in the 1630s hardly seemed to recommend the island to newcomers, yet those with an acquisitive spirit and a thirst for adventure did well in voyaging there. In 1635 Barbados had been settled for only eight years by the English, who had lagged well behind other European nations in forays into the Caribbean, and the English island colonies were new and vulnerable. Repeated agricultural experimentation yielded frustratingly meager results to impatient English planters, yet the very uncertainty of the colony's economic viability contributed to the opportunities available to newcomers.

In the years before sugar emerged as the island's crop of choice, a brief opportunity existed for freed servants, who succeeded in gaining modest holdings, and, in some cases, clinging to them during the land consolidations of the emerging sugar magnates. As fortunes waxed and waned in the volatile 1630s and 1640s, planters evacuated the island and left land available for both newcomers with money and servants freed after years of indenture. Achievements for many were modest. Nonetheless, the experiences of many servants in this easternmost island of the Lesser Antilles reveal an unexpected success story in a society that few would have labeled a good poor-man's country.

The careers of the men and women who reached Barbados in 1635 temper some commonplace assumptions about Barbadian society. England's Caribbean settlers, described so vividly by Richard Dunn, Richard Sheridan, and the Bridenbaughs, founded societies based on abuse and excess.[68] In Dunn's memorable words, they

> had geared themselves for wealth, excitement, and violent combat, so they fought and played feverishly in the enervating heat, exploited the labor of white servants and black slaves, risked sudden death from mysterious diseases or the annihilation of their profits in smashing storms and buccaneering raids. The expectations the English brought with them and the physical conditions they encountered in the islands produced a hectic mode of life that had no counterpart at home or elsewhere in English experience. This is what it meant to live beyond the line.[69]

In Barbados, the plantocracy emerged at the expense of white servants and black slaves, who suffered under the grueling production of sugar in its unrelenting annual cycle. The lethargy and self-indulgence of the white planter class gained few admirers even among those who made their fortunes off sugar. New research has done little to alter this bleak view.[70] The lives of the servants who comprised the majority of the migrating population in 1635, however, suggest an alternative perspective on Barbadian society as it painfully took shape in the 1630s and 1640s.

The travelers of 1635 reached Barbados at a critical period of the island's economic development, when political strife accompanied economic instability and when opportunities existed for the hardy and fortunate. The perilous conditions that eventually encouraged many planters to leave combined fortuitously to create openings for the early comers. They overcame proprietary mismanagement and achieved modest success by ascending from servitude to land ownership.

Throughout the 1630s the Earl of Carlisle, the proprietor of Barbados, seemed singularly inept at managing the Barbadian planters or the Council. He could neither persuade the planters to acquiesce to his wishes in political matters nor deter them from continuing to plant tobacco of such poor quality that the Barbadians themselves would not smoke it, nor, indeed, could aspiring planters persuade even their fond relations to purchase a product so "ill conditioned, fowle, full of stalkes and evill coloured."[71] When Carlisle appointed as his agent his whining and ingratiating cousin Peter Hay, who cursed the planters as a "malignant cruell & evill disposed people," he only exacerbated his poor relationship with the planters.[72]

What made relations between Carlisle and the planters particularly acrimonious were the repeated failures of Barbadians to profit from their crops and the desperate efforts of investors, primarily private figures such as the Earl of Carlisle and English and Scottish merchants, to profit from taxes levied on the population and its produce. Until the cultivation of sugar, Barbadians failed to find a crop capable of commanding or sustaining high prices on an international market. The quality of Barbadian tobacco was deplorable, and as Bermuda planters had found earlier, bad tobacco could not be sold profitably in a saturated market. When the planters switched to cotton, they soon overproduced it. Between 1640 and 1642, indigo fared little better. The value of tobacco and cotton was so low that merchants had no incentive to supply the island; and discouraged planters, "being so wearied out with the small profits they reaped in their toylsome labours," left the island.[73] The agent Peter Hay complained in typical fashion about the recalcitrance of indignant planters who were "soe unfaithfull, that I can have no payment of them but by violence."[74]

Unappealing and acrimonious as these economic conditions would seem, the volatile nature of Barbados society and the devaluation of its crops ultimately worked to the advantage of those fortunate few who survived. Despite institutional and economic obstacles, some newcomers to Barbados in the 1630s found real opportunities for modest economic success. Land was limited in quantity but still available, and beginning in the 1630s, it was distributed to planters under a system devised by the Earl of Carlisle and carried out by his governor, Henry Hawley. Land grants in the first decade were not grants of land to be held in freehold. Instead, the Earl of Carlisle adjured that land be granted for no more than seven years or, rarely, for life. Ample conditions were built into land grants to ensure the return of land for any perceived offense on the part of the grantee. Leaving the island without permission, for example, or nonpayment of fees, ensured the return of the land to Carlisle.[75]

Table 4.3 depicts the total distribution of land in Barbados and the size of average grants from 1629 to 1638. The amount of land granted in the first two years of recorded grants and the average size of the grants certainly suggest advantages to early residence in Barbados, but land still remained inexpensive and available for newcomers in 1635, when 106 grants were distributed. A total of eighty-one of the travelers from London to Barbados in 1635 are known with certainty to have owned land, goods, or servants over

Table 4.3. Barbados land holdings, 1629–1638

Year	No. grants	Total acres	Average size (acres)
1629	140	15,872	113
1630	45	14,235	316
1631	31	2,749	89
1632	63	4,138	66
1633	20	905	45
1634	64	3,511	55
1635	106	9,055	85
1636	98	9,810	100
1637	139	7,604	55
1638	1	50	50
Total	707	67,929	96

Source: Compiled from William Duke, *Some Memoirs of the First Settlement of the Island of Barbados* (Barbados, 1741), pp. 13–20.

the course of their lives.[76] The amounts held were modest: few of the 1635 travelers owned more than sixty acres, while it was more common to hold only twenty acres, often in partnership with other planters. At least twenty people possessed land within three years of their arrival in Barbados; they probably arrived with sufficient funds to purchase it. Fifteen names appear on a valuable 1638 land list of all island residents who held at least ten acres in 1638, while the other five men appear in other records of land transactions. Table 4.4 lists these twenty people, their ages at arrival, and the amount of land that each held.

Table 4.4. Barbadian landholders by 1638 (1635 cohort)

Name	Age in 1635	Land held (acres)
John Batt	23	30
William Bulkeley	26	10+
John Ducker	31	30
Robert Dunstan	34	10+
Hugh Evans	18	50
William Haymond	36	40
Philip Henson	21	10+
John Key	30	60
Robert Mills	19	10+
Edmund Montgomery	26	40
John Nix	23	10+
Richard Peers	40	900+ (at death)
Robert Pendred	45	10+
Thomas Plunkett	28	40
William Seeley	29	10+
Richard Speed	35	30
Dorothy Symonds	40	25+
Joseph Thomlinson	26	30
William Weston	26	70+
Arthur Yeomans	24	80+

Sources: The 1638 land list, printed in William Duke, *Some Memoirs of the First Settlement of the Island of Barbados* (Barbados, 1741), pp. 51–62; land sales in Hay Papers, SRO; and Barbados deeds at the Barbados Archives.

The 1638 land list, combined with other land records, demonstrates how newcomers both young and middle-aged gained—and lost—land on Barbados. Dorothy Symonds ventured to the island at the age of 40 and in 1638 possessed at least twenty-five acres of land. Symonds was probably a widow when she reached the island, since she traveled alone, and was referred to as a widow in a deed of 1640 when she sold twenty-five acres of her land. Although she brought neither husband nor children with her, Symonds was not without friends on the island: she had important connections with wealthy planters, and she appointed as her executor her friend James Drax, who was Barbados's first great sugar magnate. Symonds's attention to her estate and investments is suggested by her will, which is dated 1649. This document was at least the third version she drafted. Although the will did not record the amount of land she left, her bequests make clear that she had shifted to sugar cultivation.[77]

Like Dorothy Symonds, young men came to Barbados with sufficient funds to invest and to trade actively in the Barbadian economy. Joseph Thomlinson, 26 years old when he traveled to Barbados, purchased with his partner Michael Cox a storehouse and thirty acres of land only two years after he had reached Barbados.[78] Another young early-achiever was Arthur Yeomans, described in the colony's deed books as a gentleman and a merchant. Yeomans was 24 when he migrated to Barbados. By 1637 he had a servant indentured to him for four years, and deeds of his land transactions are numerous between 1640 and 1643. In 1644 he mortgaged his plantation, and after he sold to Richard Dunn of Barbados twenty acres of land in St. James Parish, he disappeared from the records.[79]

As Yeomans's disappearance suggests, when once acquired, land was not easily retained by newcomers disappointed in their hopes for easy wealth and a speedy return to England. Tom Verney, who did not last a year in Barbados, reported enthusiastically to his father in 1639 that he had obtained one hundred acres of land and hoped to "rais my fortunes in a few years; nay, I shall be able in one yeares time to returne back the principall."[80] Likewise, James Dering, who adventured to Barbados in the 1630s, described both his labors to succeed and his reasons for migrating. Dering hoped to make money in Barbados by dint of his "industry and good husbandry." He had harvested 2,000 pounds of tobacco, with which he hoped to return to England. When Dering learned to his chagrin of the poor price of tobacco, he was compelled to stay on the island. The island's planters had agreed to stop cultivating the unsuccessful crop for two years, and Dering decided to delay his return to England in hopes of returning with fortune in hand.[81] Both the lofty aspirations of Dering and Verney and their financial failures symbolized the precarious fate awaiting Barbadian planters. It is no surprise, then, that by

1647, of the fifteen planters who had reached Barbados in 1635 and appeared on the 1638 land list, ten (67 percent) had vanished—by death, financial ruin, or success—from surviving colony records.

Most travelers to Barbados, however, did not arrive with funds sufficient to plunge into the whirl of land transactions in the 1630s. Instead, most travelers were young servants. Many of them, newly freed by 1640 after the customary five-year term had been completed, sought land of their own and benefited from economic circumstances on the island. In that dismal year the agent Peter Hay complained about the poor cotton crop and said that "the Inhabitaunts is like to be starved." He repeatedly warned his cousin James Hay in 1641 that many people had left Barbados for Trinidad, and more would go unless their grievances were redressed.[82] The conditions that encouraged people to move on made it easier for those who stayed, and for those newly freed, to get land. Of the eighty-one known landholders, the timing of land acquisition and the age at the time of migration suggest that thirty-five (43 percent) of these landowners were servants in 1635 (see Appendix B, Table B.2). These men drew on fortuitous circumstances, credit, and partnerships to obtain land.

Credit enabled former servants to acquire land before sugar cultivation caused land prices to soar. Occasionally the terms of the extension of credit were obvious as in the deed of sale for a plantation of one hundred acres with six servants, sold to the 1635 traveler Walter Jago and his partner, William Gale, for 34,000 pounds of cotton and tobacco due.[83] Credit was central to the economic development of the colony, and a planter's personal attributes, such as diligence and integrity, often secured it. The extension and use of credit both within the colony and across the Atlantic reveal the flexibility of the Atlantic economy during its early development.

Credit, however, carried great risks. Richard Ligon emphasized the extent to which the availability of credit was both essential for success and acutely vulnerable to disasters. A planter who suffered reverses of fortune due to natural disasters such as fire or loss of his stock at sea experienced at the same time a fall in credit, "so as, if he be not well friended, he never can entertain a hope to rise again."[84] Creditors and debtors were often the same people, as Nicholas Foster observed in his *Briefe Relation*. During the years when the island produced only cotton and tobacco, the poor value of island crops discouraged merchants from supplying the island. Disgruntled and pessimistic planters left Barbados, "being very much indebted both to the Merchants, and also to one another."[85]

Foster's and Ligon's comments illuminate the risks of accepting credit, even for those with friends capable of assisting in paying debts. Tom Verney begged his brother for money and lamented that if his father did not pay his debts, he would "lye and starve in prison."[86] James Dering purchased a plantation of one hundred acres, with nine servants and stock, on credit for £150 due in England. Anxious that he would not be able to repay the debt because of the poor quality of tobacco, Dering pleaded that his cousin assist him in repayment.[87]

Debt proved more perilous for those who had little or no collateral, as was the case for those servants newly freed from indenture with perhaps a shirt, some tobacco or cotton, or, rarely, pounds sterling. The only collateral available was the labor of the man himself. The first stage, then, was for a man to offer his own services to secure a debt. The 1635 passenger Richard Richardson and his partner Middleton Cooper arranged for Thomas Branie and Samuel Terrent to build them one house, or else to serve four years apiece.[88] Once new planters secured their position with land or goods, they could then offer these items as collateral—but the cost of nonpayment was high. Thomas Plunkett, another 1635 traveler who appears on the 1638 land list as a landholder of more than ten acres, owed William Williamson 6,995 pounds of cotton in 1641 and therefore loaned his plantation, servant, and important stock to Williamson until the debt was paid. The difficulty of repaying a debt with no visible means of support probably explains why this deed marked Plunkett's last appearance in the surviving Barbados records.[89]

Credit provided the central ingredient to procure a plantation and to participate in Barbados's agrarian economy. Partnership was also employed by newly freed servants and others seeking to gain land on the island.[90] The risks of high levels of indebtedness made partnerships attractive to new planters. And for two planters, partnership was the ingredient necessary to end a period of indebtedness. In 1641 John Mills sold to John Weston and William Hanyes 12½ acres, which made up the plantation where they lived. The two men had presumably been renting the use of the plantation and managed either to obtain enough credit or to persuade Mills to sell it to them.[91] Of the thirty-five former servants who acquired land between 1640 and 1643, fourteen (40 percent) did so with at least one other man. Other travelers to Barbados in 1635 who may not have been servants also found it expedient to join with other men in buying and planting land. The size of the estates purchased was often tiny. The passenger Ralph Harwood joined with Thomas Ferrier to purchase ten acres of land from Edward Wilkinson in 1640.[92] Another 1635 traveler, Felix Line, and his partner also purchased only ten acres.[93] Owning any land, however, was clearly sufficient to merit the honorific of planter for these former servants in the colony's records.

For new landowners, then, strength lay in numbers. In some cases men created multiple partnerships. Arthur Winde joined forces with two other men when he purchased a plantation of twenty acres in 1643.[94] Walter Jago used his partnerships for larger ventures. In May of 1640, he and William Gale purchased a plantation of one hundred acres with six servants. By 1641 Gale and Jago had acquired other partners and had sold off their plantation in Christ Church.[95]

With land, as was true in Virginia, increased local responsibilities and privileges ensued, as the careers of Edward Ash and Francis Dene demonstrate. Edward Ash reached Barbados in 1635 at the age of 20, probably as a servant. His name does not appear in any of the extant deeds of the 1640s. But by 1658 he owned land in St. John's Parish, and by 1656 he had been appointed one of its churchwardens.[96] Ash managed even to marry.[97] Francis Dene, another probable servant in 1635, rose to the status of gentleman. He traveled to Barbados at the age of 21, and in 1641, with his partner John Davis, recorded a debt to William Haitshorne and used their plantation as security. Dene apparently was a man who spoke his mind and acted on his beliefs, for in the 1650s his name appeared on a list of nonconformists to be banished. If banished, he soon returned to the island, for in 1653 he and his son were mentioned in the will of John Turner, and by 1659 Dene was called "gentleman" in a transaction in which he sold half his plantation in St. Thomas for 15,000 pounds of sugar. His stature within the Barbadian community was recognized by the Council when he was appointed the guardian of the children of Captain Robert Hooker in 1654.[98]

Those seeking similar opportunities later in the decade of the 1640s would find credit and land much harder to obtain. With the onset of sugar cultivation in 1643, the island became a place that tempted the adventurous and the avaricious with the possibility, however remote, of quick and easy profit. As one foreign visitor commented by 1654, "they came here in order to become wealthy."[99] Richard Ligon fueled the expectations of fortune-hunters by urging those to come to Barbados who were not content to sit at home but who "can by [their] own Industry, and activity, (having youth and strength for friends,) raise [their] fortune, from a small beginning to a very great one." Even the map that Ligon drew of Barbados would entice an observant viewer (Figure 10). His map delineated in a neat row the plantations along the island's leeward coast but showed plenty of empty space still available on the island's windward side and in the hilly interior. In Ligon's depiction, Europeans traveled the island on horseback, a sure indication of privilege and status, while two fleeing black figures reminded the reader of the slave population waiting to serve successful planters. Native Americans, symbolized here by a single naked figure armed with a bow and arrow, also labored for English planters on the island. According to the map, the island even boasted camels. To Ligon's readers in England, Barbados might seem a strange and exotic place with such unlikely inhabitants, but it was a place that promised enor-

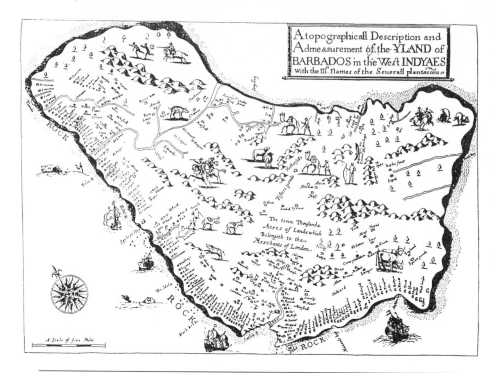

Figure 10. Richard Ligon's map of Barbados, circa 1650. From *A True and Exact History of the Island of Barbadoes* (London, 1657). Courtesy of the Beinecke Lesser Antilles Collection, Hamilton College.

mous profit and the status that came with having one's name adorn the rim of the island to mark one's property.[100]

Colonists from other places journeyed to Barbados in search of the fortune Ligon promised. The New England merchant and 1635 traveler William Vassall moved to Barbados in 1648 after his personal and political failure in Massachusetts. Others preferred to live elsewhere, but traveled frequently to Barbados and occasionally owned estates there. The Bermudians Christian and Martin Welman and Severin Vicars lived temporarily on Barbados and cultivated sugar.[101] Two New Englanders in the 1635 contingent, the Boston merchants Robert Nanney and Edward Rainsford, were heavily invested in Barbados sugar: Nanney, indeed, made provisions in his will for his "houses and land" on Barbados.[102] Most of these new arrivals and absentee planters were involved in sugar and profited from it.

The result of the sugar boom and the reality of rapid and immense fortunes to be accrued by the industrious and fortunate meant that Barbados soon became too crowded and land too expensive to sustain freed servants or those of modest means with aspirations for financial success. Land values had soared with the transition to sugar cultivation. In 1640, 4,000 pounds of tobacco procured an improved plantation of twenty acres. In 1641 ten acres could be purchased for 5,000 pounds of tobacco. In his systematic assessment of land values, Richard Dunn detected that prices increased ten times between 1640 and 1646.[103] The enthusiastic acquisition of land by those planters with sufficient capital to procure both the land for sugar and the labor and equipment necessary to raise the crop drove prices up. Planters who had already achieved modest success from tobacco, cotton, or indigo marshaled their available credit and funds to buy as much land as possible from the small planters who could neither resist the appeal of high offers, nor market their crops profitably, nor muster up sufficient funds to cultivate sugar themselves. Indeed, even those who had gained land in the 1640s did not necessarily cling to it.

Not all Barbadians who had arrived in 1635 and had secured land by the 1640s weathered the transition to sugar. Many planters, of course, left the island with money in hand before the sugar revolution. Thomas Dabb probably returned to England in 1642 after he had sold his whole estate for £70.[104] Likewise, William Levyns probably left Barbados after he had sold a plantation of thirty acres and a servant in 1640 for the astounding sum of £160.[105] Others seem to have been pushed out during the early sugar years. Philip Philpott sold his home plantation, stock, and servants in 1646.[106] By that same year the planter Henry Berrisford had sold off his estate as well. Berrisford had reached Barbados in 1635 at the age of 32. Between 1641 and 1646, three deeds record land transactions between him and other Barbadians identified as planters. After the 1646 transaction no further records appear for Berrisford. He, like many other small planters, probably sold off all his property and left the island.[107]

References to sugar that appear in wills and deeds reveal that of the 118 landholders, only sixteen (14 percent) shifted successfully to sugar. The most spectacular success story of the 1635 cohort was Richard Peers, who accrued 900 acres by the time of his death and was clearly one of the winners in the land consolidations of the 1640s and 1650s. Yet Peers had reached Barbados as a well-connected and privileged planter. Unlike most travelers to the island in 1635, Peers had lived in Barbados before that year and had acted as governor for his brother-in-law Henry Hawley in 1633 and 1634, when he earned the enmity of Father White on his way to Maryland for his inflated corn prices.[108] Peers apparently had traveled to England in 1634 but stayed there only briefly, leaving London in January of 1635. Peers had the funds and connections to ensure his success on the island. How successfully he retained his position is another story—one that in the case of most of the

1635 travelers remains obscure for lack of sources. Studies of planter persistence have tended to focus on later periods with better sources. Richard Dunn, however, has argued that there was little apparent advantage to early residence on the island. Dunn found that the men who became the leaders—political, economic, and social—of the island arrived between 1640 and 1660. Only 39 percent of the top Barbados families had settled the island by 1638.[109] The small number of the passengers of 1635 who converted their holdings to sugar plantations seems consistent with Dunn's findings. Planters such as Dorothy Symonds, Francis Dene, Edward Ash, and Richard Peers, whose careers have previously been described, stand out as exceptions in their ability to turn from tobacco, cotton, indigo, and servants to sugar and slaves.

Those travelers of 1635 whose names disappeared from the extant Barbados records by the middle of the 1640s probably employed a range of strategies. One strategy was involuntary: given the high rates of mortality on the island, especially after 1647, many of those planters whose names vanish probably died. Others simply left the island, as in the cases of Henry Berrisford or Philip Philpott. Out-migration has become a recurring theme in the evolution of small plantation societies. Especially on small islands such as Barbados and Bermuda, migration was a necessary strategy for economic survival. Small planters moved on, prodded by the large planters who coveted their holdings. Diplomatic necessity also dictated patterns of movement. The small Caribbean islands changed hands repeatedly as the victims of rivalries between European powers with competing claims to the islands—a barrier to economic stability and expansion not experienced with such frequent and devastating force by English counterparts on the mainland.

By the 1650s the new shape of the island's economy secured Barbados's role as England's most valuable colony in the seventeenth century. The configurations of the sugar islands with their small and self-indulgent planter elite firmly in place presiding over a large and ill-treated slave majority became a familiar pattern in the Caribbean. Less familiar, however, are the mechanisms that permitted these configurations to emerge and the patterns of migration, labor, and land acquisition that predated sugar. The careers of the travelers of 1635 provide a context for the evolution of plantation society in the Atlantic and Caribbean. In the 1630s and 1640s, Barbados was a haven not only for the wealthy. Newcomers with money and freed servants alike found opportunity in the presugar years. Those who failed to prosper employed the privileged strategy of residents in all parts of the Atlantic world: they moved on.

In the case of Barbados, we see most clearly through the island's extant land deeds the strategies of partnership and credit that permitted servants and other men to acquire land on their island home. In Virginia, land was more readily available, as thousands of unclaimed headrights suggest, and servants free from their indentures could obtain it more easily than their West Indian counterparts. On Bermuda it was goods, not land, that marked a man's accomplishments. Each colony had its distinct measures of success, whether in land, office, live stock, or servants, and the men who ventured overseas in 1635 as servants and free men struggled to secure them.

Almost from the moment of their first settlement, these colonies moved in different directions, a pattern that reflected the quickly improvised nature of colonial life. By the 1620s, for example, each colony shared the cultivation of tobacco, a crop that seemed well adapted to the environment of different regions of the Atlantic world. Although a common tax was imposed on colonial tobacco, the price of the crop could not be uniform given the varying qualities produced in Bermuda, Barbados, and Virginia, and given the insurmountable barriers to controlling colonial supply. The differences in each of these colonies, signaled in the quality of tobacco crops—but also reflected in the changing composition of the laboring population over time, in soil, in location, in the threat of indigenous or international rivalries—point to the wholly incomplete integration of the Atlantic in these early decades of the Atlantic world's creation. Although men ventured from one colony to another, as the invasion of Barbados by men from other colonies indicates, they were unable to transfer the expertise of one colony to somewhere else. They could bring with them experience in controlling labor or organizing a farm, but they could not replicate the worlds, colonial or metropolitan, that they had left behind. No colony embarked on an irrevocable trajectory, of course: future events would alter agricultural and labor configurations in different parts of the Atlantic, and differences in agricultural production and economic structure did not preclude integration in a later period. But that integration would be profoundly challenged by the long-standing divergences between colonies. Only networks of migration and communication across the Atlantic and among the different colonies, established with each colony and tightened when planters from one region ventured to another to exploit its distinctive riches, would help overcome these differences.

5 | *Piety and Protest in the Puritan Diaspora*

Edward Johnson, one of seventeenth-century Massachusetts' most aggressive promoters, remarked in his history of New England that beginning in 1635, the time soon approached "wherein the Lord Christ would have his people come from the Flaile to the Fan, threshing out much this yeare, increasing the number of his Troopes, and valiant Leaders, the Ships come thicker and faster filled with many worthy personages."[1] Johnson's parochial zeal did not mislead him in this instance: the cleric Robert Baillie concurred with Johnson's assessment. Like other observers he recognized the connection between ecclesiastical affairs in England and the movement of men and women to the colonies. Reflecting on this process, he noted that beginning in the years 1634 or 1635, "when the yoke of Episcopall persecution in England became so heavie on the necks of the most of the godly . . . many thousands of them did flee away . . . to joyn themselves to these American Churches."[2]

The people who traveled from London to New England in 1635 were, if not all exceptionally worthy, as Johnson would have had his readers believe, certainly unusually contentious and eager to act upon their religious convictions. Johnson and Baillie recognized a transformation in the character of passengers from the old to the new England, a shift from the utopian migration of the Winthrop fleet to the persecution migration that commenced with the appointment of William Laud as Archbishop of Canterbury in 1633. The enactment of Laud's policies and his vigorous ecclesiastical visitations heightened the pace and character of this migration. Puritanism was not a homogeneous movement, and many of those who reached New England in 1635 brought with them a zealous piety and labored over the course of a decade to broaden, challenge, and shape the congregational uniformity articulated in John Winthrop's vision for Massachusetts.

Providence Island and Bermuda, two remote island outposts at the edges of English settlement, received similar populations of puritan exiles. Accommodation, characterized by the acceptance of puritan habits and, more assertively, by church membership, enabled many new arrivals to demonstrate

132

their commitment to piety. For others, that commitment could be achieved only through individual or collective acts of defiance. Puritanism in the Atlantic world proved sequentially fissiparous, and the 1635 travelers were disproportionately represented in major and minor disputes in all the puritan colonies in British America. On Providence in the 1630s and on Bermuda in the 1640s, the religious conflicts that emerged all over England found their own remote Atlantic settings. Providence's stubborn minister Hope Sherrard, who created an Independent congregation and refused to perform the sacraments for many island residents, and Bermuda's new Independent congregation of the 1640s provided focal points of controversy that, as in the Antinomian Controversy in New England, witnessed the creation of political factions around doctrinal perspectives. In both tumultuous periods the travelers of 1635 played central roles, demonstrating that for many newcomers to England's Atlantic colonies in the 1630s, piety was a central impetus to plantation, and faith was the essential ingredient for survival.

The turmoil in the different puritan colonies, moreover, illuminates the tensions and ambiguity latent in puritanism in these critical decades. Puritanism, defined only in opposition to Church of England policies since its inception, in the 1630s found itself the dominant form of worship in parts of England's Atlantic world as it would soon be in England itself. Unfamiliar with positions of political and ecclesiastical power, clergy and laity alike struggled to define the nature of their faith. The result was a decade of dispute and of transformation in ecclesiastical polity, puritanism, and relations between ministers and laity.

The experiences of these travelers to New England, Providence, and Bermuda draw together four strands in the recent historiography of puritanism in old England and New England: a fresh appreciation of the diversity of puritan beliefs carried to New England in the 1630s;[3] an awareness of the importance of timing in the character and composition of the exodus;[4] a strengthened emphasis on the transatlantic aspects of puritanism; and the suggestive delineation of high rates of geographic mobility by New England's first generation,[5] a pattern of removal that was the culmination of diversity of belief and intensity of zeal. The varieties of puritanism and their changing expression introduced to the Americas by the Laudian exiles of 1635 brought conflict in political and religious spheres to all the colonies. No colony, no matter how broad and inclusive its form of worship, was immune to the squabbles of the 1630s and 1640s, and these conflicts could be sparked by a mere handful of people. Many travelers who arrived in 1635 demonstrated both a passionate commitment to their understanding of puritan belief and a willingness to take on sacred and secular authorities in its defense. Those who had willingly uprooted themselves and their families for a three-thousand-mile voyage over turbulent seas were equally willing to sacrifice harmony and comfort for their beliefs in their colonial laboratories where puritan practices evolved in unpredictable ways.

This zealous puritan population, however, was not destined only for the colonies profiled here. The puritans' "errands," as Karen Ordahl Kupperman has reminded us, took them to many different wildernesses.[6] The puritan exodus from England was a true diaspora. The Netherlands had been the initial refuge for puritans disgruntled by the practices of the Anglican church. But by the 1630s, while some puritans continued to venture east to the continent, thousands of others journeyed west across the Atlantic, to the Chesapeake, the Caribbean, New England, and Bermuda.[7] All colonies received puritans. Virginia, for example, contained puritan enclaves in Nansemond, or Upper Norfolk, and Isle of Wight Counties. By 1642 there were enough nonconformists there to justify a request to John Winthrop for "a supply of faithful ministers" from New England.[8] Even Barbados by the 1650s possessed its own share of sectarians. When Philip Bell took over as governor there, he passed an act to suppress "certayne sects and separatists."[9] An act probably passed between 1642 and 1650 was directed against people with "erroneous opinions," who met in private and endeavored to seduce others with their views. They were ordered to conform to the public (Anglican) worship.[10]

Although all colonies received puritans, not all colonies were puritan. The distinction is important. Although Virginia probably contained far more puritans than inhabited Providence or Bermuda, it was the latter two that, along with New England, were puritan colonies. The puritan nature of Providence and especially of Bermuda has long been overshadowed by the historical interest accorded the New England colonies.[11] What made Bermuda and Providence Island puritan colonies was the company leadership, the strenuous efforts of company members to recruit puritan settlers, each colony's perception of itself as a puritan haven, and the religious controversies that erupted on each island and intruded on the political process to dangerous degrees.

The composition of company membership was a central factor in shaping a colony's religious life. Members of the Somers Islands Company were not exclusively puritan, but there was from the beginning of the Company "a definite Puritan trend." This attribute of company personnel was important because shareholders were responsible for sending out their own settlers. Puritan investors tended to recruit sympathetic settlers, as when Robert Rich wrote his brother Nathaniel in 1618 and reminded him that in light of Nathaniel's desire "to have religion . . . planted amonge us," he should "have a speciall respect, not to send any but those that are of honest and discreet carrage."[12] The Somers Islands Company was strongly committed to constructing a complete cultural life for the colony. Although in 1622 there was only one minister on the island, by 1640 the company had built nine churches, one chapel, and five houses for the island's ministers.[13]

Despite its puritan leanings the Somers Islands Company sought to avoid the appearance of nonconformity in the 1630s. Indeed, although in that troubled decade Bermuda received ministers who became avowed Independents within a few years, religious affairs on the island remained superficially consistent with Anglican practice. Not until 1638 were ministers voyaging to Bermuda expected to take the oaths that passengers to New England had already been required to take for three years: this omission permitted five ministers, all of whom would play a role in the conflicts of Bermuda's version of the Civil War, to travel in that year.[14] In 1638, however, the Privy Council deplored the free departure of those ministers who hoped to "preserve their factious and schismaticall humors" in Bermuda and ordered not only the regulation of departing clergy but also the return of all who had previously left England without passes.[15] A year later the Somers Islands Company came under direct attack for nonconformity because of reports of improper liturgical practices on the island.[16] By 1639 the Company had populated the island with several nonconforming clerics whose presence created an environment conducive to schism and dissent.

The Providence Island Company demonstrated a comparable ambivalence about its puritan role. This joint-stock venture was composed of men who became zealous parliamentarians in the 1640s. They were almost to a man strongly identified with the puritan cause—men such as John Pym, Lord Brooke, Robert Rich (the Earl of Warwick), Lord Say and Sele, Sir Thomas Barrington, and John Gurdon, the son of the Suffolk county sheriff Brampton Gurdon, and the brother of two Massachusetts-bound passengers in 1635, Murial Gurdon Saltonstall and Edmund Gurdon. In the absence of a parliament during the 1630s, Company members found outlets for frustrated political participation in the creation of a new society in the tropics.[17] This society was to embody puritan ideals in its religious organization and by proselytizing to the native population. The colony, moreover, was to generate wealth from a range of enterprises: it was to serve as a privateering base, raid Spanish settlements, initiate trade on the mainland, and profit by marketing such luxury goods, procured through either trade or plantation production, as flax, silk, indigo, and madder, for which planters would receive one-third share of their labor. As sole proprietors of this colony, the investors were responsible for sending out men to cultivate crops; for organizing ships to supply the colony, transport these men, and return laden with marketable goods; for representing the colony's interests at the court of Charles I of

England; and for shaping every aspect of the society they devised in the tropics.

Its attention to profits, however, did not distract the Company from matters of the spirit. To encourage ministers, the Company agreed by the end of their first year as proprietors not to limit clerical salaries to £40 per annum, as originally had been decided, but rather to offer between £40 and £100 in money in England or the equivalent in commodities on the island. The minister, furthermore, was not to be on the island Council, in order that political activities not "hinder his more serious studyes."[18] The minister's salary reflected his importance to the community: in comparison, Richard Lane, who traveled to Providence in 1633, and again with his family in 1635, was to be paid only £30 for one year of service.[19]

The Company was not interested in just any English settler for its West Indian utopia. Both Bermuda and Providence leaders sought to distract colonists who intended to go to New England. The Bermuda Governor Roger Wood made this point forcefully in 1634, when he sadly observed the flight of people from England to New England: he maintained that these people would be better served in Bermuda, "where they should find a loving people a sweet and holesome clymate but no p.secuton."[20] By 1635 the Providence Island Company emulated Bermuda in trying to entice "some godly familyes" destined for New England. The Company offered such families special privileges, initially in 1635 permitting godly planters to keep two-thirds shares of their produce, compared with the customary half-share, and later enticing them with positions on the council, suffrage, and autonomy in congregational affairs. In 1638 the Company launched a more vigorous campaign to persuade the minister Ezekial Rogers, who ultimately settled in New England, to travel instead to the island with his congregation.[21] Successful efforts were recorded with glee: the Providence Island Company minutes noted in 1638 that "diverse that were going to New England did now declare their willingnes to goe to providence," and enumerated the seven passengers carefully.[22] The proprietor Lord Say and Sele, according to a petulant John Winthrop, essayed "by disparaging" New England "to divert men from coming to us."[23] And Lord Say not only enticed some men in England to Providence instead of New England but indeed lured New England residents away from their recently acquired mainland home to journey to the remote island. Although Providence and Bermuda often had difficulty distracting settlers bound for New England, subsequent events on the islands indicated that Bermuda and Providence had siphoned off the luminaries migrating to the American mainland some zealots of their own.

It is fortuitous indeed that it is possible to employ the 1635 London port register to examine in a systematic fashion the beliefs and behavior of some of the men and women who reached puritan destinations just as the nature of puritanism and, consequently, the puritan migration, changed. Although the ships bound for the puritan colonies contained large numbers of servants whose necessity may have overshadowed their religious sensibilities, religious concerns combined with economic necessity to spur many families to leave England for the puritan colonies of New England, Bermuda, and Providence Island.[24] For some men, religious reform could inspire a renewed commitment to colonial outposts. Richard Norwood fled England in 1637 for his former home in Bermuda. He recalled later that "the times were dangerous in England, by reason of many innovations in Religion brought in by the Bishops (the Lord be blessed for that happy reformation wch we heare and hope of) and at that time I was in danger my selfe to have bene called in question, wch occasioned me to move the honoble Company for this place."[25] For other men and women, the ecclesiastical changes of the 1630s prompted a first exile. In 1635 Philip and Nathaniel Kirtland, two yeomen of Sherington, Buckinghamshire, ventured to New England. They lived in a region of Buckinghamshire noted for nonconformity: Mr. Worcester, the minister of Olney, an adjacent parish, was a nonconformist. In 1633 seven parishioners in the area were excommunicated, while others were presented for attending the Olney services. The Kirtlands' mother, Rose, was herself presented for nonconformity.[26] In this climate of increased regulation, the Kirtlands, accompanied by twenty-two other people from their region in Buckinghamshire, left England.

These tales of flight were repeated over and over in parishes throughout England. Together, the religious migrants defined—by virtue of their numerical superiority, economic hegemony, intellectual pedigrees, and emotional tenacity—the character and impact of the migration of 1635. The diverse experiences of these hopeful voyagers once they reached their colonial destinations reveal a spectrum of religious behavior, from accommodation to disruption. Although some responded to the moral suasion of the puritan community, others brought and developed religious notions that proved to be in conflict with newly accepted conceptions of congregational worship, and these people sought to alter the community. The percentage of settlers in each region who were committed to puritanism varied significantly and shaped the impact of the zealous minority.

The disputes that these zealous travelers sparked in their new homes open a window to a wider view of puritanism in a critical decade. In the 1630s both Providence Island and New England witnessed vituperative congregational conflicts that foreshadowed those of England in the next decade. In the case of Massachusetts, these conflicts led to the gradual emergence of an identifiable and enforceable puritan orthodoxy at the expense of a vocal and enthusiastic minority. Conflicts on Providence, which centered around the Independent congregation gathered by one minister and his supporters, never achieved a clear resolution because of the Spanish invasion in 1641. In the 1640s, congregational conflict made a vigorous appearance in Bermuda, signaled by the creation of an Independent church by three of the island's ministers. These conflicts, considered together, permit a number of conclusions about religious affairs in the different colonies. First, the pronounced and, in the case of New England, disproportionate involvement of the travelers of 1635 attests to the zealous nature of the Laudian exiles. Second, these disputes reinforce the theme of the simultaneous creation and elaboration of the Atlantic world. They illuminate the varied ways in which congregational worship and gathered churches evolved in different colonial settings: the New England way was neither understood nor welcomed by all residents of the island colonies. On Providence, congregationalism was strenuously opposed by colony governors. Moreover, these disputes confirm the great range of puritan expression that was possible in the 1630s and 1640s. Reformation of the church did not necessarily entail a commitment to a gathered congregation. Indeed, the conflicts delineated later make apparent the anguish experienced by those who were left behind by the progressive separatism of their neighbors: the New Englander William Vassall and the Bermudian Richard Norwood faced ostracism for their inclusive philosophies. Third, ministers played different roles in these conflicts, depending largely on the amount of sanctioned authority they had and on their unofficial relationship with political leaders in London and in the colonies.[27] Above all, the doctrinal range of these disputes reveals the disorganized nature of ecclesiastical reform in the 1630s and 1640s, and this spectrum of puritan beliefs boded ill for subsequent efforts for reformation in England itself.

Because in New England there was, for the most part, agreement at least on the legitimacy of a gathered church, the story starts there. The anomaly of the New England way emerges in the subsequent assessment of conflicts on the islands of Bermuda and Providence, where ministers railed against each other and against colony governors in their efforts to establish Independent congregations.

A contemporary estimate reckoned that approximately 3,000 people emigrated from England to New England in 1635.[28] Approximately half of these voyagers left from the port of London. These new arrivals included a vocal minority whose earnestly held beliefs challenged the existing church and state structures in Massachusetts Bay. They arrived at a time when a rigid orthodoxy was taking shape, and they confronted this emerging and precarious orthodoxy in both religious and secular ways: as some new arrivals questioned notions of church membership, others raised questions of political legitimacy. Their failure to amend Massachusetts' institutions in the 1630s was a result less of the tenacity of their beliefs than of the simple reality that a majority of the new arrivals embraced the emerging orthodoxy and that the dissenters were not unified in their opposition. However willing to express its beliefs, the articulate minority could not, in the end, compel colony leaders to subvert their original vision of sacred uniformity.

Many settlers communicated an initial desire to accommodate New England mores by joining the church. The New England system of gathered churches rejected membership in a church simply by virtue of birth or baptism: in New England, pious men were culled from a community to inspect each other's souls and attest to their sanctity before joining in a church covenant and then admitting other members. It was no easy task to join a congregation and to subject oneself to the unforgiving scrutiny of the saints. Church membership was an arduous procedure that demanded public professions of faith. After they had been privately examined by their minister, individuals rose before the congregation and related their moment of sanctification. Moreover, beginning in 1635, procedures became stricter, and authorities expected visible evidence of sanctification.[29]

New Englanders confronted powerful incentives to join churches. For those who had abandoned homes and friends in England to pursue their chosen faith in a new world, membership symbolized the completion of that quest. Church membership also provided access to the sacraments: children could not be baptized unless their parents were church members. Awareness of this constraint surely motivated Alexander and Elizabeth Baker, who joined the Boston church a full decade after their arrival in 1635. The day following their membership, the Bakers brought their five Boston-born children to church for baptism.[30] Furthermore, in the Massachusetts and New Haven colonies, church membership was a prerequisite to political participation, and church members were rewarded with political status.[31]

Membership itself was no simple measure of piety; nor, indeed, did it signify an unquestioning or uniform acceptance of congregational discipline or doctrine. It did, however, represent an important commitment to both faith and community. Altogether, 252 (21.6 percent) of the travelers from London are known to have joined churches. Only 61 women, as compared with 191 men, were among this group, but the few surviving records dictate that bias. For Massachusetts and New Haven, it is easy enough to determine the church membership of freemen but much harder to determine the behavior of their wives; it is virtually certain that women joined churches at rates equal to or greater than their husbands, as any examination of a single congregation's records reveals. From 1636 to 1646, for example, 236 people joined the second church gathered at Dorchester under the ministry of Richard Mather. Of these, 128, or 54.2 percent, were women. The Dorchester church's sex ratio was not atypical. The list of church members maintained by John Fiske at Salem until 1640 contains 177 names, of whom 88 (49.7 percent) were women.[32] Clearly, then, women joined churches at a rate comparable to that of men.

With the opportunity to track both men and women through church records in a variety of towns, moreover, the rate of church membership among adult passengers to New England in 1635 proves higher than some New England historians have estimated.[33] In 1635 33 adult passengers from London settled in Dorchester. Of these, 17, over half of the total eligible adult population, joined the town's church. Of the 16 adults who did not join the Dorchester church, some did join other churches on subsequent moves: 6 people joined churches in Milford, New Haven, Salem, and Ipswich. Thus in this well-documented sample group, 23 out of 33 people, or 70 percent, actually joined churches through the rigorous methods of testimony.[34] A comparison with the town of Roxbury confirms that Dorchester was not atypical: there, 17 out of 22, or 77.3 percent, adult first generation settlers from London in 1635 joined the Roxbury church or removed to other towns where they joined the church.

These sample groups not only attest to high rates of membership but also remind us that church membership did not occur immediately upon arrival. The exact or approximate date of membership is known for 183 (73 percent) church members who were adults in 1635.[35] For 69 (27 percent) of the 252 church members, either the date is unknown, or the traveler was only a child in 1635. Table 5.1 portrays the rate of church membership for this group of adult passengers. The average length of time waited was under three years. Some adults joined churches as soon as they arrived in New England. Four newcomers, for example, joined the Boston church in October of 1635, and three more joined in January of 1636.[36] Others waited. Robert Browne, who traveled in 1635 on the *Truelove,* did not join the Cambridge church until 1648, thirteen years after he had reached Massachusetts. The delay in his membership and the description of his conversion in his narrative illustrate the important role that the religious climate in New England played in encouraging people to join churches.

In his confession, which is typical of its genre, Browne described first his sinful past, his struggles to reform, his backsliding, his despair, his turn to the Bible to seek means for salvation, the ensuing strength of his faith, and, finally, his departure for New England. In New England he avowed, "God hath endeared my heart more to himself, hath showed me more of my vileness and wretchedness." For Browne, New England played an essential role

Table 5.1. Speed of church membership for adults in the 1635 cohort (New England)

Year joined	N
1635	30
1636	50
1637	29
1638	15
1639	11
1640	15
1641	7
1642	4
1643	5
1644	3
1645	9
1646	2
1647	2
1648	1
Total	183

Sources: Freemanship records for Massachusetts and New Haven; published church records for Dedham, Dorchester, Hingham, Roxbury, Charlestown, Boston, Salem, Braintree, Cambridge, and the Second Church of Scituate; reconstructed records for New Haven; manuscript transcription of Milford records at the New Haven Colony Historical Society, New Haven, Conn.; and various genealogical sources.

in his lengthy quest for grace. Whereas he lamented at great length his association in England with "wicked men" and regretted the "evil of company keeping," he acknowledged the benefits of associating with those who observed the Sabbath.[37] For sinners struggling to eschew frivolous recreations, companions who heeded God's word were exemplary role models who exerted unrelenting pressure to seek grace. In New England, where the company of saints outnumbered that of sinners, it is little wonder that those who wrestled with demons in the old world found comfort among the cherubim in the new. Other 1635 travelers noted the power of individual ministers and recorded particularly resonant Bible verses that encouraged, inspired, and aided them in their quests for salvation.[38]

Confessions and spiritual autobiographies illuminate the influence of that community on newcomers. The moral suasion of the puritan community was overpowering. Merchants in particular were vulnerable to accusations of impropriety in their behavior and, moreover, embraced the mores around them. One settler, Dennis Geere, who traveled in 1635 with his wife and daughters from Sussex on the *Abigail,* recorded in his will that "the Lord our God of his great goodness, since my coming into New England, hath discovered to me all usury to be unlawful." Geere, who had learned this lesson within months of his arrival, instructed his executor to reimburse any who could prove the charge of usury against him.[39] Others learned such lessons more painfully, as in the case of Geere's fellow traveler Robert Keayne. A London merchant, Keayne voyaged to New England in 1635 on the *Defence,* a star-studded ship that transported several puritan divines, as a prosperous man with between £2,000 and £3,000. He was also a pious man, whose attendance at London area sermons and lectures was diligently recorded in a book of sermon notes.[40] In Boston, Keayne served in numerous public offices on town committees, as a selectman, and as a representative to the General Court. His attention to Massachusetts' orthodoxy was most vividly symbolized in his assiduous note-taking during the Antinomian trials. But Keayne was to imperil the orthodoxy he so lovingly and zealously embraced and defended. In 1639 Keayne was accused of overcharging, admonished by the church, and fined by the Court.[41] Keayne remained preoccupied by this ordeal for the rest of his life, and his extraordinary will was a lengthy and pained defense of the charge.

As some signaled their appreciation of the moral values of the puritan community in their attitudes toward commercial practices, other new arrivals communicated their commitment to their new home in naming practices. William Preston traveled in 1635 from Buckinghamshire with his wife, Mary, and their six children, Elizabeth, Sarah, Mary, John, Daniel, and Edward. After the family's removal to the orthodox New Haven Colony by 1639, four more children were born. In contrast to the names of their English-born siblings, these children were christened Jehiel, Hackaliah, Eliasaph, and Joseph.[42] A second family, the Munnings from Denge Hundred, Essex, demonstrated a similar trajectory in naming their children. The two oldest were christened Anna and Mary. The third child, born in Essex in 1632, was christened Michelaliel. In Dorchester were born Takeheed, Hopestill, and Return.[43] The family's new preference for hortatory names for their New England–born children might reflect the preponderance of residents in that town with instructive names: for example, the 1635 London traveler Hopestill Foster lived in Dorchester with his mother, Patience. Evidence suggests, however, that the family did consider the meaning of the names: it is probably no accident that the Munnings family departed for England sometime after the birth of Return. Both the Preston and the Munnings families embraced aspects of the religious culture around them, and they expressed their incorporation into a new puritan world in naming their New England–born children.[44]

New names for children born in a new England—such a practice shows individuals coming to terms with the collective values of New England culture. But these values were also contested, and new understanding of religious matters did not always result in shared symbols of community harmony. As newly arrived New Englanders enjoyed liberation from religious persecution and uncertainty in England, they ranged in their beliefs into areas unanticipated by colony rulers. The unflagging attention devoted to doctrinal issues preoccupied not only the clergy, but the laity as well, especially those who arrived during the period of the persecution migration that began in the mid-1630s. Individual and collective challenges to church authorities required new mechanisms for control and altered the role of the English ministry in the colonies. The following episodes reveal the relationship between theological conflict and community fission, while also demonstrating the range of disciplinary methods chosen by puritan polities, including fining, censure, excommunication, banishment, and execution, in efforts to restore the harmony of the founders' utopian expectations. The travelers of 1635 journeyed doctrinally as they had geographically. In their acts of defiance, church members communicated with conviction their rejection of clerical and congregational authority. Disproportionately represented in major and minor conflicts throughout New England, these troubled puritans attest to the dynamic nature of New England society in the 1630s and to the means by which orthodoxy was created and enforced during a period of precarious stability.

The experiences of three London travelers, Thomas and Marie Olney and the peripatetic cleric Hugh Peter, who had been strangers in England but who met in the course of a church trial in Salem, demonstrate the spectrum of theological positions occupied by the new arrivals of 1635. Where some assaults on congregational order could be subdued by meting out fines, the challenge that the Olneys posed called for sterner measures. Excommunication was employed for particularly severe cases of individual disruption, as Thomas and Marie Olney discovered in Salem, Massachusetts. The Olneys had traveled from London aboard the *Planter* with their two young children, Thomas and Epenetus. They were separatists who embraced the ideas of the Salem minister Roger Williams, as had most of the Salem congregation at first. After Williams's banishment, however, only the Olneys and a few others remained staunch in support of his beliefs, and they aspired to establish their own separatist congregation in Salem. Although Thomas Olney's name appeared on the 1636 Salem church covenant, he refused to abandon his earlier "heresies" and was tried with others before the church in 1637, by which time Hugh Peter was minister and John Fiske was teacher. It was Peter who instigated the trial.

Hugh Peter was one of the most illustrious newcomers to New England in 1635.[45] In matters of faith and government, Peter struggled to achieve reconciliation where he noticed duress. His plans invariably backfired. Concerned, for example, by what he perceived to be great disagreement between John Winthrop and Thomas Dudley and their respective supporters, Peter, in company with his fellow traveler from London, the gentleman Henry Vane, forced the two parties to meet. The two newcomers remind us by their actions of William Hunt's keen observation that a "Puritan who minds his own business is a contradiction in terms."[46] Peter influenced the course of Massachusetts politics sufficiently through his uninvited intervention to ensure the eclipse of Winthrop, who had already lost the governorship in 1634, in favor of Vane, "a yonge gentleman of excellent partes," who won the election of 1636 as governor of the colony and captivated Massachusetts with his youthful charm.[47]

Fortunately for affairs of state, Peter was soon called by the Lynn church. Although Peter did not accept this job, he did accept the position of minister in the Salem church, where he replaced Roger Williams. In Salem, Peter exerted himself, as he had on behalf of colony politics, to remedy church divisions and to rid the town of its separatist dissenters. It was at this moment that the Olneys and Peter, who had reached the colony simultaneously from the port of London, confronted each other across a widening theological chasm.

Thomas Olney's exchange with Peter and the church elders neatly articulates the way in which the 1635 travelers embraced contrary positions and pursued their theological beliefs to the detriment of community harmony and personal comfort. Peter sacrificed Olney and other separatists to restore the purity of the threatened Salem church. Olney maintained that he had to separate from the church because he witnessed practices he felt should not be tolerated. In particular, Olney complained that "such as have ben defiled with idolatry have ben hx [here?] admitted without washing yr hands by repts [repentance]." Olney asserted that all New England settlers could legitimately be accused of idolatry for their previous participation in Church of England rites. Although the Salem church members replied that such people had given satisfaction and had joined with the true church of Christ, Olney doubted the legitimacy of such conversion, warning these members that "they may yet retayne Babilon in yr hearts."[48]

For Olney adult baptism offered the only solution to the contamination of the Anglican church, and for this act, Olney, his wife, and eight others were censured by the Salem church.[49] Of the dissenters Hugh Peter later reported, "these wholly refused to hear the church, denying it, and all the churches in the bay, to be true churches, and except two, are all re-baptized."[50] Ordered out of the Bay Colony with the Hutchinsonians, the Olneys left Salem for Providence in 1638, where Thomas Olney was one of twelve original members of the First Baptist Church.[51] Olney served as pastor of that church and baptized new members. Removal to Providence, however, did not end religious conflict. The First Baptist Church subsequently split, with Olney at the helm. Olney withdrew from the church and formed a separate congregation. The issue was sacramental and theological: the dispute concerned the laying on of hands (the so-called Sixth Principle), which Olney and his supporters rejected.[52]

The experiences of the Olneys in Salem suggest the variety of problems that New England authorities faced as colonists pursued their own divisive beliefs or took on clerical leaders. Salem could survive the separatist challenge only by ridding the church of its dissenters. Individuals posed threats to society that had to be greeted harshly. In a society permeated by faith, in which every action was endowed with sacred significance and in which all deeds were performed for the glory of God, an individual's religious challenge was not a matter for only the church authorities to address. Still more dangerous were those conflicts that permitted organized opposition to lay and ecclesiastical structures. Two incidents in particular, the Antinomian Controversy and a division in the Scituate church over the practices of the minister, demonstrated the ways in which religious and enthusiastic New Englanders found themselves embroiled in controversies with lay and church authorities. Both incidents, furthermore, were numerically dominated by the zealous puritans who traveled in 1635.

Undoubtedly the most dramatic example of the upheaval provoked by theological disputes in early Massachusetts is the Antinomian Controversy, in which the 1635 cohort was well represented. Indeed, the Antinomian Controversy of 1636 to 1638 brought Massachusetts virtually to the brink of war. Three ministers who arrived from London in 1635 took particular issue with the Antinomians: Thomas Shepard, Peter Bulkeley, and Hugh Peter all shared an important role in the exacerbation and, finally, the resolution of the controversy. Twenty-one other travelers from London, including the colony's new governor Henry Vane, aligned themselves against these divines.[53]

The role of ministers in the controversy, which rapidly assumed political dimensions, reveals the peculiar transition experienced by New England ministers in their relocation to a new world setting. The historian David Hall has observed that migration to New England changed the nature of ministers' work. Whereas in England, puritan ministers had tended to a small, self-selected portion of the population, in New England, ministers were responsible for saints, sinners, and unsaved souls.[54] Those who had been expelled from pulpits in England or persecuted for carrying out the dictates of their consciences sought in Massachusetts the purity of worship denied them in England. For some, expectations could not hope to compete with reality, and the disputes of the first decade were unexpected for these colonists.[55] The Antinomian Controversy forced ministers, many newly arrived to the colony, to change from their erstwhile role as victims of Laudian persecution to enforcers of an emerging and, at times, confusing, orthodoxy. In so doing, they altered not simply their previously adversarial relationship to political authority but also their relationship to churchgoers. The former fugitives Thomas Shepard, Hugh Peter, and Peter Bulkeley now joined with Winthrop and other secular authorities to reinforce habits of political deference, restore pure worship, and punish theological speculation.

Shepard and Bulkeley, both men who bore that cherished puritan badge of honor, expulsion from an English pulpit,[56] chaired the synods that gathered to discuss the issues raised in the controversy. Both men were, as the historian and 1635 passenger William Hubbard noted, "two as able and judicious divines as any the country afforded."[57] They were also unusually devoted throughout their careers to uniformity in worship and resisted attempts at liberalization or toleration. The Antinomian Controversy enabled them to cut their teeth on the religious issues that would long preoccupy them in the new world.

Both men labored with the Boston minister John Cotton to clarify points of doctrine. Thomas Shepard, furthermore, met three times with Anne Hutchinson, whom he considered "a verye dayngerous Woman to sowe her corrupt opinions to the infection of many."[58] Hugh Peter, although not officially appointed as were Shepard and Bulkeley to remedy the conflicts in the Boston church, characteristically assumed responsibility for sorting out his misguided Boston colleague John Cotton. In May of 1636 Peter preached at Boston and urged the church to spare Mr. Cotton so that he might study the Bible and make marginal notes "upon all the knottye places of the Scripture." Quickly identifying one segment of the population most drawn to Hutchinson's pernicious opinions, Peter also recommended that employment be found for women and children, lest "idleness . . . be the ruin both of church and commonwealth."[59] Peter then identified another source of the colony's unrest: its leader. He pointed out to Governor Vane that "before he came, within less than two years since, the churches were in peace." Peter, who surely made few friends with his abrupt, public, and intrusive corrections of character deficiencies, also cautioned Vane to "beware of peremptory conclusions, which he perceived him to be very apt unto."[60]

Although the presence of Peter, Shepard, and Bulkeley, who were prominent members of the 1635 clerical contingent, on the side of Winthrop's law and order might suggest that those new arrivals involved in Massachusetts' great controversy were all supporters of Winthrop, far more of the 1635 newcomers were drawn to Anne Hutchinson and John Wheelwright. Most celebrated was Henry Vane, who had joined the Boston church within months of his arrival. In the wake of the controversy, as it became increasingly clear that Vane's side was losing political control, the young governor, in a teary outburst, attempted to resign his office. Persuaded to stay on until the next election, Vane finally returned to England in the summer of 1637, one year before his original three-year license for New England had expired.

Although the most celebrated supporter of Hutchinson, Vane was hardly alone in his advocacy of her ideas. Statistics compiled by Emery Battis confirm that New England residents who arrived in 1635 were disproportionately drawn to Antinomianism (Table 5.2). The number of participants from two key years, 1630 and 1635, stands out in this table. The passengers in the Winthrop fleet of 1630 were people of extraordinary commitment to the puritan experiment whose faith in their undertaking or desperation to leave England prompted them to move to the new world without waiting to see how the colony fared. That they would find themselves embroiled in controversy over the appropriate expression of piety is not surprising. The presence of the 1635 group is striking as well.[61] Of the people who traveled from London in 1635, twenty-one can be identified as supporters of Hutchinson: four were servants; eight were craftsmen, with more in cloth trades than other areas (four tailors, one glover, one draper); and four were merchants. Eleven are known to be church members, and nine were freeman. One, Henry Vane, was the governor of the colony. The wives of some of these men were probably also supporters of Anne Hutchinson, who with "her fluent Tounge and forwardness in Expressions" succeeded in attracting many people, "espetially simple Weomen of her owne sex."[62]

Why did these colonists embrace the controversy so early in the process of settling into their new communities? One explanation can be at best suggestive: religious men and women who left England in 1634 and 1635 were, as Robert Baillie noted, Laudian exiles, driven from their homes by the enhanced ecclesiastical regulation of the Archbishop's rule. These travelers, then, in their flight to America recaptured the zeal of the Winthrop fleet of 1630. In this respect, these two particular cohorts of settlers shared a passion for matters of faith likely to land them in extreme positions at odds with neighbors and pastors. A second interpretation, more easily demonstrated, supports Emery Battis's argument about the important inversion of customary authority heralded in the Antinomian Controversy. We see this in the case of two servants who ventured from London to New England in 1635. Ralph

Table 5.2. Antinomians by year of arrival

Year of arrival	No. of supporters
1628	3
1629	1
1630	38
1631	1
1632	4
Before 1633	12
1633	10
Before 1634	13
1634	10
Before 1635	10
1635	27
Before 1636	13
1636	3
Before 1637	4
1637	12
Before 1638	19
1638	6
Total	187

Source: Emery Battis, *Saints and Sectaries: Anne Hutchinson and the Antinomian Controversy in the Massachusetts Bay Colony* (Chapel Hill: University of North Carolina Press, 1962), p. 295.

Hudson, a draper, voyaged to New England from Yorkshire on the *Susan and Ellen* with five servants. One of these servants, Henry Knowles, exceeded his master's fervor when both men supported Hutchinson. Hudson recanted, while Knowles moved on to Rhode Island, thus terminating his apprenticeship and separating himself from his master.

Another servant, Henry Bull of Roxbury, clung to his beliefs and sacrificed his family and friends for his convictions. Bull was praised in John Eliot's church records because "he lived honestly for a good season," but Eliot sadly recorded that "on the suddaine (being weake & affectionate) he was taken & transported wh the opinion of familisme & running in that siszme he fell into many & grosse sins of lying &c."[63] Among the list of doctrinal faults that caused Bull's excommunication was a revealing comment about his demeanor: the ministers Thomas Weld and John Eliot observed that "he did publiquly Expresse, but shifted, and was loath to argue or defend it, but would not unsay it againe," and, above all, his views were "obstinately held." His behavior was "impudent and contemptuous . . . unseemly in any especially in a young youth." Bull, like the Boston servant Henry Knowles, unflinchingly challenged authorities. Finally, Bull declared that he would not repent and that he would consider it "a great mercy, to be cast out of ye Church." The church happily obliged him.[64]

The costs that Bull was willing to pay and his continued religious engagement testify to the strength of his faith. His protest was not simply a matter of youthful rebellion. Like Bull and Knowles, many other supporters of Hutchinson were excommunicated and removed to Rhode Island with their families. In fact, of the twenty-one Antinomians in the London cohort, sixteen, along with their families, permanently left Massachusetts for New Hampshire or Rhode Island. For those who would not recant, allegiance to their faith disrupted their families and their callings. Removal to Rhode Island did not end disputes for the Antinomians: first settled at Portsmouth, the Antinomians disagreed about matters of church discipline, and some of the group moved to what became Newport, carrying the church records with them in a time-honored and prudent strategy in ecclesiastical disputes. Many of those who removed to Rhode Island with the Antinomian controversy continued to seek their own version of faith, and they were attracted to the Baptists and, later, the Quakers. Henry Bull, for example, became a Friend in Rhode Island.[65]

But other Hutchinson supporters recanted. After the signers of a petition in support of John Wheelwright discovered that the General Court ordered all signers who did not recant to be disarmed, many yielded.[66] Among these were several London travelers, including the shoemaker George Burdin, the cooper/merchant Edward Rainsford, the draper Ralph Hudson, and the tailor Thomas Savage, all of Boston, and Thomas Ewer of Charlestown.[67] One can imagine that the situation was awkward for some. Ralph Hudson, for example, had been elected constable of Boston only one month before.[68]

The men in the 1635 cohort who recanted were easily reintegrated into the Boston community after their flirtation with heresy as it was defined in Massachusetts. Their reunion with the community reflects the fluid nature of Massachusetts orthodoxy in the decade of the 1630s and of Boston in particular.[69] The rigidity of the new orthodoxy required the excommunication of "heretics," but the fluidity of it enabled penitent men to be rehabilitated. Edward Rainsford even achieved the distinction of serving as a deacon of the Boston church in 1667. Perhaps most spectacular was the rehabilitation of Thomas

Savage, the son-in-law of Anne Hutchinson. He moved only briefly to Aquid-neck, and once back in Massachusetts, he became a colony Assistant. Thomas Savage not only recanted but also turned from his seeking origins. In a convenient switch from hunted heretic to enforcer of orthodoxy, Captain Thomas Savage diligently reported to the Magistrates in 1662 an illicit "tumultuous" meeting of Quakers held one Sunday.[70]

Less politically debilitating than the Antinomian controversy, but equally trying socially and theologically, were conflicts five years later in Scituate, where once again the new arrivals and one returned zealot of 1635 challenged congregational authorities. The town of Scituate in the Plymouth colony was the site of two ministerial upheavals. That Plymouth, generally identified as more liberal in forms of worship than neighboring Massachusetts, experienced such acrimony reveals the pervasiveness of conflict in all parts of New England. The majority of church members in Scituate removed to Barnstable in 1639 with their minister, Mr. Lathrop, ostensibly over non-ecclesiastical matters but possibly as a result of conflicts over baptism.[71] Lathrop's removal left eight stalwart members of the church behind. Those who remained included the Vassall, Stockbridge, and King families, who had settled in Scituate soon after their arrival from London in 1635. Others joined the remnant of the Scituate church, and a small majority of church members called the mettlesome Mr. Chauncey as their pastor.

A preacher at Ware in England, a town that sent several residents to Roxbury in 1635, Charles Chauncey had reached Plymouth in 1638 after numerous disputes with the Laudian regime in England.[72] Conflict followed him to his post in Plymouth. While serving there, Chauncey disturbed his congregation by his beliefs concerning baptism. Maintaining that "sprinkling was unlawful," Chauncey insisted that full immersion was necessary for baptism. The Plymouth church conceded that immersion was lawful but refused to accept that sprinkling was not. The church generously agreed that when administering baptism, Chauncey could perform the sacrament as he wished, provided that he extend the same courtesy to John Rayner, the other Plymouth clergyman. Chauncey refused this arrangement, and instead "removed himself" to the church at Scituate.[73]

In Scituate, Chauncey invoked the displeasure of some members of the recently diminished congregation. Conflict over baptism attended him at this new post, too. A sizable minority opposed complete immersion, and Chauncey requested that they not appear at communion.[74] Those who had opposed Chauncey's appointment and were subsequently excluded from communion refused to enter a new covenant with the church under Chauncey. Instead, they renewed their old covenant and organized their own church in February of 1643. Leading the opposition to Chauncey were six figures, five of whom had left London in 1635: Thomas and Susan King, William Vassall, Judith Vassall (William's daughter), and Ann Stockbridge, who led her husband, John, into the controversy as well.[75]

Issues of sacrament and lay control intermingled in the Scituate church dispute. The Stockbridges were sufficiently distressed by Chauncey's insistence on immersion that they took their child to Boston to be baptized in 1642. Chauncey obligingly provided them with a letter recommending Ann Stockbridge to the Boston church in order for her child to be baptized.[76] For William Vassall a fundamental issue in the division was that of liberality of church policy. Vassall noted in a letter to John Wilson that he had been accused of inclining "toward Scottish discipline." He defended himself against this charge but reaffirmed his inclusive policies in his insistence that people other than church members alone should be welcomed at the communion table.[77]

The separate and competing church in Scituate formed by the Vassalls, Stockbridges, and Kings distressed not only the first church but also Plymouth Colony officials, who labored to achieve a reconciliation. Vassall, in a series of letters to Massachusetts divines defending his actions, argued that his church was the old church, whereas it was Chauncey's church that was the new church.[78] The two Scituate churches coexisted uneasily until they reconciled following the removal of Chauncey in 1654.[79]

William Vassall extended his inclusive philosophies of church membership to the political sphere with the drafting of Child's Remonstrance of 1645. The timing of Vassall's political assault coincided with Massachusetts' insecurity during the Civil War. The 1640s comprised a decade of crisis for the fragile orthodoxy that had emerged in Massachusetts in the 1630s: England promised greater religious toleration and experimentation for Protestant sectarians during the Civil War than did the colony that had projected itself as the most godly community of all. Instead, New England retrenched and reaffirmed its commitment to intolerance.

The effect of the Civil War in both England and the New England colonies was greater attention to the repressive New England way. One expression of this tension was Child's Remonstrance. Originally in Massachusetts during the 1630s, Robert Child returned to England in the 1640s, and when he went once again to New England, he carried with him the zeal for toleration and presbyterianism that infused the Parliamentary side.[80] Child's Remonstrance was a mouthpiece for the inclusive philosophies of William Vassall. According to John Winthrop, it was William Vassall who orchestrated the entire petitioning effort. John Winthrop dismissed Vassall as "a man of a busye and factious spirit, & allwayes opposite to the Civill Governmentes of this countrye, & the waye of our Churches." He accused Vassall of approaching non–church members and persuading them to petition appropriate provincial bodies and parliament.[81] Indeed, Vassall did not even live in Massachusetts but rather in Plymouth, where he had made a similar proposal to the Assembly there in 1645. Vassall insisted that colonists should be governed by English laws, a possibility that Winthrop found anathema to his vision of Massachusetts as a colony governed by God's laws. Vassall left Plymouth for England to plead his case before Parliament.[82] Winthrop maintained that Vassall later left England for Barbados in 1648 because he found few sympathetic ears for his petitions.[83] But it is possible that Vassall, "a man of a pleasant and facetious wit, and in that respect complacent in company,"[84] could no longer stomach the rigid New England way, and that he had tired of his years of struggling in the church to include all worshipers in communion and in the government to broaden political rights. William Vassall was a powerful and persuasive man who was able to mobilize those around him in formal protests against ministers and magistrates, and his fights with Chauncey in Scituate and with Winthrop in Massachusetts reveal his unrelenting efforts to make institutions in New England as inclusive as possible.

Few in New England, however, were interested in inclusion. The collective struggles just described reveal the ease with which New England communities split and congregations divided into ever smaller and increasingly righteous bodies. The founding of new towns symbolized not the success of the puritan mission but, in many cases, its failure to remedy division or to accommodate an unanticipated diversity of beliefs. For those profiled here, the pursuit of faith led to banishment, censure, and exile. Authorities, for their part, learned that the greatest threats posed to the community were internal ones.

This was a lesson authorities learned with great pain from the first planting of the New England colonies. While threats to the colony charter or adversarial relations with the indigenous inhabitants of southern New England constantly reminded colonial leaders of the ferocity and potency of external challenges to mere survival, the assaults launched from within by seemingly God-fearing and pious people compelled authorities to retrench and retreat. What enabled the young New England colonies to withstand such challenges was the fact that so many of the newcomers allied themselves with religious and political institutions. As church membership signaled acceptance of aspects of the reigning orthodoxy, so too did the acquisition of political office herald an implicit acceptance of existing authority. Over eighty men in the 1635 cohort held town and colony offices (see Appendix B, Table B.7). The fervent and vocal, yet disorganized, minority of malcontents and zealots could not compete successfully with the more numerous colonists who chose to reaffirm the emerging orthodoxy of early Massachusetts, and as a result, however exuberant this minority's protests were, their impact was smaller than their enthusiasm promised.

The power of the vocal minority was also diminished by its members' decisions to abandon the colonial experiments and rigid hierarchies that so poorly met their expectations, as William Vassall and Henry Vane did. Moving on provided many dissatisfied New Englanders with a mechanism for remedying the endless conflicts and disagreements generated in a society where people battled over matters of faith on which, all concurred, there could be no compromise. For those who could not alter community institutions to accommodate their aspirations, physical mobility, which was the distinguishing characteristic of first generation settlers to New England, provided a preemptive alternative to the possibility of civil and ecclesiastical confrontations.

Few in New England openly questioned the legitimacy of church order or the relationship between ministers and elected officials. On the islands, however, this church order itself was challenged. What made orthodoxy and congregational worship in New England possible was an alliance of ministers and officials who quelled dissent and enforced conformity. An orthodoxy could be created only with the support of the state, which island ministers lacked. Even on Bermuda, where ministers themselves served on the island Council, Independent churches emerged over the opposition of colony leaders and despite the internal disputes among island clergy. Where island governors sought order and would compromise to achieve it, island ministers sought salvation, for which there could be no compromise. The result was acrimony and division. The eruption of religious conflict, moreover, was fraught with political danger because there were few places on the islands where enemies could be avoided. Both islands are small—Providence Island is twenty-four square miles, and Bermuda is twenty. Poor mechanisms for resolving disputes and a reluctance by company members to alienate island leaders played an important role in intensifying the island's religious difficulties.

Religious conflict on Providence Island centered around one man, the cleric Hope Sherrard, and the political faction that developed around his supporters, who included influential councilors such as the 1635 traveler Richard Lane. The appointment of Hope Sherrard ensured that religious matters would painfully remain in the forefront of Providence Island Company concerns. Sherrard had attended the Cambridge bastion of nonconformity, Emmanuel College, and by 1633 he had been appointed by the Company as a minister on the island.[85]

Sherrard was one of many ministers, most unsatisfactory, sent to Providence Island. The first minister, the Welshman Lewis Morgan, stayed for no more than a year before he was dismissed as a "seditious and malignant spirit" and arrested on the Company's orders and returned to London.[86] He was followed in 1634 by Arthur Rous, Hope Sherrard, and one Mr. Ditloffe. Ditloffe returned in May of 1634, and Rous's stay proved equally brief and unsatisfactory.[87]

Because of this history of difficulty in both obtaining and retaining suitable ministers, the Company in London made strenuous efforts to keep Sherrard on the island. Sherrard found loyal supporters on the island as well. Richard Lane insisted, when he contemplated not returning to Providence or Association in 1635 because of disputes that he had there with the organization of government, that he would return only if Mr. Sherrard's fiancée accompanied him, "thatso Mr. Sherheard may be ye more ingaged to stay upon the Island."[88] The presence of his fiancée, who traveled to Providence in 1635 in the company of Lane, his wife, children, and servants, may have placated Sherrard but of course did little to appease his many enemies. By 1635 there were ranged against Sherrard Captain Hooke and others, who, he complained, "joyned together to foment a faction against mee in the church." Although Sherrard assured Sir Thomas Barrington that he could produce twenty or thirty men to testify on his behalf, Governor Philip Bell himself opposed Sherrard, whom he had imprisoned in 1635 for two months.[89] This tension between the governor and the minister boded ill for island harmony.

Sherrard's activities on the island suggest that he was hoping to erect a gathered church similar to those in New England, in which sacraments were reserved for a privileged few. Sherrard initially satisfied his puritan proclivities by suspending some people from communion and excommunicating others. Island residents complained to the Company in London: in 1636, the Company assured Sherrard he had their support but implored him to employ "Christian moderacon" in his interactions with island residents. The Company urged Sherrard to reconsider the state of those whom he had excommunicated, and to be sure, if he continued to suspend people from communion, that those suspended knew well beforehand that they would be denied the sacrament. The appointment of a new governor, Captain Robert Hunt, to replace Philip Bell briefly gave Sherrard an ally. In 1636 Sherrard still offered communion, but by the late 1630s Sherrard ceased performance of the sacraments altogether.[90]

Sherrard enjoyed a monopoly in island ecclesiastical affairs. For a while he was the only minister on the island, and if he chose to reorganize worship on puritan lines, there was little his concerned detractors could do aside from complain to Company members whose sympathies lay with Sherrard. In 1639 the Company wrote to Hunt's replacement, Governor Nathaniel Butler, obviously in response to his complaints, that it had tried to find a minister who would remove the inconvenience posed by nonadministration of the sacraments but could not find one. The Company urged Butler to be happy with Sherrard and to give him "and his particular Congregation all Liberty and favour."[91] This reference to a particular congregation is significant: Sherrard had successfully established an Independent congregation by 1639. At the same time, the Company wrote to Sherrard and reported that it was trying to find another minister to perform baptism for those who desired it. The Company urged Sherrard not to "desist yor Publick labour for the Instruccon of the Island" but pleaded with him not to antagonize others "that Unity may bee mayntayned in the Island and all may concurr in the beating downe of Sinn, and building up the kingdome of God."[92]

Sherrard found an unfortunate enemy in Governor Nathaniel Butler, who was an experienced soldier and colonial governor. He had served first on Bermuda, reaching the island in 1619. His skills would be fully tested during his sojourn on Providence. In his diary Nathaniel Butler described the island's troubled religious life starting in February of 1639, about the time Mr. Nicholas Leverton arrived as a second minister.[93] Butler noted Leverton's presence with relief: Leverton performed the sacrament of communion, "wch hadd nott bin administred in the Iland, for some yeares past." Sherrard had refused to perform other sacraments as well. With much surprise Butler recorded that Sherrard had christened a child in March of 1639, "(that wch I never seene him before doe, but untill now ever refused) . . . but in deed itt was ye child of an especiall favorite of his."[94]

Butler's initial enthusiasm at Leverton's arrival proved premature. Leverton was soon influenced by Sherrard, whose nonconformity he increasingly shared. Sacred and secular relations on the island progressively deteriorated. Butler recorded one Sunday that he went to Sherrard's church for both morning and afternoon services and "found him strangely possest wth a streine of uncharitable and dangerous suggestions out of ye pulpitt." Butler did not elaborate, unfortunately, on what these suggestions were, but he clearly found Sherrard's preaching to be troublesome. In January of 1640, he noted that Sherrard "preached tollerably in the morneinge, and intollerably in ye afternoone," and a week later, Butler found Sherrard's preaching so offensive that he resolved to spend the afternoon at home rather than in church. In the following week, he did not go to service at all, and one week later, having optimistically returned to church, Butler dismissed Sherrard's sermons as "malicious Invectives."[95]

Butler's dislike of Sherrard was more than simply doctrinal or sacramental: his diary provides evidence of personal animosity. Butler recorded regularly the efforts of Sherrard's servants to flee their master: runaways were not frequently mentioned in the diary, but Butler assiduously noted the times when Sherrard's black servants and English servants "came awaye in a bote," once in company with a servant of Sherard's ally, Richard Lane. The servants always chose to escape during Sunday services, a fact that obviously titillated Butler.[96]

What made Sherrard particularly menacing to Butler was the alignment of political sentiment around a puritan faction. Butler referred to "the three Sherrardian counsellers" whom he found intractable.[97] The leader of Butler's opposition was the 1635 traveler Richard Lane.[98] By 1640 four Providence residents, including Lane and the two ministers, were sent back to England in chains as prisoners for opposing the deputy governor of the island.[99] Arrested as the Spanish attacked the island in 1640, the four men were vindicated by the Company in London. But the arrest of the councilors and ministers and their vote of no confidence in the deputy governor revealed the intimate relationship between religious disputes and political factions and the disintegration of authority on the island. The Spanish seizure of the island in 1641 would dictate an unexpected resolution to congregational conflicts.

Providence's decade of struggle, at least according to extant records, took place at the very top of society. On this island, ministers created and enforced a new puritan orthodoxy, one defined by a gathered church, over the opposition of the governors. The disputes, then, were debilitating for the harmony of the fragile island polity, and they revealed dangerous fissures in a colony with enough challenges posed by disgruntled island laborers and Spanish neighbors to need whatever unity it could achieve.

During Providence's turbulent decade, Bermuda had attempted to maintain the appearance of consistency with Anglican practice. As the Spanish seized Providence Island, however, Bermuda's latitudinarian policies disintegrated. The New England pattern of religious conflict and migration was echoed in Bermuda in the 1640s. Religious conflict in Bermuda had two phases. The first dispute witnessed growing disagreement over the practices of ministers on the island. In particular, the strenuous efforts of some Bermuda clergy to catechize all adults on the island distressed clergy and laity alike, and signaled a growing, and to some, an inappropriate, commitment to a puritan vision. The second dispute centered around the culmination of this extensive catechizing, the emergence of an Independent congregation.

In its *Orders and Constitutions* of 1622, the Somers Islands Company had ordered the governor and council to suppress "all factious and seditious Preaching, teaching, and disputing, as well in private, as publike."[100] But this injunction ultimately proved impossible to enforce. The church itself was an important focus of community life and thus a potential site of conflict, as a seating controversy in 1627 revealed. The island's prescient governor, Philip

Bell, detected in the vituperative fervor of this conflict the seeds of future "factions and disorder."[101] Religious conflict on the islands was endemic. The combination of a vigorous puritan company, vigilant nonconformist ministers eager to exert authority in church matters on the island, and the ability of these ministers to assume political authority through their seats on the island's governing council ensured that religious disagreements were frequent and, ultimately and characteristically in this period, inseparable from political conflicts.

As in New England the settlers of 1635 found themselves arrayed on both sides of religious controversy. These controversies can be traced in part through the experiences of the five ministers who had migrated in 1635, George Stirke, Henry Jennings, John Oxenbridge, Daniel White, and Isaiah Vincent. Although George Stirke died a few years after this trip and Henry Jennings seems to have returned to England after his tour of three years ended, the three other ministers suggest the range of puritan sentiment among the most committed members of the population.

The creation of an identifiable puritan faction was instigated by the 1635 passenger and cleric John Oxenbridge, who was a zealous independent. His education at Emmanuel College would have been sufficient to suggest his puritan inclinations: his behavior in England and on the island confirms this suspicion. Like his New England compatriots Thomas Shepard, Hugh Peter, John Jones, and Peter Bulkeley, Oxenbridge had attracted Archbishop Laud's attention. Oxenbridge served after he had left Emmanuel as a tutor at Magdalen College, Oxford. His unorthodox approach included requiring his students to swear an oath that they would conform to strict style in matters of personal appearance and behavior. Such zealous oversight cost him his job. Laud deprived Oxenbridge of his position, and the young puritan cleric left for Bermuda soon after.[102]

Oxenbridge played an important role on Bermuda in the reformation of the church. Within a few years of his arrival, he had transformed the liturgy into a puritan template. A Spaniard shipwrecked on Bermuda in 1639 described church services there: what he unknowingly delineated were practices typical of nonconformist worship. He noted that there were five or six churches, to which people flocked twice on Sundays, in the morning and evening, to hear sermons during services that lasted more than three hours. Singing that was distinguished more by its great volume than by its tunefulness launched the services, followed by the minister's "long prayer," "a chapter" out of "a book," and then a sermon in which the minister, as this Roman Catholic observer understood, explained "the meaning of the Bible as he (fancied) it to be." The Spaniard remarked particularly that all islanders, "men, women, youths, boys and girls and even children all carry their books to church." Sabbatarian rules prevailed, forbidding even children's games. And only three feast days were observed, and even then only as if they were normal Sundays: Ascension, Christmas, and the Feast of the Incarnation.[103]

But reorganizing services was only part of the process of reformation. Mr. Oxenbridge was particularly concerned about the knowledge of his parishioners, most evident in the 1630s through his active catechizing: he even composed a catechism intended not only for children, as was customary, but also for adults. His actions in and out of the pulpit riled some neighbors and colleagues: in 1639, one Vincent Sedgewick was presented at the Assizes "for that he had slanderously reported that Mr. John Oxenbridge should speake false Latine in the pulpitt & in a slyghtinge traducinge manner sayd that he had a brother would whippe him about the piggmarket."[104] Sedgewicke's complaint against Oxenbridge is too vague to indicate a substantive religious dispute, but the complaint coincided with Oxenbridge's controversial catechizing throughout the island. Few of his peers opposed him. As early as 1641 his colleague Daniel White stood alone among island clergy in opposition to the new practice of extensive catechizing.[105] On Bermuda by 1641, one critic noted, it became common "to catechise constantly, all men and women throughout the Iland." Lay complaints fell on deaf ears. Two of the Reverend William Golding's parishioners, a couple in Smith Tribe, complained to him, "intreating him that they might be spared from that his weekly exercise, as not beeing in conscience well perswaded of it." Richard Norwood, the Bermuda surveyor and teacher, wrote Oxenbridge directly to complain of the practice and received in reply an unsympathetic epistle lambasting Norwood's "captious cavills" and "bitterness."[106]

Its association with radical puritan interests made catechizing particularly insidious to critics. Indeed, affairs on the island moved further away from Anglican practice. Reformation of the service and extensive catechizing were the first steps of church reform. The next step was the creation of an Independent congregation. Oxenbridge, who returned to England in 1641 to lobby Parliament on behalf of the colony, left the island before the actual creation of an Independent church "but left the cursed seed or fruit of [his] faction behind [him]." One critic wrote of Oxenbridge that he and his wife "were the first ground work of this [Independent] faction."[107] As early as 1643, substantive concerns were raised about church discipline: Richard Norwood, in a petition to Governor Forster, asked despairingly how much authority ministers were supposed to have; by what system a minister could sit in judgment of others; and who had authority over a minister.[108]

The second phase of religious convulsion occurred when three people gathered to form an Independent church. For Bermudians as for New Englanders, changes in English politics and religion influenced events on the island. The trial and subsequent execution of Archbishop Laud were a signal to puritans everywhere to pursue their own sacred visions unencumbered by the ecclesiastical regulation of the unfortunate archbishop. In Bermuda, a small island with only a few strong-minded ministers, the struggle to erect Independent congregations mirrored on a tiny scale the battles fought elsewhere in England then and later. What happened in Bermuda was the rapid creation of an Independent church by three ministers, Nathaniel White, William Golding, and Patrick Copeland, who renounced their ties to the Church of England and entered into a covenant among themselves in 1643 or 1644. White had apparently replaced Oxenbridge as the leader of the extreme puritan faction. These ministers claimed that they were subject to no human authority, so it did not matter what Parliament ruled about the Bermuda church. Sacraments were offered only to those who were members of the new church. The island soon became divided into two parties, and no one, Richard Norwood reported, had moderate feelings on the subject.[109] The island was run at this time by a triumvirate, and two of the three men joined the Independent church, as did one of the island's councilors.[110]

Religious controversies erupted quickly in Bermuda. Aggrieved parishioners complained that their children died unbaptized and that they themselves were deprived of the sacraments. Adopting a stance as strict as that of Providence's minister Hope Sherrard, Nathaniel White declared that children would not be baptized if their parents were ignorant of church teaching: even Governor Josias Forster's child—John Oxenbridge's own cousin—was reportedly denied baptism because Forster would not make his confession.[111] One staunch critic of the Bermuda Independents, Richard Norwood, described at length the affairs on the island. He complained that the ministers had taken over the government: "Our Governor Capt Sayle hath bene I thinke wholy guided by them . . . Whereby we have seene an experiment here of that wch very few I suppose in England have seene namely of the superiority or goverment of Ministers." Norwood wrote that many had left for Trinidad because of these conflicts, and he remarked with great surprise at the extent of the controversy. "Indeed it is incredible," he commented, "it should grow to such a height in so short a time."[112]

The governor who replaced the poorly united triumvirate tried to silence the ministers unless they conformed to services as ordered by Parliament: the ministers then refused to preach at all until they could "preach unmanacled."[113] Other lay residents on the island opposed the Independent church and petitioned for redress. Indeed, the conflict in Bermuda was played out in pamphlet literature in England. Nathaniel White, Richard Norwood, William Prynne, Josias Forster, and the Earl of Warwick himself published works addressing Bermuda's gathered church, while numerous anonymous pamphlets as well attested to strong feelings on the subject. In a petition of 1644, island-ers complained that one councilor and two of the island's governors had joined the Independent church.[114] The minister Daniel White went home to England in 1644 because of his disagreement with the puritan party.[115] Oth-ers, however, supported the new church. In a counterpetition, ninety resi-dents of the island disavowed the general petition of 1644 that opposed the Independent church and indicated their own support for the new church.[116]

As in New England, religious conflict led to physical mobility. The Ber-mudian exodus to the Bahamas was prompted by religious conflict on Ber-muda: in 1645, the first group of Independents left Bermuda. Another con-tingent set out in 1648. The London passenger Robert Ridley, an active lay preacher in the 1640s, was involved in the 1648 migration. He had been brought before the Council in August of 1648 by "divers of the Countrey" who disliked Ridley's "teaching and drawing the people from the discipline set forth *in the church* to be observed." Two ministers, the Reverends Viner and Hooper, said at the time that they would "preach noe longer" unless Ridley's behavior were suppressed. The Governor and Council proclaimed that "none shold soe convene hereafter, uppon paine of imprisonment. And afterwards to be banished out of the land if they will not conforme."[117]

The religious controversies sapped the energies of Bermudians, but what savaged the precarious stability of the small island's polity was the execution of Charles I, which overstepped the limits of Bermudian support for Parlia-ment. The island's government fell into the hands of royalists. The appalled islanders called for the administration of an oath of allegiance to the king and to the established church: although few quibbled with the oath to the king, the support of the church did provoke opposition. In a final royalist frenzy, in September of 1650 the "countrey in general rose up in Arms," evicted Gover-nor Turner, and forced Nathaniel White and members of his congregation to flee to Sagatea, "a most barren Rock, shallow Earth."[118] Parliament later forced Governor Forster to rescind their banishment, but several Inde-pendents remained on the Bahamas.[119]

Distinguished from New England by the personal and political divisions be-tween political leaders and clergy and, especially, among the clergy them-selves, the disputes of Providence and Bermuda nonetheless shared central defining features of the birth-pangs of a distinct political puritan stance. Puritans, unaccustomed in the 1630s and 1640s to possessing legitimate power, found different ways of exercising it and distributed that power to the clergy in opposing ways as well. The clergy themselves could not agree on appropriate sacramental obligations or even on the organization of congrega-tions: as opinions varied among lay and clergy alike, the precarious colonial polities settled on shifting quicksand. One place's heresy was another's ortho-doxy—at one time or another. Each person defined his or her puritanism in opposition to someone else's heterodoxy: Richard Norwood, the opponent of Bermuda's Independent faction, was a supporter of reformation in the church of England, and at the same time as he criticized Bermuda's own ecclesiastical organization, he wrote with delight of the news of the "happy reformation" under way in England.[120]

It was precisely this uncertainty that made those who had authority react venomously and uncompromisingly to ecclesiastical challenges, whether they appeared as a faction around a popular minister, as an individual's challenge to the legitimacy of church organization, or as a collective rejection of scrip-tural interpretation. For the clergy, division in the ranks was unexpected and painful: the anguish with which Daniel White fled Bermuda and the perceived necessity of exiling rival congregations or ministers to inhospitable reef is-lands or to unsettled regions of New England suggested the surprise and fear with which politically astute clergy clung to their positions of power and shed the burden of troublesome colleagues.

Had anyone in England sought a lesson in colonial experiences, it would have been ominous indeed for the possible successes of puritanism in old England. Some observers appreciated the perils of puritanism in its more uncompromising forms. The wonderfully perceptive and acerbic cleric Robert Baillie explored ecclesiastical organization and difficulties in the colo-nies in his study, *A Dissuasive from the Errours of the Time* (London, 1646). The great exodus to New England that commenced in 1634 and 1635, Baillie believed, marked "when that new way [Independency] began first to be dangerous to the rest of the World."[121] A strenuous opponent of the Independents, Baillie found ample evidence for his argument in colonial ex-periments. Baillie admired the Independents in London, where they proved "a uniting Principle," casting none out of the church, in sharp contrast to New England. Baillie held New England ministers particularly responsible for spreading their rigid and exclusive notions to Bermuda, whose gathered church Baillie abhorred.

Baillie appreciated, as too few did, the contagion of radical religious ideas. He delineated their spread throughout the Atlantic world, from old England to New England by 1635, then to Bermuda by 1641, from whence, Baillie argued, the Bermudian gathered church hoped "to dissolve and annull all the Churches of England. yea of the world."[122] As formerly exiled ministers flocked from Holland and their colonial outposts to London, Baillie trembled for the continued harmony of English Independents.[123] Baillie cannily appre-hended the Atlantic context of puritanism and the ways in which colonial outposts in the 1640s and 1650s provided laboratories for puritan experiments that could then be reexported, like tobacco or sugar, back to England for processing or transplantation. Puritanism, in short, was a disorganized and divisive affair in the colonies—and only the most self-deceptive Parliamentarian could imagine that its achievements in England, with its larger population of radical puritans, would be any more coherent or lasting.

6 | *Persistence and Migration in Old and New England*

Only two days after he had reached Massachusetts Bay from London in 1635, Thomas Shepard traveled to Newtown (Cambridge) from the home of the colony's treasurer, William Coddington, who had hosted Shepard and his family on their arrival. Newtown was in a state of upheaval. Many of the residents there had already removed to Hartford, Connecticut, to follow their minister, Thomas Hooker, leaving "many houses empty and many persons willing to sell." Shepard and his companions resolved to rest temporarily in Newtown, "until we should see another place fit to remove unto." But soon inertia set in. Several members of his company, enjoying the fellowship of the Newtown church, decided to stay put. Moreover, settled snugly with their goods in their newly acquired homes, "they thought their lives were short and removals to new plantations full of troubles."[1] And indeed they were. As one colonial planter wrote tersely following his forced move from Surinam to Antigua, "Resettling is hard."[2]

New plantations on the mainland required more than brave hearts and strong backs: they demanded unceasing optimism, preparation to make peace or some type of accommodation with new Indian or Dutch neighbors, and a vision of the future that could picture shelter and a cultivated field along English models where there stood forests cluttered with brush and fields crowded with rocks. Clearing arable land in the older settlements around Boston was arduous enough, in a region where rocky ledges and quagmires jostle for prominence. Land farther afield in New England's interior or along the region's southern coast posed still greater challenges. Moreover, colonists traveled across New England at great peril: in the same year that Thomas Shepard arrived in the Bay Colony, two shallops sent from Massachusetts to Connecticut laden with goods foundered, and all the men on board drowned. And one party of seventy people that reversed the trip, traveling by sea from Connecticut to Massachusetts aboard the *Rebecca,* had to unload its goods after running aground, causing some of her passengers to starve to death before they reached Massachusetts. The land route proved no friendlier.

Twelve men who traveled overland from Connecticut lost one of their company on the way, and all would have starved to death had they not "lighted upon an Indian wigwam."[3] Yet for all the dangers of travel and the weariness of Shepard's Newtown neighbors, removals to new and old plantations alike were normative in early America, as indeed migration was customary in England.

Movement within a single colony and to adjacent colonies was the migration that most closely replicated English patterns of migration. Because of surviving sources, the emphasis here is on geographic mobility in only one region of England's Atlantic world, New England.[4] The longevity of its inhabitants and the richness of its sources make New England an ideal place to undertake a study of internal migration. Movement in other English colonies was often preempted by an early death: where second migrations occurred, they have been lost for the seventeenth century in haphazard records. But the relative longevity of New Englanders permits a systematic examination of mobility. The individuals who reached New England from London in 1635, 80 percent of whom appear in extant New England records, moved at least once and typically twice in New England. And the propensity to move was not determined by wealth alone. Large landholders as well as landless laborers moved on.[5]

The 1635 travelers to New England enjoyed in the colonies an unfamiliar religious climate that liberated them from the strictures of Anglican worship while constraining them to new and contested visions of puritan orthodoxy. In many respects these colonists created for themselves a world vastly different from the one left behind, a difference fully embodied in their gathered churches. Nonetheless, a defining characteristic of the 1635 migrants—their mobility throughout the New England colonies—was wholly consistent with English patterns of mobility. In this respect the migrants to the new world transported with their motley assortment of goods, chattels, and expectations the traditional mechanisms for accommodating economic distress, religious discontent, pessimism about future opportunities, and real reversals of fortune. It should not be surprising to find New England residents moving frequently. They came, after all, from a land in which migration permeated all ranks of society. They were newcomers to a strange and evolving land, and new to the whole enterprise of colonization. When the soil proved rocky or inadequate, when a commercial enterprise failed, or when a church changed to the distress of its members, geographic removal offered the sure way to preempt conflict.

As the lure of London to people from all over England makes clear, migration in England was common: young adults moved to new communities when they married, families picked up their stakes for better opportunities elsewhere, a child moved to find a domestic position or to commence an apprenticeship. Judith Phippen made such a lengthy migration. She journeyed to New England in 1635 as a servant, probably with the family of Nicholas Davis, and was certified in the London port register under Davis's name with a license from Stepney, Middlesex. But Phippen herself was originally from the county of Somerset, and had completed a long trek to her post outside London.[6]

Evidence of Phippin's travels on a larger scale comes from a variety of counties. In Elizabethan Buckinghamshire, 80 percent of people who deposed in courts had moved at least once. In the Weald of Kent and Sussex between 1580 and 1649, 77 percent of people had moved at least once.[7] But rates of migration varied regionally. David Souden has determined that in seventeenth-century Devon, almost half of all witnesses in court attested that they still resided in the parish of their birth. In Somerset and Wiltshire, that figure dropped to one-third of the men and one-quarter of the women; in Oxfordshire and Leicestershire, the numbers were lower still, and finally in Norfolk fewer than 20 percent of the men and 15 percent of the women lived in the parish of their birth.[8] These numbers attest to a great range in the extent of movement and to the gendered experience of migration. Yet overall, even in the most geographically entrenched county, movement was the norm for well over half the population. Much of this movement occurred within small areas, within the region of the hundred, or across county lines, but still to or from adjacent parishes.

Examples of such local movement abound among the travelers to New England in 1635, as the experiences of two men—a farmer and an innkeeper—attest. The husbandman Simon Stone emigrated with his wife and five children to Watertown, Massachusetts, in 1635. Stone had married Joan Clarke in Great Bromley, Essex, on August 5, 1616. Stone himself was of Great Bromley, where his father David was a yeoman. Three of the Stones' children were baptized there between June of 1617 and October of 1620. After that year, the family disappeared from sight, not to resurface again in the extant records until 1629, some ten miles away in Boxted, Essex, when Simon Stone was assessed 20s. in lands for the county lay subsidy.[9]

Robert Long was of a similar age to Stone. Long, his wife, and ten children were certified in the London port register with their servant Luce Mercer from the town of Dunstable, in Bedfordshire. Dunstable lies on the main London-Chester Highway, just thirty-two miles outside London. Before they lived in Dunstable, however, the Longs dwelled twenty miles away in St. Albans, Hertfordshire, where Robert and Sara Long were married at the great abbey in 1614. Six of their children were baptized there between the years 1615 and 1629. Robert Long, a tavern keeper in St. Albans, obviously acquired a certain degree of status, for in 1618, he was appointed constable.[10]

By 1630, however, the Long family had relocated to Dunstable,[11] where Robert's first wife, Sara, died in 1631.[12] In Dunstable, Robert Long was still an innkeeper. Both St. Albans and Dunstable were major stopping places for travelers on the London-Chester road: Watling Street, the highway, ran through Dunstable and St. Albans, and was "one of the chief thoroughfares in the kingdom."[13] As a result of this constant traffic, both towns had many inns, whose growth was fostered by the passing of travelers. It is not clear exactly why Long moved from St. Albans, but his choice of Dunstable as his new home enabled him to continue his career as an innkeeper. Despite his new residence in Dunstable, Long maintained his ties to St. Albans, for in 1633 he apprenticed his son Robert to Fromabove Done of St. Albans, a dyer.[14] In 1635, however, Robert Long, Jr., broke his apprenticeship to accompany his family on yet another move, this time to Charlestown, Massachusetts.[15]

One segment of the English population was accustomed to vast migrations across England. Ministers and their families traveled from one end of the country to the other to find employment and, among this particular population, to evade authorities. Of the ministers in this cohort, Peter Bulkeley demonstrated the least mobility. The son of a parish minister, he was born in Odell, Bedfordshire, was educated at Cambridge, and returned to Odell to succeed his father as rector there.[16] Other clerics were far more active in their English peregrinations. Thomas Shepard was born in Northamptonshire, educated at Cambridge, employed in Essex, married in Yorkshire, settled briefly in Northumberland, and hid from authorities in London.[17] By the time he set sail from London in 1635, Thomas Shepard had traversed much of the country's north-south axis.

For magnitude and celerity of internal migration, however, Shepard met his match in Hugh Peter. Peter was born in Foy, Cornwall, and went to Cambridge University at the age of 14, where he stayed for eight years. He moved from Cambridge to London, and then to Essex, where he preached and married, before returning to London "to ripen [his] studies." He was solicited by friends to preach and received a license to do so from the Bishop of London, where he preached at St. Sepulchre.[18] He had a falling out, however, with the Bishop, George Montaigne, in 1626: Montaigne took Peter into custody "for some undutiful and bold speeches" against the Queen.[19] Peter moved to Holland, where he served in Rotterdam until June of 1635. In that month he sneaked back to London from the Netherlands and secretly boarded a ship for New England.

In the new world Robert Long settled permanently in Charlestown, where he established himself again as an innkeeper; Thomas Shepard stayed put in Cambridge, Massachusetts, until his death; Peter Bulkeley moved once within Massachusetts to take up his position as the minister of Concord, although his son John returned to England; Bulkeley's fellow minister John Jones settled at Concord and then Fairfield, Connecticut, but his son John moved on to the island of Nevis; and Hugh Peter ultimately returned to England. These examples suggest that there was not necessarily a correlation between movement in old England and New England for single individuals, who might have moved around in England but then settled happily in one town in New England. But there was a correlation, among the population as a whole, in the propensity to move. As migration was the norm in old England, so was it the norm in New England.

What sharply distinguished mobility in New England from English patterns was the distance traveled and the onerous task of building new homes and clearing new fields. In England whole families rarely ventured long distances, and they lived in a world whose intense pressure on arable land offered few opportunities to learn how to clear densely wooded tracts. The Long family journeyed along the Watling road from St. Albans to Dunstable only some twenty miles and in this change was typical of those families who moved around from one settled parish to another.[20] In New England, the distances traveled were usually much longer and those who ventured from a newly settled town rarely had the opportunity to purchase a cleared parcel of land: instead, the laborious process of building a home and clearing land for planting started anew. There were also real hazards posed by moving to new territories. Even close to the centers of English settlement, the hazards of colonial life were vivid. Farther afield, new dangers presented themselves. The trek itself through New England was physically daunting as newcomers adapted Indian travel paths to their needs or constructed new roads and bridges. Circumstances in new towns were equally uncertain. Those who removed to Connecticut in 1635 found themselves at war within one year of their arrival. Lion Gardiner, an engineer sent to erect a fort at Saybrook, was an officer in the Pequot War, and at least fourteen other men in this cohort served as soldiers, a handful of them in the infamous massacre of Pequot men, women, and children at Mystic.[21] Gardiner was able to rescue the two daughters of another passenger, William Swaine, who had been taken by the Pequots.[22] The risks, then, of secondary migrations across New England were myriad, yet time and again residents of the colonies took those risks in long and perilous journeys to land wrested from indigenous control. The long and arduous overseas voyage itself clearly heralded the new manifestation of migration patterns. Once in the colonies, New Englanders moved hundreds of miles to new homes, from Lynn to Long Island, from Cambridge to Hartford, from Roxbury to New Haven, from Portsmouth to Monmouth.

Table 6.1 describes the frequency of removal among the people who reached London in 1635 and then boarded ships for New England. Not included here are the temporary way stations that offered hospitality to new

Table 6.1. Geographic mobility of 1635 cohort within New England (number of moves)

No. moves[a]	No. people	%
D. at sea	1[b]	
0	340	36.2
1	338	36.0
2	154	16.4
3	66	7.0
4	28	3.0
5	10	1.1
6	2	.2
Total	939[c]	99.9

a. Zero moves means that the traveler settled in the town of first arrival, one means that the traveler moved to a second town, and so on. The town of first arrival is not necessarily a port town. All newcomers had to endure a waiting period when they first reached Massachusetts: many nestled temporarily in Boston and Charlestown.

b. One child, Thomas Jones, died at sea.

c. The total is derived from the total number of arrivals for whom there is complete information (434) and for whom there is some information (505). "Complete" here means simply that date and place of death are known.

arrivals in port towns. Some new arrivals sojourned with friends, some boarded temporarily with strangers, and others nestled in wigwams and other temporary shelters erected to accommodate newcomers. I have calculated only those towns where a settler actually maintained a residence and practiced a trade, however transitory that residence proved to be. Some people moved after only brief stays. Clement Chaplin, for example, first settled in Cambridge. He was immediately appointed a selectman in 1635, an office indicating some commitment to the town, but a year later he was in Connecticut.[23] Chaplin's migration to a second town was typical of most residents of the New England colonies: just over one-third of the passengers in this cohort moved once in New England, out of their first home. In fact, given the incomplete information available for many colonists, one third is the upper limit on persistence: for many of these people, there is no information beyond the town of first planting, and whether the settlers died or moved on is unknown. This table underestimates mobility by assuming that when an individual no longer appears in extant records, he or she stayed in the last known town.

Just over one-third of passengers who reached New England from London in 1635 stayed in their first town of settlement. The majority of travelers, then, moved on, most only once more, but a significant minority moved more frequently. Within single families there were divergences. Married daughters were more likely to move than their parents or brothers. Hester Ballard, for example, reached New England at the age of two. She settled with her parents in Lynn. Although her parents never moved from Lynn, Hester married a Lynn man and removed first to Pawtucket, then to Providence. Likewise, Mary Jostlin, who settled in Hingham with her parents and four siblings when she was a toddler, removed in 1654 with her family to Lancaster. Whereas her parents remained in Lancaster, Mary married and lived in Dorchester and Milton.

Other residents, the "frequent flyers" of early New England, greatly exceeded the average of two moves. One such man, Thomas Blackly (or Blatchly) distinguished himself with his mobility. He left London at the age of 20. Where he settled first is not known, but by 1637 when he served in the Pequot War he was in Hartford. By 1645 he lived in New Haven. Blackly's subsequent migration to Newark in 1665 might have been a response to the Half-Way Covenant of 1662, which sufficiently distressed many members of New Haven churches that they moved to New Jersey, where they could practice traditional (restrictive) church admissions. He was back in Hartford by 1670, when the Court granted him sixty acres, but the next year he was granted liberty to depart. He did not stray far: he was a deputy for Branford, Connecticut, in 1672 and was still in Branford as late as March of 1674. Presumably he then traveled to Boston, where he died later that year, leaving estates in both Boston and Connecticut, and having dwelled in at least four different colonies.[24]

Blackly's transplantations suggest the extent to which residents of New England traveled among the different adjacent colonies. Tables 6.2 and 6.3 depict the ways in which colonists dispersed themselves not only within Massachusetts but also throughout New England and even farther afield. As in Table 6.1, only colonies of actual residence are counted here. Table 6.2 describes the distribution of the 1635 settlers when they first reached the colonies. For 939 of the 1,169 passengers who left London, the town of settlement within two years of arrival is known. For 118 of the 939, the very first town is unknown; however, I have found a town of settlement within two years of arrival. Most of these 118, I suspect, lived in Massachusetts.

Although most colonists first settled in Massachusetts, not all did. Puritan New England in 1635 contained alternatives recognized by astute travelers, and these migrants chose places of settlement thoughtfully and knowledgeably. Published promotional literature available for travelers distinguished

Table 6.2. Initial colony of settlement (1635 cohort)

Colony	N	%
Massachusetts	743	79.1
Maine	14	1.5
New Hampshire (Dover)	1	.1
Plymouth	41	4.4
Connecticut	22	2.3
Unknown[a]	118	12.5
Total	939	99.9

Sources for Tables 6.2 and 6.3: James Savage, *A Genealogical Dictionary of the First Settlers of New England,* 4 volumes (Boston, 1860–1862); Charles Edward Banks, *Topographical Dictionary of 2885 English Emigrants to New England, 1620–1650,* ed. Elijah Ellsworth Brownell (Baltimore: Genealogical Publishing Company, 1937, 1969); Charles Henry Pope, *The Pioneers of Massachusetts* (Baltimore: Genealogical Publishing Company, 1900, 1965); published colony and town records; and various genealogical sources.

a. Unknown is a category of people for whom place of settlement soon after 1635 is known, but not necessarily the original town. Those who settled in Concord or Dedham, for example, were obviously not there in 1635 before the towns were settled, but they were there soon after.

between different New England towns. William Wood's *New England's Prospect,* published in London in 1634, offered a compendium of information about particular towns. Wood helpfully informed potential planters that Dorchester was "the greatest Towne in New England," while in Roxbury the residents were "all very rich," and Newtown (Cambridge) boasted a huge common pasture and "many handsome contrived streets."[25] Particularly fortunate in 1635 were those travelers on the *Hopewell* who accompanied Wood on his return to Lynn from London and could profit from his experience.

Initially these choices of settlement were made primarily among different Massachusetts towns. Only 7 percent of the London cohort settled out of the Bay Colony on their arrival in New England. Within a few years, however, these figures altered significantly as people who had first settled in Massachusetts moved on to other colonies (Table 6.3). Whereas 61 percent of the London cohort are known to have remained in the Bay Colony, 39 percent chose to leave. Table 6.3 echoes various dramas of New England's first decade of settlement. The movement of people into Rhode Island, for example, reflects the enforced exodus of Antinomians and their families. Population dispersal into Connecticut and Long Island stemmed from a combination of religious and economic factors. The center of English population shifted from the Atlantic coast of Massachusetts as the population moved south into

Table 6.3. Migration out of Massachusetts Bay by 1635 travelers who had settled first in Massachusetts

| | Second colony or region | | | | | | | |
First colony	Massachusetts	Plymouth	Conn.	New Haven	New Hampshire	R.I.	Long Island	Other[a]
Massachusetts (743)	486	69	52	28	8	30	24	46
Unknown (118)	44	7	37	11	10	6	0	3
Total	530	76	89	39	18	36	24	49

a. This category includes those who returned to England or moved to the West Indies and the Chesapeake. Some, such as William Vassall, who moved outside the region did so in third or fourth migrations, so they are not included in this category.

Rhode Island and southwest into Connecticut and New Haven, clinging to the coastline and to the banks of the Connecticut River (Figure 11).

For all its frequency, migration within New England seemed to some contemporaries to threaten the puritan experiment and to signal a covetousness and dissatisfaction at odds with the founders' harmonious visions. Edward Johnson was harsh indeed in his record of the first removal from Newtown to Hartford. The people of Cambridge, he noted, "seeing that tillage went but little on, Resolved to remove." Johnson chastised those preoccupied by "thoughts of removing" for their criticism of the soil around them and remarked cuttingly that "they only waited now for people of stronger Faith than themselves" to buy their property.[26]

As Johnson observed, there were some common reasons for removing. Scarcity of land in conjunction with family size, occupational opportunity, and religious discontent were three major reasons for migration in New England. Many people moved because of economic and occupational considerations. Poor planting soil in an economy almost entirely dependent on farming for subsistence, for example, dictated both sparse settlements and repeated movement. The Plymouth colony, with its sandy soil and scrub trees, was particularly plagued by frequent removals. William Bradford lamented there "the straightnes and barrenes" of the town of Plymouth. The problem was so severe that at one point in 1644, the Plymouth church itself considered removing as a body rather than suffer such a depleted membership.[27]

In other cases it was not the quality of the soil but rather its quantity that forced people to move on. The migration of hundreds of Massachusetts Bay residents to Connecticut in 1635 and 1636 was prompted in part by per-

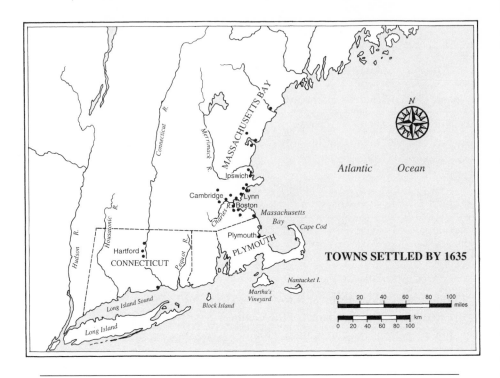

Figure 11. English settlement patterns in New England through 1650

ceived land shortages in increasingly crowded first-generation towns. Certainly this was how the 1635 traveler William Hubbard recorded the removals. He noted that when the towns of Watertown and Roxbury first petitioned the General Court in 1635 for permission to remove, "the occasion of their desire . . . was for that all the towns in the Bay began to be much straitened by their own nearness one to another, and their cattle being so increased, together with the addition of many families."[28] This request, which was made before many of the London cohort had landed in Massachusetts, boded ill for newly arrived families seeking land in some of the more congested towns. Men who were farmers and who instructed their children in husbandry especially needed land in order to provide for their sons and daughters. It was the pressure of land constraints, for example, that may have prompted the removal of the eight-member Burchard family from Roxbury to Hartford, or the seven Kilbournes to Wethersfield, or the seven Marvins to Hartford, or seven of the eight Prestons to New Haven. The largest families in the 1635 cohort were disproportionately likely to move from towns that were already settled in 1635, when they had the chance to develop newly opened areas.

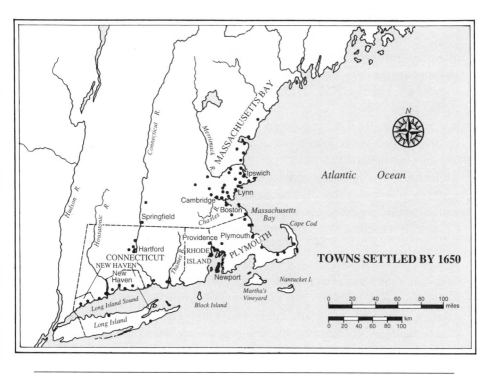

Figure 11. Continued

Other families sacrificed proximity for land. The family of Thomas Lord, with seven children, moved once from Cambridge to Hartford, Connecticut, in 1636. With one exception, the Lord children moved within the Hartford area to Wethersfield, Stonington, and Saybrook, but the entire family chose not to relocate so as to ensure property for the second generation in adjacent lots. Indeed, one of the Lord sons removed himself to Virginia, where he achieved prominence as a county justice.

Family size alone, however, was not the sole determinant of migration. Occupation mattered as well. Robert Long, an innkeeper, had greater flexibility than a farmer had. Long's family numbered thirteen when he reached New England with his wife, ten children, and one servant. The Longs continued to have more children in Charlestown, but the family did not move on from that town. Right after his arrival in Charlestown, Long received license to keep a "house of entertainment."[29] Furthermore, his oldest son, Robert, had been apprenticed to a dyer in England. Long clearly did not expect his children to adopt farming as a vocation in the new world, and he was certainly ill qualified to train them in husbandry. Likewise, Richard Hollingsworth reached Salem with eleven dependents and settled in permanently. Hollingsworth was a shipbuilder, and his children were engaged in various maritime ventures. Turning their backs to the land altogether, the Hollingsworths looked to the sea for their maintenance.

Removals were generally couched in terms of inadequate land and opportunity, but clearly the religious conflicts that permeated this region shaped patterns of migration. The decentralized establishment of New England towns, in which town polities varied as greatly as did forms of congregational worship, guaranteed that not all people would find all towns to their liking. Although New Englanders could not shop in a free marketplace of ideas, they could shop for residences. And so they did, voting with their feet with a speed and vigor that dismayed observers. Such religious disputes launched the settlement of Hartford. For Thomas Hooker, the clerical progenitor of the Connecticut migration, theological concerns clearly shaped his decision to relocate. Massachusetts was not big enough for both Hooker and John Cotton. With significant areas of disagreement between the two men, most notably Hooker's more restrictive ideas about baptism, it was expedient for Hooker to move on.[30] Many families in Cambridge followed Hooker to Connecticut, and it is not clear whether they too embraced Hooker's position or simply desired to follow their minister to his new home.

Shorter migrations across colonial borders could allow New Englanders to join a different ecclesiastical polity. Connecticut, unlike its neighbors Massachusetts and New Haven, did not require freemen to be church members. For those seeking greater religious liberty, Plymouth was more lenient than neighboring Massachusetts: the Plymouth colony did not enforce church attendance until 1651.[31] Rhode Island had no established church and promised greater religious tolerance to those who fled to her borders, although the radical Samuel Gorton tested even those limits.

Religious exiles continued to face conflict and removal. Although it was settled by religious refugees, Rhode Island did not promise ecclesiastical harmony. Providence was peopled by Baptists and separatists, many from Salem under the leadership of their exiled minister Roger Williams, while the island of Aquidneck, encompassing the communities of Portsmouth and Newport, was settled by Antinomian exiles from the Massachusetts colony. The Antinomians, whose ideas about faith and its practice were as diverse as one would expect given their notions of received truth, did not long remain together. Newport was founded by a group from Portsmouth that disagreed about matters of church discipline and moved to the western end of the island of Aquidneck, carrying the town records with them.[32] The Newport population desired a more organized church polity than did the group at Portsmouth, which seemed content with a vague religious structure. Portsmouth had neither a meeting house nor a minister in its early years, whereas Newport church members promptly hired a permanent minister, Robert Lenthall.[33] Of the 1635 cohort who moved with the Hutchinsonians to Aquidneck, fifteen settled in Portsmouth, and fifteen settled in Newport. Connecticut and New Haven towns also experienced religious conflict that necessitated the removal of substantial numbers of settlers. The town of Wethersfield and its church divisions spawned no fewer than six new towns in Connecticut, in New Haven, and on Long Island. Each new division followed a dispute in the church, and all disputes derived from an original conflict among the six founding members of the church, a three-year conflict so intensely divisive that men were sent from three colonies to try to resolve it.[34] Thus ecclesiastical conflicts in a single town, which were exported with its residents to other communities, caused the dispersal of Wethersfield residents throughout southern New England.

The configurations previously outlined—land, family size, religious concerns—are all general reasons why people moved in early New England. What prompted particular decisions for removal, and what kinds of towns compelled what types of people to move on? Table 6.4 compares the rates of mobility in and out of nine different first-generation towns in the Massachusetts colony.[35] Profiling only the passengers who sailed from London in 1635, the table depicts overall rates of removal by comparing the total number of departures with the total number of arrivals, yielding a percentage that measures the rate of mobility from a particular community for this one cohort of travelers.[36]

The range of overall rates of removal is large, from 18.8 percent for Boston to 72.5 percent for Watertown, reflecting both the different economic opportunities and congregational options available in local communities and the overall tendency toward high rates of migration. Boston was clearly atypical, with fewer than 20 percent of the 1635 residents moving on and fifty-one people actually moving into the town after 1640. Ipswich and Charlestown are the next comparable towns to Boston. At the other extreme was the town of Watertown: almost three-quarters of the people in the 1635 cohort moved away. Five of the towns shared rates of removal between 60 and 66 percent. Although these statistics are based entirely on the activities of those passengers who reached New England from London in 1635, the numbers generated and displayed here do not seem inconsistent with the New England population as a whole. A study of the town of Charlestown found that fully half of those who settled in the community during the first decade eventually moved on, a proportion that closely matches the rate of removal of 51.3 percent for Charlestown for the 1635 cohort.[37]

The statistical comparison of New England towns in Table 6.4 directs

Table 6.4. Rates of removal from selected Massachusetts towns (1635 cohort)

Town	Total settlers in town in 1635 sample (N)	Total departures from town in 1635 sample (N)	Total departures (%)
Boston[a]	186	35	18.8 (2 returned)[b]
Ipswich	120	54	45.0 (2 returned)
Charlestown	80	41	51.3
Roxbury	58	35	60.3 (2 returned)
Dorchester	74	46	62.2
Cambridge	96	62	65.6 (2 returned)
Lynn	102	66	66.0 (4 returned)
Dedham	24	16	66.7
Watertown	69	50	72.5

a. Boston includes Braintree, Muddy River (Brookline), and Romney Marsh (Chelsea).
b. "Returned" here means returned to town in question after moving out.

inquiry into the local context of geographic mobility. Table 6.1 tells us that most people moved once: scrutiny of these selected towns in Table 6.4 helps understand who moved and why. There prove to be as many reasons for second migrations as there were variations in town polities in New England. Alienation from the church and insufficient land were the central causes. But the table also suggests why portions of the population stayed put, as two sizable cohorts did in Roxbury and Dorchester: there the success of family and parish transplantations from England encouraged people to remain in one town in New England. In such cases, transplantation enhanced geographic stability.

The removals from the town of Dedham are particularly intriguing because of the date of the town's founding in 1636. Only twenty-four people in the cohort settled there, a tiny number, yet it is a portion of the population worth considering particularly because of the opportunities available to them as town founders. The 1635 cohort had ample opportunity, for example, to gain land, yet Dedham lost sixteen out of its twenty-four original settlers in the 1635 cohort. Of the nine household heads in this group, eight had signed the town covenant, as had two adult sons.[38] Seven of these householders moved out of Dedham. Those few individuals in the 1635 cohort who moved to Dedham were women who married Dedham men. In fact, of those nineteen people who had arrived by 1640, only four, the Eaton family and Robert Onion, stayed in Dedham, making the actual rate of departure of town founders and their families 75 percent.[39]

There were many reasons why people should have remained. Of the original founders and their families, all but one person came from Watertown, so that the first settlers benefited from bonds of neighborliness that transcended their new experience in Dedham. As founders of the town, these families stood to share in all land divisions: at the very first town meetings, for example, Ralph Shepard, Philemon Dalton, Samuel Morse, and Joseph Morse received land.[40] If being there first counted in land acquisition, as it demonstrably did in seventeenth-century New England, these families should have been well positioned. What is striking, however, about the role of the ten covenant signers in this cohort is that although active in the town's secular affairs, they played only a modest role in Dedham's religious affairs. When the church was organized, eight men were charged to gather the church. None of the London cohort were selected for this process, although some of them were already church members in Watertown.[41] Dismissed to the church at Dedham, the former Watertown worshipers nonetheless took an active role in the organization of the Dedham church, as Philemon Dalton did when he challenged a neighbor's admission.[42] Given Dalton's concerns over the integrity of new church members, it is surprising that he was not selected to gather the church. The denial of religious status or recognition to the Dedham town covenant signers might have prompted their removal.

The town of Lynn shared Dedham's high removal rates, but for different reasons. Whereas for Dedham the surviving evidence intimates that the people who moved on were those shut out of the church, in Lynn the frequent removals of town inhabitants were not accompanied by acrimony. Instead, Lynn families moved out of necessity, returning to Lynn when subsequent opportunities allowed. Within ten years of Lynn's planting, six other towns had been founded by Lynn people, and in 1640 a seventh was settled.[43] Lack of land was the overriding concern—at least for some of the wealthier families in the town. Few early Lynn records have been located, but there is an extant land distribution list compiled in 1638. Table 6.5 lists the land holdings, occupations, family size, and removal of those residents who traveled in 1635 and settled in Lynn. Not included on this list are those families, such as the Almys, Freemans, Woods, and Geeres, who had already removed from the town to Sandwich by 1638.

The farms that these largest landholders maintained were of reasonable

Table 6.5. Landholding in Lynn, 1638 (1635 cohort)

Name	Acres	Occupation	Family	Moved?
Edward Howe	210	Farmer	5	d. 1639
Edward Farrington	200	Farmer/Miller	6	Yes
John Cooper	200	Farmer	5	Yes
John Wood	100		2	Yes
Henry Collins	90	Starchmaker/Farmer	5	
William Ballard	60		4	
Hugh Burt	60		5	
Christopher Foster	60	Farmer	5	Yes
Thomas Laighton	60		1	Yes
Thomas Marshall	40	Innkeeper	1	Yes[a]
Samuel Bennett	20	Carpenter	1	Yes
Jeremy Howe	20	Farmer	1	Yes
Ephraim Howe	10	Farmer	1	Yes
Edward Ireson	10		2	
Edmund Bridges	10	Blacksmith/Cobbler	1	Yes
Philip Kirtland, Jr.	10		1	Yes[a]

Source for acreage: Lynn book of land distribution, 1638, in Alonzo Lewis, *The History of Lynn, including Nahant* (Boston: S. N. Dickinson, 1844), pp. 103–105.
   a. Returned to Lynn.

size, but they moved from Lynn at the same rate as small landholders. Altogether eleven of these Lynn men moved on. The largest landholder in this cohort, Edward Howe, died in 1639, but his two sons, Ephraim and Jeremy, who in 1638 owned a modest thirty acres together and could reasonably have expected to farm their father's land, moved on to the New Haven colony by 1645 and started fresh. Edward Farrington and John Cooper, both with two hundred acres, moved to Southampton, Long Island, in 1640, as did Christopher Foster, who owned sixty acres. It was, in fact, some of the modest landowners in 1638 who stayed behind. What this seeming incongruity might suggest is marked deviation in expectations. The Farrington, Cooper, and Foster families were large; and with children to provide land for, these farming families might have anticipated that Lynn would not be able to ensure sufficient land in subsequent divisions for their children. The Howe brothers, for example, were the oldest sons in a large family. Their migration to New Haven ensured that the family land in Lynn would remain intact for their younger siblings.

Moreover, those men of more modest holdings who did stay in Lynn were not farmers by training. Instead, they devised strategies to succeed in a land-poor town. Henry Collins had been a starch maker in London. In Lynn he took up farming. In 1638 when Lynn petitioned the General Court for more land, Henry Collins received ninety acres. Collins obviously succeeded in Lynn: in the 1681 assessment of the town, he paid the third highest assessment out of forty men. His son Henry, however, was a carpenter.[44] This shift in occupation suggests the flexibility that families needed to remain together in crowded towns. Although historians have found similar occupational and familial decisions made in New England in later periods, New Englanders had to weigh family proximity with personal expectations in the region's very first decades of settlement. Those people who did move into the town were not farmers. Benjamin Keayne, who moved from Boston to Lynn in 1642, was, like his well-known father, Robert, a merchant who did not depend on the land for his support. And Benjamin eventually left Lynn for England.

What distinguished the Lynn removals was the distance that Lynn settlers traveled in their pursuit of new homes. In each incident of removal, Lynn residents moved out of the Bay Colony for new settlements in Plymouth or in distant Long Island. In all, twelve of the 1635 settlers in Lynn traveled on to Sandwich in 1637. But this was a short trip compared with the 1640 exodus for Long Island. In that year John Winthrop noted that the people of Lynn found themselves "straitened."[45] Forty families moved to Long Island.

Among these forty families were three who had traveled together in 1635 from three parishes in Newport Hundred in Buckinghamshire. Newport Hundred is in the western region of the county, about sixty miles from London. Five families altogether—the Griggs, Cooper, Farrington, Purrier, and Kirtland families—entered their names on the same day at the port of London and presented their licenses to travel. Sixteen of the group came from the parish of Olney: John and Wibroe Cooper with their three children, Edmond and Elizabeth Farrington with their four children, and William and Alice Purrier, with their three daughters. George and Alice Griggs with their four children came from the parish of Lavendon, and the brothers Philip and Nathaniel Kirtland were from Sherington. Olney and Lavendon are adjacent parishes on the River Ouse, and Sherington is nearby.[46]

Newport Hundred was a center of dissent in the 1630s: the parishes of Olney and Newport were particularly attractive to nonconformists, with people from communities like Sherington forsaking their own parish services to attend services elsewhere. The minister of Olney, Mr. Worcester, was presented for "seldom or never" coming to church "till the psalm be almost sung." In other words, Mr. Worcester ignored the Anglican liturgy preceding the sermon but came to church only to preach.[47] Seven parishioners at Olney were excommunicated in May of 1633, and then in August of 1633, three men of Sherington were presented for attending church at Olney and Newport.[48] The intensified enforcement of Laudian policies heralded by the 1634 visitations may have warned the worshipers away from the region.[49] Worcester himself emigrated to New England in 1639. The Buckinghamshire contingent may well have been sympathetic to Mr. Worcester's sentiments. In fact, Rose Kirtland, of Sherington, the mother of Philip and Nathaniel, was presented for nonconformity, and William Purrier joined Mr. Worcester in Salisbury, Massachusetts.

Perhaps in response to these hardships, the Farrington, Cooper, and Kirtland families left Newport Hundred in Buckinghamshire together in 1635. They settled first in Lynn and then traveled together again in this second removal to Long Island. They were soon joined in Long Island by the family of William Purrier, also of Buckinghamshire, who left his Massachusetts home in Salisbury and settled in Southold. Thus a second migration within New England reunited these English neighbors.[50] The Lynn exiles eventually relocated to Southampton on Long Island, where they retained strong ties with Lynn: four men in this Buckinghamshire group returned to their first New England home. What these returns to Lynn suggest is that town residents did not leave Lynn because of bitter divisions or painful quarrels, as was the case in so many removals in New England. Rather, people moved out of necessity and returned when opportunities elsewhere proved disappointing, prospects in Lynn improved, or old attachments to kin and friends supplanted other concerns.

If most of the travelers of 1635 moved out of these first-generation towns, who then were the people who remained behind? They tended to be men who had accumulated religious and civil offices, but these alone were not sufficient. Evidence for the towns of Roxbury and Dorchester suggests that those who remained behind enjoyed not only the high regard of their New England neighbors but also the proximity of old England family and friends. The London travelers who settled permanently in Roxbury found there a community similar in personnel to that in England. Roxbury's minister John Eliot was from Nazing in Essex. Many of the 1635 travelers were from Nazing and from the parishes of Ware and Great Amwell just over the Essex border in adjacent Hertfordshire. In 1635 twenty-one residents of Stanstead Abbot, Ware, and Amwell in Hertfordshire, and Nazing in Essex traveled on the *Hopewell:* twenty settled in Roxbury.[51] Of these twenty, almost all remained in Roxbury or did not move out of the town for several years. The only members of this group who left Roxbury were three women who married men in other towns and one man who moved to Dorchester after 1648. Thus, 75 percent of this selected group within the 1635 cohort remained in the town, compared with 39.7 percent of total arrivals in the 1635 cohort who stayed in Roxbury. Chain migration to New England played an important role in circumscribing behavior in the new world.

The Nazing group not only benefited from family connections with the leaders of the community but also established themselves instantly at the center of Roxbury affairs. Eight of the adults promptly joined the church, re-creating the community of old England, "where many of the church injoyed society together." Isaac Heath became a church elder. The minister John Eliot knew his parishioners well and was able to describe them lovingly in his church records. John Ruggles, he noted, was "a lively christian," while John's wife Barbara was commended as "a Godly Christian woman." When Barbara Ruggles died giving birth to her second child, John Eliot memorialized her and added that "the powr of the grace of Christ did much shine in her life & death."[52]

The Nazing travelers of 1635 soon acquired political status to rival Eliot's spiritual accolades: John Astwood and Isaac Heath were freemen by 1636, and John Ruggles, Lawrence Whittamore, and Giles Payson became freemen in 1637. Isaac Heath was a deputy to the General Court as early as 1636.[53] The Nazing men also supported huge households. Isaac Heath received 256 acres and had a household containing twenty-one people. Philip Eliot supported twenty-five people. Not all, however, were the "very rich" inhabitants whom William Wood had described in *New England's Prospect* (1634).[54] Giles Payson and John Ruggles supported far more modest households of two and three people, respectively, which in Ruggles's case was the exact size of his nuclear family.[55] But the Nazing community, or as Eliot called it, "the knot . . . of the Nazing Christians," was strong, and bonds of kinship and old English neighborhoods ensured the tenacity of the new community.[56] In Roxbury those people who, through family connections, good fortune, religious status, and economic advantages, were able to establish themselves at the center of community life, stayed put in rates disproportionate to persistence rates for the travelers of 1635 as a whole.

The two towns that stand out as anomalies in Table 6.4 are Boston and Ipswich. On the basis of statistics compiled about the experience of the 1635 travelers, Boston lost only 18.8 percent of its sampled population and unlike all the other sampled towns, actually attracted fifty-one people after 1641. Ipswich's population turnover comprised less than half the sampled population. It is possible that both towns were more selective in allowing people in and thus contained a population better able to accommodate themselves to local mores. The Boston town meeting, for example, decided in 1635 "that noe further allotments shalbe graunted unto any new comers, but such as may be likely to be received members of the Congregation." Residents needed permission, furthermore, to sell their plots or houses to newcomers.[57] This aspiration for homogeneity, however, remained increasingly unfulfilled as Boston became a town more concerned with the claims of Caesar than of God.

More important to persistence rates than Boston's vaguely enacted preselection process was the mercantile orientation of both towns. Boston and Ipswich were communities in which artisans who migrated from England could continue to practice their trades. Both were commercial communities in an agrarian new world setting. As early as 1634, before the London travelers had arrived in New England, Boston proper lacked sufficient woods and meadows.[58] Boston grew quickly: its population doubled from 1635 to 1638, until it passed 2,000 people by 1640, by which year the 1635 cohort comprised almost 7 percent of the town's population.[59] The residents of this awkwardly configured village with its strangled neck who wished to farm possessed land in remote Mount Wollaston (Braintree) or Muddy River (Brookline). Farmers often moved to live on their land, leaving the peninsula in the hands of tradesmen and merchants.

Although Boston did not offer farmers convenient access to their land, it did provide craftsmen with the rare opportunity to practice their vocations. Darrett Rutman has described Boston as poorly suited to John Winthrop's model for Massachusetts. Winthrop's communal ideal, Rutman asserted, was consumed in Boston by "the acquisitive instincts of the contemporary Englishman."[60] Certainly fortunes could be made in Boston, as the success of merchants attested. More importantly, however, a tradesman could continue to work at his craft without shifting to husbandry as craftsmen elsewhere in New England were obliged to do. Artisans who migrated to Boston continued to be identified in town and colony records by a single occupation, in contrast to those men in other New England towns who were described by a variety of occupations. Philip Drinker of Charlestown, for example, was a potter who also ran a ferry. Nicholas Davis, also of Charlestown, was a tailor, merchant, and tavernkeeper; and the carpenter John Gould also farmed.[61] Henry Tibbetts of Dover, New Hampshire, performed such diverse crafts as shoemaking, lumbering, and farming.

In contrast, even if they supplemented their artisan work with farming, Bostonians continued to identify themselves primarily as craftsmen. Tradesmen in Boston quickly organized themselves into guilds, and the Massachusetts General Court records are replete with petitions from tradesmen seeking special privileges. In 1648 Robert Turner and eight other Boston shoemakers petitioned the General Court for permission to create a company "as wee were in our native country" to maintain standards of craftsmanship. Edward Rainsford and the other coopers of Boston and Charlestown lagged behind the assertive shoemakers; but they finally petitioned the General Court in 1668 to complain that unqualified people were making casks, and they sought permission to form a society and regulate themselves.[62] Of twenty-four Bostonians from the 1635 cohort for whom occupation is known, only two were identified as husbandman. One of these men, the tailor Robert Mere, carried on a trade and farmed extensively. The others were exclusively tradesmen.[63] Those tradesmen identified with other crafts were in overlapping trades: George Burdin, for example, was both a tanner and a shoemaker, a combination that was appropriate for one whose working material was leather.

The tradesmen of Boston diversified their economic interests in two main areas: intercolonial and transatlantic trade, and investment in local industries. The commercial success of the tailor Thomas Savage and the cooper Edward Rainsford signals such economic breadth. Bostonians of all occupations invested in what little industry existed in the young colony. The joiner Ralph Mason, the shoemaker George Burdin, and the merchant/tailor Thomas Savage all invested in the ironworks.[64] Tradesmen also assumed important town offices. Bostonians were able to influence local politics without being church members, because Boston allowed non–church members to participate in town affairs. Furthermore, artisans were able to translate their professional skills into civic responsibilities. William Courser, a shoemaker, served for several years as the town's leather sealer, and the glover and merchant Thomas Buttolph was the clerk of the market.[65]

Like Boston, Ipswich adopted an aggressive stance to encourage the town's nonagrarian industries, especially those oriented toward the sea. The town decreed in 1641 that a neck of land should be set aside "for the advancement of fishing." Every boat that went to the neck was to have sufficient room to fish, and all newcomers were to receive equal privileges.[66] Merchants were readily granted permission to build warehouses and wharfs, as William Payne discovered in 1641.[67] In that same year, the town established a committee for furthering trade, on which the London passenger John Tuttle served.[68]

For new arrivals in 1635, Ipswich proved an extremely attractive place. Land was abundant, and people were relatively few. William Wood declared in 1634 that it was "one of the most spacious places for a plantation . . . In a word, it is the best place but one, which is Merrimacke." Wood noted that there was room in these two plantations for twice as many people as lived in New England as a whole.[69] Indeed, his perception was apparently accurate, for the residents who reached Ipswich in 1635 acquired large holdings of land. In a community where the average size of land grants was ninety-seven acres, all of the people who reached the town from London in 1635 flourished with larger than average holdings.[70]

Land, however, was not the only important source of wealth in Ipswich. Both Ipswich and Boston offered opportunities to amass considerable fortunes in a variety of ways. Merchants were attracted to the commercial towns: Robert Keayne moved from Lynn to Boston, for example, soon after he had reached Massachusetts. William Payne and William Hubbard moved as well, from Ipswich to Boston. Even tradesmen could acquire sizable estates. Compared with the average estate value of all known estates for travelers to New England in 1635, which was £399.9s.4d., the wealth amassed by Boston residents is impressive.[71] The average for Boston decedents was £950.7s.6d., whereas the average for Ipswich was £548.4s.6d. (Table 6.6).

Other well-heeled merchants for whom inventories are not available include John Tuttle, Jeremy Belcher, and William Hubbard, all of Ipswich. Jeremy Belcher noted in 1658, for example, that he had recently suffered great financial losses, including a £400 loss when he was last in England.[72] Likewise, John Tuttle, who reached New England with a large estate, had left Ipswich for Ireland in the 1650s, and his estate is not included here. Only two other inventoried first-generation adults could match these wealthy Boston and Ipswich men for estate size: John Proctor, Sr., first of Ipswich and later of Salem, who left £1,200 in 1672, and the Connecticut resident Thomas Bull, whose estate was worth £1,284.11s. in 1684.

In explaining the uniqueness of Boston and Ipswich, some historians have rightly made much of the regional origins of some of the influential settlers of the two towns.[73] It is certainly significant, for example, that some of the settlers of Boston were Londoners, true metropolitans, who lived together in Boston in patterns similar to those they had displayed in London and who remained oriented toward that city. In fact, the 1635 travelers who settled in Boston were disproportionately likely to come from London. Of 120 known places of origin for Boston residents for the 1635 cohort, thirty-eight, or almost one-third, were from the greater London area. Merchants who were well connected in London made Boston their home: Thomas Savage, Robert Keayne, and Robert Nanney all conducted Atlantic trade from a Boston base and shared the advantage of connections to London creditors and relations.[74] Both Keayne and Thomas Buttolph, a glover, who were from London Cornhill, lived in Boston's Cornhill. Boston enabled merchants to reaffirm ties they had known in London and to draw on their Atlantic trade connections to expand elsewhere. Nanney and Rainsford owned property in Barbados, whereas the Ipswich and Boston resident William Paine, who was particularly active in starting the Saugus ironworks, had trade connections in Virginia.[75] In the case of Ipswich and Boston, there were clear advantages for those who

Table 6.6. Total estate value of Ipswich and Boston decedents (1635 cohort)

Name	Total estate value (£.s.d)	Date	Town	Occupation
William Adams	218.00.00	1659	Ipswich	
Thomas Blackly	218.00.00	1674	Boston	
Ann Buttolph	115.19.7	1680	Boston	Widow
Thomas Buttolph	1,598.18.10	1667	Boston	Glover
Thomas Crosby	1,091.16.00	1702	Boston	Minister
Robert Day	478.10.00	1683	Ipswich	
Simon Eires	577.05.00	1658	Boston	Surgeon
George Giddings	1,021.12.06	1676	Ipswich	Merchant
Jarvice Gold	66.08.07	1656	Boston	Shoemaker
Martha Haffell	349.16.6	1668	Ipswich	Widow
Richard Hubbard	1,457.05.00	1681	Ipswich	
Robert Keayne	2,427	1657	Boston	Merchant
Edward Loomis	119.15.9	1682	Ipswich	Weaver
Robert Mere	349.00.00	1667	Boston	Tailor
Robert Nanney	1,089.14.4	1663	Boston	Merchant
William Payne	4,239.11.05	1660	Ipswich	Merchant
Allen Perley	320.2.6	1675	Ipswich	Farmer
Edward Rainsford	1,638.07.11	1680	Boston	Merchant
Christopher Stanley	349.16s	1646	Boston	Tailor
William Wild	225.14.6	1662	Ipswich	Carpenter

Average estates:
Boston	950.7.6			
Ipswich	548.4.6			
All known decedents	399.9.4			

Sources: Suffolk County Wills: Abstracts of the Earliest Wills upon Record in the County of Suffolk, Massachusetts (Baltimore: Genealogical Publishing Company, Inc., 1984); and *The Probate Records of Essex County, Massachusetts*, 2 volumes (Salem: The Essex Institute, 1916). All values have been deflated.

elected to stay put. Even so, almost half of Ipswich residents moved on, and Boston was clearly an anomaly in the sedentary patterns of its residents and in the ability of the town to attract newcomers with its commercial opportunities.

Thus New Englanders moved on and in some instances profited from their mobility.[76] Demonstrating the frequency of migration is one thing, however: delineating its significance in New England society is another. The effects of high geographic mobility were varied. For individuals the process of removal brought its own confusion in administrative detail, sentimental attachment, and church attendance. People in a new town frequently maintained contacts with their old community, especially if the towns were adjacent. The surgeon Simon Eires, for example, moved from Watertown to Boston in the 1640s. Eires had been appointed clerk of the writs for Watertown, but "being generally at Boston," Eires was replaced by another man in 1645.[77] Those who removed to distant towns often retained land in their former communities. Edmund Munnings continued to own land in Dorchester after he had returned to England. Nicholas Davis owned land in Charlestown well after he had departed for Rhode Island. In 1642, four years after he had left Charlestown, he sold off six acres to John Fisenden of Cambridge.[78] Likewise, many responsibilities followed people after they had left. Richard Saltonstall, Jr., was appointed executor of the estate of John Dillingham, but in his absence in England, his duties were discharged, and others appointed in his stead.[79]

For local institutions the implications of removal were far more profound. Odd intimations survive about the legal inconvenience posed by removal. For example, in Massachusetts in 1644, only five out of twelve accused men were available for trial in the Mary Latham–James Britton adultery case. The other seven men had already departed the jurisdiction. Thus this celebrated adultery trial revealed a persistence rate of 42 percent, not different from those rates revealed for the 1635 cohort who settled in first-generation towns.[80] The difficulty posed to legal bodies when important individuals were absent is not hard to appreciate. Likewise, it is easy to imagine how other institutions were defined by the heavy turnover in leadership. It was not only the destitute who moved on, but also wealthy people with lofty expectations, recalcitrant divines, and simple people of steadfast faith. Towns lost both their best and brightest and their most meek and lowly in the regular removals throughout New England.[81]

Much of the impact of these removals has been obscured in the community studies that remain such a popular and important genre in the history of early New England. Many New Englanders, however, could not be identified with any single community over the course of their lives. Thomas Hooker fled

Cambridge; and John Winthrop, who tried to define Boston even before he settled there, was dismayed by the unintended direction his town took, and he labored to redefine Boston's increasingly wayward path from grace to commerce. The repeated removals through New England were not always affirmations of community but rather were symptoms of the profound disarray in early puritan efforts to translate sacred visions into political entities.

This disarray, signaled in the migrations of men and women who crisscrossed the region alone, with friends, or in search of family, brought together diverse people in towns newly created out of the remnants of fractured or overcrowded first-generation communities. Although in some cases one region of England might retain a political or religious hegemony in new towns, as in the case of Roxbury, this was more often the exception. Mixtures of people and rates of removal demonstrate the dynamic nature of life in early New England. And there was no clear predictor of settlement based on place of origin in England, as the dispersal of the five families from Newport Hundred, in Buckinghamshire, to Lynn, Ipswich, and Boston reveals.

High mobility, finally, underscores the resemblance of New England to old England. Comparisons of persistence rates in different communities make this point clear, although such comparisons are fraught with difficulty, given the variant sizes of towns, parishes, and counties, and the fundamental difficulty of tracking who died, who moved, and who vanished from the records. The most mobile towns in New England, like Charlestown or Lynn, prove in such comparisons to resemble London's persistence rates more than those of any other place in the English Atlantic world. These puritans in New England may have been seeking a certain kind of ecclesiastical order, but they hardly shed the old patterns of mobility. Table 6.7 compares persistence rates for different Virginia counties and old and New England communities.

A table that essays to compare persistence rates in places with widely varied sources almost begs criticism. Admittedly, comparisons are fraught with difficulty. The samples employed are different for each town or parish. First and foremost, my study includes all people, not just men, not just adult taxpayers, and not just householders. Studies of only householders increase rates of persistence. Moreover, the increased mobility of women (who moved additionally for marriage) is part of this study, as is the mobility of children as they left home for apprenticeships, marriage, or education. But to say that such an approach *distorts* New Englanders' experiences is to suggest that the study of *all* New Englanders, whether servants or aged relations, is less accurate than a study of male householders and ratepayers. Second, the best studies of persistence are those for parishes that possess good records for demographic history in general and family reconstitution in particular.[82] Ideally, one should be able to trace particular individuals within towns or par-

Table 6.7. Comparative persistence rates

Location	Date	Population sampled	N	Persistence rate (%)
England				
Clayworth, Notting.	1676–1688	Householders	?	50
Cogenhoe, Northnts.	1618–1628	Householders	187	50
London				
Deponents	1580–1640			14–22
St. Christopher[a]	1580–1590	Householders	58	52; 33
St. Bartholomew	1635–1645	Householders	76	55; 33
St. Margaret	1642–1652	Householders	125	50; 30
Virginia				
Accomack-Northampton,Va.	1646–1655	Householders	?	53–57
Lancaster County,Va.	1669–1679	Householders	?	39
Surry County, Va.	1668–1678	Householders	?	46
New England				
Windsor, Conn.	1676–1686	Male taxpayers	165	57
Dedham, Mass.	1648–1660	Adult males	98	52
Rowley, Mass.	1643–1653	Householders	?	59
Boston, Mass.	1635–1660	All 1635 passengers	186	82
Ipswich, Mass.	1635–1660	All 1635 passengers	120	55
Charlestown, Mass.	1635–1660	All 1635 passengers	80	49
Roxbury, Mass.	1635–1660	All 1635 passengers	58	40
Dorchester, Mass.	1635–1660	All 1635 passengers	74	38
Cambridge, Mass.	1635–1660	All 1635 passengers	96	35
Lynn, Mass.	1635–1660	All 1635 passengers	102	34
Dedham, Mass.	1635–1660	All 1635 passengers	24	33
Watertown, Mass.	1635–1660	All 1635 passengers	69	27

Sources: James P. Horn, "Migration in the Chesapeake," in Thad W. Tate and David L. Ammerman, eds., *The Chesapeake in the Seventeenth Century: Essays on Anglo-American Society and Politics* (Chapel Hill: University of North Carolina Press, 1979), p. 195; Roger Finlay, *Population and Metropolis: The Demography of London 1580–1650* (Cambridge: Cambridge University Press, 1981), pp. 46–47; Laura Auwers Bissell, "From One Generation to Another: Mobility in Seventeenth-Century Windsor, Connecticut," *WMQ* 31 (1974), p. 102; Table 6.4, earlier.

a. The first measurements for St. Christopher le Stocks, St. Bartholomew by the Exchange, and St. Margaret Lothbury, all London parishes, depict the percentage of householders who were still present five years after the date depicted; the second percentage denotes those still present ten years after the starting date.

ishes. The towns employed in this study of the London travelers do not contain such records. Nor, indeed, do the Virginia counties highlighted earlier contain comparable records. My study is of particular individuals within one town at one point in their lives; others of these studies are of the people of a town. I do not know what the overall persistence rates for all inhabitants of the nine towns that I profiled are because, as noted before, the records do not permit such analysis, especially for the first decade of settlement. Therefore, these comparisons are made under less than ideal conditions. Yet the comparisons revealed in this table are nonetheless suggestive. The overall thrust of this table is that half of all people commonly moved out of their first towns of settlement, just as they did in England. Moreover, the London cohort demonstrated rates of persistence in Massachusetts far lower than those found in studies of contemporary Windsor, Dedham, and Rowley. A full picture of migration by men and women over the life cycle enhances rates of migration in the same way that studies of householders, taxpayers, and landowners tend to emphasize persistence. Thus such puritan order as was created in New England did not lie in the geographic stability of church adherents, and whatever the puritans rejected about English culture, it was not the endemic patterns of migration that demarcated points in the life cycle as fully as did sacraments and hiring fairs.

It should be no surprise that responses to adversity molded in old England continued to dictate movement in New England. Once we appreciate migration as normative, the social or political significance of migration recedes.[83] Migration neither heralded a new outlook nor rejected one: migration was both the humdrum consequence of the most homely actions and the painful consequence of religious or economic strains. Like old Englanders, New Englanders transplanted themselves throughout their life cycles for any number of reasons, although they clearly tended to move greater distances and to undertake grueling and dangerous journeys. The consequences for individuals, who escaped religious difficulties or economic strains, who joined family while bidding farewell to friends, were many and varied. But the consequence for the region lay in the enduring familial and affectionate connections that New Englanders created and maintained, not only to their kin in old England but within New England itself. The newest towns in the region, although often geographically remote, were hybrid communities that were formed by second and third migrations by people from many places in both old and New England. New England towns were not isolated, for all their unusual opportunities for religious and political autonomy. The same process of migration that separated people from friends by thousands of miles across the Atlantic served within New England to tie the region's new and precarious settlements together.

7 | *Migration and the Atlantic World*

The English men and women who settled optimistically in Surinam between 1652 and 1666 confronted the same challenges that had thwarted English attempts to plant the region since the late sixteenth century. A harsh disease environment ravaged colony after colony, at one point reducing the number of men able to bear arms from 1,500 to 500 in the space of a single year.[1] Five earlier settlements had failed altogether.[2] But this particular effort met with greater initial success. Promises of freedom of worship accompanied indications of modest economic stability. The colony's chief town, Torarica, boasted one hundred houses and a chapel, with some five hundred plantations extending thirty leagues upriver by 1667.[3] What curtailed this auspicious start was the Dutch, who in the Treaty of Breda gained the South American colony in a seemingly advantageous swap for New Netherland. By 1668 the Dutch had assumed control of the colony, and English planters suffered legal and economic disadvantages under new Dutch rulers who essayed to drive the English away. One English woman detailed these problems in a letter in 1674. Bathsua Scott, a daughter of the 1635 traveler and minister John Oxenbridge, wrote this letter from Boston, where she had joined her father after fleeing Surinam by way of Barbados. Scott had left her husband in Surinam, where he had been confined by the Dutch and saw his plantation ruined. He was, reported James Banister, "the only subject his Majtie hath now left in that colony." Communications between husband and wife, between Boston and Barbados and Surinam, were difficult. Letters repeatedly miscarried in these tumultuous times, and three years elapsed before Bathsua Scott heard from her husband. For his part, Mr. Scott had failed to receive the sixteen or seventeen letters his wife had sent him. At long last, Bathsua Scott received word that her husband was alive and that he was eager to go to Jamaica to start planting anew. Mr. Scott was, in Bathsua's words, "in a posture fitt for removall."[4]

His aspirations in Surinam sacrificed to international rivalries, Mr. Scott's plans to evacuate the colony seem reasonable indeed. He was hardly alone in his flight from Surinam. In 1668 another planter, William Byam, had fled the "unfortunate colony" for Antigua, where he reported that he was reluctantly "hewing a new fortune out of the wild woods."[5] Bathsua Scott's phrasing of her husband's aspirations, however, is significant. For as her husband was poised and eager to move on to a new English colony, his "posture fitt for removall" was replicated again and again by thousands of other residents of the colonial world who moved within their first colony of settlement or from one colony to another.

These migrations through the Atlantic and Caribbean made it impossible for any part of the colonial world to evolve in isolation. The westward flow of passengers from England to the colonies comprised one dimension of the slow and fitful process of Atlantic integration that had begun in the seventeenth century. A second dimension was embodied in Mr. Scott's "posture fitt for removall." Second and third migrations or visits within the Atlantic allowed repeated and sustained contact with England and with other colonies, migrations that ultimately cemented colonial connections as fully as did the overlapping nature of company members in London and of experienced officers in the colonies. Whether this movement was deliberate, accidental, or even, as in Scott's case, reluctant, its pervasiveness tied together the disparate and distant regions of the Atlantic world. The connections embodied in this movement, moreover, were reinforced by letters and by the many personal ties that colonial residents maintained on both sides of the ocean. Together these associations created and sustained the English Atlantic world.

Regular contact by colonial residents and visitors with England and with different colonial societies ensured that this new Atlantic world was balanced on a fulcrum between remote colonial outposts and frequent interaction. It is obvious that variety characterized England's colonies. Households and houses varied as much as did forms of congregational worship. But these colonial variations did not evolve in isolation either from each other or from England. Geographic mobility was not part of a conscious effort to ensure conformity in the colonies to a broader English culture. Indeed, such an effort was futile: although English people brought with them a multitude of English ways, colonial exigencies forced other patterns upon them. But frequent movement did enable colonial residents and visitors to retain contact with old England and with other colonies, and for all their geographic distance, this contact enabled them to remain a part of England even as England itself was ultimately altered by its colonial holdings. In their repeated journeys from one colony to another and from the colonies to England, many of these voyagers signaled an understanding of a large and varied colonial world that offered myriad compelling opportunities of different sorts, whether the pursuit of piety or the quest for riches and status. When one venture failed or disappointed, another awaited.

Although migration cemented the scattered parts of England's colonial holdings into a larger, albeit still tenuous, union, migration also distinguished the colonies from England. For Atlantic migrations brought a defining cultural heterogeneity to colonial life that was absent in English parishes. Central to Atlantic societies was the variety of people who dwelled therein. The migration of English people from different parts of Britain to single places in the colonies comprised one aspect of this new heterogeneity. But the English were only one small part of the new Atlantic world, and English migration comprised only one of many flows of people. Many other people, including Scots, Welsh, Irish, continental Europeans, Africans, and Native Americans, also inhabited and shaped this new Atlantic world. The coexistence and co-residence of many different cultures were a source of considerable apprehension in the seventeenth century. The English found themselves living with men who were sworn enemies in Europe; with indigenous people whose diverse cultures were so rich and varied that the lessons the English learned in one location could rarely be applied elsewhere and whose relationship with uninvited English neighbors was always uncertain; and with Africans, both from Africa and from Spanish, Dutch, and Portuguese colonies, whom the English purchased with alacrity whenever opportunity and fortune permitted. Thus even as the English geographic mobility highlighted here literally connected England and its colonies, the heterogeneous and polyglot nature of each colonial society derived from global migration patterns that ultimately reinforced colonial differences from England.

Indeed, the varied configurations of Atlantic societies were embodied in Bathsua Scott's experiences. Her family was scattered throughout the colonies—her father and herself in Boston, her husband in Jamaica, their abandoned property in Surinam. In each colony they found themselves in vastly different worlds. In Surinam the Scotts lived in an international society with Dutch neighbors, on plantations worked by enslaved Africans, and in close proximity to a large indigenous population. In Boston Mr. Oxenbridge and his daughter would enjoy the familiar solace provided by a dense English presence, with lives regulated by the enduring symbol of New England's departure from England, the gathered church. But they lived there jumbled together with men and women from all over England—at least thirty English counties were represented in the 1635 migration to New England—and with refugees like Mrs. Scott from other colonies as well. Although the intimacy and immediacy of English and Native American habitation had receded somewhat in four decades of English settlement in Massachusetts, indigenous populations continued to make their presence known. In Boston where Oxenbridge lived and labored in the 1670s, they appeared primarily as traders, diplomats, and servants; but within two years several powerful New England tribes, led by Metacom, a man whom Bathsua Scott knew derisively as

King Philip, destroyed thirteen towns of the southern New England frontier, damaged six others, killed several thousand settlers, and rolled back the line of English settlement for decades.[6] On Jamaica, Mr. Scott joined a colony under English rule for just over a decade. Although the previous Spanish planters evacuated the island when the English invaded, they left behind a community of maroons in the island's mountainous interior. Ambitious English planters sought to reap their own fortunes in Jamaica's verdant soil, but they could do so only through the aggressive recruitment of experienced planters from other colonies and of likely Irish men and maids displaced by Oliver Cromwell's new plantations in Ireland and by the massive acquisition of slave laborers. They were joined in their exploitative endeavors by buccaneers, whose presence made their pleasure palace of Port Royal "the wickedest city in the West."[7] Thus this single family spanned the Atlantic, separated by thousands of miles and divergent experiences but linked by affection, kinship, and colonial adventures. They demonstrated the cosmopolitan nature of colonial life, the importance of family connections that spanned the ocean, the persistence of ties in the face of extreme duress, and the episodic connections embodied in frequent migration. The Atlantic Ocean contained more than a world in motion; it was also a world created by migrations that connected distant places and brought diverse people together into new hybrid worlds.

English Migrations

An initial voyage across the Atlantic represented an enormous undertaking, if not in financial preparation, at least in courage. Subsequent migrations, however, were facilitated by the very nature of these first voyages. Atlantic crossings required sojourns in numerous colonies and ports to replenish dwindling supplies of food and especially water or to load colonial products. Thus Father White, during his first voyage to Maryland, stopped at Scilley, the Canary Islands, Barbados, and St. Christopher.[8] And as Lord Delaware journeyed home from Virginia, he planned to go to Nevis, "famous for wholesome (sic) Bathes," but his discomfort at the southerly winds that buffeted the ship encouraged him to go to the western islands instead, thereby giving him a sightseeing tour instead of the intended health cure.[9] Thus men such as Lord Delaware who returned to England from colonial outposts brought with them information about other islands and existing or future settlements. Necessity often sparked these short stays, but visits could lead to new plantations. Indeed, John Hilton explained of Nevis's first settlement, it was when Anthony Hilton was on his way to Virginia and stopped by Saint Christopher, "as they knew no other way," that the islands came to his attention and sparked his interest in colonization there.[10]

Many of these visits to other colonies were of only short duration, yet there was a clear connection between travel and a permanent migration. Richard Norwood became a permanent resident of Bermuda only after a series of shorter stints on the island. He first came to Bermuda in 1613, stayed long enough to survey the islands, and then returned to England within four years. By 1637 he had decided to leave England once again for Bermuda, where he established himself as a schoolmaster and a planter.[11] For one man, travel for business was itself part of the *process* of transplantation. Such was the case for Barnaby Davis, who arrived in New England on the *Blessing* in the fall of 1635 to investigate the affairs of William Woodcock, an active investor in various colonial enterprises and a member of the Providence Island Company. After Davis had landed in Boston, he set out on the arduous overland route for Connecticut to talk to Francis Stiles, newly settled at Windsor. When Davis reached Windsor, he found that Stiles himself had already left for England, at which point Davis boarded another ship and set off for England with Captain Thomas Babb, on what was presumably the return voyage of the *Hopewell*'s second trip to New England in 1635. Davis pursued Francis Stiles to England, an Atlantic crossing that permitted him to indulge in a brief visit to his wife in Tewkesbury, but Stiles had apparently returned to Connecticut within a month of his arrival in London. At last Davis reached Boston and set out again for Connecticut, where he presumably located the errant Stiles. In Connecticut, Thomas Hooker and others provided Davis with letters to deliver to England. Waylaid to serve in the Pequot War, Davis finally reached England in 1637, delivered his letters, and proceeded to spend just under two years running errands for Mr. Woodcock. In his regional travels Davis apparently found New England to his liking and was not dismayed by the prospect of repeated ocean crossings, for he decided to retrieve his wife and children and goods to go to New England as a planter.[12]

Firm evidence of the frequency of the transatlantic travel embodied in Davis's numerous voyages lies in the number of people registered on London ships in 1635 who were making second or third trips back to the colonies in that year. Although their number cannot compare with the 308 people who traveled home from London to the continent in that same year, the impact of these voyagers was nonetheless significant. Altogether at least 37 people are known with certainty to have been making such trips in 1635 (see Appendix B, Table B.8, and Table 1.4). This group contained individuals who had already made a commitment, either emotionally, financially, or physically, to the Atlantic world. In this category fall those passengers who already lived in the colonies but were returning home; those who had lived in the colonies at one time and in 1635 were expressing a renewed commitment to the colonies; and experienced company agents and colonial employees. Although comprising only a small proportion of the total number of travelers, this peripatetic cohort stands out by virtue of its wealth and the political and economic power that it wielded in the colonies. This important group of frequent travelers and experienced colonists symbolized the dynamic nature of the early English Atlantic world.

Some repeat voyagers had gone to England to collect their families or chose in that year to give life overseas a second chance. At least ten New England–bound travelers had lived in Massachusetts before their journey from London in 1635. William Vassall, for example, had traveled with the Winthrop fleet in 1630, whereas William Almy was in Saugus by 1631. By 1634 Almy failed to attend the Court of Assistants, probably because he had already sailed to England.[13] William Vassall's stay was far shorter. An original patentee of the colony, he left Massachusetts on the *Lyon* when the Winthrop fleet returned to England in 1630.[14] Five years later Vassall brought with him his wife and five children, and Almy transported his wife and three children, in new efforts to settle permanently in Massachusetts.[15] Richard Saltonstall, Jr., brought along a new wife and his wife's brother in his return to Massachusetts. Saltonstall's marriage signals the importance of seeking brides in old England: both John Winthrop, Jr., and Edward Ireson also brought new wives with them to the new world in 1635.[16] Altogether these ten men brought at least nineteen relatives with them, in addition to numerous servants and other dependents.

Experienced company and colony officers comprised a second part of this population. Eight such men traveled in 1635. Like the New England–bound men, they traveled with entourages of servants and relatives. Richard Lane returned to Providence Island in 1635 after less than a year in England, which he had reached on the *Elizabeth* in 1634. He had journeyed to England to approach the Providence Island Company for payment of half a year's wages due him for his labors in the Bay of Darien, where he had worked for a year-and-a-half.[17] Lane was loathe at first to return to Providence, as the Company hoped he would do, because of "some Miscariages in the Govermt there." The Company concurred with his assessment of island affairs, and he returned to Providence armed with the Company's support, "he being reputed honest and industrious leaving him at libty to make choice of any ground in the Island." To encourage his return, the Company granted Lane permission to bring his wife and three children with him.[18]

Lane's mission was typical of that of many company employees and high-ranking officers: these men spent long years in colonial service and traveled back and forth across the ocean currying favors, aggrandizing colonial status, and redeeming wages and land. Accompanying Lane, for example, was Isaac Barton. Sent out with six servants by the Providence Island Company as the colony's sheriff in 1635, Barton had been on the island at least as early as December of 1633.[19]

On Bermuda individual proprietors had their own island representatives. George Hanmer and Hugh Wentworth, who traveled on the *Truelove,* were employed by the Rich family. Wentworth had lived on Bermuda since 1620, when he was welcomed as a "very true labouringe man." Hanmer, only 24 years old in 1635, was a more recent arrival. In 1634 Hanmer, Wentworth, and a third man, Thomas Durham, were appointed as agents of Sir Nathaniel Rich, "for the managing of [his] business in the Islands." Rich urged young Hanmer "to answer (his) good opinion with fidelity," and hoped all three men would be particularly attentive to the condition of his fruit trees. Employment for the Rich family required occasional personal attendance on the family at its Essex seat: George Hanmer was in England by June of 1635, and apparently Wentworth was there then as well, since the family's secretary William Jessop hoped in a subsequent letter sent by the *Dorset* that Wentworth had arrived home safely. Indeed, the duties of agency required numerous trips: Wentworth was back in England by 1638. Hanmer, however, had by then been relieved of his responsibilities.[20]

For some repeat travelers, motives for the journey to London remain obscure. This is particularly the case for three travelers to the West Indies who returned home to the colonies in 1635.[21] Richard Peers, the sometime governor of Barbados, journeyed back to the island in that year; and Luke Stokes and Captain Jacob Lake, praised as a "discreet and honest Gentleman," traveled on the *Peter Bonaventure* to Nevis, where Lake had lived since the late 1620s.[22] Peers, who acted as governor in place of his brother-in-law Henry Hawley in 1633 and 1634, apparently then made a short trip to England, departed London on January 6 aboard the first ship of the year bound for Barbados, and took office again for Hawley in September of 1635 when Hawley set off for England. No direct evidence survives to explain the reasons for the initial voyages to London, but the numerous excursions of Hawley and Peers from Barbados suggest the importance of personal reports to the proprietors on affairs in the colonies.

Travel to old England for business and personal reasons was common even for those who did not hold colonial offices. The Virginians Christopher Boyes, Richard Rutherford, John Gater, Bartholomew Hoskins, Richard Townshend, Robert Sabin, and Robert Scotchmore were repeat voyagers in 1635. John Gater had come to Virginia in the *George* in 1620, the same year that Richard Townshend reached the colony in the *Abigail.* In 1635 each man traveled from London with his wife and a child. Sabin and Scotchmore, however, traveled alone. Both men had been in the colony for at least thirteen years, but Sabin made his permanent home in England: in 1638, he deposed before the High Court of Admiralty as a tallow chandler of Mardes Mill, Hertfordshire.[23]

Because they voyaged so regularly, some planters maintained residences in London. The planter Bartholomew Hoskins, first in Virginia by 1616, if not earlier, maintained a home in the London area for at least two decades. That he made repeated visits to London from Virginia is attested by parish records. He was married in Stepney, Middlesex, in 1628. Five years later, his son was baptized there. His wife, furthermore, may never have left England to join her husband in Virginia.[24] Clearly, to some men, personal and financial connections in London were important enough to success in their colonial ventures that they warranted the inconvenience of Atlantic travel and the difficulty of chronic family separation.

Moreover, these transatlantic residences enabled one colonial planter to fuse a new Atlantic identity. Precisely when Walter Jenkins first appeared in Virginia is not known, but by 1635 when he boarded the *Constance* to return to Virginia, he had resided in the colony at least long enough to own land there and to have commenced the laborious process of tobacco cultivation. In 1637 Jenkins deposed in London before the High Court of Admiralty regarding his failed voyage to Virginia in 1635. His deposition, prefaced with the ritualistic incantation of occupation and residence, revealed the conflation of America and England that was a product of such frequent Atlantic migrations. Jenkins described himself as a planter not of Virginia, but of Westminster, Middlesex. From the heart, then, of England's fragile empire, Walter Jenkins defined himself as a planter, not just one who cultivated tobacco but rather one who, in the more pervasive meaning of the time, settled colonies. He assumed the occupation of a provincial tobacco farmer but claimed his primary residence in England itself, thereby anticipating the appellation that would describe absentee planters in later decades.[25]

Whereas colonial residents ventured east across the ocean to procure goods and favors for their American homes, London merchants reversed the process. They voyaged west to secure the annual flow of lucrative colonial products. London merchants comprised anywhere between 5 and 10 percent of the population of travelers from England to the colonies in the early decades of settlement. These men, or their factors and representatives, voyaged to cement commercial ties with colonial merchants and planters and to ensure their own share of the colonial spoils. The new American colonies required any product that a merchant chose to export, and in return, merchants imported colonial crops such as tobacco, sugar, cotton, and indigo in the 1630s and 1640s. Indeed, one did not even need to be a member of a merchant guild to trade with the colonies because the North American trade was not restricted. Thus, in Jacob Price's words, a "huckster horde" traveled to the colonies with a motley assortment of goods to barter for colonial crops.[26]

London merchants aboard ships in 1635 traded in both tobacco and sugar. John Chappell was an importer of Virginia tobacco and in 1635 boarded a boat to travel there. Nathaniel Wright had imported sugar to London in 1633: two years later, he boarded a ship to Barbados.[27] Later records reveal three other Virginia-bound travelers, John Redman, Thomas Bradford, and John Butler, to have been tobacco merchants.[28] Possibly their voyages in 1635 launched their careers. Thus we see in the case of these five men the importance of personal trips to the colonies for those merchants engaged in marketing colonial products. Other merchants traveled in that year, including Abraham Johnson, George Grace, and Nathaniel Braddock, bound for Virginia. At least one of these men, George Grace, found himself resident in Virginia for at least three years after his entrepreneurial voyage in 1635, presumably still waiting to recoup his fortunes.[29]

According to extant sources for all the passengers of 1635, the most enthusiastic travelers back and forth across the Atlantic were residents of Bermuda. Bermuda had been planted by the English since the disastrous hurricane that wrecked the Virginia-bound *Sea Venture* there in 1609. During Virginia's troubled years in the 1610s, Bermuda remained a focus of colonizing activity, although by the time these voyagers traveled in 1635, Virginia had long since eclipsed its sister colony in the Atlantic. Bermuda, which is still an English colony, possesses a remarkable collection of seventeenth-century records, second only to those of New England in their depth and variety. Moreover, low mortality rates and several surviving lists of people who departed the island in certain years permit fuller reconstructions of life histories and of migration than is possible for other places. What the colony's records reveal are high rates of migration. Of the thirty-seven passengers making return trips home to all the colonies from London in 1635, ten were Bermuda residents returning to the island.[30] Thus whereas passengers to Bermuda comprised only between 4 and 5 percent of the total number of passengers to the colonies in 1635, they comprised 27 percent of the known repeat voyagers.

Bermuda was the destination for two ships in 1635, the *Dorset* and the *Truelove,* carrying a total of 218 passengers. A full 20 percent of those Bermudians for whom supplemental information has been located were actually returning home to the island in that year. These people included one minister, George Stirke, on his way home from an unsuccessful effort to extract more money from the Somers Islands Company; two agents of the Rich family; three women in their forties who had lived on the island for some twenty years each; and four other longtime planters. Some of these individuals had already made trips to England before, including George Stirke, who had ventured to England in 1631 or 1632 to take the cure at Bath.[31] Christian Wellman, one of the women returning home to Bermuda in 1635, had been a resident of the island since at least the 1620s. She had made at least one other trip to England sometime between March of 1623 and March of 1626.[32]

Another 20 percent of Bermudians for whom information is available subsequently moved off the island to settle in England, the Bahamas, Jamaica, Barbados, and Massachusetts (Appendix B, Table B.9). Two ministers, Daniel White and John Oxenbridge, returned to England as a result of various ecclesiastical conflicts; and a lay minister, Robert Ridley, fled to the Bahamas during Bermuda's own Civil War in the 1640s. Many men emigrated for greater economic opportunity than the densely settled island promised.[33] The regularity of such movement is suggested by family separations: the sister-in-law of the 1635 traveler and island governor Josias Forster had a husband who lived on Barbados.[34] Christian Wellman and Severin Vicars made shorter forays to Barbados. Christian Wellman and her husband Martin returned from there with their servants and slaves in 1657, whereas Severin Vicars traveled to Barbados at least twice, and his wife, once.[35]

As their Barbados investments indicate, not only did many Bermudians leave permanently for other homes, but also many Bermudians traveled off the island frequently. Twenty out of the fifty travelers for whom there is some evidence (40 percent) left the island at least once to travel to England or to other colonies. In 1657, for example, George Hubbard, Edward Chaplin, and Severin Vicars left Bermuda to sell tobacco, and in October of that year, Bernard Coleman returned to Bermuda from a trip away.[36] Bermuda's rates of repeat migration to other colonies might be high—no other colony in this period has records adequate to provide any sustained comparison. Economic opportunities were few on this small island, and the voyage to London was particularly easy and short for these travelers, although the voyage home to Bermuda was long and grueling. So the 40 percent of Bermudians in this sample who are known to have ventured off the island for short visits or for new homes might represent a higher rate of migration that we can identify elsewhere. But even if rates for other colonies are only one-half or one-quarter of Bermuda's rate, the result is still considerable movement within the Atlantic from colony to colony and on to England.

The energetic Bermuda cohort demonstrates that despite the vast discomforts of Atlantic voyages, English men and women journeyed from colony to colony and between England and its colonies with, if not comfort and ease, at least frequency. Yet the frequency of ocean travel hardly indicated safe voyages. The danger of the seas required men and women to confront their mortality in a most tangible way. Deaths at sea from disease and misfortune were common occurrences: George Whittacre had to write his will aboard the *William* of London on his way to England, John Robinson drowned on his way from Barbados to Surinam, John Davis died on his way from London to Barbados in 1659, and John Collins was lost at sea.[37] Some ships simply vanished. Yet a voyage to America, for all its dangers and despite the preparations undertaken by most families and the frequent liquidation of all English assets to fund the crossing, did not in itself signal a commitment to any single part of the Atlantic world. The pattern of relocation from one colony to another was established early on. Bermudians, for example, moved on to Virginia (1634), St. Lucia (1638), Tobago (1640), Trinidad (1642), the Bahamas (1640s), and Providence (throughout the 1630s).[38] Providence also attracted residents from New England, including one sizable contingent in March of 1640.[39] Indeed, such movement was essential for the success of some colonies. Proposals for the settlement of Jamaica centered on recruiting experienced residents of other colonies. A ship was to be sent to Barbados "and the other Caribe Islands" to inform people of the subsequent arrival of a ship bound for Jamaica; and from New England might "reasonably be exported good store of men willing to change their climate."[40] Indeed, there seems to have existed a core group of men—both colonial officers, soldiers, and planters—who were avid partakers in colonial experiments.[41] Ministers were particularly eager colonizers, combining a quest for employment, evangelical impulses, and adventure in their various overseas outposts. The cleric John Oxenbridge left Bermuda in 1641 after six years there but later tried his hand at settlement in Surinam, whose plantation he encouraged in a promotional pamphlet, before journeying to Barbados and ending his career in Boston.[42] Oxenbridge had a good model for such travels in the experiences of the cosmopolitan minister Patrick Copeland, who had worked for the East India Company, acquiring in his labors a cherished Japanese language catechism, before his career took him to Bermuda.[43]

For all its frequency, however, colonial leaders contested migration to other colonies, regretting both the loss of able men and their taxes, and the humiliation that extensive emigration could bring. Thus Peter Hay tried to prevent Barbados residents from moving on to Tobago, but the Governor and Council told him his request was "unresonable."[44] At various times, colonial governments required people to register for their voyages. In Virginia the Governor and Council ordered people bound for England to enter their names at their county courts. Evidence of this order survives in the Norfolk County records, where in 1641 the 1635 travelers Thomas Brittayne and Robert Boddy entered their names to go to England.[45]

Because colonial governments occasionally resented the departure of their subjects, the right to move on from one colony to another was protected by Charles I in a 1641 proclamation. King Charles expressed his concern that colony governors, misunderstanding his intentions, were forbidding people from leaving colonies. "By wch restraint," he complained, "our subjects are deprived not onely of that due liberty of free subjects which wee are gratiously pleased to allowe them but also of those opportunities of advanceing their estates, wch in other pts of our domynions might possibly occur unto them." He reiterated his desire that those free of "debt, service, or otherwise" be permitted to remove "out of the several Islands and places of their residence." He particularly instructed all the officeholders of the West Indies colonies to permit all subjects to go to any other plantation.[46]

When Robert Boddy and Thomas Brittayne had their names inscribed in the Norfolk County Minute book, they left a tangible record of migration that for hundreds of others has been lost. Many of those whose first voyage overseas was recorded in the 1635 London port register traveled on again within the Atlantic. In the absence of records detailing departures and arrivals, evidence of frequent voyages comes from a variety of other sources. We know, for example, that Jeremy Belcher traveled back to England at some point between 1635, when he reached New England from London, and 1658 because he refers to this trip in a court petition, but other records of his voyage are missing.[47] Commercial interests were often so important that personal attention to transport items across the ocean and to transact business in London motivated people to travel across the Atlantic themselves, even within weeks of their arrival in America.[48] Francis Stiles, for example, left Windsor, Connecticut, as soon as he could after his arrival in May or June of 1635 for a brief trip to England.[49] The array of such errands was great. Edmund Freeman returned to Plymouth from one trip to England in 1639 laden with a supply of hats.[50] The tobacco planter Bartholomew Hoskins of Virginia presumably accompanied his crop when he was in England in 1628, paying duty on tobacco imported to London in the *Thomas and John*.[51] Likewise, when George Hubbard left Bermuda in July of 1657, he explained in a deed that he was "bound forth to sea . . . to seake sale for my tobacco in the ship Marie." On the same ship were his fellow 1635 travelers Edward Chaplin and Severin Vicars.[52] And planters accompanied petitions as well as tobacco. A petition signed by sixty-eight Bermuda tobacco planters, both men and women, was delivered in person to the Privy Council by many of its signers.[53]

Where commercial transactions encouraged frequent travel, employment difficulties prompted second and third migrations. Education often required the first relocation for colonial residents aspiring to the ministry. The son of the Bermuda minister George Stirke ventured from the island to Massachusetts to commence his education at Harvard, as did other Bermuda sons. A Harvard degree, however, sadly offered no promise of employment close to home. Ministers trained at Harvard soon outnumbered the attractive posts available in New England and thus were forced to look farther afield for positions. The tumult of the Civil War and Commonwealth, moreover, prodded Harvard-trained ministers versed in congregationalism to take the place of episcopal ministers expelled from their English pulpits. Altogether over one-third of the Harvard graduates in the College's first seventeen classes sought employment in Europe.[54] Of the 1635 contingent, at least two of the seven sons of Harvard traveled abroad. John Bulkeley went to England, and John Jones, Jr., moved on to Nevis.[55]

Other men who were poorly suited to the labor of their new homes moved on. Thomas Goad, brought as a servant to serve John Winthrop for four years, stayed at most only months in New England before he boarded a ship and was last heard from in Spain. Goad could have reached New England no earlier than late August, but already by March of 1636, his kin in London knew he had left Massachusetts. He apparently left New England on a ship bound for Spain, and Winthrop's friend Francis Kirby regretted that his cousin Goad "did not prove a fit servant" for him.[56]

A range of personal concerns enticed colonial residents home to England. Some men and women who returned to England were, in Richard Ligon's words, "desirous to suck in some of the sweet air of England."[57] Such homesickness might have prompted Ann and Jasper Arnold of Stepney, Middlesex, to return to England after a voyage to New England: they returned so quickly that they left no record of their presence in colonial records.[58] Their return may have indicated an inability to adjust to the primitive conditions of frontier life after the bustling melee of the metropolis. The sudden death of a spouse early in an overseas enterprise led others to terminate their colonial efforts. Following the death of her husband only two years after she had reached New England, Sara Geere returned to Lewes, Sussex, with her two daughters.[59] There she settled with family members.

Those traveling for personal reasons could be implored to serve many public functions while on their journeys. John Astwood intended only a visit of short duration to England in 1653 when he was delegated by the New Haven colony as its agent, "the court understanding that Capt. Astwood is speedily to take a voyage thither aboute his owne necessary occasions."[60] When Hugh Peter left New England after six busy years there, he was sent on a commission by the Massachusetts leaders to negotiate for New England, "both in furthering the work of reformation of the churches there which was now like to be attempted, and to satisfy our countrymen of the true cause why our engagements there have not been satisfied this year." He and his companions were also charged with other economic concerns, most particularly how to obtain cotton from the West Indies.[61]

For many of those who returned to England or moved on in the 1640s, the reason was clear, and the story familiar: the outbreak of the Civil War signaled to committed puritans in all colonies an opportunity to serve God and preserve the faith in the home country, not in a wilderness periphery. Travelers in the New England cohort who are definitely known to have returned to England or to have moved to other parts of the Atlantic world from New England number only 73, out of a total of 1,169, but I would estimate that anywhere between 8 and 17 percent of the population returned (Appendix B, Table B.10).[62]

The Civil War exacted a heavy toll among the top ranks of New England's leaders. Colony assistants, deputies, ministers, church elders—all found their role in God's service redirected by the Civil War. The 1635 contingent included some committed Parliamentarians. Henry Vane, the former governor of the colony, participated in both the short and the long parliaments. Hugh Peter was a chaplain in Cromwell's army, whereas John Tuttle, Samuel Shepard, and George Cooke moved to Ireland, thereby joining two colonial enterprises through their experience and zeal. Some paid a heavy price for their participation: George Cooke died in Ireland in a skirmish that made him a Protestant martyr, and both Vane and Peter were executed in 1662 for their prominent roles in the Civil War.[63]

But not all those who returned to England were illustrious participants in momentous events. Edmund Munnings, of Tillingham, Essex, a parish in Denge Hundred, had migrated in 1635 with his wife, Mary, and their children Anna, Mary, and Michelaliel to Dorchester, Massachusetts.[64] Although Goodman Munnings was still in Dorchester in 1651, when he requested "to have the land about his howse recorded," he apparently concluded that Dorchester offered little that he had not gained and could not yet recover in England, where he had served on the manorial court for Tillingham.[65] Edmund Munnings and some of his children returned to Tillingham by 1653. Munnings and his son Hopestill built new lives in old England. Hopestill married an English woman, Sara Smith, in 1659. At least one of Edmund's children returned to New England. Michelaliel traveled on the *Speedwell* from England in 1653, and unlike other members of his family, seemed committed to life in Massachusetts. He represented his father in court in 1654.[66] Return, inappropriately disregarding the injunction of his name, also remained in the new world and married Sarah Hobart, daughter of the Hingham minister Peter Hobart, in 1664. Two years later, on the other side of the Atlantic, Edmund Munnings, a "very ancient man of Dengey," was buried in Tillingham.[67]

Like the Munningses, many families were split as colonial parents traveled back to England, leaving children in the new world. Richard Saltonstall left behind his son Nathaniel, and Thomas Parish left his son Thomas. Samuel Shepard trusted his daughter Jane to the care of Edward Collins.[68] The Massachusetts General Court addressed the problem of separations when it expressed its concern for those married people whose spouses were in England or elsewhere and who found themselves subject to temptations. The Court insisted that "all such married psons as aforesaid shall repair to their relations . . . upon ye paine or penalty of 20£."[69] There were risks involved in leaving a spouse, as Joseph Faber learned at great pains. After four years in New England, Faber returned to England by 1639 without his wife, who then became embroiled in an infamous adultery trial involving Captain John Underhill.[70]

Faber's domestic misfortunes offer tangible reminders of the difficulties associated with migration and family separation. Some New Englanders lamented their returns to England and felt guilty for abandoning New England. Edward Bullock of Dorchester, Massachusetts, was sufficiently troubled by his relocation to England that he justified it in his will of 1649, recording carefully his "calling and determinacon to goe for England," signaled by "the Providence of God."[71] Richard Saltonstall, Jr., pondered at length his decision to return, and sought the advice of the Boston minister John Cotton. Saltonstall had made a vow to continue in the colonies, but then his wife became sick and went to England to seek help. His wife was told to remain in England, and Saltonstall's loyalties were torn. Cotton assured him that in such circumstances, it was permissible to return to England.[72] Those who returned to England could salve their troubled consciences by the many ties—familial, financial, and legal—that they retained with New England. Vincent Potter, for example, served as a factor and agent for his brother-in-law, Thomas Fowle of Boston, after his return to England.[73]

Because of family separations, those undertaking return trips to England planned their voyages with the same care that had preoccupied the London mercer Nathaniel Braddock when he wrote his will in London before venturing to Virginia in 1635.[74] Samuel Shepard, in anticipation of his return to England, requested the General Court to relieve him of his duties as deputy in attending the court in 1645.[75] Shepard was held in such high esteem by the Cambridge church that even after he and his wife were living in Ireland, the church records described them as still "in Memberly Relation to us."[76] George Burdin did not leave New England until 1652 and was uncertain enough about this trip with his wife and family that his will recorded his trepidation. He made arrangements for the dispersal of his property should he die in England: Burdin's will also accommodated the uncertain preferences of his wife, with stipulations for her portion should she be in England or New England.[77]

The result of these patterns of migration, as men initially ventured to colonies to investigate their prospects, then returned to claim their families, and then moved on again within the colony or overseas, all the while leaving family and friends behind in England and in other colonies, resulted in families that were themselves Atlantic in interest and experience. Two of the families of the 1635 cohort, the Vassalls and the Winthrops, illustrate the breadth of family experiences. William Vassall was a merchant in England and the son of a wealthy London merchant: his father, John, perhaps sparked his son's colonial ambitions with his own investment in the Virginia Company; moreover, a second son, Samuel, invested in the Levant and East India Companies as well as, like his brother William, the Massachusetts Bay Company.[78] William Vassall first migrated to New England in 1630. Daunted, he immediately returned to England, but then in 1635, accompanied by his wife and five children, he traveled to New England again, residing first in Massachusetts before moving quickly to Plymouth. Vassall found himself embroiled in political and religious controversies in New England, most notably as the instigator of Child's Remonstrance. In 1648 William Vassall moved to England. From there this cosmopolitan man, whose family's varied investments perhaps disposed him to a second colonial adventure, turned his thoughts to Barbados. While Anna, Margaret, and Mary Vassall moved with their father to Barbados, his daughters Frances and Judith remained in New England. His son John had moved to Barbados as well but eventually moved on to settle Cape Fear, North Carolina. William's will, drafted in 1655, reflected his expansive interests when he mentioned his property on Barbados, in New England, "or any other part or place in the world."[79] The family diaspora of the Vassalls was a common occurrence: as families had been severed by the original migrations to the colonies, so did they remain severed as families transplanted themselves.

The Winthrop family was similarly dispersed. With John Sr. as the founder of Massachusetts and John Jr. the governor first of Saybrook and later of Connecticut, the family had important centers of power in New England. But the founder's son Samuel Winthrop took the family's interest to the Indies: he planted sugar in St. Christopher and finally settled in Antigua. Another son, the ill-fated Henry Winthrop, had also tried the islands during a brief and utterly unsuccessful sojourn on Barbados in 1627. And the Winthrops knew England's first colony well: John Jr. was educated at Trinity College in Dublin, a haven for zealous puritans in the 1620s. Winthrop relatives, particularly the Downings and the Reads, were scattered in England, Scotland, and Holland during the 1650s. Moreover, although John Sr. spent nineteen years in Massachusetts, he was intensely engaged in a larger colonial world, as his journal and letters indicated, while John Jr. thrived in a cosmopolitan Atlantic world that embraced scientists and naturalists in London, Pequots on his own property in Connecticut, and the Dutch governor of New Netherland. For families with Atlantic commercial and political interests, such as the Vassalls and the Winthrops, such patterns of dispersal placed family factors advantageously in important ports.[80]

The many families whose members were scattered around the Atlantic world were navigated by letters, deeds, and wills. Wills are perhaps the most tangible expression of enduring Atlantic ties. Bequests knit together family members who had not seen each other in decades and who had no familiarity with each other's lives; indeed, bequests were a great expression of optimism in a document grimly prompted by thoughts of its author's mortality. Bassel Terry, a Barbadian planter who had first reached the island in 1635 after his journey from London, fell ill in 1650 and wrote his will. He left four hundred pounds of "good merchantable sugar" to his father in England "to bee sent him as soone as conveniently it may." The difficulties of regular communication were highlighted in Terry's provisions for the sugar should his father be dead.[81] The Concord minister Peter Bulkeley wrote his will at the age of 76. In it he arranged two possible bequests for his son Edward, depending on whether he stayed in New England or left for England: the bequest in England could be paid there by another son, John, who had already removed himself to England.[82]

The consequences of the Atlantic migrations were an enhanced familiarity by travelers, visitors, and colonial residents with different colonies, visited on business or on the way back and forth to England: this familiarity seduced men to leave one colony for another and enticed others overseas as settlers. Repeat migrations, although often born of failure and disappointment, gave fresh opportunities for success. In that migration to the colonies enabled colonies to prosper, migration permitted the creation of the Atlantic world. But that men and women traveled frequently within and among colonies meant that this Atlantic world could ultimately become a coherent entity to the English.

A Hybrid World

The English were neither the only residents of this colonial world nor the only ones to travel within it. We see this heterogeneity in three respects: the presence of people from all over England in single colonial towns or farms, the uncomfortable neighborliness of Europeans in the colonies, and the confrontation of all the people of the Atlantic—European, African, and indigenous Americans—in the colonies. The societies that the English joined and created in the first half of the seventeenth century were shaped by the inhabitants of four continents. As a result, the colonies were characterized by a cultural heterogeneity unrivaled in the most active ports of Europe. Even the most humble English inhabitant in the most remote colony found himself living in a world far more culturally complex than anything he would have experienced in England. In this respect, we do no service to the nexus of variables shaping these triracial and polylingual worlds if we regard English colonies as the "New England" and "Little England" that their English inhabitants intended them to be.

In the early seventeenth century, the English were relatively new to colonization and to settlement in the Atlantic and Caribbean. The very success of their entrepreneurial efforts was almost entirely dependent on the massive mobilization of English men and women overseas: as a consequence, seventeenth-century colonies were migrant societies populated by individuals who had personally experienced the journey from England to America. In these volatile first decades of settlement, the English who ventured across the Atlantic learned that old rules held little sway overseas. Relations between Europeans proved highly fluid in the Atlantic world, as necessity and diversion in the Americas occasionally overrode old enmities from Europe. And the level of uncertainty and misunderstanding that characterized English relations with Native Americans did not always engender the armed conflict more frequently memorialized by participants than were diplomatic, commercial, and labor relations. When the English first met Native Americans, they reacted with diplomatic incompetence and social uncertainty: episodes of harmony demonstrate possibilities that ultimately failed to be pursued. Old enemies dined festively, old friends found new enmities in newly competitive and dangerous circumstances, and previous interactions could not predict future encounters.

Nowhere is the ambiguity of cultural encounters in the Atlantic world more evident than in the unlikely friendships between the Spanish and the English in the Atlantic. With each nation the self-appointed defender of its respective faith at home and abroad, the Spanish and the English were inveterate, although in this turbulent period, intermittent, enemies in Europe. Indeed, many colonists and several colonial governors had served as soldiers against Hapsburg forces on the continent, and some had fought at sea in naval engagements. Within the Atlantic, the hostilities continued, with English and Spanish privateers engaged in private skirmishes for coveted goods and for local control over trade and smuggling routes. The presence of Spanish ships offered a vivid reminder to the English of the hazards of life in the Caribbean, where caution was always necessary for safe passage on the seas. During his voyage to and within the Caribbean, the Englishman Henry Colt remarked on the need for vigilance there and particularly criticized the casual security he observed on Barbados. His own vessel was chased by Spanish ships during his travels, to the detriment of Colt's private supply of libations so laboriously packed and transported for his enjoyment and consumption overseas.[83] Nothing signaled more fully the hostility between these rival empires than the numerous Spanish attacks on the Providence Island Company holdings of Providence and Tortuga, the two most precariously situated English islands.[84]

Yet individual English and Spanish travelers and residents in the Caribbean could find space for amity and friendship, evident in a number of improbable domestic interludes. Despite the frequent Spanish attacks on his own colony, the Providence governor Nathaniel Butler, himself a military veteran of continental campaigns in the Thirty Years War, was able to dine on Easter day with two Spanish friars who were temporarily imprisoned on the island: on the night of Holy Saturday, they gave Butler the "buena pasca."[85] In this ecumenical feast Butler exploited English religious and political sensibilities to lash out at his island enemy, the puritan minister Hope Sherrard, whose piety was violently assaulted by this Catholic sacrament. But he was also able to enjoy an entertaining diversion in a colony plagued by internal religious and political strife and by the simultaneous dangers of a large and hostile enslaved labor force and nearby Spanish ships, poised to attack the island. The desire for entertainment encouraged these international contacts. Henry Colt's sojourn on St. Martin gave him an opportunity to dine with the island's Dutch governor, a man clearly eager for the company that foreign travelers provided, whom Colt applauded as "ye only temperate Hollander yt ever I saw, or heard of, & a man of good appearance."[86]

Henry Colt and Nathaniel Butler were well-traveled men before they ventured to America. But these cosmopolitan dinner parties could also achieve a more modest setting, bringing provincial men and women from rural England into intimate contact with foreigners in their new colonial homes. In 1639 a group of shipwrecked Spaniards was farmed out to several Bermuda households before funds could be raised to replace their ship and send them home. Bermuda was a puritan colony, already by this year experiencing religious conflicts as nonconformist ministers struggled to enforce strict comportment on island residents: the island's Protestant householders harbored these Catholic castaways, doubtless at considerable peril to the sanctity of their households but with the compensation of bolstering their modest financial resources. One castaway recorded his impressions of life on the small island, marveling at the modesty of island houses, the length and rigor of the puritan liturgy, and the youth of the island's servants. For their part the English remain silent: Bermuda children raised in Protestant households, newly accustomed to the vigilant catechising of the island's ministers, must have wondered at the presence in their homes of these Catholic men, of a faith long-villainized by their English hosts. To guard the colonial world from Catholic invasion or subversion was a central preoccupation of English colonists; yet harbored in their small huts, protected by the rules of the sea that safeguarded castaways, were the very enemies they feared, salvaged from the sea like the wrecked goods that Bermudians eagerly scavenged. These are precisely the encounters that heralded the departure of life in the colonies from life in England.[87] Thus in Bermuda and on Providence, inveterate enemies lived amicably for short periods.

But where old enemies could share their quarters as the lion lay down with the lamb, old allies could equally find new enmities, especially when they competed for land. The English and the Dutch were in regular contact in the colonies, especially in the Caribbean but also in New England, where John Winthrop documented the arrival of Dutch ships and traders. In May of 1635, for example, a Dutch ship reached Boston from Saint Christopher, laden with salt and tobacco. Winthrop's keen interest in affairs in other colonies was reflected in his journal entry, where he carefully recorded the Dutch merchant's report of St. Christopher. Two weeks later two Dutch ships arrived straight from Holland, bearing horses, heifers, and sheep.[88] But essential trade did not secure harmonious relations between the two groups. Only five years later, the first English settlement on Long Island was inauspicious indeed: although the two nations were at peace with each other, the Dutch in New Netherland imprisoned and interrogated six men who had moved from Lynn, Massachusetts, to try their fortunes in a new plantation.[89]

The mixture of Europeans in the Americas was hardly the only measure of the new colonial world. Relations between Native Americans, Africans, and Europeans proved equally ambivalent. The grueling labor necessary to turn American terrain into cultivated English fields brought together the people of the Atlantic world. In all the seventeenth-century colonies, English indentured servants toiled next to Indian or African servants and slaves. The inequities of colonial society were thereby imposed on bound laborers of different cultures, clans, lineages, tribes, kingdoms, and nations. Nowhere were these labor hierarchies more evident than in the presence of Indian servants and slaves on colonies with no indigenous populations. The English shuffled Indian populations around the Atlantic world. Estate inventories from a number of colonial households reflect the hybrid worlds that colonists inhabited. By 1676, for example, Richard Norwood's Bermuda estate included five black adults, "one old indian woman," one "indian negrow girle called Nann," and four other black children. His household was a veritable melting pot of new world exploitation, especially vivid on an island that before English settlement had no indigenous inhabitants.[90]

Providence Island, like Bermuda with no indigenous population when the

English claimed the island, demonstrates the variety of people and labor systems that could coexist in English colonies as early as the 1630s. Although the presence of enslaved Africans was meager in most English colonies, the first English plantations to achieve a slave majority did so as early as 1636 (on Tortuga) and 1638 (on Providence).[91] The advantageous location of each island in close proximity to slave trade routes made slaves accessible and affordable. As the Providence Island Company put it perfunctorily, "Negroes being procured at cheap rates, more easily kept, and perpetually servants," planters seemed unable to resist the temptation.[92] Thus the English settlers on Providence were the first English people overseas to live in a triracial society, where Africans outnumbered the English, and English indentured servants labored alongside Indian and African servants and slaves.[93] On these islands the English found their first experience as a minority population within a society of their own creation. This demographic situation proved precarious for English planters, whose slaves rebelled[94] and who were forced to accept a maroon population in the island's mountainous interior. But divisions in the island were not drawn rigidly along racial lines. Both servants and slaves resisted their labor, most frequently by running away, sometimes together, and the slave population itself was divided into factions loyal to the English and to the maroon population.

Although this island contained a slave majority, African and English laborers were joined by Native Americans from the Mosquito coast and from New England. Because the people of the nearby Mosquito coast were both trade partners and targets for conversion, indigenous laborers received particular attention from the Company in London. Children, both boys and girls, were to be taken from the mainland to Providence and given a Christian education if they "may be had wth their parents good likeinge." These children, according to a 1632 order, were to be raised as if they were English children, in English families.[95] Some Native American women were apparently on the island as well.

Not all Native Americans were accorded the delicate treatment given Providence's indigenous trade partners. At the end of the Pequot War in New England, after the English had finished destroying Pequot villages and murdering those fortunate enough to have survived the rampages and ravages of the war, the English colonists shipped seventeen of the surviving Pequots, fifteen boys and two women, off to the West Indies in 1637. The Pequots were actually bound to Bermuda, but the captain of the ship somehow missed his elusive destination and ended up in Providence, where the Pequots were sold as slaves.[96] The Pequots found themselves not only in an alien tropical environment, far from their home in southern New England, but also forced to make accommodation with Mosquito Indians, Africans, and Englishmen.

They were referred to by Company members in London—who had presumably never seen a Pequot although they were certainly likely to have encountered Africans in England—as the "cannibal Negros" from New England.[97] The use of language here is revealing. Cannibalism intrigued Europeans throughout the period of conquest and settlement. And by calling these exiled Pequots "Negros," the Company suggested that the categories shaped by seventeenth-century notions of race or color were contained within a larger category denoting laboring status. These seventeen Pequots were, unequivocally, slaves, who had been captured in war and sold by the captor for reasons of security and revenge. Thus they were, in English eyes, "Negros." On Providence, then, we see the complex nature of colonial encounters in the Atlantic world, where some Native Americans had a privileged status while others were enslaved; and where the Spanish regularly attacked the island and chased Providence ships, yet the island's governor dined and worshiped with two Spanish friars.

This colonial heterogeneity was described in colorful detail in a book printed in London in 1607, *An Houre Glasse of Indian Newes*. This tale recounts the adventures of a Guiana-bound ship that, after seventeen miserable weeks at sea, finally landed its surviving passengers on St. Lucia, in answer to their plaintive pleas to be set ashore. The island was inhabited by people described by the author John Nicholl as "a companie of most cruell Caniballs and man eaters," who, in apparent contradiction of Nicholl's description of them, brought food to the ship. The Englishmen subsequently purchased a little village for the price of a hatchet. The English spent their time on St. Lucia leveling trees and erecting fortifications to prepare for an assault by the hosts who proved so relentlessly hospitable. Before English stupidity provoked the complete disintegration of relations on the island, the English hosted a party, during which one English member of the party, a Master Tench, "fell a singing of Catches with the Carrebyes," and another Englishman, Master Alexander, went arm in arm through the island with two other Caribs. A subsequent assault, paced by truces during which the Indians brought the English food, drove the English from the island. They fled in a boat, and after a lengthy and parched journey, they found the mainland, where a party of Spaniards, traveling with Native Americans and blacks, discovered the English and took them along on their journey from Caracas to Coro. The Spanish even generously allowed the weakened English to ride while the Spaniards walked alongside on foot. In Coro the English were presented to the Governor, "a flemming which could speake a little English," who distributed the English to different families, where they were well cared for and nursed back to health. Determined to return home, the English left after five months, but once they reached Cartagena, they were imprisoned as spies. Once freed, the men embarked on various ships for Havana, and from there to Spain, and finally back to England.[98]

This single tale introduces all the people of the Atlantic world and the entire spectrum that accommodated their interactions, from singing songs together to staging sieges. It demonstrates that however reluctantly many English men and women ventured across the Atlantic to new colonial homes, they were forced to make rapid and unfortunately often inadequate adjustments to a new and unexpected world. John Dane tried to make such accommodations when he moved to New England in the mid-1630s. Soon after his arrival he settled in Roxbury, Massachusetts. A journey he took to Ipswich in anticipation of relocating there impressed itself on his mind not only because it signaled God's providence but also because of his encounter with the region's indigenous people. He walked to Ipswich "alone when thare was no path but what the ingens had made." He found the path difficult to follow, recalling later "sumtimes I was in it, sumtimes out of it, but god directed my waie." Along his uncertain way he met "forty or fiftie indiens, all of a Roe." Dane offered a friendly if apprehensive "What chere" as he went by, to which "with a loud voise, laughing" they "cryd out, What chere, What chere."[99] In a few short years of English settlement, the new world was already blurred, with one nervous Englishman adopting an indigenous path and the Native Americans adopting an English greeting. Dane's previous life in the provincial English towns and villages of Berkhamstead, Hertford, Wood Roe, and Hatfield held nothing to guide him in these new world exchanges: necessity took him on the path, and security guided his affable greeting.[100] But exchanges were not always so benign, and the 1635 passenger, engineer, and military officer Lion Gardiner, who lived and worked among the different indigenous populations of southern New England, treating with them in war, peace, and trade, observed these strains. He captured the ambivalence of colonial–Native American relations in southern New England when he wrote in 1660, reflecting on his experiences in the Pequot War and his subsequent dealings with Narragansett, Mohegan, and Long Island Indians, that he "would fain die a natural death, or like a soldier in the field, with honor," than to suffer the tortures some Indians visited on captives, with their skin flayed or their flesh roasted. Yet even as he conjured this violent image, he hoped to guide his fellow New Englanders to more responsible dealings with their indigenous allies.[101] It was central to the uncertainty of life in the Atlantic world that men who traded one day, whether English, Dutch, Spanish, Mohegan, or Pequot, might the next day be at war.

Within this chaotic world, with its new footpaths, its truncated families, its exotic visitors, its uncomfortable neighbors, and its unfamiliar products, English residents labored to surround themselves with some familiar trappings of

English society. Perhaps especially in those colonies where perils loomed largest, as in Providence where Spanish attacks marked the change of seasons as regularly as did hurricanes, it was particularly important to devise occasions for relaxation and fellowship. Governor Nathaniel Butler of Providence recorded in his detailed journal just such an occasion. He was rowed by his servants to the leeward part of the island, "to dine at a great feast made by all the welshmen in the Ilande."[102] These very recreations, however, make clear that the diversions available on Providence derived from the heterogeneous nature of Atlantic American societies. A St. David's Day feast might have been difficult for Butler to attend in England, but in England's colonies from Ireland to America, people from all parts of Britain lived jumbled together, from Irish Catholic prisoners from Cromwell's Ireland in Protestant households in Barbados, to neighboring Welsh and English settlements on Newfoundland, in strange, hybrid worlds.[103]

We see the complexities of life in the Atlantic in the estate inventory of John Baddum. Taken in February of 1661, Baddum's inventory reflected a significant accumulation of wealth in the twenty-six years since he had left London for Virginia in 1635. Baddum possessed an estate valued at almost 8,000 pounds of tobacco, a measure of value symbolic of Virginia's cash crop and of the colony's difference from England, where Baddum's estate would have been reckoned in pounds sterling. His estate included several cows, steers, and oxen, essential ways to store a family's capital in the precarious colonial environment, and such household items as chairs and stools. Baddum also possessed some unusual creature comforts. His inventory included a fiddle, curtains, and a valence.[104] If Baddum knew how to play his fiddle, he could entertain his neighbors with familiar tunes from England. Perhaps he enabled them to dance after a hard day's toil or to hear tunes that would induce homesickness for England. His fiddle would also introduce African and Native American neighbors, servants, or slaves to entirely different melodic and rhythmic patterns, harmonic relations, and modes; his music would reinforce orally the many profound differences between these component cultures of Virginia society. With his curtains and valence, John Baddum framed his world in a way deemed fashionable in England, yet the world he framed was vastly different from the one left behind. Perhaps instead of mounting his curtains and valence properly on a bed, he used them to decorate the window hewn out of his cabin's walls. Through his window Baddum could see tobacco fields, worked mostly by English servants, but perhaps cultivated as well by African laborers. Baddum had survived one attack by the Native Americans in 1644 and would come to know them as his neighbors, likely learning some Algonquian to facilitate trade. He lived in a society peopled by men and women from three continents, Europe, North America, and Africa, who cultivated a crop distinctive to, and indeed, symbolic of, the new Atlantic world. Through his window, framed by his English valence, as he viewed the complicated society around him, Baddum would have to wonder: where did England end, and where did America begin? It was in that space between that the Atlantic lay—not just an ocean connecting these varied places, but an entire world, however fractured and fractious, that ultimately transformed each of its component parts.

The multiracial and heterogeneous societies that the English inhabited in the Atlantic world reflect the complexities of colonial life. Viewed from the context of the English societies that spawned them, colonial societies, especially in the seventeenth century, look like simplified renditions of England, with truncated social and economic hierarchies, imprecisely transferred and stripped down legal and ecclesiastical systems, and the intimate scale of community life. Yet if we look at these societies not from the benchmark of an English parish but rather from somewhere on a precarious perch in the middle of the Atlantic, we see fully that the English colonies contained people from a vastly expanded range of cultural, linguistic, and national groups. The heterogeneity characteristic of the Atlantic colonies would ultimately be transferred to England itself, as colonial products and the diverse people of the Atlantic world circulated to the metropole in a process that continues to this day. But in these first decades of English colonization in America, it was the small and precarious colonies of the Atlantic, containing societies more diverse than any their inhabitants had previously experienced at home and created by global migration patterns, that signaled most fully what it meant to live in an Atlantic world.

During the reigns of Elizabeth I and James I, a number of people imagined a world in which England's reach encompassed the globe. Some of these men, such as Samuel Purchas, had themselves never strayed far from home in England, and their expectations of global power were derived from the experiences of others and their own vivid imaginations.[105] This vision gained force in the first decades of the seventeenth century but remained illusory until English men and women left England for overseas colonies in numbers sufficient to make permanent claims to distant plantations. By the 1630s, men and women who spanned the economic spectrum had realized this vision. Indeed, they literally experienced a world that spanned from the Caribbean to North America, and farther afield to India and Africa, a world whose reach earlier promoters had only imagined. At this juncture, as experience matched imagination, the English Atlantic world emerged. But it did so chaotically, resembling in these early decades of the seventeenth century nothing so much as a patchwork, a collection of disjoint and loosely connected pieces of a haphazardly homespun whole.

The extraordinary diversity within and between colonies points to the imperfect integration of England and its new colonial holdings across the ocean. Both historians of the Atlantic world and those who participated in and observed its creation have exploited a common metaphor to describe this relationship: they have likened the Atlantic Ocean to a bridge.[106] When the minister William Crashaw delivered a sermon in 1610 to the Virginia adventurers, this was precisely the metaphor he embraced. He avowed from the easy comfort of a London pulpit that the voyage to Virginia "is in that true temper so faire, so safe, so secure, so easie, as though God himself had built a bridge for men to passe from England to Virginea."[107] Experienced travelers might have disputed Crashaw's depiction of ocean travel: discomfort aside, the Atlantic bridge connected what one colonial promoter called the "the out-borders and skirts of the Empire."[108] Comparing the Atlantic to a bridge reinforces the prevalence and importance of the two-way travel that connected the different parts of the Atlantic world. A complex pattern of migration evolved to accompany and sustain colonial enterprises as men and women voyaged from one colony to another and on to a third.

But this bridge did not ensure an easy and automatic integration between the different parts of the Atlantic. Here other contemporary borders offer illuminating parallels. Like the Atlantic Ocean, the Irish Channel connected England to some of its oldest colonies, the plantations of Munster, Londonderry, and Ulster. Offa's Dyke likewise stood as an archaic remnant of a long-vanished national barrier between England and Wales, whereas Hadrian's Wall offered a tangible reminder of the novelty of English and Scottish union under a common monarch. But these barriers endured in the richly varied local cultures on either side of these internal British "bridges" and in the intermittent but heartfelt resistance that accompanied English rule. The work of internal conquest remained incomplete. So thought the educator John Brinsley. His book, *A Consolation for our Grammar Schooles* (London, 1622), outlined his own national standards for education and addressed the importance of educating "those of the inferiour sort, and all ruder countries and places." He enumerated those places: "Ireland, Wales, Virginia, with the Sommer Ilands," and dedicated his work to those in charge of settling these areas, including the Governors of the Channel Islands. For Brinsley, English plantations on Bermuda and in Virginia were simply part of a larger national enterprise that spanned from "the ignorant countrie of Wales" to "that poore Irish nation."[109] But what Brinsley particularly noted and lamented was that the British world remained imprecisely integrated in the early seventeenth century.

Similarly incomplete, indeed, only just beginning, was the integration of the American portion of England's Atlantic world with England itself. The English Atlantic world only just emerged in this part of the seventeenth century, with each new venture building a new layer of complexity and offering a new colonial pattern. In part because of this imprecise integration, the story told here is one peculiar to the early seventeenth century, when it was not yet clear what these colonial holdings might mean for England, or which type of plantation would become a dominant colonial model. The Atlantic world remained a poorly defined region, composed of a series of disparate and chaotic colonial adventures. English people abroad did not set out to create an Atlantic world any more than there was any coherent effort to form an empire. Instead, a mélange of private and frequently competing efforts provided the impetus for overseas commercial and colonial activity that precipitated, in turn, the English migrations detailed here. Although the process of migration and remigration gradually made different parts of the Atlantic world familiar to many travelers and adventurers, the integration of this Atlantic world by any number of measures would be slow. The English people who inhabited it and traveled within it provided a crucial commonality that connected and sustained this odd and uncertain world. But in the seventeenth century the English Atlantic world remained, above all, a wild and chaotic place, one where servants rocked alone in hammocks strung between cedar posts under palm branch roofs; where puritan saints reigned; where children were bartered with other trade goods and livestock measured secure wealth; where desperate, brave, and ambitious people clambered between a fragile ship's decks and ventured over 3,000 treacherous miles for something better than the pittance they found at home; and where, above all, new accommodations were essential for survival.

Appendixes

Notes

Archival Sources

Index

Appendix A
Calculating Travelers

Invaluable as it is for measuring migration out of London in the early seventeenth century, the 1635 port register is not without its flaws and limitations, and as a result it has been little used by other historians interested in travel to the colonies. Other port registers more fully document traveling populations, delineating consistently and in great detail occupation and English origins.[1] The London register provides names and ages for all travelers to the colonies and to the continent, and for most soldiers; and all ministers to non–New England colonies are identified as such. Fully described as well are those travelers to the continent whose place of residence was included more frequently than for New England travelers and whose names were scrupulously indicated, as well as their reason for traveling. Beyond these scraps of information, the port clerks recorded home parish and occupation for only some of the New England passengers (317, or just over 25 percent) and for none of the passengers to the other colonies.

The register also contains some inaccuracies, with some travelers counted twice by the harried port clerks, while other names were missing from the register for reasons documented in Chapter 2. In many cases the clerks' neglect seems to have been accidental. Certainly the haphazard way in which individuals appeared on ships indicated both confusion about the colonial world and general indifference to destination. Only those individuals known by name to have traveled are included in the revised figures: that is, the total number of passengers is actually higher, as there are 83 travelers known to have traveled on four New England ships who are not included here because their identities are not known. The adjusted New England total would then be at least 1,252; but given the fact that the other 14 New England ships were probably also undercounted, speculation on accurate numbers would be somewhat futile. Table A.1 illustrates the corrected figures for the travelers to the American colonies. What is clear is that the inaccuracies are neither egregious nor distorting. Although the clerks may have missed some people, especially those whose sole purpose was to elude royal officials, and counted others twice, a close scrutiny of the London port register reveals that clerks at

Table A.1. Adjusted statistics by destination for travelers to America

Colony	Ships	Original listing	Adjusted listing	%
Virginia	20	2,005	2,009	41.2
New England	17	1,178	1,169	24.0
Barbados	8	983	983	20.2
St. Kitts	5	423	423	8.7
Bermuda	2	219	218	4.5
Providence Island	1	72	76	1.6
Total	53	4,879	4,878	100.2

Source: London port register, E157/20 1-e, PRO.

England's busiest single port managed to record a migration that even in a country characterized by extensive internal migration must have seemed enormous.

Appendix B
Supplementary Tables

Table B.1. Bermuda travelers: officeholders and owners of land or goods
(1635 cohort)

Name	Year	Comment
John Casson	1662	1 share and tenement
Edward Chaplin	1662	1 share and tenement
Bernard Coleman	1639	17-year land lease
Josias Forster	1635	Land, slaves
Anthony Gilliard	1630	Debt owed him
George Hanmer	1634	Agent for Rich family
William Holt	1638	Lost suit in court
George Hubbard	1662	3 shares
Sampson Lort	1638	Won suit in court
Samson Meverill	1638	On jury
John Miller	1626	On jury, council,
John Oxenbridge	1635	Minister; owned slave
Timothy Pindar	1639, 1662	Lost suit, occupied shares
Robert Ridley	1638	On jury
George Stirke	1623	Minister, on council
Edward Stoughton	1626	On council
Arthur Thorne	1639	Called goodman
Robert Varvell	1662	2 shares
Severin Vicars	1670	2 shares in whale fishing, called Mr.; Owned land in Barbados

Table B.1. (continued)

Name	Year	Comment
Hugh Wentworth	1623	7-year lease, 2 slaves, 2 servants
Daniel White	1635	Minister, on council
John Yates	1626	By 1631, had servant; in 1641, 11-year lease

Source: All tables in Appendix B are based on the database compiled for this project. Sources include colonial records, information from several periodicals with a genealogical focus or which include genealogical information, especially including the *New England Historical and Genealogical Register;* the first and second series of the *William and Mary Quarterly, The American Genealogist, Virginia Genealogist, Tyler's Quarterly Historical and Genealogical Magazine, The Virginia Magazine of History and Biography, Caribbeana, Bermuda Historical Quarterly,* and *The Journal of the Barbados Museum and Historical Society;* and many genealogies, some cited in this book's footnotes and others cited more fully in my dissertation, "Venturers, Vagrants, and Vessels of Glory: Migration from England to the Colonies under Charles I (Ph.D. Dissertation, University of Pennsylvania, 1992).

Table B.2. Barbados landholders (1635 cohort)

Name	First evidence	Age in 1635	Amount of land in acres	Partner?
Edward Ash	1658	20	18+	
John Ashurst	1645	24	10+	
Daniel Baker	1640	20	20	
Edward Banks	1651	35	?	
John Bathe	1638	23	30	
William Beaton	1640	24	20	Y
James Bell	1665	19	?	
John Belton	1652	48	two plantations	Y
Henry Berrisford	1641	32	36	Y
George Blacklock	1644	32	20	Y
Thomas Bromby	1640	59	50	Y
Henry Broughton	1652	20	10	
William Buckley	1638	26	10+	
Philip Cartwrite	1664	20	?	

Table B.2. (continued)

Name	First evidence	Age in 1635	Amount of land in acres	Partner?
Richard Chapman	1644	40	300+ (merchant)	
John Compton	1651	26	?	
William Corser	1639	24	20	
Richard Cribb	1642	19	10	
Marmaduke Crosby	1640	28	30	Y
Thomas Dabb	1642	25	95	Y
Robert Davers	1654	14	8	
John Dellahay	1642	27	60+	
Francis Dene	1641	21	?	
Richard Dent	1643	17	20	
John Dukkarth	1638	31	30	
Robert Dunstarr	1638	34	10	
John Etherington	1643	17	33+	Y
Griffin Evans	1640	40	40	Y
Hugh Evans	1638	18	50	
Henry Gilder	1640	18	?	
James Goldingham	1649	32	60	Y
Farford Goldsmith	1640	22	30	Y
William Hamond	1638	36	40	
Richard Hannis	1643	21	20	
Ralph Harwood	1640	23	10	Y
Philip Henson	1638	21	10+	
John Hogg	1664	21	?	
William Huckle	1654	20	?	
Robert Hurt	1679	19	?	
Walter Jago	1640	20	100	Y
Edward Kemp	1640	19	50	Y
John Key	1638	40	60	
Thomas Lamberd	1656	23	6+	

Table B.2. (continued)

Name	First evidence	Age in 1635	Amount of land in acres	Partner?
John Lawnder	1650	16	?	
Edward Layton	1640	30	40	
William Levyns	1640	22	30	
Thomas Love	1651	19	67	Y
Philip Lovell	1640	34	30+	
Felix Lyne	1642	25	10	Y
Robert Mills	1638	19	10+	
Edmund Montgomery	1638	26	40	Y
James Montgomery	1646	19	40	Y
Pierce Morgan	1671?		?	
Christian Mynnikin	1643	19	?	
Richard Newbold	1647	28	80+ (merchant)	
John Nicks	1638	23	10+	
James Pallister	1641	28	10	
Richard Peers	1630?	45	900	
Robert Pendred	1638	40	10+	
Philip Philpott	1640	30	20	Y
Thomas Plunkett	1638	28	40	
William Powell	1647	19	?	
Edward Pullin	1640	27	20	
Henry Rawlins	1658	25	?	
Leonard Robinson	1640	20	40	Y
William Seely	1638	29	10+	
George Selman	1645	16	?	
Anthony Skooler	1665	20	?	
Richard Speede	1638	35	30	
Dorothy Symonds	1638	40	25+	
Basil Terry	1643	22	20	
Joseph Thomlinson	1637	26	30+ (merchant)	Y

Table B.2. (continued)

Name	First evidence	Age in 1635	Amount of land in acres	Partner?
John Thurrogood	1645	20	20	
Thomas Trigg	1641	21	50	
John Usher	1643	26	20	Y
Richard Walton	1643	21	50	
Nicholas Watson	1648	26	?	
William Weston	1638	26	70+	
Edward Wilkinson	1641	17	30	
Arthur Wynd	1643	17	20	Y
Arthur Yeomans	1637	24	80+	

Table B.3. Luminaries and clergy in New England (1635 cohort)

First generation	Second generation
Luminaries	
John Astwood (Asst, Mass.)	
Clement Chaplin (Trsr, Conn.)	Christopher Almy (Asst, R.I.)
George Cook	Henry Bull (Gov, R.I.)
Joseph Cook	Caleb Carr (Gov, R.I.)
Edmund Freeman (Asst, P.C.)	John Lawrence (mayor, NYC)
Lyon Gardiner	John Wincoll (JP, Me.)
Roger Harlakenden	William Hubbard[b] (historian)
Edward Howe (depty)	
Robert Keayne (mcht)	
Robert Nanney (mcht)	
Thomas Olney (Asst, R.I.)	
William Paine (mcht)	
Richard Saltonstall [a] (Asst)	
Thomas Savage (Asst)	
William Swayne (Conn.)	
Henry Vane (Gov, Mass.)	
William Vassall[a] (mcht)	
John Winthrop, Jr.[a] (Gov, Conn.)	
William Wood[a] (author, *New Englands Prospect*)	
Clergy	
Peter Bulkeley (Concord)	John Bulkeley[b] (England)
Thomas Carter (Woburn)	Thomas Crosby[b] (Eastham, Harwich)
John Jones (Concord; Fairfield, Conn.)	Edward Drinker (Baptist, Charlestown)
Thomas Millet (Brookfield)	William Hubbard[b] (Ipswich)
Thomas Olney (Baptist, Providence, R.I.)	John Jones[b] (Nevis)
Hugh Peter (Salem)	Thomas Olney (Baptist, R.I.)
Thomas Shepard (Cambridge)	Thomas Shepard (Charlestown)
Zachariah Whitman (Milford)	
John Wilson[a] (Boston)	

a. Second trip to New England in 1635.

b. Harvard graduates.

Abbreviations: Asst (Assistant); Trsr (Treasurer); depty (deputy); mcht (merchant); Gov (Governor).

Table B.4. Dissenters and contentious spirits in New England (1635 cohort)

Name	Belief	Settled
Jeremy Blackwell	Antinomian	Exeter, N.H.
Henry Bull	Antinomian, Quaker	R.I.
George Burdin	Antinomian	Mass.
Caleb Carr	Antinomian	R.I.
Robert Carr	Antinomian	R.I.
John Davies	Antinomian	R.I.
Nicholas Davies	Antinomian, Quaker	R.I., P.C.
Sara Davies	Antinomian	R.I., P.C.
Edward Drinker	Baptist	Mass.
Rodolphus Elmes	Quaker	P.C.
Thomas Ewer	Antinomian	Mass.
Thomas Ewer, Jr.	Quaker	P.C.
Joseph Fludd	Baptist	Mass.
Ann Gillam	Quaker	Mass.
Benjamin Gillam	Quaker	Mass.
Job Hawkins	Antinomian	R.I.
Ralph Hudson	Antinomian	Mass.
Edward Jeoffries	Antinomian	R.I.
Marie Jeoffries	Antinomian	R.I.
Robert Jeoffries	Antinomian	R.I.
Susan King	Scituate controversy	P.C.
Thomas King	Scituate controversy	P.C.
William King	Antinomian	Mass.
Henry Knowles	Antinomian	R.I.
Adam Mott	Antinomian	R.I.
Sara Mott	Antinomian	R.I.
Robert Nanney	Antinomian?	N.H.
Marie Olney	Baptist	R.I.
Thomas Olney	Baptist	R.I.
Edward Rainsford	Antinomian	Mass.
James Roger	Baptist	Mass.
Thomas Savage	Antinomian	Mass.
Anthony Stannion	Antinomian	N.H.
Ann Stockbridge	Scituate controversy	P.C.
John Stockbridge	Scituate controversy	P.C.
George Taylor	Baptist	Conn.
Henry Vane	Antinomian	Mass./Eng.
Judith Vassall	Scituate controversy	P.C.
William Vassall	Scituate controversy	P.C.
John Warner	Gortonist	R.I./Eng.
Michael Williamson	Antinomian	R.I.

Sympathizers
Thomas Buttolph

Table B.4. (continued)

Name	Belief	Settled
Edmund Freeman		
Robert Titus		

Others excommunicated

Simon Bird	Boston (lewd conduct)	
Lydia Eliot	Roxbury (1655; restored 1656)	
William Potter	New Haven (executed for bestiality)	
William Preston	New Haven	

Accused witches

Ann Burt (Lynn, 1669, accused)
John Carrington (Wethersfield, 1651, executed)
Rachel Haffield Clinton (Ipswich, 1687, accused; Salem 1692, convicted and freed)
Mary Holman (Cambridge, 1659, accused)
Winifred Holman (Cambridge, 1659, accused)
John Proctor, Jr., (Salem, 1692, executed)

Table B.5. New England church officers (1635 cohort, first generation)

Name	Office	Church
John Astwood	Elder	Milford
Richard Champney	Elder	Cambridge
Clement Chaplin	Elder	Wethersfield
Philemon Dalton	Elder	Hampton
John Freeman	Deacon	Eastham
Jasper Gunn	Deacon	Milford
Isaac Heath	Elder	Roxbury
Edward Howe	Elder	Lynn
Thomas King	Elder	Scituate
Thomas Parker	Deacon	Reading
Giles Payson	Deacon	Roxbury
Daniel Preston	Deacon	Dorchester
Edward Rainsford	Deacon, elder	Boston
Simon Stone	Elder	Watertown
Zachariah Whitman	Elder	Milford

Table B.6. Luminaries and clergy: Bermuda and Providence Island (1635 cohort)

Bermuda	Providence Island
Clergy	
Henry Jennings	
John Oxenbridge	
Robert Ridley (in 1640s, self-appointed)	
George Stirke[a]	
Isaiah Vincent	
Daniel White	
Officers	
Edward Chaplin	Isaac Barton[a]
Josias Forster (governor)	Richard Lane[a]
Anthony Gilliard[a]	Nicholas Riskinner (governor, Association)
George Hanmer[a]	William Thorp[a]
George Hubbard	
John Miller[a]	
Edward Stoughton[a]	
Hugh Wentworth[a]	
John Yates[a]	

a. Second trip to colonies.

Table B.7. Sample offices held in New England (1635 cohort)

Name	Place	Year	Office
Christopher Almy	R.I.	1680	Elected governor; did not serve
		1693	Agent
John Almy	R.I.	1658	Commissioner (Portsmouth)
William Almy	R.I.	1648	Deputy (Portsmouth)
		1656	Commissioner (Portsmouth)
John Astwood	New Haven	1643	Deputy (Milford)
		1648	Rep. to N.E. confederation
		1653	Magistrate (Milford)
		1654	Agent
James Bates	Mass.	1640	Deputy
William Beardsley	Conn.	1649	Deputy
John Birchard	Conn.	1673	Clerk
Thomas Birchard	Conn.	1650	Deputy (Saybrook)

Table B.7. (continued)

Name	Place	Year	Office
Thomas Blackly	Conn.	1672	Deputy (Branford)
John Briggs	R.I.	1648	Deputy (Portsmouth)
Thomas Brigham	Cambridge	1639	Constable
Henry Bull	Portsmouth	1638	Corporal
		1639	Sergeant
	Newport	1640	Sergeant
		1655	Commissioner
	R.I.	1666	Deputy
		1674	Assistant
		1685	Governor
Thomas Bull	Conn.	1651	Lt., captain
Thomas Buttolph	Boston	1647	Constable
Caleb Carr	R.I.	1654	Commissioner
		1661	Treasurer
		1695	Governor
Clement Chaplin	Cambridge	1635	Selectman
	Mass.	1636	Deputy (Cambridge)
	Conn.	1638	Treasurer
	Conn.	1643	Deputy (Wethersfield)
Henry Collins	Lynn	1664	Selectman
Henry Collins, Jr.	Lynn	?	Selectman
George Cooke	Mass.	1636	Deputy
Joseph Cooke	Cambridge	1635	Selectman
	Cambridge	1645	Lt.
Simon Crosby	Cambridge	1636	Selectman
Timothy Dalton	Dedham	1638	Deputy, General Court
Robert Day	Ipswich	1679	Selectman
Simon Eires	Watertown	1636	Selectman
	Mass.	1641	Representative
		1645	Clerk
Hopestill Foster	Dorchester	1645	Selectman
		1665	Deputy, "Captain"
Edmund Freeman	Plymouth	1640	Assistant
John Freeman	Eastham	1653	Deputy, selectman
	Plymouth	1667	Assistant

Table B.7. (continued)

Name	Place	Year	Office
Lion Gardiner	Easthampton	1650s	Magistrate
George Giddens	Ipswich	1639 1655	Selectman Deputy (Mr.)
Jasper Gunn	Conn.	1663	Deputy (Milford)
Roger Harlakenden	Cambridge Mass.	1635 1636	Selectman Assistant
Isaac Heath	Mass.	1636	Deputy
Edward Howe	Mass.	1638	Representative (Lynn)
Richard Hubbard	Ipswich	1663	Selectman
William Hubbard	Ipswich	1639	Selectman
Ralph Hudson	Boston	1637	Constable
Robert Jeoffries	Newport	1639 1642	Treasurer Captain
Thomas Jones	Dorchester	1645	Selectman
Thomas Joslin	Hingham	?	Town officer
Robert Keayne	Mass.	1638	Deputy
John Kilborn	Conn.	1660	Deputy (Wethersfield)
Thomas Laighton	Mass.	1649	Representative (Lynn)
Robert Long	Charlestown	by 1638	Selectman
Edward Lumas	Ipswich	1661	Constable
Thomas Marshall	Mass.	1650s	Representative (Lynn)
Mathew Marvin	Conn.	1654	Deputy (Norwalk)
Marvin, Mathew Jr.	Conn.	1690s	Deputy (Norwalk)
Samuel Morse	Dedham	?	Town officer
Adam Mott	Portsmouth	1642	Clerk
Thomas Munson	Conn.	1665	Militia officer
Thomas Olney	R.I.	1648	Deputy (Providence)
William Paine	Ipswich	1639	Selectman
Thomas Parish	Cambridge	1639	Selectman
Francis Peabody	Topsfield	1659	Selectman
Thomas Pell	Conn.	1665	Deputy

Table B.7. (continued)

Name	Place	Year	Office
William Purrier	New Haven	1653	Deputy (Southold)
Edward Rainsford	Boston	1663	Selectman
William Read	Mass.	1636	Deputy
Richard Saltonstall	Mass.	1637	Assistant
Martin Saunders	Braintree	1640	Deputy?
		1642	Selectman
Thomas Savage	Boston	1651	Selectman
		1655	Deputy (Capt)
	Mass.	1659	Speaker of house of deputies
	Mass.	1680	Assistant
Samuel Shepard	Cambridge	1638	Selectman
Anthony Stannion	Exeter	1647	Clerk of the writs
John Stedman	Cambridge	1645	Ensign
John Stockbridge	Scituate	1643	Constable
William Swaine	Mass.	1636	Deputy
	Conn.	1636	Assistant
	Conn.	1641	Deputy (Wethersfield)
	New Haven	1656	Deputy (Branford)
Edward Thomlins	Lynn	1643	Clerk of the writs (Mr.)
Henry Tibbetts	Dover	1642	Constable
Robert Turner	Boston	1646	Constable
John Tuttle	Ipswich	?	Selectman
	Mass.	1644	Representative
John Tuttle	Boston	1652	Constable (Romney Marsh)
Richard Tuttle	Boston	1637	Constable
Henry Vane	Mass.	1636	Governor
William Vassall	Mass.	1630	Assistant
John Warner	R.I.	1648	Deputy (Warwick)
Zachariah Whitman	New Haven	1644	Deputy (Milford)
John Whitney	Watertown	1637	Clerk
John Winkoll	Kittery	1655	Deputy (Mr.)
Deane Winthrop	Groton	1655	Selectman

Table B.7. (continued)

Name	Place	Year	Office
John Winthrop, Jr.	Mass.	1632	Assistant
	Saybrook	1635	Governor
	Conn.	1656	Governor
William Wood	Mass.	1636	Representative (Lynn)
	Sandwich	1637?	Clerk
		1640	Constable

Table B.8. Age profile of selected merchants and colonial residents in 1635 (**Boldface** denotes people who had already lived in the colonies before their voyage from London in 1635)

Name	Age	Ship
To Bermuda		
Judith Bagley	58	*Dorset*
Ellen Burrows	30	*Truelove*
Anthony Gilliard	38	*Truelove*
George Hanmer	24	*Truelove*
John Miller	47	*Dorset*
Edward Staughton	50	*Truelove*
George Stirk	40	*Dorset*
Christian Wellman	43	*Dorset*
Hugh Wentworth	44	*Truelove*
John Yates	49	*Truelove*
Average age: 42.3		
To Barbados and Nevis		
Lancelot Bromley	44	*Expedition*
Jacob Lake	30	*Peter Bonaventure*
Richard Peers	45	no name
Luke Stokes	35	*Peter Bonaventure*
Nathaniel Wright	32	*Falcon 1*
Average age: 37.2		
To Providence		
Isaac Barton	27	*Expectation*
Joan Filby	50	*Expectation*
Richard Lane	38	*Expectation*
William Thorp	30	*Expectation*
Average age: 36.3		

Table B.8. (continued)

Name	Age	Ship
To New England		
William Almy	34	*Abigail*
Edward Ireson	32	*Abigail*
Robert Jeoffries	30	*Elizabeth and Ann*
Thomas Knore	31	*Abigail*
Edward Rainsford	26	*Abigail*
Richard Saltonstall	23	*Susan and Ellen*
William Vassall	42	*Blessing*
John Wilson	35	*Defense*
John Winthrop	27	*Abigail*
William Wood	27	*Hopewell 2*
George Woodward	35	*Hopewell*
Average age: 31.1		
To Virginia		
Christopher Boyes	38	*Constance*
Nathaniel Braddock	31	*Merchant Hope*
Thomas Bradford	40	*Merchant Hope*
John Butler	50	*Assurance*
John Duncombe	46	*Assurance*
John Gater	36	*Assurance*
Rice Hooe	36	*America*
Bartholomew Hoskins	34	*Safety*
Walter Jenkins	30	*Constance*
John Redman	46	*Globe*
Richard Rutherford	40	*Constance*
Robert Sabin	40	*America*
Robert Scotchmore	39	*George*
Benjamin Symes	42	*Thomas*
Richard Townshend	28	*Globe*
Average age: 38.4		
Average age for entire group: 37.1		

Note: Not included in this table are first-time company officers: Lion Gardiner, Nicholas Riskinder, or Robert Evelin, for example.

Table B.9. Return migrants and sojourners: Bermuda (1635 cohort)

Name	Comment
William Alberry	Left Bermuda with family for Eleutheria, 1661.
Judith Bagley	On Bermuda by 1617; traveled to England c. 1634.
Ellen Burrows	On Bermuda before 1635.
Josias Forster	Left Bermuda repeatedly for London.
Anthony Gilliard	On Bermuda by 1630; in England c. 1634–1635.
George Hanmer	On Bermuda by 1634; back in London c. 1634.
Henry Jennings	Bermuda minister, probably returned soon.
John Miller	On Bermuda by 1626; traveled to England c. 1634.
John Oxenbridge	Bermuda; England; Barbados; Surinam; Boston.
Robert Ridley	Lay preacher, banished to Bahamas.
James Rising	Went from Bermuda to Salem, Mass., by 1662
Francis Russell	Went from Bermuda to Jamaica, 1658
George Stirke	Bermuda minister, on island by 1623; traveled to Bath 1631/2, c. 1634.
Edward Stoughton	On Bermuda by 1626; traveled to England c. 1634.
William Thorpe	Lieutenant in Bermuda; in 1635 to Providence.
Severin Vicars	Bermudian; business in Barbados, traveled there with wife at least twice by 1660.
Edward Vincent	Went from Bermuda to Jamaica, 1658.
Christian Wellman	Bermuda by 1618; traveled to England c.1625, again c.1635; property in Barbados, lived there and returned from Barbados to Bermuda in 1657 with servants and slaves.
Hugh Wentworth	In Bermuda by 1623; traveled to London again 1634, 1638, etc.; agent for Rich family
Daniel White	Bermuda minister; went back to England in disgust with Independents.
John Yates	On Bermuda by 1622; traveled to England c. 1634.

Table B.10. Return migrants and sojourners: New England (1635 cohort)

Name	Comment
Christopher Almy	Returned 1693 R.I. colony agent; lived in Monmouth, N.J., briefly.
William Almy	In Saugus by 1631; by 1634, had returned to England, and with family traveled from London in 1635.
Ann and Jasper Arnold	Returned by 1644 to London.
John Astwood	Returned 1654 as New Haven colony agent; died in England.
Jeremy Belcher	Mentioned in 1658 a trip to England. Merchant.
John Bulkeley	Returned circa 1645 to England permanently. Minister.
Henry Bull	Returned soon?
Edward Bullock	Returned by 1649.
George Burdin	Returned by 1652.
Edward Burt	Lived in London area by 1667.
Clement Chaplin	Returned 1640s; treasurer of New Haven colony.
George Cooke	Returned 1640s. Soldier. Died in Ireland, 1652.
Joseph Cooke	Returned after 1653.
Barnaby Davies	Returned in 1635; then settled in Charlestown after three years.
Isaac Disborough	Returned 1640s?
Rodophus Elmes	Returned to England; then moved back.
John Emerson	
Joseph Faber	Returned 1639; his wife involved in adulterous affair with Capt. John Underhill.
James, John, and Abigail Fitch	Returned 1640?
Joseph Fludd and family	Returned circa 1646?
Edmund Freeman	Returned 1639; went to purchase hats.
Elizabeth Geere and her two daughters	Returned 1637 after death of husband.
Thomas Goad	Returned 1635; servant to Winthrop.

Table B.10. (continued)

Name	Comment
Edmund Gurden	Returned 1637; brother-in-law of Richard Saltonstall.
Samuel Hall	Returned soon.
Elizabeth Harlakenden	Went back to N.E.
Edward Ireson	Was servant in N.E.; in 1635, returned there with wife.
Henry Jackson	?
Robert Jeoffries	In Charlestown in 1630 (possibly in his capacity as mercer?) Traveled in 1635 with his family from London.
John Jones	Minister in Nevis, 1651.
Benjamin Keayne	Merchant; returned to England, leaving wife in Massachusetts.
Thomas Knore	In New England before his 1635 trip.
Robert Lord	Removed to Virginia.
Thomas Marshall	Went to fight for Parliamentary army; returned later to Lynn.
Munnings family	1650s returned to Denge Hundred, Essex.
Thomas Parish	1654 returned to England; clothier of Suffolk.
John Pelham	Returned soon? brother of Herbert Pelham.
Hugh Peter	Returned 1642? Salem minister; chaplain in Cromwell's army; executed 1660.
Vincent Potter	Returned 1639.
Edward Rainsford	First in Boston in 1630; in 1635 returned to N.E. from London.
Mabel Read	Later returned to N.E.
William Read	Returned to England 1652, leaving children behind.
Richard, Murial, Sr., and Murial, Jr., Saltonstall	Richard was with his father in Massachusetts in the early 1630s. Returned to England in 1649.

Table B.10. (continued)

Name	Comment
John Sedgewick	Died in Jamaica 1656.
Samuel Shepard	Returned 1645, served under Cromwell. In Ireland 1658. Left daughter in Massachusetts.
Francis Stiles	Returned 1635; brief visit to England.
Elizabeth Streaton	Returned in 1668 with husband?
Edward Thomlins	Returned 1644.
Abigail Tuttle	
John and Joan Tuttle	Returned 1650s; John died in Ireland 1656.
Henry Vane	Returned 1637; prominent in Civil War. Executed 1662.
John Vassall	To Cape Fear and Jamaica.
William Vassall and family	1630, 1646 William Vassall traveled with Winthrop fleet; returned with fleet to England; traveled again to New England in 1635 with his family; in 1646, went first to England, then to Barbados with his wife and three daughters.
John Warner	Returned 1652.
Josua Wheat	Returned 1640.
John Winthrop, Jr.	Numerous voyages.
William Wood	Author of *New Englands Prospect* (London, 1634); returned to New England in 1635 from London
George Woodward	Returned 1635; fishmonger, on business in 1635.

Note: Other suspected returners from family groups with no records in New England number 32.

Table B.11. Local offices held in Virginia (1635 cohort)

Name	Office	Year of office	Age in office	Age in 1635
William Allinson[a]	Constable (NB)	1651	41	25
Thomas Ap Thomas	Jury (SU)	1654	49	30
John Baddum	Jury (NH)	1645	50	40
Handgate Baker	Jury (NH)	1648	35	22
Robert Baldry	JP (YO)	1657	40	18
Henry Banister	Jury (NF)	1653	50	22
	High sheriff (YO)	1669	66	
William Berry[a]	Arbitrator (AC)	1645	27	17
Christopher Carnoll[a]	Jury (MD)	1643	31	23
Giles Collins	Constable (NF)	1655	40	20
	Jury (LN)	1652	37	
Robert Crouch	Jury (YO)	1661	41	15
Christopher Dixon[a]	Jury (NH)	1654	43	24
Hugh Fouch	Jury (NB)	1657	39	17
Savill Gaskins[a]	Jury (LN)	1666	60	29
Francis Gray[a]	Jury (MD)	1644	24	15
John Gresham	Jury (NB)	1647	37	22
Henry Haler	Jury (NB)	1651	38	22
William Hardish	Jury (NB)	1652	39	22
Reginald Hawes	Undersheriff (AC)	1645	35	25
Capt. H. Higginson	Viewed tobacco crop (JC)	1639	32	28
	JP/Commissioner (JC)	1654	47	
Anthony Hoskins	High sheriff	1660	47	22
Rice Hooe	Viewed tobacco crop (CC)	1639	40	36
	JP (CC)	1655	56	
Bartholomew Hoskins	Vestryman (Linhaven Parish, LN)	1640	39	34
Jasper Hoskins	Constable (NF)	1648	37	24
Nicholas Jurnew	Vestryman (NB)	1655	48	28
Thomas Kedby	Undersheriff (NB)	1653	43	25
David Kiffin	Jury (NH)	1651	40	24

Table B.11. (continued)

Name	Office	Year of office	Age in office	Age in 1635
Christopher Kirke	Jury (NH)	1651	39	23
Alexander Maddox	Jury (NH)	1651	37	21
Edward Major	JP (NA)		19	
Anthony Parkhurst	Viewed tobacco crop (CR)	1639	46	42
Arthur Raymond[a]	Jury (NH)	1649	34	20
Simon Richardson	Jury (NB)	1651	39	23
William Spicer	Jury (NB)	1655	40	20
Mr. Oliver Sprye	Viewed tobacco crop (UN) JP Commissioner (NA)	1639 1646	25 32	21
Peter Starkey	Constable (YO)	1659	46	22
William Starling[a]	Jury (NH)	1658	41	18
Richard Townshend[a]	Justice (YO) Viewed tobacco crop (CR)	1633 1639	26 32	28

a. Former servant. County and colony abbreviations: AC (Accomack); CC (Charles City); CR (Charles River); JC (James City); LN (Lower Norfolk); MD (Maryland); NA (Nansemond); NB (Northumberland); NF (Norfolk); NH (Northampton); SU (Surrey); UN (Upper Norfolk); YO (York).

Notes

Abbreviations

Barb. Arch.	The Barbados Archives, Lazaretto, Barbados
Berm. Arch.	The Bermuda Archives, Hamilton, Bermuda
BHQ	*Bermuda Historical Quarterly*
BL	The British Library, London
BRO	Buckinghamshire Record Office, Aylesbury, Buckinghamshire
Caribbeana	Vere Langford Oliver, ed., *Caribbeana: Being Miscellaneous Papers Relating to the History, Genealogy, Topography, and Antiquities of the British West Indies,* 6 volumes (London: Mitchell, Hughes, and Clarke, 1913–1919)
CO	Colonial Office Records, Public Record Office
Conn. Records	J. Hammond Trumbull, ed., *Public Records of the Colony of Connecticut* (Hartford: Case, Lockwood, and Brainard, 1850–1877)
CSPC	W. Noel Sainsbury, ed., *Calendar of State Papers, Colonial Series, 1574–1660* (London: Green, Longmans and Roberts, 1860)
CSPD	*Calendar of State Papers, Domestic Series 1547–1704* (London: Green, Longmans and Roberts, 1856–1872)
EIHC	*Essex Institute Historical Collections*
ERO	Essex Record Office, Chelmsford or Colchester, Essex
Hay Papers	Hay of Haystoun Papers, Scottish Record Office, Edinburgh
HRO	Hertfordshire Record Office, Hertford, Hertfordshire
JBMHS	*Journal of the Barbados Museum and Historical Society*
Jessop Letterbook	Letterbook of William Jessop, Add. 63,854, British Library
Lefroy, *Memorials*	John Henry Lefroy, *Memorials of the Discovery and Early Settlement of the Bermudas or Somers Island, 1515–1685,* 2 volumes (London: Longmans, Green, and Company, 1877, 1879)
Mass. Records	Nathaniel B. Shurtleff, ed. *Records of the Governor and Company of the Massachusetts Bay in New England, 1628–1686* (Boston: William White, 1853–1854)
MD Archives	William Hand Browne et al., eds., *Archives of Maryland . . .* (Baltimore: Maryland Historical Society, 1883–1925)
MHS	The Massachusetts Historical Society, Boston, Massachusetts

MHS Coll.	*Collections of the Massachusetts Historical Society*
MHS Pro.	*Proceedings of the Massachusetts Historical Society*
NEHGR	*New England Historical and Genealogical Register*
NEQ	*New England Quarterly*
Nugent	Nell Marion Nugent, ed., *Cavaliers and Pioneers: Abstracts of Virginia Land Patents and Grants, 1623–1666* (Baltimore: Genealogical Publishing Company, 1979)
PCSM	*Publications of the Colonial Society of Massachusetts*
Plymouth Records	Nathaniel B. Shurtleff and David Pulsifer, eds., *Records of the Colony of New Plymouth, in New England* (Boston: William White, 1855–1861)
PRO	The Public Record Office, Kew
Rich Papers	Vernon A. Ives, ed., *The Rich Papers: Letters from Bermuda, 1615–1646* (Toronto: University of Toronto Press, 1984)
RI Records	John Russell Bartlett, ed., *Records of the Colony of Rhode Island and Providence Plantations in New England* (Providence: A. Crawford Greene and Brother, 1856–1865)
Savage, *Dictionary*	James Savage, *A Genealogical Dictionary of the First Settlers of New England,* 4 volumes (Boston: Little Brown, 1860–1862)
SRO	Scottish Record Office, Edinburgh, Scotland
VCRP	Virginia Colonial Records Project
VHS	Virginia Historical Society, Richmond, Virginia
VMHB	*Virginia Magazine of History and Biography*
VSL	Virginia State Library and Archives, Richmond, Virginia
Winthrop, *Journal*	Richard S. Dunn, James Savage, and Laetitia Yeandle, eds., *The Journal of John Winthrop, 1630–1649* (Cambridge, Mass.: Harvard University Press, 1996)
Winthrop Papers	Allyn B. Forbes, ed., *The Winthrop Papers, 1498–1654,* 6 volumes (Boston: The Massachusetts Historical Society, 1929–present)
WMQ	*William and Mary Quarterly,* 3rd Series

Introduction

1. Petition to the Admiralty and Navy, 1634, printed in Jennings Cropper Wise, *Col. John Wise of England and Virginia (1617–1695)* (Richmond, Va.: The Bell Books and Stationery Co., 1918), pp. 29–30. John Wise and William Hudson were listed twice in 1635: first, as passengers on the *Bonaventure* on January 2; second, as passengers on the *Transport* on July 4. My suspicion is that they actually traveled on the *Transport* in July. The *Bonaventure* carried passengers bound for Maryland, and Wise and Hudson certainly ended up in Virginia. It is possible, albeit unlikely, that the pair actually made a round-trip crossing between January and July.

2. The original register, E 157/20 1-e, is located at the Public Record Office, Kew. The portion of the list comprising the Atlantic migration was published by John Camden Hotten, *The Original Lists of Persons of Quality, Emigrants . . . and Others Who Went from Great Britain to the American Plantations, 1600–*

1700 (London: Chatto and Windus, 1874). The London register is hardly unknown to other historians, who have used Hotten's compilation to count the number of travelers to the colonies in 1635. Although the London register provides the largest listing for one port for a single year, other historians have examined larger populations, most particularly the 9,868 people who departed from ports in England and Scotland over a three-year period, profiled in Bernard Bailyn, *Voyagers to the West: A Passage in the Peopling of America on the Eve of the Revolution* (New York: Knopf, 1986); and the long run of Bristol registers detailing the departures of over 10,000 people employed so effectively by David Souden, "'Rogues, Whores and Vagabonds'? Indentured Servant Emigrants to North America, and the Case of Mid-Seventeenth-Century Bristol," *Social History* 3 (1978): 23–41; Abbot Emerson Smith, *Colonists in Bondage: White Servitude and Convict Labor in America 1607–1776* (Chapel Hill: University of North Carolina Press, 1947); and David W. Galenson, *White Servitude in Colonial America: An Economic Analysis* (Cambridge: Cambridge University Press, 1981).

3. Roger Finlay has estimated the population of the city of London, Liberties, and outparishes somewhere between 301,000 and 351,000. *Population and Metropolis: The Demography of London 1580–1650* (Cambridge: Cambridge University Press, 1981), p. 60.

4. Nicholas Canny has estimated that 100,000 people migrated to Ireland before 1641. Canny, *Kingdom and Colony: Ireland in the Atlantic World, 1560–1800* (Baltimore: The Johns Hopkins University Press, 1988), p. 96.

5. Henry A. Gemery's estimate of total migration for the decade is 69,000: "Emigration from the British Isles to the New World, 1630–1700: Inferences from Colonial Populations," *Research in Economic History* 5 (1980), 216. My own estimate for the decade is slightly higher, based on various statistics on the total number of passengers from London, estimates for other ports, and extrapolations for the decade as a whole: I would set the total number of travelers to the colonies in the 1630s somewhere between 80,000 and 90,000. Although only seventeen ships departed London for New England in 1635, for example, at least thirty ships are known to have arrived in New England in that year by July alone, when ten of the ships bound from London had not yet reached New England (John Winthrop to Sir Simonds D'Ewes, 20 July 1635, *Winthrop Papers,* v. 3, p. 208). The thirty ships included four from Weymouth, one from Sandwich, three from Bristol, one from Southampton, one from Ipswich, and two Dutch ships, and ranged in size from the immense 400-ton *Great Hope* of Ipswich to the hardy 25-ton *Batchelor* of London.

6. Gemery, "Emigration from the British Isles," p. 212.

7. Bernard Bailyn, *The Peopling of British North America: An Introduction* (New York: Knopf, 1986); and Bailyn, *Voyagers;* and David Hackett Fischer, *Albion's Seed: Four British Folkways in America* (New York: Oxford University Press, 1989).

8. Such, indeed, is the ambition of the Great Migration Study Project. This immensely valuable undertaking seeks to centralize our information on the men and women who participated in the Great Migration. See Robert Charles An-

derson, *The Great Migration Begins: Immigrants to New England, 1620–1633* (Boston: New England Historic Genealogical Society, 1995), 3 volumes, for the first results of this project. Superior records and strong genealogical sources for that region have drawn historians to studies of New England settlement. Migrating cohorts analyzed by other historians for New England include the 273 travelers from Great Yarmouth and Sandwich in 1637 described by T. H. Breen and Stephen Foster in "Moving to the New World: The Character of Early Massachusetts Immigration," *WMQ* 30 (1973): 189–222; 110 passengers from Wiltshire between 1635–1638 profiled in Anthony Salerno, "The Social Background of Seventeenth-Century Emigration to America," *Journal of British Studies* 19 (1979): 31–52; and 693 passengers from Sandwich, Weymouth, Southampton, and Great Yarmouth in 1635, 1637, and 1638 in Virginia De-John Anderson, "Migrants and Motives: Religion and the Settlement of New England, 1630–1640," *NEQ* 58 (1985): 339–383; and *New England's Generation: The Great Migration and the Formation of Society and Culture in the Seventeenth Century* (New York: Cambridge University Press, 1991).

9. A preliminary effort, one that has had huge ramifications on Chesapeake scholarship, to sketch the contours of the different migrations that made Virginia society can be found in Wesley Frank Craven, *White, Red, and Black: The Seventeenth-Century Virginian* (Charlottesville: University Press of Virginia, 1971). James P. Horn, in *Adapting to a New World: English Society in the Seventeenth-Century Chesapeake* (Chapel Hill: University of North Carolina Press, 1994), has traced the experiences of migrants in Virginia by examining the parallel histories of Virginia and two counties in England. See also Russell R. Menard, "British Migration to the Chesapeake Colonies in the Seventeenth Century," in Lois Green Carr, Philip Morgan, and Jean B. Russo, eds., *Colonial Chesapeake Society* (Chapel Hill: University of North Carolina Press, 1988), pp. 99–132.

10. With the exception of Bailyn's *Voyagers,* most of these projects have focused on New England. See Breen and Foster, "Moving to the New World"; Bailyn, *Voyagers;* and Anderson, *New England's Generation* (and most particularly Anderson's Ph.D. dissertation, "To Pass Beyond the Seas: The Great Migration and the Settlement of New England, 1630–1730" [Harvard University, 1984], which she kindly permitted me to examine as I started my own research) for approaches that have helped shape the strategy followed here.

11. Nicholas Canny, "The British Atlantic World: Working Towards a Definition," *The Historical Journal* 33 (1990): 479–497; Alan Karras, introduction, to Alan Karras and J. R. McNeill, eds., *Atlantic American Societies: From Columbus through Abolition, 1492–1888* (London: Routledge, 1992), pp. 1–15; and Bernard Bailyn, "The Idea of Atlantic History," *Itinerario* 20 (1996): 19–44, have especially shaped my thinking about Atlantic history. Quotation from Ian K. Steele, "Exploding Colonial American History: Amerindian, Atlantic, and Global Perspectives," *Reviews in American History* 26 (1998), 83.

12. Helen Nader, "The End of the Old World," *Renaissance Quarterly* 45 (1992): 799.

13. J. H. Elliott, "Final Reflections: The Old World and the New Revisited," in Karen Ordahl Kupperman, ed., *America in European Consciousness, 1493–1750* (Chapel Hill: University of North Carolina Press, 1995), p. 401.

14. The absence of sources for St. Christopher, Nevis, and Antigua in the 1630s and 1640s has made it impossible for me to follow the careers of all but a few passengers to these islands.

15. Here I hope to modify one important line of analysis of colonial migration, which holds that place of origin in England and the context of migration across the Atlantic dictated in fundamental and immutable ways the settlement patterns and cultural configurations in America. For an early exploration of the important connections between old and new Englands, see Sumner Chilton Powell, *Puritan Village: The Formation of a New England Town* (Garden City, N.J.: Anchor Books, 1965). See more recently Horn, *Adapting to a New World*; David Grayson Allen, *In English Ways: The Movement of Societies and the Transferal of English Local Law and Custom to Massachusetts Bay in the Seventeenth Century* (Chapel Hill: University of North Carolina Press, 1981); and Fischer, *Albion's Seed*. I propose that we consider the ways in which migration created not only particular regional settlements but also a broader Atlantic world.

1. Clearinghouse and Countinghouse

1. Letters from William Booth to John Booth, 1628–1647 (F.c.6–16), quotations from F.c.6, F.c.7, F.c.11, F.c.14, Folger Shakespeare Library, Washington, D.C. Military service did little to ease William's financial difficulties. Subsequent letters found him begging money from his brother again—he wanted £5 to buy clothes to look presentable, and helpfully informed his brother that a sergeant on his way to London for "a supplie of men" would be a reliable bearer of this modest sum. William Booth obligingly provided John with £10 to relieve him of his debts. William made a career of the military: the final letter in the collection, dating from 1647, reveals William asking brother John yet again for money, this time for £50 to £60 to raise a company. John refused. F.c.16. An earlier version of this chapter appeared in "The English Atlantic World: A View from London," Nicholas Canny, Joseph E. Illick, Gary B. Nash, and William Pencak, eds., *Empire, Society and Labor: Essays in Honor of Richard S. Dunn, Pennsylvania History* 64 (1997) (special supplemental issue): 46–72.

2. E. A. Wrigley, "A Simple Model of London's Importance in Changing English Society and Economy, 1650–1750," *Past and Present* 37 (1967): 44–70.

3. This is the estimate of the population of the city of London, Liberties, and outparishes. Roger Finlay, *Population and Metropolis: The Demography of London 1580–1650* (Cambridge: Cambridge University Press, 1981), p. 60.

4. William Cookes, "The Cheating Age: Or Leonard of Lincolnes Journey to London to Buy Wit" [1625], facsimile in W. G. Day, ed., *The Pepys Ballads*, v. 1 (Cambridge: D. S. Brewer, 1987), pp. 158–159. See also "A Merry Progress to London to See Fashions, by a Young Country Gallant, That had More Money then Witte" (London, c. 1620), also in *Pepys Ballads*, v. 1.

5. Wesley Frank Craven and Walter B. Hayward, eds., *The Journal of Richard Norwood* (New York, 1945), passim, quotations from pp. 14–15. Norwood's disruption of his apprenticeship was not atypical given his trade. Citing studies of Norwich and Salisbury, Peter Clark points out that significant percentages of apprentices never became freemen, particularly in urban trades of lower status.

Three-quarters of the apprentices in contemporaneous Salisbury and Norwich failed to achieve their freedom at the same time that Richard Norwood sailed off to see the world. Peter Clark, "Migrants in the City," in Peter Clark and David Souden, *Migration and Society in Early Modern England* (Totowa, N.J.: Barnes and Noble Books, 1988), pp. 269–270. The Bermuda Proprietors believed that there were pearls in their distant colonial investment.

6. See Paul Slack, "Metropolitan Government in Crisis," for a discussion of mortality rates during plague years and of the government's response to the recurring problem of the plague, in A. L. Beier and Roger Finlay, *London 1500–1700: The Making of the Metropolis* (New York: Longman, 1986), pp. 60–81.

7. See John Wareing, "Migration to London and Transatlantic Emigration of Indentured Servants, 1683–1775," in *Journal of Historical Geography* 7 (1981): 356–378; David Souden, "English Indentured Servants and the Transatlantic Colonial Economy," in Shula Marks and Peter Richardson, eds., *International Labour Migration: Historical Perspectives* (Hounslow, Middlesex: Published for the Institute of Commonwealth Studies by M. Temple Smith, 1984), pp. 19–33; and Abbot Emerson Smith, *Colonists in Bondage: White Servitude and Convict Labor in America, 1607–1776* (Chapel Hill: University of North Carolina Press, 1947), chapter 3.

8. Robert Hume, *Early Child Immigrants to Virginia* (Baltimore: Magna Carta Book Co., 1986), pp. 39, 40.

9. Warrant to the sheriffs of London and Middlesex and the Keeper of Newgate, 8 July 1635 (Docquet), *CSPD* v. 93 (Charles I, Domestic), p. 262. Only four of these fourteen names appeared on Virginia passenger lists. My efforts to track down the original warrant have proved unsuccessful.

10. My interpretation of London in the 1630s and of the London port register indicates that the social and economic origins of the majority of travelers in 1635 were humble at best. For other interpretations see among others Mildred Campbell, "Social Origins of Some Early Americans," in James M. Smith, ed., *Seventeenth-Century America* (Chapel Hill: University of North Carolina Press, 1959), pp. 63–89; David Galenson, "'Middling People' or 'Common Sort'? The Social Origins of Some Early Americans Reexamined," *WMQ* 35 (1978): 499–524; and David Souden, "'Rogues, Whores, and Vagabonds': Indentured Servant Emigrants to America, and the Case of Mid-Seventeenth-Century Bristol," *Social History* 3 (1978): 23–41. I believe that any consideration of origins of migrants must be very time- and place-sensitive: origins could diverge greatly from one decade to the next, depending on a range of circumstances in England, including population growth, economic cycles, harvest failures, and local urban opportunities.

11. Ann Kussmaul, *Servants in Husbandry in Early Modern England* (Cambridge: Cambridge University Press, 1981).

12. Brian Dietz, "Overseas Trade and Metropolitan Growth," in Beier and Finlay, *London 1500–1700*, pp. 115–140.

13. According to Wrigley and Schofield, the estimated population of England was 3,597,670 in 1581 and rose to 5,091,725 in 1640. E. A. Wrigley and R. S. Schofield, *Population History of England, 1541–1871* (Cambridge, Mass.: Harvard University Press, 1981), pp. 208–209.

14. B. E. Supple, *Commercial Crisis and Change in England, 1600–1642: A Study in the Instability of a Mercantile Economy* (Cambridge: Cambridge University Press, 1959), pp. 5–6.

15. Peter Clark, "The Migrant in Kentish Towns, 1580–1640," in Peter Clark and Paul Slack, eds., *Crisis and Order in English Towns 1500–1700* (Toronto: University of Toronto Press, 1972), pp. 117–163 (quotation from page 145); and John Patten, "Patterns of Migration and Movement of Labour to Three Pre-industrial East Anglian Towns," *Journal of Historical Geography* 2 (1976), p. 118.

16. Paul A. Slack, "Vagrants and Vagrancy in England, 1598–1664," *Economic History Review* 27 (1974): 360–379; and A. L. Beier, *Masterless Men: The Vagrancy Problem in England 1560–1640* (London: Methuen, 1985).

17. Clark, "Kentish Towns"; and Souden, "'Rogues, Whores, and Vagabonds'," p. 161.

18. M. J. Power, "East London Housing in the Seventeenth Century," in Clark and Slack, *Crisis and Order,* p. 237.

19. Jeremy Boulton, "Neighbourhood Migration in Early Modern London," in *Migration and Society,* p. 108; Finlay, *Population and Metropolis,* pp. 64, 66. In a study of emigrants to the colonies from London in the eighteenth century, by which time internal migration had subsided substantially, 65 percent of migrants came from over 100 kilometers away. Wareing, "Migration to London and Transatlantic Emigration of Indentured Servants."

20. Irene Scouloudi, *Returns of Strangers in the Metropolis 1593, 1627, 1635, 1649: A Study of an Active Minority, Publications of the Huguenot Society of London* 57 (1985), p. 96.

21. *A Proclamation Declaring His Majesties pleasure concerning Sir Walter Rawleigh* (London, 1618); and *A Proclamation declaring His Majesties pleasure concerning Captaine Roger North* (London, 1620).

22. Charles I, *Against Travellers without Licenses 19 November 1630* (London, 1630).

23. On accommodation under James I, see Nicholas Tyacke, *Anti-Calvinists: The Rise of English Arminianism, c. 1590–1640* (Oxford: Oxford University Press, 1987), p. 3.

24. Derek Hirst, *Authority and Conflict: England, 1603–1658* (Cambridge, Mass.: Harvard University Press, 1986), p. 165; and Tyacke, *Anti-Calvinists,* p. 246.

25. Robin Clifton, "Fear of Popery," in Conrad Russell, ed., *The Origins of the English Civil War* (London: Macmillan, 1973), p. 146.

26. See, for example, the series of actions against the 1635 traveler Thomas Shepard and Mr. Anger for their purported preaching without licenses in Earls Colne, in the Archdeaconry of Colchester Act books, 1627–1633, microfiche at the Institute of Historical Research, London.

27. R. J. Acheson, *Radical Puritans in England 1550–1660* (London: Longman, 1990), p. 44. Puritans emphasized preaching and the Bible, deplored and feared Catholicism, and sought to secure the conformity of society within a "culture of discipline." This is William Hunt's definition of puritanism, taken from *The Puritan Moment: The Coming of Revolution in an English County* (Cambridge, Mass.: Harvard University Press, 1983), p. x. For a narrower definition, see Paul Christianson, "Reformers and the Church of England under Elizabeth and the Early Stuarts," *Journal of Ecclesiastical History* 31 (1980): 463–482.

28. Quoted in Michael MacCarthy-Morrogh, *The Munster Plantation: English Migration to Southern Ireland, 1583–1641* (Oxford: Oxford University Press, 1986), p. 203.

29. Richard Saltonstall, Jr., to John Winthrop, Jr., 22 June 1632, Robert Moody, ed., *The Saltonstall Papers, 1607–1815* (Boston: The Massachusetts Historical Society, 1972), v. 1, p. 119.

30. 31 December 1634, Commission for Foreign Plantations, *The Winthrop Papers*, v. 3, pp. 180–181. Laud, as Archbishop of Canterbury, sat on the Privy Council and was a Commissioner for Foreign Plantations. For the February decree of the Privy Council, see W. L. Grant and James Munro, ed., *Acts of the Privy Council (Colonial)*, v. 1 (London: H. M. Stationery Office, 1908), pp. 199–201. Objections by the planters of New England to such regulations can be found in CO 1/8, items 40 and 41, PRO. Laud was also concerned about English congregations on the continent. In June of 1634 he and Bishop Juxon of London instructed the English merchants who lived at Delft about their newly appointed preacher and their conformity to the Church of England (*CSPD*, Charles I, v. 7, 21 June 1634, no. 3, p. 87).

31. In addition to the uses of *traveler* in some of the legal restrictions cited earlier, see especially Thomas Palmer, *An Essay of the Meanes How to Make Our Travailes, into Forraine Countries, the More Profitable and Honourable* (London, 1606). Palmer divided travelers into three parts: involuntary (those voyaging on missions of church, state, or law), nonvoluntary (those who traveled for reasons of religion), and voluntary (merchants, mechanics, artisans, tradesmen). My thanks to Cynthia Van Zandt for calling my attention to this book.

32. Nicholas Canny, *Kingdom and Colony: Ireland in the Atlantic World, 1560–1800* (Baltimore: The Johns Hopkins University Press, 1988), p. 96 (population estimate), p. 77 (quotation).

33. John Winthrop to John Winthrop Jr., 20 April 1623, *Winthrop Papers*, v. 1, p. 281; and Nicholas Canny, "The Origins of Empire: An Introduction," in Canny, ed., *The Origins of Empire* (Oxford: Oxford University Press, 1998), p. 6.

34. M. Perceval-Maxwell, *The Scottish Migration to Ulster in the Reign of James I* (London: Routledge and Kegan Paul, 1973), p. 313.

35. About 2,000 cloth workers migrated from the Weald in 1616 to the Palatinate, whereas smaller numbers migrated in the 1630s. C. W. Chalklin, *Seventeenth-Century Kent: A Social and Economic History* (London, 1965), p. 35; and James Horn, *Adapting to a New World: English Society in the Seventeenth-Century Chesapeake* (Chapel Hill: University of North Carolina Press, 1994), pp. 104–106.

36. A note in June of 1634 detailed the number of ships in each of England's vice-admiralties. London's port accounted for 154 ships and vessels, including 8 large East India Company ships. Other vice-admiralties contained more ships (such as Suffolk's 233 or Hants's 166), but no single port was as active as London. *CSPD* Charles I, v. 7, p. 101–102, item 64.

37. Clark, "Kentish Towns," p. 138.

38. William Booth to John Booth, 16 July 1629, F.c.14, Folger Shakespeare Library, Washington, D.C.

39. Wrigley and Schofield, *Population History*, p. 216. Some of those New England-ers in the 15 to 24 age category were children traveling with their parents, young tradesmen, and young married couples.

40. See entry for 20 February 1634/5, E 157/20 1-e.

41. "Gallants, to Bohemia. Or, let us to the Warres again: Shewing the forwardnesse of our English Souldiers, both in times past, and at this present" [1632], in W. G. Day, ed., *The Pepys Ballads*, v. 1, pp. 102–103.

42. See especially Nicholas Canny, "The Ideology of English Colonization: From Ireland to America," *WMQ* 30 (1973): 575–598.

43. L. M. Cullen considers the relationship between military service and emigration in "The Irish Diaspora" in Nicholas Canny, ed., *Europeans on the Move* (New York: Oxford University Press, 1994), pp. 120–126.

44. Commission for Foreign Plantations, December 1634, *Winthrop Papers*, v. 3, p. 180.

45. None of the passengers to Providence, Virginia, Bermuda, Barbados, or Saint Christopher were registered with place of residence indicated, and attempting to seek English residences with no evidence at hand is probably a more daunting task than seeking the proverbial needle in the haystack. A total of 317 New England passengers recorded their place of residence in the port register, but even these parishes are misleading. Some people were listed from one particular parish, but they had moved there recently from other counties or had demon-strated such repeated mobility in England that to attribute them to one county is misleading.

46. Canny, *Kingdom and Colony*, p. 100.

47. See *The Registers of St. Katharine by the Tower, London,* Part I (Baptisms, Mar-riages, Burials, 1584–1625), and Part II (Baptisms, Marriages, Burials, 1626–1665), transcribed and edited by A. W. Hughes Clarke, *Publications of the Har-leian Society* vv. 75, 76 (London, 1945–1946).

48. London Port Books, E 190/38/1, E 190/41/5; will of Nathaniel Braddock, Pile, 55, PRO. Admittedly, the bias of extant records favors those who lived in London and could conveniently attend court sessions there. Of those Virginia passengers testifying at the Admiralty hearings for the failed voyage of the *Constance,* all were from London or metropolitan Middlesex.

49. Attestation of William Alberie, 22 February 1658/9, Bermuda Colonial Re-cords, v. 2, pp. 312–313, Berm. Arch; Glassington and Meverill were born in London, Vincent was married there, International Genealogical Index, The Guildhall, London. Vincent was a minister, and the other three were servants.

50. A younger Van Heck son, born in Virginia, was naturalized in Maryland by Act of Assembly in 1669. Edward C. Papenfuse et. al., eds., *A Biographical Diction-ary of the Maryland Legislature, 1635–1789* (Baltimore: The Johns Hopkins University Press, 1979–1985), v. 2, p. 849.

51. A. P. Newton, *The Colonising Activities of the English Puritans* (New Haven: Yale University Press, 1914), p. 16. Rich apparently sailed ships with commis-sions from several different sources.

52. Accounts of tobacco shipped in the *Abraham,* June 1637, HCA 30/636, PRO.

53. Jacob M. Price observes in *Perry of London: A Family and a Firm on the Seaborne Frontier, 1615–1753* (Cambridge, Mass.: Harvard University Press,

1992) that by the end of the seventeenth century, among traders and the lesser gentry a "peripatetic, migratory . . . subculture" emerged (p. 1). The evidence here suggests that that subculture was in place much earlier in the century, at least on the continent.

54. In October of 1635 two men named Peter or Peeter Deboyse (Deboyses) were listed as residents in London. The first one, Peeter, was a weaver, who with his wife had lived in England six years. They were born in Hainault, in Valenciennes, and had three children, who were born in England. They lived with one John Deboyhe, born in Ypres. The second man, also a weaver, lived with his wife. They were Flemish and had lived in London for two years. Scouloudi, *Strangers,* p. 266.

55. In the year 1635, for example, there were a total of 2,499 "strangers" dwelling in the city of London alone, with another 1,134 living in metropolitan Middlesex, Surrey, and in Westminster. Their occupations were dominated by cloth making, which accounted for a total of 713 of the strangers altogether (609 were weavers): a remaining 129 were clothes makers (104 were tailors). See Scouloudi, *Strangers,* pp. 124–125, 133. Amidst the economic strains of the period, the presence of strangers trading and working in the city was a source of conflict with native-born workers, who complained to the Privy Council that foreigners were stealing their custom. In response to these complaints, in September of 1635 a record was undertaken of all the strangers in the city, resulting in the detailed Return of 1635, which named the strangers and their occupations. Scouloudi, pp. 96–97.

56. The clerks recorded the three destinations as Amsterdam, Cave, and the Low Countries.

57. Simon Schama, *The Embarrassment of Riches: An Interpretation of Dutch Culture in the Golden Age* (New York: Knopf, 1987), pp. 193–195. In the 1630s the Dutch started domestic cultivation of tobacco.

58. Babette Levy, "Early Puritanism in the Southern and Island Colonies," *American Antiquarian Society Proceedings* 70 (1960), 81.

59. See the Gay Transcripts, Peter Papers, v. 4, for documents concerning the English ministers in the Netherlands in the 1630s, MHS.

60. Peter Coldham, *English Adventurers and Emigrants, 1609–1660: Abstracts of Examinations in the High Court of Admiralty with Reference to Colonial America* (Baltimore: Genealogical Publishing Company, 1984), depositions *re* the *Elizabeth* of London, p. 72. See also the deposition of Thomas Young, HCA 13/53, f. 132, PRO, who was captain of the *Elizabeth*. He deposed about the ship's difficulties departing from the Chesapeake back to England. The ship reached Point Comfort, and all the company refused to go to sea again because of its poor condition.

61. John Chappell and Nathaniel Wright had imported goods from the colonies— Virginia tobacco and muscavado (unrefined) sugar—to London in 1633. In 1635 Chappell boarded a ship for Virginia, whereas Wright traveled to Barbados. Three other Virginia-bound travelers, John Redman, Thomas Bradford, and John Butler, were tobacco merchants. Wright imported sugar, 25 January 1632/3, whereas Chappell imported Virginia tobacco, 17 May 1633, E

190/38/1, f. 12 recto, f. 59 recto, London Port Book 1632–1633, PRO. For John Redman, see Thomas Gower v. William Anthony, 9 May 1637, HCA 13/111 (no page numbers); for John Butler, E 190/41/5, f. 48verso, lists his tobacco imports in 1637, PRO; for Thomas Bradford, see petition, c. 1644, of merchants, grocers, and others dealing in tobacco, Harley 1238, f. 9, BL. On the circumstances that inspired and bedeviled these tobacco merchants, see John Pagan, "Growth of the Tobacco Trade between London and Virginia, 1614–1640," *Guildhall Studies* 3 (1979): 248–262.

62. Petition of Agnes Grace to House of Commons, State Papers, Domestic, Charles I, SP 16/475, VCRP reel 356, VSL. George Grace appears in the London port books: see, i.e., E 190/8/1, London Port Book listing exports and imports by denizens, f. 11recto, 23 January 1632/3, in which Grace shipped linen, PRO.

63. David Hancock, *Citizens of the World: London Merchants and the Integration of the British Atlantic Community, 1735–1785* (Cambridge: Cambridge University Press, 1995), p. 85.

64. Agreement for the settlement of the plantation in Ulster, 28 January 1609/10, EL 1740; and list of moneys collected in London for the plantation in Ulster, 1613, 1614, 1615, 1745, Ellesmere Collection, Huntington Library, San Marino, Calif.

65. T. K. Rabb, *Enterprise and Empire: Merchant and Gentry Investment in the Expansion of England, 1575–1630* (Cambridge, Mass.: Harvard University Press, 1967), p. 89.

66. Robert Brenner, *Merchants and Revolution: Commercial Change, Political Conflict, and London's Overseas Traders, 1550–1653* (Princeton: Princeton University Press, 1993), pp. 114–115.

67. Rabb, *Enterprise and Empire,* Table 12, p. 108.

68. Court held for Providence, 3 December 1631, CO 124/2, p. 43, PRO.

69. Court held 4 February 1634/5, CO 124/2, p. 190; and letter to Captain Philip Bell by the *Expectation,* 20 April 1635, CO 124/1, f. 76verso, PRO.

70. Letter to Captain Philip Bell, CO 124/1, f. 79, PRO.

71. Richard S. Dunn, *Puritans and Yankees: The Winthrop Dynasty of New England 1630–1717* (New York: Norton, 1971), pp. 63–72.

72. Letter to Captain Henry Ashton and the commissioners of Barbados, 27 March 1640, Hay Papers, GD34/922, SRO.

73. John Rolf, "Certain Reasons touching ye most convenient times & seasons of ye yeare for ye magazine ship to set forth for Engld towards Virga," Brock Collection, Brock 583, p. 88, Huntington Library, San Marino, Calif. See also R. M., *Newes of Sr. Walter Rauleigh* (London, 1618), p. 25.

74. Virginia Company, *A Note of the Shipping, Men, and Provisions Sent and Provided for Virginia . . . in the Yeere 1621* (London, 1622).

75. Winthrop, *Journal,* p. 147.

76. The unfortunate Tom Verney, who failed after nine months in the colony, was aboard the *Merchant's Hope* on its 1634 voyage and wrote his aunt and uncle a letter only hours before the ship departed. John Bruce, ed., *Letters and Papers of the Verney Family Down to the End of the Year 1639* (London: Camden Society, 1853), p. 163.

77. Joan de Rivera, "Shipwrecked Spaniards 1639: Grievances Against Bermudians," L. D. Gurrin, trans., *BHQ* 18 (1961), p. 17.
78. Ordinary courts held for Providence Island, 4 February 1634/5 and 9 February 1634/5, CO 124/2, pp. 190–192, PRO.
79. A number of the *Bonaventure*'s passengers were listed in *A Relation of Maryland* (London, 1635).
80. Henry Fetherston and Thomas Babb v. Thomas Stanley, 16 March 1635/6 to 15 June 1636, HCA records, in Coldham, *English Adventurers and Emigrants,* pp. 63–64.
81. Deed of Richard Lambert, 15 May 1635, HCA 30/547, PRO. Lambert, of Colchester, Essex, was the master of the *Thomas and John.*
82. John Onions v. the *Hope,* Coldham, *English Adventurers and Emigrants,* p. 105.
83. Instructions to Thomas Punt, 8 May 1632, CO 124/1, f. 43recto, PRO.
84. William Woodcock and Joseph Yonge v. John Thierry, 28 February 1635/6, HCA records, printed in "Notes on New England Voyages," *NEHGR* 104 (1950): 17–18. There is no indication of where these thirty people boarded the *Love:* only eight passengers were registered in London.
85. Henry A. Gemery, "Emigration from the British Isles to the New World, 1630–1700: Inferences from Colonial Populations," *Research in Economic History* 5 (1980), 180, refers to seventeenth-century emigration as one of the "darker corners" in England's economic history.

2. The Colonial Travelers of 1635

1. Mercers' Company Court Records, 1619–1625, f. 87; 1625–1631, f. 224recto, Mercers' Company Archives, Mercers' Hall, London; will of Nathaniel Braddock, Pile 55, PRO.
2. Mercers' Company Court Records, 1631–1637, ff. 7verso, 37recto, 129recto, 143recto, Mercers' Company Archives, Mercers' Hall, London.
3. On the "new men," those merchants who lacked Company affiliation and through sheer hard work invested in Virginia plantations in order to initiate their trading careers, see Robert Brenner, *Merchants and Revolution: Commercial Change, Political Conflict, and London's Overseas Traders, 1550–1653* (Princeton: Princeton University Press, 1993), chapter three, and p. 114.
4. Jacob Price, "Transaction Costs," in James D. Tracy, ed., *Political Economy of Merchant Empires* (Cambridge: Cambridge University Press, 1991), p. 280.
5. Michael McGiffert, ed., *God's Plot: The Paradoxes of Puritan Piety, Being the Autobiography and Journal of Thomas Shepard* (Amherst: University of Massachusetts Press, 1972), p. 60.
6. Sarra Simes may have been regarded by the Harlakenden family as a maidservant of sorts, but she was also a family friend with well-placed relations. She referred to John Stedman and William French as her brothers in her will ("Genealogical Gleanings," *NEHGR* 48 [1894], 126).
7. In his study of migration from East Anglia, N. C. P. Tyack suspected that Samuel Shepard was actually Thomas Shepard in disguise (Tyack, "Migration from East Anglia to New England before 1660" [Ph.D. Dissertation, Univer-

sity of London, 1951], p. 271). My belief is that Thomas Shepard was disguised as one John Shepard, a husbandman, whereas this Samuel was truly the brother.

8. The quotation comes from William Hubbard's *History,* revised first chapters, 2 *MHS Coll.* 5, 6, 1878 additions, p. ix. Hubbard himself had traveled as a thirteen-year-old child from London in 1635, so perhaps he recalled the discussions that had transpired before his own family relocated in that year. The contrast depicted here does not by any means intend to suggest that financial considerations did not also shape departures for New England. The phrase "vessels of glory" appears frequently in writings of the period. See Thomas Shepard to Mr. Secks, 19 December 1646, Add. 4,276, f. 138, BL, in which Shepard hoped that God would prepare the native people of New England to be vessels of glory. John Winthrop's paternal exhortations to his oldest son John while the boy was enrolled at Trinity College in Dublin included the father's fervant desire that God "hath pleased to make thee a vessell of glorye." Winthrop Papers, reel 1, 26 April 1623, MHS.

9. Winthrop, *Journal,* p. 270; *Suffolk County Wills: Abstracts of the Earliest Wills Upon Record in the County of Suffolk, Massachusetts* (Baltimore: Genealogical Publishing Company, Inc., 1984), pp. 6–8.

10. Irene W. D. Hecht, "The Virginia Muster of 1624/5 as a Source for Demographic History," *WMQ* 30 (1973): 70.

11. Again, for a comparison with the Virginia Muster: in 1624/5, 34.1 percent of the population fell between the ages of 15 and 24, still significantly higher than the population of England (Hecht, "Virginia Muster," 71). There was, however, a higher percentage of children resident in the colony in 1625 than traveled there from London in 1635.

12. See David Galenson, *White Servitude in Colonial America: An Economic Analysis* (Cambridge: Cambridge University Press, 1981), p. 95, for differential skill levels correlated with age on Barbados.

13. It is hard to believe that all thirty-one children could have been children of first marriages with different surnames from remarried parents.

14. Robert Hume, *Early Child Immigrants to Virginia, 1618–1642* (Baltimore: Magna Carta Book Co., 1986), pp. 40–41.

15. Lewis Hughes, *To the Right Honourable, The Lords and others of his Majesties most Honourable privie Councell* (London, 1625?), B1 recto-verso.

16. Joan de Rivera, "Shipwrecked Spaniard 1639: Grievances against Bermudians," trans. L. D. Gurrin, *BHQ* 18 (1961), 26.

17. Court for Providence Island, 3 December 1631, CO 124/2, pp. 42–43, PRO.

18. Only two youths in this age bracket were dependent children.

19. This is almost identical to the figure that Ann Kussmaul ascertained for youths between the ages of 15 and 24 in England, 60 percent of whom were servants. See Ann Kussmaul, *Servants in Husbandry in Early Modern England* (Cambridge: Cambridge University Press, 1981), pp. 3–4.

20. Providence Island Committee held 5 March 1634/5, CO 124/2, p. 201, PRO. It is fortuitous that the most extensively discussed ship sent to the Island was the *Expectation,* which sailed from London in 1635. Unfortunately, most people

were not listed by name in the Company records, so it is difficult to attach particular occupations to individuals.

21. Providence Island Committees, held 23 March 1634/5, 10 April 1635, 17 April 1635, CO 124/2, pp. 210–214, PRO.

22. Here my statistics are able to confirm Wesley Frank Craven's estimate that 75 percent of early Virginians were servants. *White, Red, and Black: The Seventeenth-Century Virginian* (Charlottesville: University Press of Virginia, 1971), p. 5.

23. Occupations listed for New England include fifty-eight servants, forty-seven husbandmen, thirteen tailors, ten carpenters, seven shoemakers, four glovers; three each for bakers, linen weavers, masons, millers, and tanners; two each for clothiers, carriers, fishermen, joiners, and laborers; one each of the following: barber, bricklayer, butcher, cloth worker, draper, fishmonger, glazier, harness maker, innkeeper, linen draper, mercer, ostler, plow wright, soap boiler, starch maker, stationer, surgeon, tallow chandler, turner, weaver, wheelwright, and wholesale man. The information provided, however, is not consistently reliable. See Games, "Venturers, Vagrants, and Vessels of Glory: Migration from England to the Colonies under Charles I" (Ph.D. Dissertation, University of Pennsylvania, 1992), pp. 53–58, for a discussion of the adjustments to occupations recorded in the port register. Another category not considered under occupations would include statesmen, such as John Winthrop, Jr., the governor of the new Saybrook colony.

24. The actual number of servants for the New England–bound population as a whole is probably at least four times as high as that listed before, but because so many likely servants vanish in the New England records, only those individuals recorded as servants or definitely known to have crossed the Atlantic in conditions of indenture are included here.

25. Family size of Virginia passengers was much smaller than that in New England: most of the Virginia families were headed by young couples and thus contained either only one child or, at most, two children.

26. The quotations are from Robert Cushman, *A Sermon Preached at Plimmoth in New England* (London, 1622), p. 11.

27. Thomas Lawrence left his wife an estate valued at £823.1.8 by Joan, who was the estate's administrator. See the account, A25/2962, HRO. Marriage licenses in William Brigg, ed., *The Herts Genealogist and Antiquary* 1 (Harpenden, 1895), 291.

28. Draft Minute Books of the Borough Court, St. Albans Borough Records #289, 1612–1613, and Mayor's Court Book 1586–1633, St. Albans Borough Records #312, St. Albans Public Library, St. Albans, Hertfordshire.

29. Mayor's Court Book 1586–1633, St. Albans Borough Records #312, f. 101, St. Albans Public Library; and Account of the Estate of Thomas Lawrence, A25/2962, HRO.

30. Mayor's Accounts 1627–1628, St. Albans Borough Records #164, St. Albans Public Library. Of this £6, the court subsequently returned £4 to Tuttle.

31. Mayor's Court Book 1586–1633, f. 124, St. Albans Borough Records #312, St. Albans Public Library.

32. Three possible reasons for the Tuttle family exodus suggest themselves. One possibility is that John Tuttle, a draper, suffered during the cloth depressions of the period and sought greater opportunity for his large extended family in the new world. Second, John Tuttle was clearly committed to a puritan vision: he returned to England during the Civil War to serve the Parliamentary forces and died in Ireland during the Commonwealth. St. Albans itself may have had an active nonconformist community. Two fellow residents, Thomas and Marie Olney, who had also migrated in 1635 with their children Thomas and Epenetus, became Baptists in Massachusetts and followed Roger Williams to Rhode Island. Third, John Tuttle may have been influenced by his westward-looking relatives. For the Tuttle family, then, settlement in New England could have provided a solution to three vexing problems: economic insecurity, religious intolerance, and family separation.

33. *The Planters Plea or The Grounds of Plantations Examined, and Usuall Objections answered* (London, 1630), p. 32.

34. "Genealogical Research in England," *NEHGR* 69 (1915): 357–358.

35. Cornelius May, senior, had been resident in Virginia since 1616, when he arrived on the *Providence* at age 25, according to the Virginia muster. John Camden Hotten, *The Original Lists of Persons of Quality, Emigrants . . . and Others Who Went from Great Britain to the American Plantations, 1600–1700* (London: Chatto and Windus, 1874), p. 247.

36. John Bruce, ed., *Letters and Papers of the Verney Family Down to the End of the Year 1639* (London: Camden Society, 1853), p. 163.

37. G. Garrad to [Lord Conway], 18 September 1635, *CSPC*, 1574–1660, p. 214.

38. Of the ships embarked from London, size is known for only ten: the 25-ton *Batchelor;* the *Christian* (40 tons); the *Planter* of London (170 tons); the *Merchant's Hope* of London (90); the *Elizabeth* of London (220); the *Rebecca* (100); the *Hopewell* (200); the *Elizabeth and Ann* (300); the *Susan and Ellen* (240); and the *Thomas and John* (200). See lists of Trinity House Certificates for ships for the years 1633 and 1634, *CSPD*, Charles I, v. 6, p. 389, v. 7, p. 448. The range in ship size for ships plying the Atlantic suggests that in the early seventeenth century, ships had not yet become specialized in size or structure for particular carrying trades, as would be the case by the eighteenth century. Russell R. Menard, "Transport Costs and Long-Range Trade, 1300–1800," in Tracy, ed., *The Political Economy of Merchant Empires,* pp. 252–267.

39. Henry Vane to Sir Henry Vane, 7 July 1635, SP 16/293, ff. 130–131 [State Papers, Domestic, Charles I], PRO.

40. Winthrop, *Journal,* p. 157. Young Vane hardly returned the king's favor: fourteen years later, Vane would be one of the strongest advocates for the king's execution.

41. McGiffert, ed., *God's Plot,* pp. 33, 55–56.

42. McGiffert, ed., *God's Plot,* pp. 50–64. For a listing of Shepard's offenses, see the Archdeaconry of Colchester Act Book, in the Earls Colne microfiche collection, or the original at the Essex Record Office, D/A CA47.

43. The strategy of disguising prominent clerics as servants, moreover, highlights

the widespread conviction, suggested but not stated in the register itself, by travelers that the clerks had no interest in these passengers.

44. Philip Nye to John Winthrop, Jr., London, 21 September 1635, *Winthrop Papers,* v. 3, p. 211.

45. Winthrop, *Journal,* pp. 157, 162. William Woodcock and Joseph Yonge v. John Thierry, 28 February 1635/6, HCA records, printed in "Notes on New England Voyages," *NEHGR* 104 (1950): 17–18.

46. Three Essex men who traveled with their families in 1635, Simon Stone, Mathew Marvin, and Edmund Munnings, appeared in the 1629 Essex lay subsidy rolls, each one assessed for 20 shillings in land. Essex Lay Subsidies, 4 Charles I, E 179/112/638, E 179/112/632, PRO.

47. Simon and Dorothy Eires sold two messuages, one stable, and two gardens. Feet of Fines 13 April 1635, printed in *NEHGR* 69 (1915): 248–249. Philip and Anne Kirtland transferred portions of their copyhold for a total of approximately £37. Mercers' Company Court Records, Acts of Court 1631–1637, f. 178 recto-verso. Mercers' Company, Mercers' Hall, London.

48. *A Proposition of Provisions Needfull for Such as Intend to Plant themselves in New England, for one whole Yeare, collected by the Adventurers, with the Advice of the Planters* (London, 1630).

49. John Winthrop to Margaret Winthrop, 23 July 1630, *Winthrop Papers,* v. 2, pp. 303–304.

50. Edward Hopkins to John Winthrop, Jr., London, 16 August 1635, *Winthrop Papers,* v. 3, pp. 202–203.

51. William Woodcock and Joseph Yonge v. John Thierry, 28 February 1635/6, HCA records, printed in "Notes on New England Voyages," *NEHGR* 104 (1950): 17–18.

52. Mr. John Sadler to Sir Edmund and Lady Verney, 30 July 1634, Bruce, ed., *Verney Papers,* p. 161.

53. Testimony of Henry Williamson, 15 December 1635, HCA 13/52, f. 190. See also "A Proportion of the charge to furnishe and transport six men to Virginia," CO 1/1, part 2, p. 210, PRO.

54. Depositions of John Withins, gentleman of St. Andrew, Holborn, London, and John Ashcroft, embroiderer of St. Andrew, Holburn, London, HCA 13/52, PRO.

55. General Court for Providence Island, 9–11 February 1631/2, CO 124/2, p. 50, PRO.

56. *Journal of Richard Mather, 1635, Collections of the Dorchester Antiquarian and Historical Society* 3 (Boston, 1850), p. 6. It is surprising that Mather so easily received permission to sail.

57. *Journal of Richard Mather,* pp. 9–13.

58. Francis Higginson to his Friends, in England, 24 July 1629, Everett Emerson, ed., *Letters from New England: The Massachusetts Bay Colony, 1629–1638* (Amherst: University of Massachusetts Press, 1976), pp. 14–15.

59. *A Relation of Maryland* (London, 1635), p. 41.

60. Higginson to his Friends in Emerson, ed., *Letters,* p. 23; and John Winthrop to Margaret Winthrop, 29 November 1630, *Winthrop Papers,* v. 2, p. 319.

61. Winthrop, *Journal*, p. 199.
62. John Dutton to the Earl of Warwick, 20 January 1619/20, *Rich Papers*, p. 143.
63. "The Voyage of Sir Henrye Colt to ye Ilands of ye Antilles," in V. T. Harlow, ed., *Colonising Expeditions to the West Indies and Guiana, 1623–1667* (London, 1925), p. 95.
64. *Journal of Richard Mather*, p. 33.
65. John Winthrop to Margaret Winthrop, 9 September 1630, *Winthrop Papers*, v. 2, p. 313.
66. Winthrop, *Journal*, p. 152.
67. Emery Battis, *Saints and Sectaries: Anne Hutchinson and the Antinomian Controversy in the Massachusetts Bay Colony* (Chapel Hill: University of North Carolina Press, 1962), p. 93; Winthrop, *Journal*, p. 157.
68. *A Relation of Maryland*, p. 46.
69. Thomas Rous to Archibald Haye, Barbados, 26 May 1638, GD 34/923/12, Hay Papers, SRO.
70. *Journal of Richard Mather*, pp. 21–22.
71. Thomas Moore and John Digby v. John Thierry, 15 December 1635–3 July 1637, HCA 13/52, ff. 190, 213, 214, 348, 396, 410, PRO.
72. Daniel Tucker to Nathaniel Rich, 14 July 1616, *Rich Papers*, p. 8.
73. Letter from Master Wells to his people at Terling in Essex, 1633, Gay Transcripts, Miscellaneous, MHS.
74. Higginson to his Friends, 24 July 1629, in Emerson, ed., *Letters*, pp. 23–24.
75. David Cressy, *Coming Over: Migration and Communication between England and New England in the Seventeenth Century* (Cambridge: Cambridge University Press, 1987), especially chapter 6. Frank Thistlethwaite, *Dorset Pilgrims: The Story of West Country Pilgrims Who Went to New England in the 17th Century* (London: Barry and Jenkins, 1989), p. 69, talks about the formative experience, especially for children; Michael Zuckerman, "Identity in British America: Unease in Eden," in Nicholas Canny and Anthony Pagden, *Colonial Identity in the Atlantic World, 1500–1800* (Princeton: Princeton University Press, 1987), p. 119; Virginia Anderson called the voyage the "dramatic turning point in the lives of the emigrants" (*New England's Generation* [New York: Cambridge University Press, 1991], p. 88).
76. Commission to Mr. Gates and Samuell Symonds, 16 August 1634, CO 124/1, f. 75recto, PRO.
77. *A Relation of Maryland*, p. 132.
78. This tale appears in a pamphlet Nathaniel White wrote to justify the existence of the Independent faction on Bermuda, *Truth Gloriously Appearing* (London, 1646), p. 91.
79. General Court for Providence, 19 June 1634, CO 124/2, p. 151, PRO.
80. "The Answer of Thomas Babb Marchange defdt to the Bill of Complt of George Rolfe complt," in CO 1/6, pp. 224–230, PRO.
81. HCA 30/635, Book of Accompte for the Shippe called ye Tristram and Jeane, PRO.

3. Life, Death, and Labor

1. See Figure 5 for the port register entry in which the Cookes, Samuel Shepard, and William French were disguised as servants.

2. The best parallel with colonial societies would be military regiments stationed abroad. There, however, hierarchies were more elaborately defined, dictated clearly by rank, and well-established traditions of regulation, regimentation, and punishment were in place. Governor Dale of Virginia recognized the parallels when he decreed military law in the colony in 1610.

3. Ann Kussmaul, *Servants in Husbandry in Early Modern England* (Cambridge: Cambridge University Press, 1981), pp. 3–4. Kussmaul provides evidence that suggests that one English farmer differentiated between these servants and laborers. The farmer numbered his family as seventeen (twelve servants and his nuclear family), clearly not counting his ten hired laborers (Kussmaul, p. 8).

4. Richard Dunn has offered some other calculations about the extent of servitude in the colonies. Drawing on a variety of sources, he notes that in 1625, half the population of Virginia were servants; and in the West Indies by 1638, over half the Barbados population were servants. Richard S. Dunn, "The Recruitment and Employment of Labor," in Jack P. Greene and J. R. Pole, *Colonial British America: Essays in the New History of the Early Modern Era* (Baltimore: The Johns Hopkins University Press, 1984), p. 160. The higher percentage of Virginia-bound servants in the 1635 cohort might reflect an enhanced need for laborers by that year.

5. Kussmaul, *Servants,* pp. 27–28.

6. Kussmaul, *Servants,* p. 9.

7. Peter Hay letter, quoted in J. H. Bennett, "Peter Hay, Proprietary Agent in Barbados, 1636–1641," *Jamaican Historical Review* 5 (1965): 10–11.

8. Peter Hay to James Hay, Barbados, 15 October 1636, GD 34/923/3, SRO.

9. Meeting of the Providence Island Company, 22 November 1630, CO 124/2, p. 3, PRO.

10. William Jessop to Mr. Halhead, August 1634, Jessop Letterbook, letter 47, BL.

11. Thomas Durham to Sir Nathaniel Rich, October or November 1620, *Rich Papers,* p. 218. Durham's comment suggests that black workers were less expensive to purchase than were English servants to hire and maintain.

12. Robert Barrington to John Winthrop, Jr., 4 September 1635, *Winthrop Papers,* v. 3, p. 208.

13. John Dutton to the Earl of Warwick, 20 January 1619/20, *Rich Papers,* p. 143.

14. Edmund S. Morgan, *American Slavery, American Freedom: The Ordeal of Colonial Virginia* (New York: Norton, 1975), chapter 6, pp. 134–135. On rising tobacco prices, see the painstaking work of Russell Menard, especially *Economy and Society in Early Colonial Maryland* (New York: Garland, 1985), Appendix III. For an alternative interpretation, however, see David Harris Sacks, *The Widening Gate: Bristol and the Atlantic Economy* (Berkeley: University of California Press, 1991). Sacks argues in chapter nine that tobacco prices did not correlate precisely with servant registrations in Bristol later in the century. Instead, a range of variables, including especially internal political and religious

affairs in Bristol, dictated the number of servants who were registered for overseas voyages.

15. Thomas Moore and John Digby v. John Thierry, 15 December 1635–3 July 1637, HCA 13/52 and 13/53, various, PRO.

16. James Horn found similar patterns in his study of the Bristol, London, and Liverpool lists later in the century. Eighty percent of servants were contracted by small merchants and traders. See James Horn, "Servant Emigration to the Chesapeake in the Seventeenth Century," in Thad W. Tate and David L. Ammerman, eds., *The Chesapeake in the Seventeenth Century: Essays on Anglo-American Society and Politics* (Chapel Hill: University of North Carolina Press, 1979), p. 89. Evidence from Virginia land records, however, indicates that individual planters could at times pay for larger parties of laborers. Robert Freeman, a planter in James City County, claimed 700 acres in September of 1638 for transporting fourteen people, twelve of whom had traveled in 1635 on the *Assurance* from London (Nugent, p. 97).

17. Mr. John Sadler to Sir Edmund and Lady Verney, 30 July 1634, in John Bruce, ed., *Letters and Papers of the Verney Family Down to the End of the Year 1639* (London: Camden Society, 1853), p. 160. See also *A Relation of Maryland* (London, 1635), p. 52.

18. Letter from Henry Hawley to Sir James Hay, Barbados, 6 September 1636, Hay Papers, GD 34/922, SRO.

19. See William Jessop to Mr. Isaac Barton, 11 August 1634, and Jessop to Ensign Fitch, 12 August 1634, Jessop Letterbook, letters 28, 31, BL.

20. Abbot Emerson Smith, *Colonists in Bondage: White Servitude and Convict Labor in America 1607–1776* (Chapel Hill: University of North Carolina Press, 1947), p. 64.

21. Jennings Cropper Wise, *Col. John Wise of England and Virginia (1617–1695)* (Richmond, Va.: The Bell Books and Stationery Co., 1918), pp. 29–30

22. *A Relation of Maryland,* p. 52; William Wood, *New Englands Prospect* (London, 1634), pp. 53–54.

23. Thomas Verney to Sir Edmund Verney, 20 May 1639, Barbados, Bruce, ed., *Verney Papers,* p. 197.

24. Norfolk Minute Book, 1637–1646, 2 November 1640, p. 53; Will of Henry Maddin, Isle of Wight Wills, 30 March 1687, p. 266, VSL.

25. "Lieut Lion Gardener His Relation of the Pequot Warres," 3 *MHS Coll.* v. 3, pp. 136–137. As a point of comparison, ministers on Providence earned £40 (CO 124/2, p. 3), whereas Richard Lane, a Providence officer, received £30 (CO 124/2, p. 85, PRO). Providence officers also received shares of island produce.

26. J. Eric S. Thompson, ed., *Thomas Gage's Travels in the New World* (Norman: University of Oklahoma Press, 1958), p. 97,

27. Instructions from the Company to Mr. Richard Lane, 15 April 1633, CO 124/1, PRO.

28. Thompson, ed., *Gage's Travels,* p. 310.

29. Letter from Hope Sherrard to Sir Thomas Barrington, Providence, 6 January 1633/4, Egerton 2646, f. 58, BL.

30. 3 December 1631, CO 124/2, p. 43, PRO.

31. The Company managed to tempt one William Thorpe away from his duties on Bermuda as lieutenant of the King's Fort, 23 March 1634/5, CO 124/2, p. 210, PRO.

32. "A description of the island, 1635," CO 1/8, no. 83, PRO.

33. Instructions to Captain Hunt, 28 March 1636, CO 124/1, f. 90recto, PRO.

34. Committee for Providence Island, 31 January 1637/8, CO 124/2, p. 313, PRO.

35. *A Relation of Maryland,* pp. 22–23, pp. 39–40.

36. Meeting of Providence Island Company, 22 November 1630, CO 124/2, pp. 4–5, PRO.

37. General Court for Providence Island, 9–11 February 1631/2, CO 124/2, pp. 49–50, PRO.

38. *Orders and Constitutions . . . for the Plantation of the Summer-Ilands 6.Febr.1621* (London, 1622), p. 38.

39. Sir Richard Saltonstall to Emmanuel Downing, 4 February 1631/2, *Historical Manuscripts Commission 12th report, Appendix, part I, Cowper MSS* (London: H. M. Stationery Office, 1888), v. 1, p. 49.

40. Henry Adis, *A Letter Sent from Syrranam* (London, 1664), p. 7.

41. Tom Verney to Sir Edward Verney, Barbados, 10 February 1638/9, Bruce, ed., *Verney Papers,* pp. 192, 195. Verney certainly inundated his parents with these expectations of newfound virtue and zeal. He wrote his mother at the same time of his hope "by the grace of God, to lead a new life" (Bruce, ed., *Verney Papers,* p. 196).

42. Philip Nye to John Winthrop, Jr., London, 21 September 1635, *Winthrop Papers,* v. 3, p. 211.

43. "The Answer of Thomas Babb Marchange defdt to the Bill of Complt of George Rolfe Complt," CO 1/6, pp. 224–230, PRO. I am indebted to Dan Rolfe for calling my attention to this story.

44. "A Net Set for a Night-Raven" (London, 165?) and "The Woman Outwitted" (London, 1709) are in a collection of Virginia Broadsides at the Huntington Library, San Marino, Calif.

45. Bernard Bailyn, ed., *The Apologia of Robert Keayne* (Gloucester, Mass.: Peter Smith, 1970), p. 44.

46. Muriel Sedley Gurdon to Margaret Winthrop, 4 April 1636, Robert Moody, ed., *The Saltonstall Papers, 1607–1815* (Boston: The Massachusetts Historical Society, 1972), v. 1, pp. 128–129.

47. "George Donne's 'Virginia Reviewed': A 1638 Plan to Reform Colonial Society," ed. T. H. Breen, *WMQ* 30 (1973), 462.

48. John Dutton to the Earl of Warwick, 20 January 1619/20, *Rich Papers,* p. 143.

49. Lady Verney to John Sadler, 1 August 1634, Bruce, ed., *Verney Papers,* p. 162.

50. John Sadler to the Verneys, 30 July 1634, Bruce, ed., *Verney Papers,* p. 160.

51. Warrant to the sheriffs of London and Middlesex and the Keeper of Newgate, 8 July 1635 (Docquet), *CSPD* v. 93 (Charles I, Domestic), p. 262. Only four appear on Virginia passenger lists.

52. Nathaniel Butler to Sir Nathaniel Rich, 23 October 1623, *Rich Papers,* p. 194.

53. John Dutton to the Earl of Warwick, 20 January 1619/20, *Rich Papers,* p. 143.

54. Roger Hodges, John Browne, William Lawson, Benjamin Strange, and Edward Alden were the five. Robert Hume, *Early Child Immigrants to Virginia* (Baltimore: Magna Carta Book Co., 1986), p. 40. Not all indentured servants were impoverished or destitute. In 1635 the newly arrived passenger Thomas Clifton was sold with another servant, Edward Prince, to Elizabeth Caursley. The servants were sold along with all their goods, which included iron pots, pewter platters and plates, saucers, cups, three chests, one chair, a frying pan, and, most intriguing of all, two cushions of embroidered work (Deed dated 26 November 1635, presented in court 28 November 1636, Susie M. Ames, ed., *County Court Records of Accomack-Northampton, Virginia, 1632–1640* [Washington: American Historical Association, 1954], p. 63). Clifton sailed on the *Primrose*, which left London sometime after July 27, and probably reached Virginia in mid-September.

55. In the Virginia Muster of 1624/5, the Virginia population was 76 percent male.

56. Richard S. Dunn, *Sugar and Slaves: The Rise of the Planter Class in the English West Indies, 1624–1713* (Chapel Hill: University of North Carolina Press, 1972), p. 327.

57. Dunn, *Sugar and Slaves,* p. 328.

58. "A German Indentured Servant in Barbados in 1652: The Account of Heinrich von Uchteritz," edited and translated by Alexander Gunkel and Jerome S. Handler, *JBMHS* 33 (1970), 93.

59. To offer a point of comparison, in England it was normal for 10 percent of the population to remain single. Thus, measured against English standards, migration to the colonies increased chances of mortality and diminished the likelihood of marriage.

60. Carville V. Earle, "Environment, Disease, and Mortality," in Tate and Ammerman, pp. 121–123. On mortality before this period, see Morgan, *American Slavery,* p. 101; Russell R. Menard, "Immigrants and Their Increase: The Process of Population Growth in Early Colonial Maryland," in Aubrey C. Land, Lois Green Carr, and Edward C. Papenfuse, *Law, Society and Politics in Early Maryland* (Baltimore: The Johns Hopkins University Press, 1977), pp. 88–110.

61. Determining the total number of arrivals is very difficult. Twenty ships altogether came from London to Virginia: a contemporary estimate made in April of 1636 observed that a total of twenty-one had reached the colony in the preceding year. This number would seem to undercount many ships, since other English ports served the Chesapeake region as well. Richard Kemp to Sir Francis Windebanke, Point Comfort, Virginia, 11 April 1636, CO 1/9, pp. 17–18, PRO.

62. List of population numbers in Virginia, 1634/5, CO 1/8, item 55, PRO. Lorena Walsh suggests that 40 percent would be an upper limit in her study of Charles County, Maryland. See Lorena Walsh, "Servitude and Opportunity in Charles County," in Land, Carr, and Papenfuse, *Law, Society,* pp. 116–117. Morgan, *American Slavery,* p. 159.

63. This situation endured into the eighteenth century in the West Indian colonies: see Trevor Burnard, "European Migration to Jamaica, 1655–1780," *WMQ* 53 (1996): 769–796.

64. Lewis Hughes, *To the Right Honourable, The Lords and Others of His Majesties Most Honourable Privie Councell* (London, 1625), A2recto-verso.

65. Richard Norwood, "The Description of the Sommer Ilands," in Wesley Frank Craven and Walter B. Hayward, eds., *The Journal of Richard Norwood* (New York: Scholars Facsimiles and Reprints for the Bermuda Historical Monuments Trust, 1945), p. lxxiii.

66. Letter from the Company to the Governor and Council, 23 April 1638, *CSPC*, p. 271.

67. Richard Pares, *Merchants and Planters, Economic History Review Supplement* 4 (1960), p. 8.

68. *A Declaration of the Right Honourable Robert, Earle of Warwick* (London, 1645), pp. 7–8.

69. Petition of the Governor and company of London to the Commissioners for Foreign Plantations [28 July] 1639, *CSPC*, p. 301. Alarmed at this ill-prepared plantation and mindful that some 400 to 500 more people were ready to leave Bermuda, the Company requested a grant of land in Virginia between the Rappahannock and Potomoc rivers.

70. Edward Trelawney to Robert Trelawney, 10 January 1636, in Everett Emerson, ed., *Letters from New England: The Massachusetts Bay Company, 1629–1638* (Amherst: University of Massachusetts Press, 1976), p. 186.

71. ? to ?, 1637, in Emerson, ed., *Letters,* p. 214.

72. The number of studies delineating the improved material conditions of life in New England is abundant. For an overview, see Jim Potter, "Demographic Development and Family Structure," in Greene and Pole, *Colonial British America,* especially pp. 151–152.

73. Governor Thomas Dudley to the Countess of Lincoln, March 1631, in Peter Force, *Tracts and Other Papers Relating Principally to the Origin, Settlement, and Progress of the Colonies in North America* (Washington: privately printed, 1836–1846), v. 2, pp. 9–10.

74. Winthrop, *Journal,* pp. 139–163.

75. Instructions to Thomas Punt, 8 May 1632, CO 124/1, f. 43recto, PRO.

76. The Providence Island cleric Hope Sherrard suffered a similar debilitating illness that caused him to apologize for a delayed letter. He told Sir Thomas Barrington that he had hoped to send a letter by the *Charity* but had not been able to do so because he had been sick and lacked time (Egerton 2646, f. 58, BL).

77. Samuel Filby to Sir Thomas Barrington, Association, 28 August 1634, Egerton 2646, f. 67, BL.

78. Committee, 10 April 1635, CO 124/2, pp. 212–213, PRO.

79. Company letter to Philip Bell, 20 April 1635, CO 124/1, f. 79verso. These instructions were reiterated to Cornelius Billings, the master of the *Expectation,* CO 124/1, f. 81, PRO.

80. Committee for Providence and Association, 10 April 1635, CO 124/2, p. 213, PRO.

81. CO 124/2, p. 265, PRO.

82. William Jessop to Ensign Fitch, 30 March 1636, Add. 63,854, Jessop Letter-book, letter 153, BL.

83. Wood, *New Englands Prospect*, pp. 53–54.
84. Kussmaul, *Servants*, p. 31.
85. Kussmaul, *Servants*, p. 4.
86. Morgan, *American Slavery*, chapter 15; Dunn, *Sugar and Slaves*, chapter seven. Morgan and Dunn also address the harsh treatment of English indentured servants.
87. Richard Ligon, *A True and Exact History of the Island of Barbadoes* (London, 1673), p. 46.
88. Notes and extracts regarding white servants in Barbados, 26 November 1640, Davis Papers, Box 7, envelopes 21–22, Royal Commonwealth Society, London.
89. This paragraph should not be understood to romanticize service in England, where servants were beaten and assaulted and their wages docked (Kussmaul, *Servants*, pp. 44–48). The account book of the ship the *Abraham* expresses succinctly the role servants played as capital goods in a plantation culture. This record of items procured by Barbados planters delineates the servants, oatmeal, spirits, prunes, butter, and other items the planters purchased (HCA 30/636, PRO).
90. On the "custom of the country," see Smith, *Colonists in Bondage*, chapter 11; and for Barbados, see Hilary McD. Beckles, *White Servitude and Black Slavery in Barbados, 1627–1715* (Knoxville: The University of Tennessee Press, 1989), p. 17.
91. *A Relation of Maryland*, pp. 53–54.
92. Court held for Providence, 3 December 1631, CO 124/2, p. 42, PRO.
93. "A Breife Description of the Ilande of Barbados, [c. 1650]" in Vincent T. Harlow, ed., *Colonising Expeditions to the West Indies and Guiana, 1623–1667* (London: Hakluyt Society, 1925), p. 44.
94. 15 March 1640/1, 2 May 1641, Norfolk Minute Book, 1637–1646, pp. 70, 80, VSL.
95. When she left Sibsey's service, Mary possessed one green kirtle and waist coat, attested justice Francis Morgan, who significantly did not find the wardrobe of a maid servant beneath his consideration or beyond the purview of his local responsibilities: where the London port clerks let disguised nonconformists escape to New England in the guise of servants, local authorities in the colonies attended to the most intimate aspects of their servants' lives with attentive enthusiasm. 19 July 1641, Norfolk Minute Book, 1637–1646, p. 88, VSL.
96. An Act for the protection of servants, 26 July 1624, Bermuda Colonial Records, Fragment B, Berm. Arch.
97. Assizes, 7 December 1652, Lefroy, *Memorials*, v. 2, p. 36.
98. "Shipwrecked Spaniards 1639 Grievances Against Bermuda," trans. L. D. Gurrin, *BHQ* 18 (1961): 13–28, quotation p. 26.
99. Testimony of Robert Hurt, 12 March 1637/8, Bermuda Colonial Records, v. 2, p. 27, Berm. Arch. Evidence suggests that terms for servants might have lengthened on Bermuda over the decades of its settlement. When Thomas Durham wrote Sir Nathaniel Rich from the island in 1620, he requested that servants who were sent there be bound to five-year terms (*Rich Papers*, p. 218).
100. 19 June 1634, CO 124/2, p. 151, PRO.

101. [Charles Croke], *Fortune's Uncertainty* (London, 1667), p. 54. For a similar lament about "Turkish" usage, see T. H. Breen, James H. Lewis, and Keith Schlesinger, "Motive for Murder: A Servant's Life in Virginia, 1678," *WMQ* 40 (1983), 120.

102. 12 February 1635/6, *Plymouth Records*, v. 1, p. 37.

103. 11 January 1640/1, Susie M. Ames, ed., *County Court Records of Accomack-Northampton, 1640–1645* (Charlottesville: University of Virginia Press for the Virginia Historical Society, 1973), p. 64.

104. Lawrence Towner notes that servants with contracts, friends, or relations were more likely to pursue their grievances in court or through their conduct rather than running away. See "'A Fondness for Freedom': Servant Protest in Puritan Society," *WMQ* 19 (1962), p. 213.

105. Letter from Sir Richard Saltonstall to John Winthrop Jr., 27 February 1636/7, Moody, ed., *Saltonstall Papers*, pp. 125–127. Indenture dated 6 March 1634, reprinted in Henry Reed Stiles, *The Stiles Family in America* (Jersey City: Doan & Pilson, 1895), p. 15.

106. *Conn. Records*, v. 1, p. 6, pp. 8–9. Charles J. Hoadly, *Records of the Colony and Plantation of New Haven, from 1638–1649* (Hartford: Case, Tiffany and Company, 1857), p. 124.

107. 10 October 1626, H. R. McIlwaine, ed., *Minutes of the Council and General Court of Colonial Virginia* (Richmond, Va.: The Colonial Press, 1924), p. 117.

108. Inventory of Captain Ketteridge, 1635, in Hay Papers, GD 34/923/1, SRO.

109. HCA 30/635, PRO.

110. Ligon, *True and Exact History*, p. 44.

111. Extracts from Council Minutes, N. Darnell Davis Papers, Box 7, envelopes 21–22, Royal Commonwealth Society, London.

112. "A Breife Discription" in Harlow, ed., *Colonising Expeditions*, p. 44. The situation in Maryland was apparently more advantageous to servants. Russell Menard, "From Servant to Freeholder: Status Mobility and Property Accumulation in Seventeenth-Century Maryland," *WMQ* 30 (1973): 37–64.

113. On the treatment of servants in Virginia, see especially Morgan, *American Slavery*, chapter 6; and T. H. Breen and Stephen Innes, *"Myne Owne Ground": Race and Freedom on Virginia's Eastern Shore, 1640–1676* (New York: Oxford University Press, 1980), pp. 62–67. The York county records are particularly replete with servant horror stories. For a servant who hanged herself, see Northampton Order Book, 1657–1664, 28 July 1663, f. 173, VSL.

114. Ames, ed., *Accomack Records, 1640–1645*, 28 April 1643, p. 271.

115. 20 September 1642, depositions of Arthur Rayman, John Allen, and William Fisher, Ames, ed., *Accomack Records, 1640–1645*, pp. 204–206.

116. 6 August 1655, Lancaster Deeds, 1652–1657, p. 209, VSL.

117. 2 April 1638, Norfolk Minute Book, 1637–1646, p. 7, VSL.

118. Quoted in Mary C. Fuller, *Voyages in Print: English Travel to America, 1578–1624* (Cambridge: Cambridge University Press, 1995), p. 101. It is possible that the servants were taken in by local tribes.

119. Complications ensued in this purchase: the dispute in court was whether or not Pett then destroyed the indenture and freed Jarvis. See Ames, ed., *Accomack*

Records, 1640–1645, 30 January 1642/3, p. 246. For an instance of a larger group of aspiring runaways, see Breen and Innes's discussion of a 1638 conspiracy in Virginia in *Myne Owne Ground*, pp. 66–67.

120. 6 October 1635, *Mass. Records*, v. 1, p. 162. John Winthrop noted in his journal in September that six "lewde servantes" ran away in a skiff. They were retrieved at Pascataquack, returned to Boston, whipped, and fined. Winthrop, *Journal*, p. 154. Runaways plagued New England: see Towner, "'A Fondness for Freedom,'" p. 212.

121. Colt, "Voyage," in Harlow, ed., *Colonising*, p. 74.

122. 13 and 20 October 1639, Butler's Diary, Sloane 758, BL.

123. Ligon, *True and Exact History*, pp. 45–46. For more information about the servant rebellion, see N. Darnell Davis Papers, box 1, envelope 41, Royal Commonwealth Society, London. Dame Mary Peirce, wife of the governor Richard Peirce (or Peers), who traveled in 1635, testified that one of her husband's servants was hanged and two others tortured during the course of the rebellion. Depositions concerning this rebellion, moreover, suggest that the plot was closely connected to political affairs in England.

124. "Father White's Briefe Relation," in Clayton Colman Hall, ed., *Narratives of Early Maryland* (New York: Charles Scribner's Sons, 1910) p. 34.

125. For a different interpretation of the causes of the island's bellicose culture, see Gary Puckrein, *Little England: Plantation Society and Anglo-Barbadian Politics, 1627–1700* (New York: New York University Press, 1984), p. 13.

126. Captain Henry Ashton to the Hays, c. February 1645/6, GD 34/933, SRO.

127. Colt, "Voyage," in Harlow, ed., *Colonising*, pp. 65–67.

128. Thomas Verney to Sir Edmund Verney, 10 February 1638/9, Bruce, ed., *Verney Papers*, pp. 192–195. Henry Colt also commented on the "Multitude of Land Crabs" and their pesky ways (Colt, "Voyage," in Harlow, ed., *Colonising*, p. 68).

129. Jerome S. Handler, ed., "Father Antoine Biet's Visit," *JBMHS* 27 (1967), p. 68. As the evidence presented earlier in the chapter about the voyage of the *Constance* suggests, English business affairs were commonly conducted in taverns.

130. "A Breife Description of the Ilande of Barbados," in Harlow, ed., *Colonising*, p. 44.

131. Deposition of George Reed and John Kirton, in Joanne McCree Sanders, *Barbados Records: Wills and Administrations* (Marceline, Mich.: Sanders Historical Publications, 1979), p. 48.

132. Winthrop, *Journal*, p. 18.

133. *Orders and Constitutions*, p. 77.

134. Instructions to Governor Bell, 7 February 1630/31, CO 124/1, f. 15verso, PRO.

135. Instructions to Governor Bell, 15 May 1632, CO 124/1, f. 41recto, PRO.

136. A "family" is always defined by a society and has no fixed identity or universally understood definition. The inclusion of servants in a family highlights the social construct of the term.

137. There were, of course, Africans and people of African descent who lived in England, especially in the cities of Bristol and Liverpool. Philip D. Morgan, "British Encounters with Africans and African-Americans, circa 1600–1780," in

Bernard Bailyn and Philip D. Morgan, eds., *Strangers within the Realm: Cultural Margins of the First British Empire* (Chapel Hill: University of North Carolina Press, 1991), pp. 159–160.

138. Letter from the Company to the Governor, 28 March 1636, *CSPC*, p. 229; letter to the Governor and Council, 3 July 1638, CO 124/1, f. 124verso, PRO.

139. Instructions to Governor Bell, 10 May 1632, CO 124/1, f. 33recto, PRO.

140. "A Breife Description," in Harlow, ed., *Colonising*, p. 45.

141. Inventory of Richard Norwood's estate, 1676, in Norwood, *Journal*, p. 143.

142. "A Breife Description," in Harlow, ed., *Colonising*, p. 45.

143. On "building ways," see David Hackett Fischer, *Albion's Seed: Four British Folkways in America* (New York: Oxford University Press, 1989), pp. 62–68, 264–274.

144. Will and Inventory of Thomas Love, 21 January 1650/51, entered 8 July 1651, RB 6/11, pp. 475–477, Barb. Arch.

145. Thomas Verney to Sir Edmund Verney, 10 February 1638/9, Bruce, ed., *Verney Papers*, p. 196.

146. de Rivera, "Shipwrecked Spaniards," p. 25.

147. "Father White's Briefe Relation," in Hall, ed., *Narratives of Early Maryland*, p. 35. Ligon also commented on the hammocks servants slept on in his *History*, p. 44. Hammocks were also used in Surinam. Edmund Hickeringill, *Jamaica Viewed* (London, 1661), pp. 6–7.

148. Will of Philip Cartwright, 28 February 1671/2, entered 7 May 1672, RB 6/8, p. 382, Barb. Arch.

149. John Nicholl, *An Houre Glasse of Indian News* (London, 1607), E4 verso.

150. Historians of the early Chesapeake began to report on these networks in the 1970s. Rejecting the New England model of surveyed and defined physical communities with ordered families, they asserted the possibility of communities that spread across space and that rested on fictive familial ties. See especially Thad Tate and David Ammerman, eds., *The Chesapeake in the Seventeenth Century;* Darrett B. Rutman and Anita H. Rutman, *A Place in Time: Middlesex County, Virginia 1650–1750* (New York: Norton, 1984); and James R. Perry, *The Formation of a Society on Virginia's Eastern Shore, 1615–1655* (Chapel Hill: University of North Carolina Press, 1990). For Montserrat, see Riva Berleant-Schiller, "Free Labor and the Economy in Seventeenth-Century Montserrat," *WMQ* 46 (1989): 557–558. Berleant-Schiller has found, on the basis of the island census of 1677–1678, that "more than 70 percent of households included two adult men, whomever else they might also have included" (p. 557).

151. Various deeds RB 3/1, pp. 185–186, 226–227, 747, 760; RB 3/2, pp. 396–397. Deposition of Elizabeth Lovell, aged 55, 1 July 1653, Will of Hugh Jones, RB 4/2, p. 139, Barb. Arch.

152. Deed dated 27 July 1640, RB 3/1, p. 734; will of John Brombie, 19 August 1652, RB 6/11, pp. 499–500, Barb. Arch.

153. One father and son pair traveled to the island in 1635. Fourteen other related pairs, including brothers, sisters, and two mother-daughter pairs, traveled to Barbados as well.

154. The economic role of partnership will be taken up in the following chapter.

155. 22 May 1640, RB 3/1, p. 783; 23 August 1642, RB 3/1, pp. 185–186, Barb. Arch.
156. 20 April 1640, RB 3/1, p. 718, Barb. Arch. The wording of deeds does not always clarify the issue of shared dwellings. George Blacklock and Robert Taylor, for example, sold William Hodges one third of their plantation. The whole plantation contained twenty acres and three houses. Whether these were three dwelling houses, one inhabited by each man, or houses designed for servants, or simply outbuildings, is not clear from the deed (20 September 1644, RB 3/1, pp. 492–493). A deed of Philip Phillpott, for example, sold his entire plantation, including eleven acres and houses, to one William Webb: "houses" might simply mean outbuildings in the Barbadian context (6 April 1646, RB 3/1, p. 271, Barb. Arch.).
157. Will of Edward Bankes, entered 13 March 1650/1, RB 6/11, p. 466, Barb. Arch.
158. Will of William Huckle, 10 June 1672, entered 12 May 1673, RB 6/8, p. 486–488, Barb. Arch.
159. Will of Dorothy Symmonds, 8 September 1649, proved 18 April 1650, RB 3/3, p. 719–720, Barb. Arch. This will is entered in the deed books, not the will books.
160. So important were orphans' estates in the Chesapeake that orphans' courts were established to protect property. On Barbados, protection of orphans seems to have been a more informal practice.
161. Will of George Norton, 3 May 1665, RB 6/15, pp. 458–462, Barb. Arch.
162. Will of Anthony Schooler, dated 9 June, entered 30 November 1665, RB 6/15, pp. 436–438, Barb. Arch.
163. Will of James Marten, 26 January 1650/1, Sanders, *Barbados Wills*, p. 235; will of Thomas Nelson, 29 June 1651, Sanders, *Barbados Wills*, p. 256.
164. Will of Arthur Winde, 4 April 1657, RB 4/2, p. 228, Barb. Arch.
165. The legal phrase that recurs in contemporary documents is "the memory of man runneth not to the contrary."

4. The Trappings of Success in Three Plantation Colonies

1. The absence of any appropriate records for St. Kitts has made it impossible to trace passengers to that island.
2. 10 February 1643/4, Susie M. Ames, ed., *County Court Records of Accomack-Northampton, Virginia, 1640–1645* (Charlottesville, Va.: University of Virginia Press for the Virginia Historical Society, 1973), p. 238.
3. 27 December 1640, RB 3/2, p. 358; 4 June 1640, RB 3/1, p. 799, Barb. Arch.
4. 4 July 1643, Ames, ed., *Accomack Records, 1640–1645*, pp. 289–290; 23 January 1645/6, York Wills and Deeds, 1645–1649, p. 97, VSL; 10 February 1643/4, Ames, ed., *Accomack Records, 1640–1645*, pp. 327–328. See also Christopher Dixon, 28 May 1645, Ames, ed., *Accomack Records, 1640–1645*, p. 430.
5. Inventory of Michael Victor, entered at court 25 October 1647, York Wills and Deeds, 1645–1649, p. 295, VSL.

6. Will of John Parry, [oral], 24 March 1637/8, proved 30 July 1638, Lee 87, PRO.

7. Nicholas Canny, ed., *Europeans on the Move* (Oxford: Oxford University Press, 1994), p. 279. On contemporary images of America, see Jack P. Greene, *The Intellectual Construction of America* (Chapel Hill: University of North Carolina Press, 1995), chapter 2.

8. The figure 115 is equal to 48 percent of the total population for whom I have information and 6 percent of the total population of travelers to Virginia.

9. On Robert Boddy, see John Bennett Boddie, *Seventeenth Century Isle of Wight County, Virginia* (Baltimore: Genealogical Publishing Company, Inc., 1973), pp. 334–335.

10. Land patent of Christopher Boyce (or Boyes), 28 November 1653, Tayloe Papers, section three, VHS.

11. Nugent, p. 65. She had sold a hundred acres in Upper Norfolk County to James Knott by 1637.

12. Boddie, *Seventeenth Century Isle of Wight County*, p. 54. Sprye owned land in Isle of Wight and Nansemond Counties.

13. 20 May 1638, Nugent, p. 82.

14. Deed dated 28 February 1658, printed in *Tyler's Quarterly Historical and Genealogical Magazine* 5 (1923–1924), p. 209; York County Deeds, Orders, Wills, 1657–1662, p. 65, VSL.

15. Will of Thomas Whaplett, dated 6 January 1635/6, proved 7 July 1636, Pile 82, PRO.

16. For the career of the former servant Humphrey Belt, see Norfolk Minute Book, 1637–1646, 15 March 1640/1, p. 70; Norfolk Wills and Deeds B, 1646–1651, deed dated 14 January 1647/8, pp. 73–73A, 1 October 1649, p. 123, VSL; for Christopher Carnoll of Maryland, see *MD Archives* IV, p. 260; for Francis Jarvis of Accomack, see Northampton No. 3, 1645–1651, 28 April 1646, p. 31, VSL. On the easy availability of land until the 1650s, see Edmund S. Morgan, "Headrights and Head Counts: A Review Article," *VMHB* 80 (1972): 361–371.

17. The age is apparently incorrect. Gaskins deposed at court at the age of 24 in 1640, which would make him nineteen at the time of his journey from London.

18. On the swapping of headrights, see Games, "Venturers, Vagrants, and Vessels of Glory: Migration from England to the Colonies under Charles I" (Ph.D. Dissertation, University of Pennsylvania, 1992), pp. 389–390.

19. 15 November 1637, p. 2, will dated 1 February 1639/40, 30 March 1640, p. 29, Norfolk Minute Book, 1637–1646, VSL.

20. Norfolk Minute Book, 1637–1646, 16 November 1643, p. 200; 14 October 1645, p. 275, VSL. Cows were commonly deeded to children as one stable way of transferring capital. Lorena Walsh, "Till Death Us Do Part," Thad W. Tate and David L. Ammerman, eds., *The Chesapeake in the Seventeenth Century: Essays on Anglo-American Society and Politics* (Chapel Hill: University of North Carolina Press, 1979), p. 143.

21. 15 December 1654, Norfolk Wills and Deeds, 1651–1656, p. 114, VSL.

22. Northampton Order Book 1657–1664, f. 138, VSL.
23. Edmund S. Morgan, *American Slavery, American Freedom: The Ordeal of Colonial Virginia* (New York: Norton, 1975), p. 425.
24. Weynette Parks Haun, ed., *Surry County, Virginia, Court Records, 1664–1671* (Durham, N.C.: W. P. Haun, 1987), pp. 51–53.
25. Lancaster Deeds, etc., 1652–1657, p. 174, VSL. Another measure of relative success was ownership of livestock. A list of sheep owned in Northampton in 1661 has survived. The biggest sheepowners in the county (not 1635 passengers) were Edmund Scarborough, with 162, and John Custis, with 110. The average number owned on one page of the listing was 12 sheep per person. By this reckoning, the 1635 travelers do not fare too well but did have modest holdings. Anthony Hodgkins owned 13 sheep, whereas Richard Kellum owned 8, and Christopher Dixon, Richard Hanby, and William Starling each had 2 (Northampton Order Book, 1657–1664, ff. 89–90, VSL).
26. On opportunity in Virginia in the 1620s for people of humble origins, see especially Morgan, *American Slavery*, chapter 6.
27. On servant opportunity in Maryland, see Lois Green Carr and Russell R. Menard, "Immigration and Opportunity: The Freedman in Early Colonial Maryland," in Tate and Ammerman, pp. 206–242; Menard, "From Servant to Freeholder: Status Mobility and Property Accumulation in Seventeenth-Century Maryland," *WMQ* 30 (1973): 37–64; Lorena S. Walsh, "Servitude and Opportunity in Charles County, Maryland, 1658–1705," in Aubrey C. Land, Lois Green Carr, and Edward C. Papenfuse, *Law, Society and Politics in Early Maryland* (Baltimore: The Johns Hopkins University Press, 1977), pp. 111–133; and Gloria L. Main, *Tobacco Colony: Life in Early Maryland, 1650–1720* (Princeton: Princeton University Press, 1982), chapter 3.
28. Bernard Bailyn, "Politics and Social Structure in Virginia," in James Morton Smith, ed., *Seventeenth-Century America: Essays in Colonial History* (Chapel Hill: University of North Carolina Press, 1959), p. 95. I have also explored the subsequent careers of all the men listed in the Virginia Muster of 1624/5 and "the list of the living and the dead in Virginia, 16 February 1623/4" (both in CO 1/3, PRO) whom I could trace in the surviving county court records for the 1630s and 1640s in order to ascertain whether or not the passengers of 1635 were for some reason peculiar. The evidence I found for these other early Virginia residents supported my research on the 1635 passengers who had been longtime Virginia residents: they too shared humble origins.
29. Abraham Wood and Adam Thoroughgood started as servants: Thoroughgood, however, was the son of a vicar in England. Bailyn, "Politics and Social Structure," p. 95.
30. Virginia Muster, 1624/5, CO 1/3, f. 136recto, PRO; 10 October 1626, H. R. McIlwaine, ed., *Minutes of the Council and General Court of Colonial Virginia* (Richmond, Va.: The Colonial Press, 1924), p. 117.
31. W. G. Stanard, *Some Emigrants to Virginia* (1915: Baltimore: Genealogical Publishing Company, 1964), p. 83; note on councilors of state for Virginia [1637], CO 1/9, item 37, pp. 95–96, PRO. There were approximately one

hundred blacks in Virginia in 1630. John J. McCusker and Russell R. Menard, *The Economy of British America, 1607–1789* (Chapel Hill: University of North Carolina Press, 1985), Table 6.4, p. 136.

32. McIlwaine, ed., *Council Minutes,* 4 April 1625, p. 51.

33. List of viewers of the tobacco crop, 1639, *VMHB* 5 (1897): 119–123; Beverley Fleet, *Charles City County Orders 1655–1658 Abstracts* (Richmond, 1941), p. 16.

34. CO 1/8, ff. 21–22; CO 1/9, item 37, pp. 95–96, PRO.

35. Lyon Gardiner Tyler, *Encyclopedia of Virginia Biography* (New York: Lewis Historical Publishing Company, 1915), v. 1, p. 112.

36. Jon Kukla, *Speakers and Clerks of the Virginia House of Burgesses 1643–1776* (Richmond, Va.: Virginia State Library, 1981), pp. 46–47; James Branch Cabell, *The Majors and Their Marriages* (Richmond, Va.: W. C. Hill Printing Company, 1915), pp. 14–19.

37. Ames, ed., *Accomack Records, 1640–1645,* p. 145. The name was also spelled Hodgkins.

38. Northampton Deeds and Wills no. 3, 1645–1651, 6 August 1647, f. 96recto, VSL. James Horn has compiled an impressive database regarding personal property in the Chesapeake. In Lower Norfolk County, 66.7 percent of men with an estate of less that £50 owned pewter items (James P. Horn, *Adapting to a New World: English Society in the Seventeenth-Century Chesapeake* [Chapel Hill: University of North Carolina Press, 1994], Table 28, p. 311).

39. Norfolk Wills and Deeds B 1646–1651, 16 August 1647, p. 50, VSL. Hoskins was also declared exempt from public levies.

40. 24 June 1659, York Deeds, Orders, Wills, 1657–1662, p. 113, VSL.

41. David W. Jordan, "Maryland's Privy Council, 1637–1715," in Land, Carr, and Papenfuse, *Law, Society,* pp. 65–87.

42. *A Relation of Maryland* (London, 1635), p. 56. The three men were John Hill, William Sayer, and Edward Cranfield, all of whom traveled in January of 1635 on the *Merchant Bonaventure.* Cranfield brought his wife, Ann, with him as well.

43. Edward C. Papenfuse et al., eds., *A Biographical Dictionary of the Maryland Legislature, 1635–1789* (Baltimore: The Johns Hopkins University Press, 1985), v. 2, pp. 660–661. See also Jordan, "Maryland's Privy Council," pp. 70–71.

44. Despite its array of records, many of them excerpted, edited, and published (for fastidious Victorian audiences) by John Henry Lefroy in his *Memorials,* Bermuda has been the focus of only a few studies, and none has essayed to track the experiences of particular residents on the island. Portions of this chapter appeared previously in Alison Games, "Survival Strategies in Early Bermuda and Barbados," *Revista/Review Interamericana* 22 (1992): 55–71.

45. Lewis Hughes, *A Letter Sent into England from the Summer Islands* (London, 1615), n. p.

46. Champlin Burrage, ed., *Richard Norwood's Insularum de la Bermuda Detectio* (Boston: Houghton Mifflin, 1918), p. 18.

47. "The Motives and proposicons of his Highnes most humble and loyall subjects the people of the Somer Islands" [1640] CO 1/10, no. 82, ff. 204–205, PRO.

48. Court Records, October or November 1618, Bermuda Colonial Records, v. 1, Berm. Arch.

49. Assizes, 1628/9, Bermuda Colonial Records, v. 1, Berm. Arch.

50. Assizes, 23–24 March 1629/30; Assizes 17–20 July 1627, Bermuda Colonial Records, v. 1, Berm. Arch.

51. Hughes, *A Letter Sent into England from the Summer Islands,* n. p.

52. Norwood, *Insularum,* p. 6; Nathaniel Butler, *The Historye of the Bermudas or Summer Islands,* ed. J. Henry Lefroy (London: The Hakluyt Society, 1882), p. 79.

53. "Petition of the poore planters in the Sommer Islands being above Threescore to the Privy council," 4 June 1628, CO 1/4, p. 135, PRO.

54. Joan de Rivera, "Shipwrecked Spaniards 1639. Grievances Against Bermudians," trans. by L. D. Gurrin, *BHQ* 18 (1961), 26.

55. Council, 29 March 1648, Lefroy, *Memorials,* v. 1, p. 634; The Examination of Richard Anstell, 8 March 1625/6, Lefroy, *Memorials,* v. 1, pp. 365–366. All goods from the shipwrecked *Seaflower,* from which the Wellmans obtained their ambergris, were supposed to be delivered to authorities.

56. Robert Rich to Sir Nathaniel Rich, March 1617/18; Thomas Durham to Sir Nathaniel Rich, circa January 1619/20; *Rich Papers,* pp. 81, 175.

57. Will of Captain Josias Forster, 17 November 1666, Bermuda Wills, book 1, reel 272, Berm. Arch.

58. Will and inventory of John Casson, 14 November 1688, inventory dated 4 February 1688/9, Bermuda Wills, v. 3, part 1, reel 280, Berm. Arch. The land, house, and servant were not included in the inventory evaluation.

59. Postscript, those who disclaim general petition, in Nathaniel White, *Truth Gloriously Appearing* (London, 1645).

60. Grievances of the people of Bermuda, October 1622, in *Rich Papers,* p. 237; "The Motives and proposicons of his Highnes most humble and loyall subjects the people of the Somer Islands" [1640] CO 1/10, no. 82, ff. 204–205, PRO.

61. de Rivera, "Shipwrecked Spaniards," p. 25.

62. Population statistics for Barbados from Richard S. Dunn, *Sugar and Slaves: The Rise of the Planter Class in the English West Indies, 1624–1713* (Chapel Hill: University of North Carolina Press, 1972), p. 55; and Peter Hay to Sir James Hay, 13 April 1641, GD 34/923/32, SRO.

63. *Orders and Constitutions for the Plantation of the Summer-Ilands* (London, 1622) p. 82.

64. Norwood, *Insularum,* p. 14, p. 27.

65. Roger Wood's Letterbook, Fragment F, Bermuda Colonial Records, letter 53, 1634, Berm. Arch.

66. Letter to the Right Honble the Lords Comissioners for Forraigne Plantacons, published in Lefroy, *Memorials,* v. 1, pp. 557–558.

67. Letter to Captain Henry Ashton and the commissioners of Barbados, 27 March 1640, Hay Papers, GD 34/922, SRO; Richard Norwood to Viscount Mandeville, 29 June 1642, *Rich Papers,* p. 328.

68. Dunn, *Sugar and Slaves;* Richard B. Sheridan, *Sugar and Slavery: An Economic History of the British West Indies 1623–1775* (Baltimore: The Johns Hopkins

University Press, 1974); and Carl and Roberta Bridenbaugh, *No Peace Beyond the Line: The English in the Caribbean 1624–1690* (New York: Oxford University Press, 1972). Portions of this section appeared previously in Alison Games, "Opportunity and Mobility in Early Barbados," Robert L. Paquette and Stanley L. Engerman, editors, *The Lesser Antilles in the Age of European Expansion* (Gainesville: University Press of Florida, 1996), pp. 165–181.

69. Dunn, *Sugar and Slaves,* p. 45.

70. Gary Puckrein, *Little England: Plantation Society and Anglo-Barbadian Politics, 1627–1700* (New York: New York University Press, 1984), p. 13; and Hilary McD. Beckles, *White Servitude and Black Slavery in Barbados, 1627–1715* (Knoxville: University of Tennessee Press, 1989).

71. Beckles, *White Servitude,* p. 24; quotation from John Winthrop to Henry Winthrop, 30 January 1628/9, *Winthrop Papers,* v. 2, p. 67, referring to the tobacco that Henry shipped to England from Barbados.

72. Peter Hay to Sir James Hay, Barbados, 22 June 1641, Hay Papers, GD 34/923/34, SRO.

73. Nicholas Foster, *A Briefe Relation of the Late Horrid Rebellion Acted in the Island Barbados* (London, 1650), p. 2.

74. Peter Hay to Sir James Hay, 11 August 1638, Hay Papers, GD34/924/15, SRO.

75. [William Duke], *Some Memoirs of the First Settlement of the Island of Barbados* (Barbados, 1741), p. 18.

76. Eighty-one travelers represent 8.2 percent of the total population bound for Barbados and 68 percent of the total population for whom I have found some information in the colonial records.

77. Deeds 7 August 1640, RB 3/1, p. 781, 10 July 1648, RB 3/3, p. 509; and her will, dated 8 September 1649, proved 18 April 1650, in deed book RB 3/3, pp. 719–720, Barb. Arch.

78. Indenture 2 September 1637, RB 3/2, pp. 599–600, Barb. Arch.

79. Various deeds, RB 3/1, pp. 95–96, 305–306, 600–601, 613–614, 798–799, 901, 906; RB 3/2, pp. 23, 371; RB 3/12, p. 321, Barb. Arch.

80. Tom Verney to Sir Edmund Verney, Barbados, 10 February 1638/9, John Bruce, ed., *Letters and Papers of the Verney Family Down to the End of the Year 1639* (London: Camden Society, 1853), p. 192.

81. James Dering to Sir Edward Dering, "A Letter from Barbados in 1640," *JBMHS* 27 (1960): 124–125.

82. Peter Hay to [James Hay] 22 August 1640, GD 34/924/23; Peter Hay to James Hay, 13 April 1641, GD 34/923/32, Hay Papers, SRO. Henry Colt observed in 1631 that cotton was the crop of choice: presumably by 1640, the crop had demonstrated its unsuitability to island cultivation (Colt, "Voyage," in Vincent T. Harlow, ed., *Colonising Expeditions to the West Indies and Guiana, 1623–1667* [London: Hakluyt Society, 1925], p. 69).

83. 2 May 1640, RB 3/1, p. 734, Barb. Arch.

84. Richard Ligon, *A True and Exact History of the Island of Barbadoes* (London, 1673), p. 117.

85. Foster, *Briefe Relation*, p. 2.
86. Thomas Verney to his brother Ralph Verney, 20 September 1639, Davis Papers, envelope 27, Royal Commonwealth Society, London.
87. Dering, "A Letter from Barbados in 1640," 124–125.
88. Deed dated 20 April 1640, RB 3/1, p. 718, Barb. Arch.
89. Deed dated 12 January 1640/1, RB 3/2, pp. 364–365, Barb. Arch.
90. Richard Dunn discusses partnership in Barbados during the sugar years as a device to enable one partner to live on the island while other partners handled the marketing tasks in Europe. My sense is that many of the small-scale partnerships I have found for these settlers were truly team efforts in Barbados itself. Dunn, *Sugar and Slaves*, p. 65. Richard Pares talks of this tradition of "mateship" in the West Indies in *Merchants and Planters, Economic History Review Supplement* 4 (1960), p. 91n.
91. 6 September 1641, RB 3/1, p. 289, Barb. Arch.
92. 22 May 1640, RB 3/1, p. 783, Barb. Arch.
93. Deed 23 August 1642, RB 3/1, pp. 185–186, Barb. Arch.
94. 1 July 1643, RB 3/1, pp. 44–45, Barb. Arch.
95. 2 May 1640, RB 3/1, p. 734, Barb. Arch.; copy of indenture, 1 July 1641, Davis Papers, Royal Commonwealth Society, London.
96. St. John's Vestry Minutes, *JBMHS* 33 (May 1969), 36.
97. I have found no record of the marriage, but a son of Edward Ash was buried at St. John in 1659. RL 1/29, p. 2, Barb. Arch.
98. RB 3/1, p. 904, Barb. Arch.; Foster, *Briefe Relation;* Joanne McCree Sanders, ed., *Barbados Records: Wills and Administrations* (Marceline, Mich.: Sanders Historical Publications, 1979) p. 363; RB 3/5, pp. 401–402, Barb. Arch.; Council Minutes 1654–58, v. 1, p. 26, PRO.
99. Jerome S. Handler, ed., "Father Antoine Biet's Visit," *JBMHS* 27 (1967), 67.
100. Quotation from Ligon, *True and Exact History*, p. 108.
101. Bermuda Colonial Records, Fragment G; Volume 2, pp. 319–320, Berm. Arch.
102. Will of Robert Nanny, 22 August 1663, *Suffolk County Wills: Abstracts of the Earliest Wills Upon Record in the County of Suffolk, Massachusetts* (Baltimore: Genealogical Publishing Company, 1984), p. 225. Darrett B. Rutman commented on Nanney's Atlantic orientation, shared by many of his Boston mercantile neighbors, in *Winthrop's Boston: Portrait of a Puritan Town, 1630–1649* (Chapel Hill: University of North Carolina Press, 1965), p. 253. For Rainsford, see "List of Persons Who Left Barbados in 1679," in *JBMHS* 1 (May 1934): 174. Rainsford traveled to Boston on the *William and John*. See also Larry D. Gragg, "Puritans in Paradise: The New England Migration to Barbados, 1640–1660," *Journal of Caribbean History* 21 (1988): 154–167. Bernard Bailyn has noted that after 1660, New England merchants became particularly aware of "the importance to their business enterprises of membership in England's Atlantic community," *The New England Merchants in the Seventeenth Century* (New York: Harper and Row, 1964), quotation from p. 126; see more generally pp. 126–134.
103. Dunn, *Sugar and Slaves*, p. 66.

104. His estate was half of a ninety-five-acre estate he shared with Tom Bone, and it included two servants with four and five years to serve. Deed 1642, RB 3/1, pp. 121–122, Barb. Arch.

105. Deed 30 November 1640, RB 3/2, pp. 375–376, Barb. Arch.

106. Philpott sold his eleven-acre plantation in St. James for 3,500 pounds of tobacco in 1646. RB 3/2, p. 271, Barb. Arch.

107. Deeds in RB 3/1, pp. 282–283, 872; RB 3/2, pp. 46–47, 326, Barb. Arch.

108. "Father White's Briefe Relation," in Clayton Colman Hall, ed., *Narratives of Early Maryland* (New York: Charles Scribner's Sons, 1910), p. 34.

109. Dunn, *Sugar and Slaves*, pp. 78–79. My own efforts to trace any of the 1635 travelers' families to the 1680 Barbados census have proved futile. David Galenson has examined planter persistence for the period 1673–1723 and has found decreasing rates of persistence among the planter elite. See David W. Galenson, "Population Turnover in the English West Indies in the Late Seventeenth Century: A Comparative Perspective," *Journal of Economic History* 45 (1985): 227–235.

5. Piety and Protest in the Puritan Diaspora

1. Edward Johnson, *Wonder-Working Providence of Sions Saviour in New England* (London, 1654), reprinted in Scholars' Facsimiles and Reprints (Delmar, N.Y., 1974), p. 71. Johnson had reached New England in 1630. Threshing metaphors proved popular with the ardent husbandmen of the first generation: William Stoughton wrote in a sermon published in 1670 that "God sifted a whole Nation that he might send choice Grain over into this Wilderness" (*New Englands True Interest* [Cambridge, Mass., 1670]).

2. Robert Baillie, *A Dissuasive from the Errours of the Time* (London, 1645), p. 55. Baillie disagreed with Johnson in one significant particular: he found the New England way "to be dangerous to the rest of the World." Recognition of this important transatlantic nature of puritanism prompted the organization of a conference and the subsequent publication of its papers: Francis J. Bremer, ed., *Puritanism: Transatlantic Perspectives on a Seventeenth-Century Anglo-American Faith* (Boston: Massachusetts Historical Society, 1993). See Appendix B, Tables B.3, B.4, and B.5 for lists of New Englanders in the 1635 cohort who were particularly distinguished for their religious enthusiasm or participation. Table B.6 lists the prominent members of the migrations to Bermuda and Providence Island.

3. Philip F. Gura, *A Glimpse of Sion's Glory: Puritan Radicalism in New England, 1620–1660* (Middletown, Conn.: Wesleyan University Press, 1984); David S. Lovejoy, *Religious Enthusiasm in the New World: Heresy to Revolution* (Cambridge, Mass.: Harvard University Press, 1985); and David Hall, *Worlds of Wonder, Days of Judgment: Popular Religious Belief in Early New England* (Cambridge, Mass.: Harvard University Press, 1990).

4. Edmund S. Morgan, *The Puritan Dilemma: The Story of John Winthrop* (Boston: Little, Brown, 1958), pp. 73–76; Stephen Foster has developed this argument

that timing was everything in shaping degrees of puritan commitment in a number of important essays, and he pulled together his transatlantic analysis of the dynamic nature of puritanism in *The Long Argument: English Puritanism and the Shaping of New England Culture, 1570–1700* (Chapel Hill: University of North Carolina Press, 1991). But see also Susan Hardman Moore, "Popery, Purity and Providence: Deciphering the New England Experiment," in Anthony Fletcher and Peter Roberts, eds., *Religion, Culture and Society in Early Modern Britain: Essays in Honour of Patrick Collinson* (Cambridge: Cambridge University Press, 1994), pp. 257–289. My evidence modifies Foster's argument somewhat by suggesting that clergy who left England at any point from 1630 on were potential radicals: there was no immediate chronological connection between ecclesiastical sanctions in England and migration to the colonies. The laity, however, did become more radical over the course of the decade.

5. Richard Archer, "New England Mosaic: A Demographic Analysis for the Seventeenth Century," *WMQ* 47 (1990): 477–502; Virginia DeJohn Anderson, *New England's Generation: The Great Migration and the Formation of Society and Culture in the Seventeenth Century* (New York: Cambridge University Press, 1991).

6. Karen Ordahl Kupperman, "Errand to the Indies: Puritan Colonization from Providence Island through the Western Design," *WMQ* 45 (1988): 70–99.

7. On this puritan diaspora, see especially Babette M. Levy, "Early Puritanism in the Southern and Island Colonies," *American Antiquarian Society Proceedings* 70 (1960): 69–348.

8. 1642, Winthrop, *Journal*, p. 405. On the London travelers of 1635 with puritan sensibilities in Virginia and Maryland, see Alison Games, "Venturers, Vagrants, and Vessels of Glory: Migration from England to the Colonies under Charles I" (Ph.D. dissertation, University of Pennyslvania, 1992), pp. 432–434.

9. J. H. Bennett, "The English Caribbees in the Period of the Civil War, 1642–1646," *WMQ* 4 (1967), 369. The quotation is from a letter from Bell to Archibald Hay, August, 1643.

10. Barbados Acts, CO 30/1, p. 4, PRO.

11. Karen Ordahl Kupperman's *Providence Island 1630–1641: The Other Puritan Colony* (Cambridge: Cambridge University Press, 1993) is the obvious exception to this generalization.

12. Henry C. Wilkinson, *The Adventurers of Bermuda: A History of the Island from Its Discovery until the Dissolution of the Somers Island Company in 1684* (London: Oxford University Press, 1958, 2nd edition), pp. 94, 117; Robert Rich to Nathaniel Rich, 2 March 1617/18, in *Rich Papers*, p. 73.

13. "The Motives and proposicons of his Highnes most humble and loyall subjects the people of the Somer Islands" [1640] CO 1/10, no. 82, ff. 204–205, PRO.

14. These men were George Stirke, John Oxenbridge, Isaiah Vincent, Henry Jennings, and Daniel White. Isaiah Vincent was the only man not listed in the port register as a minister, but a stray reference in the surviving colony records makes it clear that he was a cleric. In 1628 he was appointed deacon by John Lincoln and was made minister in 1632 by Francis Erlye (memorandum by Josias For-

ster, secretary, entered with various deeds, 1635–1637, Bermuda Colonial Records, v. 1, Berm. Arch.). A sixth man, Robert Ridley, was a self-appointed lay preacher during the ecclesiastical conflicts of the 1640s.

15. 19 August 1638, W. L. Grant and James Munro, eds., *Acts of the Privy Council (Colonial)* (London: H. M. Stationery Company, 1908), v. 1, pp. 241–242.

16. Letter from the Somers Islands Company to the Earl of Dorset, 30 August [1639], CO 1/10, ff. 90–91, item 35; letter sent by the Company to the Somers Islands governor and council, 1 September 1639, CO 1/10, f. 92, no. 36, PRO.

17. A. P. Newton, *The Colonising Activities of the English Puritans: The Last Phase of the Elizabethan Struggle with Spain* (New Haven: Yale University Press, 1914), pp. 60–61.

18. Court held for Providence Island, 3 December 1631, CO 124/2, p. 42, PRO. This points to an extremely significant contrast to Bermuda, where ministers served as councilors.

19. Lane's initial responsibilities were to settle the mythical Fonseca, "if that Island shalbe discovered," and there to "plant his madder." Madder, which produces a red dye, was regarded by the Company as a potential source of profit. Lane was also to teach the skill of cultivating madder to the planters of Providence. The minister's larger salary symbolized his relative importance. General Court for Providence Island, 15 February 1632/3, CO 124/2, p. 85, PRO.

20. Roger Wood to brother B——, 1634, Roger Wood's Letterbook, Bermuda Colonial Records, Fragment F, letter 57, Berm. Arch.

21. Committee held for Providence Island, 20 February 1634/5, 1 March 1637/8, CO 124/2, pp. 194, 319, PRO.

22. General Court, 6 April 1638, CO 124/2, p. 331, PRO.

23. Winthrop, *Journal,* p. 324. Winthrop, for his part, firmly informed Lord Say that the Lord had clearly chosen New England, pp. 324–325.

24. On the important issue of religious versus economic motives for migration, see Kenneth W. Shipps, "The Puritan Emigration to New England: A New Source on Motivation," *NEHGR* 135 (1981): 83–97; and especially Anderson, "Migrants and Motives" and David Grayson Allen, "The Matrix of Motivation," in "Communications: On English Migration to Early New England," *NEQ* 59 (1986).

25. Richard Norwood to the Governor and Company of the Somers Island, 28 February 1641/2, CO 1/10, no. 105, ff. 227–228, PRO. Norwood was actually a longtime resident of the island: it is not clear if he had intended to remain in England in the 1630s and was thwarted in this goal by ecclesiastical changes there.

26. Archdeaconry of Buckinghamshire, Visitation Book, 1633–34, D/A/V/2, BRO. See also E. R. C. Brinkworth, "The Laudian Church in Buckinghamshire," *University of Birmingham Historical Journal* (1955–1956): 31–59.

27. The inconsistency of surviving records may make these disputes look quite different: top-heavy on the islands, and lay-driven in New England. With no church records for Providence and only vital statistics for Bermuda, it is impossible to assess thoroughly the extent of lay participation, although the occasional

reference intimates that many colonists had strong feelings about ecclesiastical organization and especially sacramental policies.

28. William Hubbard, *A General History of New England from the Discovery to 1680*, 2 *MHS Coll.*, v. 5, p. 263. Hubbard himself had traveled from London in 1635 on the *Defene*.

29. Edmund S. Morgan, *Visible Saints: The History of a Puritan Idea* (New York: New York University Press, 1963), pp. 88–106.

30. *Records of the First Church of Boston*, PCSM 39 (1961), p. 299. The children, Alexander, Samuel, John, Joshua, and Hannah, ranged in ages from 1 to 9.

31. These two colonies required that freemen be church members. Connecticut, Plymouth, and Rhode Island did not have such requirements. In fact, when New Haven joined Connecticut and adopted Connecticut's freeman standards, some injured orthodox puritans left the contaminated jurisdiction for New Jersey.

32. *Records of the First Church at Dorchester in New England 1636–1741* (Boston: G. H. Ellis, 1891); and "Extracts from the Records Kept by the Rev. John Fiske" *EIHC* 1 (1859): pp. 37–39. Kenneth Lockridge found that women joined the Dedham church in equal proportions with men; Kenneth Lockridge, *A New England Town, The First Hundred Years* (New York: Norton, 1970), p. 31.

33. The issue of rates of church membership is confounding. The dearth of appropriate records makes it extremely difficult to obtain an accurate or even remotely complete assessment of church membership. Interpretations of religiosity that depend on either rates of membership based on extant sources or even rates within a well-documented town are likely to be misleading. In the first case, rates based on extant sources are invariably low. In the second case, church membership was, in seventeenth-century New England, not the best gauge of piety, as membership was so difficult to obtain and the process could daunt the most upright of worshipers. It is my conjecture, based on the evidence of the Roxbury and Dorchester samples, that church membership was actually quite high. See Samuel Eliot Morison, *Builders of the Bay Colony* (Boston: Houghton Mifflin, 1958), Appendix, "Were the Settlers of Massachusetts Bay Puritans?" pp. 379–384.

34. It is conceivable that the Dorchester church was an anomaly. Given the decentralized structure of New England congregationalism, some towns could have more lenient practices. The Dorchester church had had problems in its initial gathering: John Winthrop noted in his journal that the men first involved in gathering the new church in 1636 were not considered sufficiently saintly by the churches and magistrates invited to oversee the new church. Winthrop, *Journal*, p. 173.

35. Approximate date of membership is assumed for freeman of Massachusetts to be the year that they received freeman status.

36. These were Henry Vane, William Courser, Rachel Saunders, Dionys Taylor, Thomas Savage, John Davis, and Ann Gillam.

37. Mary Rhinelander McCarl, "Thomas Shepard's Record of Relations of Religious Experience, 1648–1649," *WMQ* 48 (1991), 451–452.

38. For the confessions of other members of the London cohort, see also the confessions of Jane Champney, Mrs. Grene (Ellen Green), and John Jones, Jr., in George Selement and Bruce C. Woolley, eds., *Thomas Shepard's Confessions, Publications of the Colonial Society of Massachusetts* 58 (1981), and the spiritual autobiography of William Adams, MHS. For other accounts of progress toward grace, see especially Richard Norwood's lengthy description in Wesley Frank Craven and Walter B. Hayward, eds., *The Journal of Richard Norwood* (New York: Scholars Facsimiles and Reprints for the Bermuda Historical Monuments Trust, 1945), pp. 69–100.

39. Will of Dennis Geere of Saugus, 10 December 1635, proved 6 August 1637, "Genealogical Gleanings in England," *NEHGR* 37 (1883), 239.

40. Robert Keayne's book of sermon notes, v. 1, 1627–1628, MHS.

41. This discussion of Keayne is drawn from Bernard Bailyn, "The Apologia of Robert Keayne," *WMQ* 7 (1950): 568–587. Keayne's remarkable will has been edited by Bernard Bailyn in *The Apologia of Robert Keayne* (Gloucester, Mass.: Peter Smith, 1970). Likewise, Robert Long, an innkeeper of Charlestown, fell foul of the law and was fined 10s. by the General Court for selling a quart of beer for 2d. Long's sense of what the market could bear in the inflationary decade of the 1630s apparently overcame his apprehension of the Court's power: the following year he was fined for the same offense (General Court, 6 June 1637, 2 May 1638, *Mass. Records*, v. 1, pp. 199, 228).

42. Savage, *Dictionary*, v. 3, p. 483.

43. Savage, *Dictionary*, v. 3, p. 255.

44. David Hackett Fischer identifies hortatory names as characteristic of immigrants from Sussex in *Albion's Seed: Four British Folkways in America* (New York: Oxford University Press, 1989), p. 97, an argument that is consistent with the example of the 1635 migrants with hortatory names who settled in Dorchester. In the Dorchester case, many of the 1635 travelers with hortatory names were from the Weald of Kent, on the Sussex border. The Munningses, however, were from Essex. They returned to Tillingham, Essex, in Denge Hundred, by 1653. See Manorial Records of Tillingham, T/A 400/5; Tillingham Parish Registers, T/R 229/2; Dengie Parish Register, T/R 229/2, ERO, Chelmsford.

45. Much of the following discussion is drawn from Raymond P. Stearns's biography of Peter, *The Strenuous Puritan: Hugh Peter 1598–1660* (Urbana: University of Illinois Press, 1954), chapters 4–6.

46. William Hunt, *The Puritan Moment: The Coming of Revolution in an English County* (Cambridge, Mass.: Harvard University Press, 1983), p. 146. Morison's description of Peter as "an energetic busybody" seems amusingly apt (*Builders*, p. 118).

47. Winthrop, *Journal*, p. 157. My reading of this series of events follows that of Stearns, *Strenuous Puritan*, pp. 98–99. Emery Battis's view of this incident is far more charitable toward Peter and Vane, in *Saints and Sectaries: Anne Hutchinson and the Antinomian Controversy in the Massachusetts Bay Colony* (Chapel Hill: University of North Carolina Press, 1962), pp. 94–95.

48. "Extracts from Records Kept by the Rev. John Fiske, During His Ministry at Salem, Wenham and Chelmsford," *EIHC* 1 (1859), 48–49.

49. Olney's own children had been duly baptized at St. Albans Abbey in England, where he had also married. See William Brigg, *The Parish Register of St. Albans Abbey 1558–1689* (Harpenden, England: William Brigg, 1897), pp. 66, 68, 148.

50. Hugh Peter to the church at Dorchester, 1 July 1639, in 2 *MHS Coll.*, v. 9, p. 197.

51. *Mass. Records,* v. 1, p. 223.

52. John Osborne Austin, *The Genealogical Dictionary of Rhode Island* (1887: reprint, Baltimore: Genealogical Publishing Company, 1969), p. 42; Sydney James, *Colonial Rhode Island: A History* (New York: Scribner, 1975), p. 45. On the Fifth and Sixth Principle Baptists, see William G. McLoughlin, *New England Dissent 1630–1833: The Baptists and the Separation of Church and State* (Cambridge, Mass.: Harvard University Press, 1971), pp. 10–11.

53. A notable exception was the merchant Robert Keayne, who ardently opposed the Hutchinsonians.

54. David D. Hall, *The Faithful Shepard: A History of the New England Ministry in the Seventeenth Century* (Chapel Hill: University of North Carolina Press, 1972), p. 156.

55. See, for example, the Concord minister Peter Bulkeley's expression of dismay at "the want of Brother love," in his letter to his Boston counterpart John Cotton, n.d. (but written a few days before the ordination of the leaders of the church of Concord), Cotton Papers, MHS.

56. *CSPD*, Charles I 1634–1635, no. 12, pp. 204–205; *CSPD*, Charles I 1635–1636, no. 27, p. 47.

57. Hubbard, *History of New England,* 2 *MHS Coll.,* v. 6, p. 274.

58. Report of church trial in Boston, testimony of Thomas Shepard, in David D. Hall, *The Antinomian Controversy, 1636–1638: A Documentary History* (Middletown, Conn.: Wesleyan University Press, 1968), p. 353.

59. Winthrop, *Journal,* p. 175.

60. Winthrop, *Journal,* p. 203. One can well imagine the delight Winthrop experienced in recording Peter's chastisement of Vane.

61. There is a small difference in the degree of support these people provided: Battis divided the Hutchinsonians into three groups, core, support, and peripheral. The 1630 travelers fell heavily into the support group, with twenty-one in that category, while twelve were in the core group and five on the periphery. The 1635 travelers were more active in the peripheral group, which encompassed seventeen of the twenty-seven.

62. Thomas Shepard, Testimony at Boston Church trial in Hall, *Antinomian Controversy,* p. 365.

63. John Eliot's Record of Church members, in *A Report of the Record Commissioners, Containing the Roxbury Land and Church Records* (Boston: Rockwell and Churchill, 1884), p. 81.

64. "The causes of Hen: Bulls Excommunication" [1637], Photostats, Mass. Archives, Box 1, MHS.

65. Friends' records detailed Bull's marriages and death. Austin, *Genealogical Dictionary of Rhode Island,* pp. 264, 266.

66. The severity of being disarmed is perhaps hard to appreciate now. For contem-

poraries, it meant the loss of access to game and the risk of personal and family safety at a time of open warfare with the Pequots to the south.

67. See their acknowledgments of error, all c. November 22, 1637, *Winthrop Papers*, v. 3, pp. 513–516.

68. *Second Report of the Record Commissioners of the City of Boston: Containing the Boston Records, 1634–1660, and the Book of Possessions* (Boston: Municipal Printing Office, 1902), p. 20.

69. On the great disjunction between Boston and the expectations of Winthrop, see Darrett B. Rutman, *Winthrop's Boston: Portrait of a Puritan Town, 1630–1649* (Chapel Hill: University of North Carolina Press, 1965). Boston and Ipswich stand apart from most other seventeenth-century Massachusetts towns in their cosmopolitan, mercantile orientation and in the nonagrarian opportunities offered to newcomers.

70. Report of meeting of Magistrates, 27 March 1662, Photostats, Mass. Archives, Box 4, MHS. Savage's son, Thomas Savage, Jr., tried to benefit from his father's brief flirtation with heresy. In 1680, Savage, Jr., wrote to the town of Portsmouth, R.I., to seek compensation from the land his father had purchased there in 1638. See his letter to the moderator and freemen of Portsmouth, 30 August 1680, Photostats, Mass. Archives, Box 8, MHS. There is some debate about whether Savage moved to Aquidneck at all.

71. Samuel Deane, *History of Scituate, Massachusetts, from Its First Settlement to 1831* (Boston: J. Loring, 1831), p. 60. Lathrop had had problems in England over the issue of baptism. Part of his English congregation had separated from him in 1633 to form England's first Baptist church. See also Gura, *A Glimpse of Sion's Glory*, pp. 39, 106.

72. Chauncey was notorious for recanting three times. See his pamphlet, *The Retraction of Mr. Charles Chancy* (London, 1641).

73. William Bradford, *Of Plymouth Plantation 1620–1647* (New York: Modern Library, 1981), pp. 348–350.

74. Deane, *History of Scituate*, pp. 34–35.

75. John Stockbridge, a wheelwright, had already found himself on the wrong side of the Plymouth Colony government. His first offense occurred in 1638, when Stockbridge was presented "for disgracefull speeches, tending to the contempt of the government, & for jering speeches to them that did reprove him for yt." Four years later, Stockbridge was under bond for £20 for good behavior, but again in September of that year he was fined £5 for "contemptuous speeches against the government." *Plymouth Records*, v. 1, p. 87; v. 2, p. 45.

76. Joseph B. Felt, *The Ecclesiastical History of New England* (Boston: Congregational Library Association, 1855–1862), v. 1, p. 497; *Boston Church Records*, p. 289.

77. William Vassall to John Wilson, 7 June 1643, in Deane, *History of Scituate*, p. 69. The issue of church membership remained a source of much debate. Vassall's views were similar to those of the Newbury ministers Thomas Parker and James Noyes, who advocated opening membership to all people in a geographic area.

78. See, for example, letter of William Vassall to John Wilson, 7 June 1643, re-

printed in Deane, *History of Scituate,* pp. 66–70, and letters from Vassall to John Cotton, 9 March 1643/4, 6 April 1644, Deane, pp. 72–73. Both Vassall and Chauncey wrote letters to Massachusetts ministers justifying their actions.

79. Significantly, Vassall had left Scituate in 1646, and with Chauncey's removal to the presidency of Harvard, the two prime antagonists were gone (Deane, p. 89).

80. Morgan, *The Puritan Dilemma,* pp. 199–200; George L. Kittredge, "Dr. Robert Child the Remonstrant," *PCSM* 21 (1919): 1–146; and Richard S. Dunn, *Puritans and Yankees: The Winthrop Dynasty of New England, 1630–1717* (New York: Norton, 1971), pp. 50–55, for a discussion of the petition and Winthrop's response. Winthrop was acutely sensitive to criticism of New England. See David Cressy, *Coming Over: Migration and Communication between England and New England in the Seventeenth Century* (Cambridge: Cambridge University Press, 1987), chapter 1. In 1645, Child drafted his petition and presented it to the General Court. He denounced the congregational system, urged the opening of church membership, and demanded greater toleration. Rejected by the General Court, Child and his co-signers decided to petition authorities in England. John Winthrop prudently jailed the Remonstrants while he dispatched his own representatives to Parliament, thus deflating the conflict.

81. Winthrop, *Journal,* p. 624.

82. Vassall probably authored *New England's Jonas* (Edward Winslow, *New England's Salamander* [London, 1647], p. 5). See too John Child, *New England's Jonas Cast up at London* (London, 1647).

83. Winthrop, *Journal,* p. 706.

84. Hubbard, *History of New England, 2 MHS Coll.,* v. 6, p. 500.

85. John Venn and J. A. Venn, eds., *Alumni Cantabrigienses: A Biographical List of All Known Students, Graduates and Holders of Office at the University of Cambridge, From the Earliest Times to 1900* (Cambridge: Cambridge University Press, 1927), v. 4, p. 63; Hope Sherrard to Sir Thomas Barrington, Providence, 6 January 1633/4, Egerton 2646, f. 58, BL; Meeting of Providence Island Company, 21 January 1630/1, CO 124/2, p. 7, PRO.

86. Particular instructions to Governor and Council concerning Lewis Morgan, 10 May 1632, CO 124/1, f. 37recto, PRO.

87. General Court for Providence, 19 June 1634, CO 124/2, p. 151, PRO.

88. Ordinary Court held for Providence Island, 4 February 1634/5, CO 124/2, p. 190, PRO.

89. Hope Sherrard to Sir Thomas Barrington, Providence, 25 February 1634/5, Egerton 2646, f. 76, BL.

90. Letter to Mr. Sherrard, 28 March 1636, CO 124/1, f. 92, PRO.

91. Letter to Captain Butler, July 1639, CO 124/1, f. 142, PRO.

92. Letter to Mr. Sherrard, June or July 1639, CO 124/1, f. 145recto, PRO.

93. Leverton's arrival had something of a farcical air: he blew in thanks to some ill winds when he attempted to return from Tortuga to Barbados. Edmund Calamy, *The Nonconformist's Memorial: Being an Account of the Ministers Who Were Ejected or Silenced after the Restoration* (London, 1775), pp. 290–295.

94. Entries for 19 February 1638/9, 10 March 1638/9, Nathaniel Butler's Diary, Sloane 758, BL.

95. Entries for 26 January; 2, 9, and 16 February 1639/40, Butler's Diary, Sloane 758, BL.

96. 13 and 20 October 1639, Butler's Diary, Sloane 758, BL.

97. 21 February 1639/40, Butler's Diary, Sloane 758, BL.

98. Four pages of notes for letters Butler planned to write to the Company, Sloane 758, BL.

99. Letter from members of the Council of Providence (Henry Halhead, Richard Lane, Hope Sherrard, Nicholas Leverton) to the Company, 17 June 1640, Providence Island, in *Historical Manuscripts Commission, Report on the Manuscripts of Allan George Finch*, v. 1 (London: H. M. Stationery Office, 1913), pp. 51–58.

100. *Orders and Constitutions for the Plantation of the Summer-Ilands* (London, 1622), pp. 56–57.

101. Council, 18 June 1627, Bermuda Colonial Records, v. 1, Berm. Arch.

102. Above from John Stow, "Some Former Ministers," *BHQ* 16 (1954): 51–62.

103. Joan de Rivera, "Shipwrecked Spaniard 1639: Grievances against Bermudians," trans. L. D. Gurrin, *BHQ* 18 (1961), 26–27.

104. Assizes, June, 1639, Lefroy, *Memorials,* v. 1, p. 556.

105. Richard Norwood to the Governor and Company of the Somers Islands, 28 February 1641/2, CO 1/10 no. 105, ff. 227–238, PRO. Norwood, in another letter, referred to a catechism of Oxenbridge called "Baby Milk"; *An Advertisement to such as have care of the Conservation of True Religion by Richard Norwood*, 1 March 1642/3, printed in William Prynne, *A Fresh Discovery of Some Prodigious New Wandering Blasing Stars and Firebrands Styling Themselves New Lights* (London, 1645).

106. Richard Norwood to the Governor and Company of the Somers Islands, 28 February 1641/2, CO 1/10, no. 105, ff. 227–238, PRO.

107. Richard Norwood to the Governor and Company of the Somers Islands, 28 February 1641/2, CO 1/10 no. 105, ff. 227–238, PRO; Richard Beake to William Prynne [1646], in Prynne, *Fresh Discovery*, p. 4. Nathaniel White wrote a defense of Oxenbridge in *Truth Gloriously Appearing from Under the Sad and Sable Cloud of Obloque or A Vindication* (London, 1646).

108. Norwood's Advertisement, 1 March 1642/3, in Prynne, *Fresh Discovery,* p. 21.

109. Richard Norwood to the Governor and Company of the Somers Islands, 14 May 1645, CO 1/11, no. 7, ff. 11–14, PRO.

110. "Petition of Inhabitants of the Somers Island to the Committees of both houses for English plantations," summer, 1644, in *Declaration of the Right Honorable Robert, Earle of Warwick* (London, 1645), passim.

111. White, *Truth Gloriously Appearing,* p. 66.

112. Richard Norwood to the Governor and Company of the Somers Islands, 14 May 1645, CO 1/11, no. 7, ff. 11–14, PRO.

113. White, *Truth Gloriously Appearing,* p. 59.

114. "Petition of inhabitants of the Somers Island to the Committees of both houses for English plantations," summer 1644, included in *Declaration of the Earle of Warwick,* p. 12.

115. *A Declaration of the Earle of Warwick,* p. 7.

116. Postscript, those who disclaim general petition, in Nathaniel White, *Truth Gloriously Appearing*. Among the ninety names were twelve men who had traveled from London in 1635. Most of these young men were adolescents in 1635 when they reached Bermuda: for six of these men, this appearance in the disclaimer is the only record extant of their continued existence on the island. None appears on juries or in court or in any other record that would suggest the ownership of land or goods. Possibly, then, as in the case of the Antinomian Controversy, disenfranchised people found a strong outlet for their feelings in religious controversy. It is also curious that of fifteen travelers in 1635 known to have taken sides during the upheaval of the 1640s, only one man, Daniel White, opposed the Independents.

117. Council meeting, 4 August 1648, Lefroy, *Memorials*, v. 1, p. 638; Bermuda Colonial Records, v. 2, p. 29, Berm. Arch. On the exodus from Bermuda to the Bahamas, see Michael Craton and Gail Saunders, *Islanders in the Stream: A History of the Bahamian People* (Athens: University of Georgia Press, 1992), chapters 5 and 6; and Herbert Miller, "The Colonization of the Bahamas, 1647–1670," *WMQ* 2 (1945): pp. 33–40.

118. Letter from Josias Forster to the Company, 7 September 1650, published in *Copy of a Petition from the Governor and company of the Summers Islands with annexed Papers* (London, 1651), pp. 9–10; and *Servants on Horseback: or, A Free-People bestrided in their persons, and Liberties, by worthlesse men* (London, 1648), reprinted in *BHQ* 9 (1952): 181–213. This pamphlet contained a series of petitions from 1646 to 1647.

119. Forster was governor in 1642–1643, 1645–1646, and 1650–1658. His tenure in office witnessed the reconciliation with the Independent party, but he was no fan of toleration: he sold four Quakers as slaves to Virginia or Barbados in 1658 (Lefroy, *Memorials*, v. 2, p. 161).

120. Richard Norwood to the Governor and Company of the Somers Islands, 28 February 1641/2, CO 1/10, no. 105, ff. 227–238, PRO.

121. Baillie, *A Dissuasive*, p. 55.

122. Baillie, *A Dissuasive*, p. 108. Richard Beake, a schoolmaster on Bermuda, also thought that the Bermuda ministers admired New England too much. See his letter to William Prynne, [1646], printed in Lefroy, *Memorials*, v. 1, p. 616. Beake himself spent thirteen months in prison for his opposition to the Independents.

123. Baillie, *A Dissuasive*, p. 90. Hugh Peter offers one example of the Atlantic progress that Baillie describes on a personal level. He recalled in *Mr Peters Last Report of the English Wars* (London, 1646) that his Independent congregation at Rotterdam had played as important a role in his religious ideas as his time in New England, "amongst all those faithfull learned, Godly Brethren." In Gay Transcripts, Peter Papers, v. 1, MHS.

6. Persistence and Migration in Old and New England

1. Michael McGiffert, ed., *God's Plot: The Paradoxes of Puritan Piety, Being the Autobiography and Journal of Thomas Shepard* (Amherst: University of Massachusetts Press, 1972), pp. 64–65.

2. William Byam to Sir Charles Pym, 8 November 1668, Antigua, *Caribbeana,* v. 2, p. 15.

3. Winthrop, *Journal,* entries for November and December 1635, pp. 161–162, quotation from p. 161.

4. The only other region appropriate for a study of local migration for the 1635 travelers would be the Chesapeake. The absence of early records for most counties permits the full development of the careers only for residents of Accomack, Norfolk, and York counties. Moreover, the constant fragmentation of counties makes it difficult to track geographic mobility for this particular sample. Geographic mobility in the Chesapeake, however, is a well-told story in general terms, thanks to the research of James Horn. See especially "Moving on in the New World: Migration and Out-migration in the Seventeenth-Century Chesapeake," in Peter Clark and David Souden, eds., *Migration and Society in Early Modern England* (Totowa, N.J.: Barnes and Noble Books, 1988), pp. 172–212. Horn proposes rates of household turnover as high as 43 to 47 percent, for example, in Accomack-Northampton from 1646 to 1655.

5. My findings here echo the research of Virginia DeJohn Anderson, "To Pass Beyond the Seas: The Great Migration and the Settlement of New England, 1630–1670" (Ph.D. dissertation, Harvard University, 1984), and *New England's Generation: The Great Migration and the Formation of Society and Culture in the Seventeenth Century* (New York: Cambridge University Press, 1991); and Richard Archer, "New England Mosaic: A Demographic Analysis for the Seventeenth Century," *WMQ* 47 (1990): 477–502. Anderson tracked 693 passengers from England to New England, whereas Archer updated the data originally compiled by James Savage, a total "of 22,164 people who either migrated to New England before 1650 or were born there between 1620 and 1649" (Archer, p. 478).

6. Phippen's father, William Phipping, remembered his daughter "Judah" in his will, dated 22 September 1647. He anticipated that she would return to England, but her marriage to her fellow 1635 traveler James Hayward precluded reunion with her relatives. See Phipping's will, Pembroke 186 (microfilm Prob 11/214), PRO.

7. Peter Clark and David Souden, Introduction, in *Migration and Society,* p. 29.

8. David Souden, "'East, west—home's best'? Regional Patterns in Migration in Early Modern England," in *Migration and Society,* p. 315.

9. Great Bromley Parish Register Transcripts, ERO, Chelmsford. The Boxted parish records are extant only until 1616, and Boxted manor rolls do not commence until 1645 (D/DTs M27, ERO, Colchester), so Stone's first appearance in Boxted is difficult to trace. Will of David Stone, dated 1621, proved 27 April 1625, D/ACW 9/208, ERO, Chelmsford. Essex Lay Subsidies, Lexden Hundred, 19 December 4 Charles I (1629), E 179/112/638, PRO.

10. *The Victoria History of the Counties of England: Bedfordshire,* v. 3 (Foulkestone: Dawson of Pall Mall for the Institute of Historical Research, 1972), p. 349; William Brigg, *The Parish Registers of St. Albans Abbey 1558–1689* (Harpenden, England: William Brigg, 1897), pp. 50–63, 143. Mayor's Accounts 1621–22, St. Albans Borough Records #160. Records for expenditures mention dates of

meeting 26 November 1621 and 3 December 1621; Mayor's Court Book, St. Albans Borough Records #312, f. 107, St. Albans Public Library, St. Albans, Hertfordshire.

11. A child, Zachary, was christened in Dunstable on 20 October 1630, and a second child, Joshua, was baptized there on 14 September 1634. International Genealogical Index (IGI), The Guildhall, London.

12. Hallock P. Long, "Settlers Surnamed Long to New England before 1700," *NEHGR* 104 (1950): 36–40. Long's second wife was named Elizabeth.

13. *The Victoria History of the Counties of England: Bedfordshire,* v. 3, p. 354.

14. Apprenticeship enrolled in Book of Inrollmt, St. Albans Borough Records #286, St. Albans Public Library. The enrollment was dated 10 August 8 Charles I (1633).

15. Other examples of local movement for families in the 1635 cohort include the Eires, who moved from Lavenham to Bury St. Edmunds, Suffolk (*NEHGR* 69 [1915]: 248–252; Parish Register, St. Mary's Church, Bury St. Edmunds, microfiche at East Suffolk Record Office, Bury, Suffolk); Samuel Morse, born in Boxted, Essex, married at Redgrave, Suffolk, and later resident of Burgate, Suffolk (*NEHGR* 83 [1929]: 81–84); and Thomas Joslin, originally of Roxwell, Essex, but later of Barham, Suffolk (*NEHGR* 71 [1917]: 254).

16. Frederick Lewis Weis, *The Colonial Clergy and the Colonial Churches of New England* (Lancaster, Mass.: The Society of the Descendants of the Colonial Clergy, 1936), pp. 45–46.

17. McGiffert, ed., *God's Plot,* pp. 46–62.

18. Preceding from Hugh Peter, *A Dying Father's Last Legacy* (London, 1660), pp. 97–100, quotation from p. 99.

19. Letter from George Montaigne, Bishop of London, to Duke of Buckingham, 12 December 1626; The Earl of Warwick to Hugh Peter, c. December 1626, *EIHC* 71 (1935), 307–309.

20. The short distances traveled in England is a central finding of Roger Thompson's extensive research on this question. *Mobility and Migration: East Anglian Founders of New England, 1629–1640* (Amherst: University of Massachusetts Press, 1994).

21. Included among known soldiers were Barnaby Davis, Thomas Bull, Thomas Tibbalds, Thomas Barber, Thomas Stares, Thomas Stiles, Thomas Blackly, Thomas Munson, George Chappell, Palmer Tingley, William Whittred, Edward Lumis, William Swyndon, William Fuller, and, of course, Gardiner himself.

22. "Leift Lion Gardener His Relation of the Pequot Warres," 3 *MHS Coll.,* 3: pp. 131–160; Gardiner's redemption of the English girls is described on p. 147.

23. *The Records of the Town of Cambridge (Formerly Newtowne) Massachusetts, 1630–1703* (Cambridge, Mass.: The University Press, 1901), pp. 13–14; *The Register Book of the Lands and Houses in the "New Towne"* (Cambridge, Mass.: The University Press, 1896), p. 36; *Conn. Records,* v. 1, p. 6.

24. Charles J. Hoadly, *Records of the Colony and Plantation of New Haven, from 1638–1649* (Hartford: Case, Tiffany and Company, 1857), v. 1, 2 January 1644/5, p. 152; 6 October 1646, pp. 271–272; *Conn. Records,* v. 2, pp. 133, 138, 184–185, 234.

25. William Wood, *New Englands Prospect* (London, 1634), pp. 37, 39.

26. Edward Johnson, *Wonder-Working Providence of Sions Saviour in New England* (London, 1654), reprinted in Scholars' Facsimiles and Reprints (Delmar, N.Y.: 1974), pp. 75–76.

27. George D. Langdon, *Pilgrim Colony: A History of New Plymouth, 1620–1691* (New Haven: Yale University Press, 1966), p. 35; *Plymouth Church Records 1620–1859, PCSM* 21 (1920), 84.

28. Hubbard, *History of New England,* 2 *MHS Coll.,* 5, p. 177.

29. General Court 2 Sept 1635, *Mass. Records,* v. 1, p. 159.

30. Hooker wanted to limit baptism to children of communicants, while Cotton had more liberal views.

31. In that year, for example, the 1635 traveler Edmund Freeman and his wife were presented to the Grand Jury for not attending church, in opposition to the order of 6 June 1651 (R. A. Lovell, *Sandwich: A Cape Cod Town* [Sandwich: Town of Sandwich, Mass., Archives and Historical Center, 1984], p. 35).

32. Samuel Greene Arnold, *History of the State of Rhode Island and Providence Plantations* (New York: D. Appleton & Co., 1859), v. 1, p. 132.

33. Sydney V. James, *Colonial Rhode Island: A History* (New York: Scribner, 1975), pp. 34–35.

34. Winthrop, *Journal,* pp. 298–299. E. B. Huntington, *History of Stamford, Connecticut, 1641–1868* (1868; reprint Harrison, N.Y.: Harbor Hill Books, 1979), pp. 14–15; Sherman W. Adams and Henry R. Stiles, *The History of Ancient Wethersfield, Connecticut* (New York: The Grafton Press, 1904), pp. 136–152; Martha Bockee Flint, *Long Island before the Revolution: A Colonial Study* (Port Washington, N.Y.: Ira J. Friedman, Inc., 1896), p. 229.

35. A word on the choice of towns: these nine towns listed here include eight communities already established by 1635, and one, Dedham, that was not established until 1636 but that was selected because the 1635 arrivals who settled in Dedham did so as original signers of the town covenant. Other towns that the 1635 London migrants could have settled in included Medford, Newbury, Salem, Weymouth, Hingham, and Charlestown. In all cases the numbers are really too low to compare: no one settled first in Medford or Newbury, for example, whereas Weymouth attracted only one of the 1635 migrants. Eighteen people settled in Hingham, and forty in Salem. Plymouth Colony towns included Plymouth (twenty-seven settled in either Plymouth or the Plymouth Colony) and Scituate (twenty); again, the numbers are too low to offer valuable comparisons. Likewise, in Maine neither Saco nor Kittery were peopled by enough members of the 1635 cohort, nor is there adequate information on those who did settle there, to permit meaningful comparisons.

36. Those interested in examining differential rates of removal for the periods before and after 1640 for these nine towns should consult Games, "Venturers, Vagrants, and Vessels of Glory: Migration from England to the Colonies under Charles I" (Ph.D. Dissertation, University of Pennsylvania, 1992), p. 283. See especially Laura Auwers Bissell, "From One Generation to Another: Mobility in Seventeenth-Century Windsor, Connecticut," *WMQ* 31 (1974): 79–110, for a similar scrutiny of mobility. Bissell's intense focus on a single community per-

mits her to delineate and explain patterns of migration more fully than can this broader study of New England migration as a whole.

37. Ralph J. Crandall and Ralph J. Coffman. "From Emigrants to Rulers: The Charlestown Oligarchy in the Great Migration," *NEHGR* 131 (1977): 14.

38. The ten signers were the brothers George and William Beeresto, the minister Thomas Carter, the father and son Philemon and Timothy Dalton, John Houghton, the father and son Samuel and Joseph Morse, Robert Onyon, and Ralph Shepard.

39. Kenneth Lockridge, in "The Population of Dedham, Massachusetts, 1646–1746," *Economic History Review* 19 (1966): 318–344, explored these questions of migration and persistence. Lockridge found high rates of persistence but limited his analysis to the period after 1640. Between that year and 1648, for example, 60 percent of taxpayers remained in the town. What the evidence for the London sample indicates is a real upheaval in the first years of the town, when the requirements of Contentment, as the town was first called, drove many away.

40. 18 August 1636, Don Gleason Hill, ed., *The Early Records of the Town of Dedham, Massachusetts, 1636–1659* (Dedham, Mass.: The Dedham Transcript, 1892), p. 20.

41. Philemon Dalton and Thomas Carter achieved freeman status before the Dedham church was organized, suggesting that they had joined the Watertown church.

42. Don Gleason Hill, ed., *Records of Baptisms, Marriages and Deaths and Admissions . . . from the Church Records in the Town of Dedham, Massachusetts, 1638–1845* (Dedham, Mass.: The Dedham Transcript, 1888), p. 8.

43. Alonzo Lewis, *The History of Lynn, including Nahant* (Boston: S. N. Dickinson, 1844), p. 113.

44. Caroline Martino and Marcia Lindberg, "Henry Collins of Lynn and His Descendants," *The Essex Genealogist* 10 (1990): 145–152.

45. Winthrop, *Journal*, p. 326.

46. *The Victoria History of the Counties of England: Buckinghamshire* (London: Archibald Constable and Company, Ltd., 1927), v. 4; Sherington Parish Register, Bishop's Transcripts, D/A/T/157; Olney Parish Register, Bishop's Transcripts, D/A/T/144/3, D/A/T/145; Lavendon Parish Register, PR 126/1/1, 1574–1699, BRO.

47. E. R. C. Brinkworth, "The Laudian Church in Buckinghamshire," *University of Birmingham Historical Journal* (1955–1956), 38. Quotation from Archdeaconry Visitation Books for Buckinghamshire.

48. Archdeaconry of Buckinghamshire, Visitation Book, 1633–34, D/A/V/2, BRO.

49. "Declaration to be made to William Worcester," *CSPD* Charles I 1635–36, p. 47, no. 25.

50. The fifth family of the Buckinghamshire migration, the Griggs family, remained in Boston.

51. Robert Day of Stanstead Abbot settled in Ipswich.

52. John Eliot's Record of Church members, in *A Report of the Record Commission-*

ers, Containing the Roxbury Land and Church Records (Boston: Rockwell and Churchill, 1884), pp. 80, 81.

53. *Mass. Records,* v. 1, p. 185.

54. Wood, *New Englands Prospect,* p. 37.

55. *Roxbury Land Records,* June 1, 1639, pp. 4–5.

56. Eliot's Record of Church members, p. 172. A similar pattern holds true in Dorchester, where a cluster of forty-seven passengers from four parishes in the Weald of Kent settled and remained. Here the Roxbury and Dorchester residents resemble the Windsor men studied by Laura Bissell. She found that "the settler most likely to remain in Windsor was one who received over three hundred acres of land . . . He was a church member and a town officer." (Bissell, "From One Generation," p. 81). But I would add as well one more attribute: these men settled with old friends, neighbors, and relatives.

57. *Second Report of the Record Commissioners of the City of Boston: Containing the Boston Records, 1634–1660, and the Book of Possessions* (Boston: Municipal Printing Office, 1902), p. 5.

58. Wood, *New Englands Prospect,* p. 38.

59. Darrett B. Rutman, *Winthrop's Boston: Portrait of a Puritan Town, 1630–1649* (Chapel Hill: University of North Carolina Press, 1965), p. 80.

60. Rutman, *Winthrop's Boston,* p. 22.

61. Crandall and Coffman, "From Emigrants," pp. 22, 27.

62. Petition of Boston shoemakers, 15 March 1647/8, Photostats, Mass. Archives, Box 2; Petition of vintners of Boston and Charlestown, 3 March 1649/50, Photostats, Mass. Archives, Box 2; Petition to General Court, 29 April 1668, Photostats, Mass. Archives, box 5, MHS.

63. The tradesmen include glovers Thomas Buttolph and Anthony Stannion, shoemakers William Cope, William Courser, George Burdin, and Robert Turner, joiners John Davies and Ralph Mason, coopers Joseph Faber and Edward Rainsford, tailors Robert Mere, James Fitch, Thomas Savage, and Christopher Stanley, draper Ralph Hudson, blacksmith George Orris, mason Henry Stevens, carrier Martin Saunders, rope maker Alexander Baker, carpenter George Griggs, soap boiler George Woodward, and merchants Robert Keayne and Robert Nanney. Richard Tuttle was the husbandman.

64. Debt action at Boston court, 15 September 1653, Photostats, Mass. Archives, Box 3, MHS.

65. *Boston Records,* v. 1, pp. 108, 114.

66. George A. Schofield, ed., *Ancient Records of the Town of Ipswich, v. 1, 1634–1850* (Ipswich, Mass.: Chronicle Motor Press, 1899), p. 73.

67. *Ipswich Records,* p. 87.

68. Thomas Franklin Waters, *Ipswich in the Massachusetts Bay Colony* (Ipswich, Mass.: Ipswich Historical Society, 1905), v. 1, p. 80.

69. Wood, *New Englands Prospect,* p. 44.

70. David Grayson Allen, *In English Ways: The Movement of Societies and the Transferal of English Local Law and Custom to Massachusetts Bay in the Seventeenth Century* (Chapel Hill: University of North Carolina Press, 1981), p. 128, for average acreage. Source for landholding for 1635 cohort: Edward S. Perzel, "Landholding in Ipswich," *EIHC* 104 (1968), 309; and other genealogical

sources. Eight men owned land ranging from 125 to 1,600 acres, with an average of 518 acres.

71. Inventories are available for 81 decedents altogether out of the 1,169 travelers from London in 1635.

72. Petition to General Court, 6 November 1658, Photostats, Mass. Archives, box 3a, MHS.

73. Allen, *In English Ways,* and Rutman, *Winthrop's Boston,* make strong cases for the importance of local English origins in each of these New England towns.

74. Bernard Bailyn, *The New England Merchants in the Seventeenth Century* (Cambridge, Mass.: Harvard University Press, 1955), pp. 35–37.

75. See, for example, various deeds of William Paine recorded in Northampton Wills and Deeds 1651–1654, no. 4, f. 197recto; or Northampton Deeds and Wills 1655–1656, f. 74, VSL. On Paine's involvement in the ironworks and other New England industries, see various letters of his in 4 *MHS Coll.,* 7, pp. 401–410.

76. As T. H. Breen and Stephen Foster wrote, "Fortune . . . usually favored the mobile" ("Moving to the New World"). Servants also fared well in repeat migrations. Altogether some twenty-one men who had reached New England as servants gained land. See Games, "Venturers, Vagrants, and Vessels," pp. 311–315.

77. *Mass. Records,* v. 2, p. 136.

78. Copy of Dorchester Town Records, 8 March 1663/4, Misc. Bound, MHS; *A Report of the Record Commissioners containing Charlestown Land Records, 1638–1802* (Boston: Rockwell and Churchill, 1883), p. 94.

79. 18 October 1645, *Mass. Records,* v. 2, p. 145.

80. Winthrop, *Journal,* 7 March 1644, pp. 501–502.

81. Officeholding was extensive among the New England cohort: see Appendix B, Table B.7.

82. An instructive synthesis of some of the literature on persistence is provided by L. R. Poos in "Population Turnover in Medieval Essex: The Evidence of some Early-Fourteenth-Century Tithing Lists," in Lloyd Bonfield, Richard M. Smith, and Keith Wrightson, eds., *The World We Have Gained: Histories of Population and Social Structure* (New York: B. Blackwell, 1986), pp. 1–5. See also Bissell, "From One Generation," p. 103, for a discussion of comparisons.

83. A different interpretation of the significance of migration can be found in Roger Thompson's monumental study of the migration in old and New England of East Anglians: *Mobility and Migration,* pp. xiii, 3, 9.

7. Migration and the Atlantic World

1. James A. Williamson, *English Colonies in Guiana and on the Amazon, 1604–1668* (Oxford: Clarendon Press, 1923), pp. 163–164. This mortality rate for a single year far surpassed that of the Chesapeake colonies in their first years. Portions of this chapter appeared previously in Alison Games, "History without Borders: Teaching American History in an Atlantic Context," *Indiana Magazine of History* 41 (1995): 159–178.

2. These five include the plantations planned by Charles Leigh and Robert Har-

court on the Wiapoco, Thomas Roe's plantation on the Amazon, the Amazon Company's plantation under the leadership of the renegade Roger North, and the Guiana Company under Robert Harcourt. There were several other aborted settlements.

3. George Warren, *An Impartial Description of Surinam* (London, 1667), pp. 1–2; Henry Adis, *A Letter Sent from Syrranam* (London, 1664).

4. Bathsua Scott to James Banister, 13 September 1674, CO 1/31, no. 75, PRO; James Banister to the Earl of Arlington, 18 November 1674, CO 1/31, no. 76, PRO. The Scotts were among the approximately five hundred English colonists who left the colony within the first three years of Dutch rule. Victor Enthoven, "Suriname and Zeeland: Fifteen Years of Dutch Misery on the Wild Coast, 1667–1682," in J. Everaert and J. Parmentier, eds., *International Conference on Shipping, Factories and Colonization* (Brussels, 1996), p. 253.

5. William Byam to Sir Charles Pym, 8 November 1668, Antigua, in *Caribbeana*, v. 2, p. 15.

6. Douglas Edward Leach, *Flintlock and Tomahawk: New England in King Philip's War* (New York: MacMillan, 1958), p. 243.

7. Richard S. Dunn, *Sugar and Slaves: The Rise of the Planter Class in the English West Indies, 1624–1713* (Chapel Hill: University of North Carolina Press, 1972), p. 21; see p. 149 for Port Royal as the "Sodom of the Indies."

8. "Father White's Briefe Relation," in Clayton Colman Hall, ed., *Narratives of Early Maryland* (New York: Charles Scribner's Sons, 1910), p. 31; see also Robert Harcourt, *A Relation of a Voyage to Guiana (London, 1613)*, Hakluyt Society 2nd series no. 60 (London: Hakluyt Society, 1928), p. 127.

9. Samuel Purchas, *Purchas His Pilgrimes* (London, 1625), Book 9, chapter 8, p. 1763.

10. "John Hilton's Relation," in Vincent T. Harlow, ed., *Colonising Expeditions to the West Indies and Guiana, 1623–1667* (London: Hakluyt Society, 1925), pp. 4–5.

11. *The Journal of Richard Norwood*, edited by Wesley Frank Craven and Walter B. Hayward (New York: Scholars' Facsimiles, 1945), introduction.

12. The saga of Davis's travels appears in his petition to the Governor, Council, and Assistants, in the *Note-book Kept by Thomas Lechford, Transactions of the American Antiquarian Society* 7 (1885): 367–370. Davis settled in Charlestown.

13. George Walter Chamberlain, "The English Ancestry of William Almy of Portsmouth, R.I.," *NEHGR* 71 (1917): 310.

14. Gov. Thomas Dudley's Letter to the Countess of Lincoln, March 1631, printed in Peter Force, *Tracts and Other Papers Relating Principally to the Origin, Settlement, and Progress of the Colonies in North America* (Washington: privately printed, 1836–1846), v. 2, pp. 9–10.

15. Both ventures went awry. Almy's religious beliefs drove him and his family to Rhode Island, whereas Vassall, the apparent instigator of Child's Remonstrance, finally migrated from Plymouth Colony, where he had settled soon after his arrival in 1635, to England and then on to Barbados.

16. The Boston minister John Wilson had difficulty persuading his wife to join him in Massachusetts: his trip to England certainly included a visit with her.

17. Court held 17 November 1634, CO 124/2, p. 173, PRO.

18. Court held 4 February 1634/5, CO 124/2, p. 190; letter to Captain Philip Bell, by the *Expectation*, 20 April 1635, CO 124/1, f. 76verso, PRO.

19. New voyagers and officers to the island accompanying Barton included Nicholas Riskinner, who was to be the governor of Association Island, and William Thorpe, who had previously worked in the Somers Islands, to serve as a lieutenant. Letter to Captain Philip Bell, governor of Providence Island, CO 124/1, f. 79, PRO; William Jessop to Mr. Isaac Barton, 11 August 1634, letter 28, Jessop Letterbook, BL. The overlapping memberships of the Somers Islands Company and the Providence Island Company made repetition and borrowing in colonial personnel inevitable.

20. Thomas Durham to Nathaniel Rich, January 1619/20, *Rich Papers,* p. 175; Sir Nathaniel Rich to Hugh Wentworth, 19 July 1634, letter 1, Jessop Letterbook; Sir Nathaniel Rich to Mr. G. Hanmer, 19 July 1634, letter 3, Jessop Letterbook; Sir Nathaniel Rich to Thomas Durham, 1 June 1635, letter 92, Jessop Letterbook; W. Jessop to Mr. Hugh Wentworth, 21 September 1635, by the *Dorset,* Jessop Letterbook; "Instructions to be put in execution on my behalf by Hugh Wentworth after his landing at the Somers Islands," 17 August 1638, letter 179, Jessop Letterbook, BL.

21. The paucity of sources for the British islands before 1635 makes it extremely difficult to isolate repeat travelers.

22. James Hay, Earl of Carlisle, to Captain Ashton, 12 October 1641, Egerton 2597, ff. 189–191, BL.

23. Proof of earlier residence in the colony can be found for each of these men in the Virginia Muster, 1624/5, and "the list of the living and dead in Virginia, 16 February 1623/4," both in CO 1/3, PRO. See the deposition of Robert Sabin, 25 August 1638, HCA 13/54, f. 222, PRO. Sabin deposed about a voyage to Virginia in August of 1637.

24. Bartholomew married Dorcas Foster at St. Dunstan's, Stepney in 1628, and their son Bartholomew was baptized in London in 1633 (George Ely Russell, "Bartholomew Hoskins, Gen.," *Virginia Genealogist* 27 [1983], 83). Dorcas Hoskins was still in London in 1641, when she petitioned the House of Lords on behalf of her husband: Petition to the House of Lords of Dorcas Hoskins, House of Lords, Maine Papers, VCRP reel 601, VSL.

25. Deposition of Walter Jenkins, HCA 13/52, PRO.

26. Jacob Price, *Perry of London* (Cambridge, Mass.: Harvard University Press, 1992), p. vii.

27. Wright imported muscavado sugar, 25 January 1632/3, f. 12recto, whereas Chappell imported Virginia tobacco, 17 May 1633, f. 59 recto, E 190/38/1, London Port Book 1632–33, PRO. Wright, of course, was not yet importing sugar from Barbados in 1635.

28. For John Redman, see Thomas Gower v. William Anthony, 9 May 1637, HCA 13/111 (no page numbers); for John Butler, E 190/41/5, f. 48verso lists his tobacco imports in 1637, PRO; for Thomas Bradford, see petition, c. 1644, of merchants, grocers, and others dealing in tobacco, Harley 1238, f. 9, BL.

29. Jacob Price has noted that these voyages back and forth formed a family strategy

for some mercantile firms and kin: unfortunately, there is not enough evidence for these particular merchants, although clearly some families benefited from far-flung trade and kin networks. Price, *Perry of London,* p. 1.

30. An eleventh, William Thorp, was a former Bermudian who was en route to Providence Island in that year.

31. Petition from George Stirke to Lord Saye, Nathaniel Rich, etc., 1633/4, MHS Photostats, Box 1, MHS. One important clue in identifying repeat voyagers is their age: whereas the average age of travelers to the colonies ranged somewhere between a low of 21 years (for Bermuda) and a high of 23 years (for Providence), repeat travelers tended to be subtantially older, with average ages between 31 (for New England) and 42 (for Bermuda).

32. Deposition, March 1626, Lefroy, *Memorials,* v. 1, p. 366.

33. For the passage of Francis Russell, Edward Vincent, and James Rising, see List of people going to Jamaica from Bermuda on 5 January 1657/8, Lefroy, *Memorials,* v. 1; and Richard D. Pierce, ed. *The Records of the First Church in Salem, Massachusetts 1629–1736* (Salem: Essex Institute, 1974), 12 January 1662, p. 96.

34. Assizes, May 1656, Lefroy, *Memorials,* v. 2, pp. 73–74. This unfortunate woman, Mrs. Paskow, was reportedly sold by her husband in a drunken fit for £100 (Lefroy, *Memorials,* v. 2, Council, July 1657, p. 100).

35. Bond, 22 September 1657, Bermuda Colonial Records, v. 2, pp. 319–320; Attestation of Mr. John Stowe, commander of the *Elizabeth and Anne,* 1660, in Bermuda Colonial Records, v. 2, p. 374, Berm. Arch.

36. Bermuda Colonial Records, fragment G, items related to shipping, 1656–58, Berm. Arch.

37. Whittacre left tobacco to a brother living in London. Whittacre's commercial interests were obviously well diversified, since he also possessed some sugar. Will of George Whittacre, 13 May 1654, proved 26 June 1654, *NEHGR* 39 (1885): 165; Will of John Robinson, 2 March 1652/3, Joanne McCree Sanders, *Barbados Records: Wills and Administrations* (Marceline, Mich.: Sanders Historical Publications, 1979), pp. 94, 306; *The Probate Records of Essex County, Massachusetts* (Salem: Essex Institute, 1916), v. 2, pp. 372–373.

38. On the relocation to St. Lucia, see *Servants on Horseback: Or, A Free-People Bestrided in Their Persons, and Liberties, by Worthlesse Men* (London, 1648), p. 189. See also a 1640/41 letter to Captain Henry Ashton about the planting of Tobago and St. Lucia, Hay Papers, GD 34/922, SRO.

39. See John Winthrop's righteous disapproval of this exodus from New England. Winthrop mocked those with such misapprehensions, since many residents of these very colonies, "Providence and other the Caribbee Islands and Virginia," had in fact relocated to New England. Winthrop, *Journal,* p. 323.

40. Proposals concerning Jamaica by Marlborough [1660], CO 1/14, no. 50, ff. 123–124, PRO. See also letters from Governor Luke Stokes of Nevis about recruitment there in 1656 and 1657 in Thomas Birch, *A Collection of the State Papers of John Thurloe* (London, 1742, 7 volumes), v. 5, pp. 66–67, 77, 769.

41. Robert Tilghman, for example, a merchant of Virginia, petitioned Oliver Cromwell for free passage to the West Indies. Although he had lost his estate in both

England and Virginia, he was eager to try his hand again at colonial endeavors. Copy of a petition from Robert Tilghman, in Brock 685, Huntington Library, San Marino, Calif.

42. John Oxenbridge, *A Seasonable Proposition of Propagating the Gospel by Christian Colonies in the Continent of Guiana* [London, n.d.].

43. Copeland discussed his Japan adventures in a letter to John Winthrop, 9 December 1639, Bermuda, 5 *MHS Coll.,* 1, pp. 277–280. For his East India venture and his simultaneous support for the Virginia Company, see Patrick Copland, *Declaration How the Monies Were Disposed* (London, 1622). See also the career of Nicholas Leverton, described in Edmund Calamy, *The Nonconformist's Memorial: Being an Account of the Ministers Who Were Ejected after the Restoration* (London, 1775), pp. 290–295.

44. Peter Hay to James Hay, Barbados, 24 May 1639, GD 34/924/17, SRO.

45. Norfolk Minute Book, 1637–1646, pp. 100, 102, VSL.

46. Royal Proclamation allowing freedom of emigration, 20 June 1641, printed in Lefroy, *Memorials,* v. 1, pp. 566–567.

47. Petition to General Court, 6 November 1658, Mass. Archives, Photostats, Box 3a, MHS.

48. On the difficulty of transporting goods safely across the ocean, see Samuel Shepard to Sir Thomas Barrington, 1643, Gay Transcripts, Miscellaneous, MHS.

49. *Lechford Note-book,* pp. 367–368.

50. R. A. Lovell, Jr., *Sandwich: A Cape Cod Town* (Sandwich: Sandwich Archives and Historical Center, 1984), p. 28.

51. George Ely Russell, "Bartholomew Hoskins," *Virginia Genealogist* 27 (1983): 83.

52. Deeds, July 1657, Bermuda Colonial Records, Fragment G, Berm. Arch.

53. Petition of the "poore Planters in the Sommer Islands," CO 1/4, p. 135, c. 1628, PRO.

54. Ninety-eight men graduated in the College's first seventeen classes: thirty-three went to Europe, primarily England but also Ireland and the Netherlands (although some later returned to America), fifty-four stayed in North America, the fates of five are unknown (these men likely returned to England), three recent graduates were lost at sea bound for England in 1657, and three went to the island colonies. These statistics are based on an analysis of John Langdon Sibley, *Biographical Sketches of Graduates of Harvard University* (Cambridge, Mass., 1873), v. 1. The impulse to return was particularly strong in the College's first ten graduating classes: of fifty-five graduates, twenty-four returned to England.

55. Winthrop, *Journal,* pp. 600–601, commented in 1645 on the inability of many Harvard graduates to obtain positions and mentioned in that year that Bulkeley had gone to England.

56. Articles of Apprenticeship, 7 July 1635, *Winthrop Papers,* v. 3, p. 199; Francis Kirby to John Winthrop, Jr., London, 25 August 1635, *Winthrop Papers,* v. 3, p. 207; Emmanuel Downing to John Winthrop, Jr., 1 March 1635/6, *Winthrop Papers,* v. 3, p. 233; Lucy Downing to John Winthrop, Jr., 8 March 1635/6,

Winthrop Papers, v. 3, pp. 236–237; Francis Kirby to John Winthrop, Jr., London, 7 May 1636, *Winthrop Papers,* v. 3, p. 259.

57. Richard Ligon, *A True and Exact History of the Island of Barbadoes* (London, 1673), p. 22.

58. The Arnolds married in St. Dunstan in 1628. By 1644, their son Jasper was baptized at St. Botolphs, Bishopsgate. International Genealogical Index for London, The Guildhall, London. It is possible that the Arnolds never even boarded ship.

59. See the power of attorney of Anthony Stapley of Patcham, Sussex, printed in "New England Gleanings," *NEHGR* 40 (1880), 271. Sarah Geere was actually somewhat unusual in her rapid return to England. Other women who were newly widowed in New England within a few years of their families' arrivals remained in the colony. See, for example, Margaret Toothaker, Sara Ewer, Ann Crosby, Elizabeth Harlakenden, and Elizabeth Howe of the 1635 cohort. All five women made new lives for themselves in the colonies after the deaths of their husbands.

60. Charles J. Hoadly, ed., *Records of the Colony or Jurisdiction of New Haven, From May, 1653, to the Union* (Hartford: Case, Lockwood and Company, 1858), 12 October 1653, p. 47.

61. Winthrop, *Journal,* p. 346.

62. Compared with the number of passengers (939) for whom there is some information available, 7.8 percent of the population returned. When compared with the number of passengers (434) for whom there is complete information, however, 16.8 percent of the population returned. Furthermore, many entire families have left no extant evidence of their presence in New England. Although it is possible that entire families could vanish into the occasional lacunae of the New England records, it is unlikely, and it is more probable that these families simply returned to England. David Cressy has estimated that one in six, or approximately 15 percent of New Englanders, returned to old England (David Cressy, *Coming Over: Migration and Communication between England and New England in the Seventeenth Century* [Cambridge: Cambridge University Press, 1987], p. 192). Other historians have delineated return migration for New England as a whole in this period. See Cressy, *Coming Over,* chapter 8; Andrew Delbanco, "Looking Homeward, Going Home: The Lure of England for the Founders of New England," *NEQ* 59 (1986): 358–386; and William L. Sachse, "The Migration of New Englanders to England, 1640–1660," *American Historical Review* 53 (1948): 251–278.

63. See the description of George Cooke's death, letter to the Speaker of Parliament, Dublin, 13 April 1652, Firth MS, no. 5, f. 15, Bodleian Library. Those who survived the war could find their status in New England enhanced. Such was the experience of Thomas Marshall, who had received the status of freeman soon upon his arrival in New England. After he had served in the Civil War, he returned to Lynn and purchased a tavern. Marshall's experience in England transformed him. John Dunton, a traveler in Lynn in 1686, mentioned his stay at Mr. Marshall's inn. He described Marshall as "a hearty old gentleman, formerly one of Oliver's soldiers, upon which he very much values himself. He had

all the history of the civil wars at his fingers' end, and if we may believe him, Oliver did hardly any thing that was considerable without his assistance." Journal of John Dunton, 1686, quoted in Alonzo Lewis, *The History of Lynn, including Nahant* (Boston: S. N. Dickinson, 1844), p. 91.

64. *Fourth Report of the Record Commissioners of the City of Boston. Dorchester Town Records* (Boston: Rockwell and Churchill, 1896), p. 15 (land grant of eight acres, 18 January 1635/6); pp. 105–106 (school list, on which Munnings signed his mark, 7 February 1641/2).

65. *Dorchester Records,* p. 304 (called Goodman, 1651), p. 305; Manorial Records of Tillingham, T/A 400/5, ERO, Chelmsford. Munnings served on juries in the manorial court in 1628, 1629, and 1630.

66. Passenger list of the *Speedwell,* 1653, Photostats, Mass Archives, Box 3a. As a resident of Boston, Munnings, for example, signed a petition asking the court to repeal a law forbidding the importation of malt. Petition to General Court, 21 October 1659, Photostats, Mass. Archives, Box 3a, MHS; *Mass. Records,* v. 3, p. 351. Michelaliel died in 1659 of "a dread flux." Petition of Hannah Munninges, widow of Mahalaleel Munnings, 9 May 1662, Photostats, Mass. Archives, Box 4, MHS. Mrs. Munnings was left with two children and lots of debts.

67. Tillingham Parish Register Transcript, T/R 229/2, ERO Chelmsford, burials 1561–1696, marriages, 1618–1696, with gaps 1622–1625, 1632, 1633, baptisms, 1614–1679. Only Anne Munnings's baptism was found in this register, for 6 January 1625/6. Dengie Parish Register, T/R 229/2, ERO, Chelmsford, lists baptisms for the children of Hopestill Munnings. His will makes no reference to residences of his children. See will of Edmund Muninges, of Denge, Essex, 2 October 1666, proved 18 July 1667, "Genealogical Gleanings in England," *NEHGR* 37 (1883): 378.

68. Stephen Paschall Sharples, ed., *Records of the Church of Christ at Cambridge in New England, 1632–1830* (Boston: Eben Putnam, 1906), p. 5.

69. General Court, 11 November 1647, *Mass. Records,* v. 2, pp. 211–212.

70. In a deed in the *Lechford Note-book,* Faber is referred to as a cooper of London. Signaling his permanent departure, he sold his house and garden in Boston to Christopher Stanley in 1639 (Lechford, p. 147).

71. Will of Edward Bullock, 25 July 1649, *Suffolk County Wills: Abstracts of the Earliest Wills upon Record in the County of Suffolk, Massachusetts* (Baltimore: Genealogical Publishing Company, Inc., 1984), pp. 82–83.

72. John Cotton to Richard Saltonstall, esq., n.d., Cotton Papers, MHS. See also *New England's First Fruits* (London, 1643), p. 26.

73. William Aspinwall, *A Volume Relating to the early history of Boston, containing the Aspinwall notarial records from 1644–1651* (Boston: Municipal Printing Office, 1903), pp. 70–71.

74. Will of Nathaniel Braddock, Pile 55, PRO.

75. *Mass. Records,* v. 3, p. 52.

76. *Cambridge Church Records,* p. 5.

77. Will of George Burdin, dated 15 October 1652, *Suffolk Wills,* pp. 129–130. See also the arrangements of the Virginia planter William Smart for his several

stepchildren, 2 May 1660, Northampton Deeds and Wills, 1657–1666, p. 82, VSL.

78. T. K. Rabb, *Enterprise and Empire: Merchant and Gentry Investment in the Expansion of England, 1575–1630* (Cambridge, Mass.: Harvard University Press, 1967), p. 393.

79. Will of William Vassall, Barbados, 31 July 1655, *NEHGR* 51 (1897), p. 286.

80. Richard S. Dunn, *Puritans and Yankees: The Winthrop Dynasty of New England 1630–1717* (New York: Norton, 1971), pp. 50–51, 125; Bernard Bailyn, *The New England Merchants in the Seventeenth Century* (New York: Harper and Row, 1964), p. 88.

81. Will of Bassell Terry, 14 March 1649/50, RB 6/11, p. 438, Barb. Arch.

82. Will of Peter Bulkeley, 1658, *NEHGR* 10 (1856): 167–170. See also the will of John Bulkeley, 11 October 1689, *NEHGR* 45 (1891): 293.

83. "The Voyage of Sir Henrye Colt to ye Ilands of ye Antilles," in Vincent T. Harlow, ed., *Colonising Expeditions to the West Indies and Guiana, 1623–1667* (London: Hakluyt Society, 1925), pp. 71, 79.

84. Association, located off the coast of Hispaniola, was besieged twice by the Spanish, and conditions there were so uncertain that when the Company sent the *Expectation* out in 1635, the master of the ship, Cornelius Billings, was instructed to sail first to Association and to find out whether it were even still under English control. Instructions from the Company of Providence Island to Cornelius Billings, 20 April 1635, CO 124/1, f. 81, PRO. Providence was attacked in 1635, 1640, and 1641. In the final attack, the Spanish finally conquered the island. See *A Letter Written Upon Occasion from the Low-countries . . . whereunto is added, Aviso's from severell places, of the taking of the Island of Providence, by the Spaniard, from the English* (London, 22 March 1641/2), for an account of the attack.

85. 13–14 April 1639, Butler's Diary, Sloane 758, BL.

86. Colt, "Voyage," in Harlow, ed., *Colonising*, p. 94.

87. Joan de Rivera, "Shipwrecked Spaniards 1639: Grievances Against Bermudians," trans. L. D. Gurrin, *BHQ* 18 (1961): 16.

88. Winthrop, *Journal*, 21 May 1635, 3 June 1635, p. 147.

89. Winthrop, *Journal*, p. 327. The depositions survive in Kenneth Scott and Kenn Stryker-Rodda, eds., *New York Historical Manuscripts: Dutch* (trans. and annotated by Arnold J. F. Van Laer), v. 4, Council Minutes, 1638–1649 (Baltimore: Genealogical Publishing Company, 1974), pp. 77–85. My thanks to Jim Williams for calling my attention to the interrogation.

90. Inventory of Richard Norwood's estate, 1676, in *The Journal of Richard Norwood*, p. 143. Governor Nathaniel Butler remarked on one Native American woman from Virginia who lived on Bermuda by 1621, when she was married to "as fitt and agreeable an husband as the place would afford." A huge wedding feast was held, with a reported one hundred people in attendance. Butler's attention to her presence and this event suggests the small size of the Native American population on the island at this early date (Nathaniel Butler, *The Historye of the Bermudaes or Summer Islands*, ed. J. Henry Lefroy [London, 1882], p. 284). Other Bermuda estates were similarly varied. In Hugh Went-

worth's household as early as 1641, four English servants labored alongside two black slaves. Thomas Burrows owned four people identified as "negros" and two "malatos." Inventory of Hugh Wentworth [1641] in Lefroy, *Memorials*, v. 1, pp. 567–569. See the wills of Thomas Burrowes, 12 March 1658/9, and also Josias Forster, proved 17 November 1666, Bermuda Wills, Book 1, reel 272, pp. 51, 107, Berm. Arch.; Forster to the Company, 20 December 1650, Lefroy, *Memorials*, v. 2, p. 19.

91. On slavery in Providence, see Alison Games, "'The Sanctuarye of our Rebell Negroes': The Atlantic Context of Local Resistance on Providence Island," *Slavery and Abolition* 19 (December 1998): 1–21. By 1639 a Spaniard ship-wrecked on Bermuda observed the presence of "a few negroes" there, whom he believed to have been from other wrecked ships or sold by Dutch traders (de Rivera, "Shipwrecked Spaniards": 26).

92. 3 July 1638, CO 124/1, f. 124, PRO. The Company instructed Captain Can-nock as early as 1633 to buy slaves from "any dutch shipp"; slaves could also be seized as prize from passing Spanish ships. Captain Cannock's commission, 1 July 1633, CO 124/1, f. 58verso; CO 124/2, p. 265, PRO; Karen Ordahl Kupperman, *Providence Island, 1630–1641: The Other Puritan Colony* (Cambridge: Cambridge University Press, 1993), p. 172.

93. No other colony shared Providence's and Association's difficulties in this period. Incidents of alleged slave conspiracies can be found on Bermuda, but not until the 1650s. See Council, 2 November 1656; Council, 2 November 1656, Le-froy, *Memorials*, v. 2, pp. 94–95; Proclamation by the governor, 6 November 1656, Lefroy, *Memorials*, v. 2, pp. 95–97; and Proclamation by the governor, 26 July 1664, Lefroy, *Memorials*, v. 2, pp. 216–217. See also Virginia Bernhard, "Bids for Freedom: Slave Resistance and Rebellion Plots in Bermuda, 1658–1761," *Slavery and Abolition* 17 (1996): 185–186.

94. There was a rebellion on Providence on May Day of 1638. The residents of the island should not have been observing May Day, according to the restrictions demanded by puritan worship. May Day in 1638 fell on a Tuesday, so if the island residents were somehow distracted on this traditional holiday, the island-ers' noncompliance with their investors' expectations is clear. There was another alleged conspiracy in 1640, after which the English executed fifty slaves (Kup-perman, *Providence Island*, p. 172). By 1638 a maroon population was evident in the island's interior. Raids on this population proved almost wholly ineffec-tive. See Butler's Diary, entries for 27 and 30 March 1639, Sloane 758, BL.

95. Instructions to Governor Bell, 10 May 1632, CO 124/1, f. 33recto; letter to Governor Bell, 20 April 1635, CO 124/1, f. 77verso, PRO.

96. On plans to send the Pequots to Bermuda, see *Winthrop Papers*, v. 3, pp. 450, 457. The Pequots would perhaps have been better served in Bermuda, accord-ing to a letter from the Bermuda minister Patrick Copland, who informed the Massachusetts Governor John Winthrop that he "wold have had a care of them, to have disposed them to such honest men as should have trained them up in the principles of religion; and so when they had been fit for your plantation, have returned them againe, to have done God some service, in being instruments to doe some good upon their countrymen" (5 *MHS Coll.*, 1, p. 277). John Win-

throp noted that Captain Pierce had missed Bermuda in his *Journal*, July 1637 (Winthrop, *Journal*, p. 227). Another ship that missed Bermuda ended up at Hispaniola (Winthrop, *Journal*, p. 222).

97. Letter to the Governor and Council, 3 July 1638, CO 124/1, f. 124verso, PRO. A. P. Newton, *The Colonising Activities of the English Puritans* (New Haven: Yale University Press, 1914) concluded that this was a reference to Africans transported from the West Indies to New England and then brought back because they were uncontrollable (p. 261). Karen Kupperman believes that the "cannibal Negros" to have been Pequots (*Providence Island*, p. 178). The same terminology was found in Portuguese references to indigenous laborers in Brazil.

98. John Nicholl, *An Houre Glasse of Indian Newes* (London, 1607), passim.

99. "John Dane's Narrative," *NEHGR* 8 (1854), p. 154.

100. For two other intimate interactions, see the Petition to the General Court of Jeremiah Belcher, 6 November 1658, Photostats, Mass. Archives, box 3a; the Petition to the General Court of Peter Plaise of Boston, March 28, 1666, Photostats, Mass. Archives, Box 5, MHS.

101. "Leift Lion Gardener His Relation of the Pequot Warres," 3 *MHS Coll.*, 3 (1833), pp. 152–153.

102. 26 January 1639/40, Butler's Diary, Sloane 758, BL.

103. The term "hybrid" is Nicholas Canny's: he uses it to describe the failed efforts of settlers to replicate Scotland in Ulster. Nicholas Canny, "The Origins of Empire," introduction to Canny, ed., *The Origins of Empire* (Oxford: Oxford University Press, 1998), p. 14. See also William Vaughan, *The Golden Fleece* (London, 1626), part three, pp. 19–20, for a discussion of the Welsh and English settlements on Newfoundland.

104. Inventory of John Baddum, taken 7 February 1660/1, in Northampton Wills and Deeds, 1657–1666, p. 113, VSL. James Horn has done detailed research comparing the material culture of Virginians with their counterparts in the counties of Gloucester and Kent. See James Horn, *Adapting to a New World: English Society in the Seventeenth-Century Chesapeake* (Chapel Hill: University of North Carolina Press, 1994), chapter 7.

105. Samuel Purchas, *Hakluytus Posthumus, Or Purchas His Pilgrimes* (London, 1625), book 10, conclusion of whole work, p. 1970. Purchas wrote that he never strayed more than two hundred miles from his home in Norfolk.

106. David Hancock notes his debt to those works depicting the Atlantic as a bridge: see *Citizens of the World: London Merchants and the Integration of the British Atlantic Community, 1735–1785* (Cambridge: Cambridge University Press, 1995), pp. 8–9.

107. William Crashaw, *A Sermon Preached in London before the right honorable the Lord Lawarre . . . and others of his Majesties Counsell for the Kingdome, and the rest of the Adventurers in that Plantation* (London, 1610), E1verso.

108. R. M., *Newes of Sir Walter Rauleigh* (London, 1618), p. 45. A second reference to the colonies as the "skirts of America" occurs in William Castell, *A Petition of W.C. Exhibited by the high Court of Parliament now assembled, for the propagating of the Gospel in America, and the West Indies* (London, 1641), p. 10.

109. John Brinsley, *A Consolation for Our Grammar Schooles* (London, 1622), title page, dedication, pp. 14–15.

Appendix A

1. See especially the 273 passengers from Great Yarmouth and Sandwich in 1637 described by T. H. Breen and Stephen Foster in "Moving to the New World: The Character of Early Massachusetts Immigration," *WMQ* 30 (1973): 189–222; 110 travelers from Wiltshire between 1635–1638 profiled in Anthony Salerno, "The Social Background of Seventeenth-Century Emigration to America," *Journal of British Studies* 19 (1979): 31–52; and 693 passengers from Sandwich, Weymouth, Southampton, and Great Yarmouth in 1635, 1637, and 1638 in Virginia DeJohn Anderson, *New England's Generation: The Great Migration and the Formation of Society and Culture in the Seventeenth Century* (New York: Cambridge University Press, 1991) for examples of studies based on stronger port registers.

Archival Sources

In the United States

American Antiquarian Society, Worcester, Massachusetts
Bulkeley Family Notes, 1550–1800.
Shepard Family Papers, 1636–1681.

The Folger Shakespeare Library, Washington, D.C.
Booth Letters, 1628–1647.

The Huntington Library, San Marino, California
Brock Collection.
Ellesmere Collection.
James Hay, Earl of Carlisle, Papers relating to land granted Merchant Adventures (1628–1630).

Massachusetts Historical Society, Boston, Massachusetts
Adams, William. An Account of his Experiences. Transcribed from his own hand-writing, 1659.
Cotton Papers.
F. L. Gay Transcripts.
Keayne, Robert. Sermon Notes, 1627–1628; 1643–1646.
Massachusetts Archives, 1600–. Photostats.
Miscellaneous Bound documents. 1501–1700.
Oxenbridge, John. The Conversion of the Gentiles. c. 1670.
Winthrop Papers.

The New Haven Colony Historical Society, New Haven, Connecticut
Milford Church Records, copy.

Virginia Historical Society, Richmond, Virginia
Charles City County Records, 1642–1842. Charles City County Order Book, 1641/2.
Land patent of Christopher Boyce. Tayloe Family Papers, Section Three.

Virginia State Library and Archives, Richmond, Virginia
Charles City County Records, microfilm, reel 13. Two pages of Charles City County orders, 10 January 1650/1.

Henrico County Miscellaneous Court Records, 1650–1807. Reel 1.

Isle of Wight County Deeds, Wills, Guardians Accounts Book A, 1636–1662, microfilm 1.

Lancaster Deeds, etc., 1654–1702, part 1.

Lancaster Deeds, etc., 1652–1657.

Norfolk Minute Book, 1637–1646.

Norfolk Wills and Deeds B, 1646–1651.

Norfolk Wills and Deeds, 1651–1656.

Norfolk County Wills and Deeds D, 1656–1666.

Northampton Deeds, Wills, etc., No. 3 1645–1651.

Northampton Wills and Deeds, No. 4, 1651–1654.

Northampton Deeds and Wills, No. 5, 1654–1655.

Northampton Orders, 1655–1656.

Northampton Deeds and Wills, etc., 1657–1666.

Northampton Orders, Deeds, and Wills, No. 7, 1656–1657. Bound with No. 8.

Northampton Deeds and Wills, No. 8, 1666–1668. Bound with No. 7.

Northampton Order Book, 1657–1664.

Northumberland Deeds and Orders, 1650–1652.

Northumberland Order Book, 1652–1665.

Northumberland Record Book, 1652–1658.

The Virginia Colonial Records Project, indexes and microfilm.

Warwick County Orders, Fragments, 1646–1650.

Westmoreland Deeds and Wills, No. 1, 1653–1671.

Westmoreland Deeds, Wills, Patents, etc., 1653–1659.

York Deeds, Orders, Wills, 1633–1657; 1691–1694.

York Wills and Deeds, No. 2, 1645–1649.

York County Deeds, Orders, Wills, etc., No.3, 1657–1662.

York County Deeds, Orders, Wills, etc., No. 4, 1665–1672.

In Barbados

Barbados Archives, Lazaretto, St. Michael, Barbados

RB 3/1–3, 5–8, 11–12: deeds.

RB 3/48, 49: deed indexes.

RB 4/2, 6: original will books.

RB 6/1, 2, 8–15, 30, 41, 42: wills.

RL 1/68: indexes.

Christ Church Burial Register, RL 1/21, film.

St. John's Burial Register, RL 1/29, film.

St Michael's Parish Register, RC 1/1, film.

In Bermuda

Bermuda Archives, Hamilton, Bermuda

Bermuda Colonial Records. 13 pieces, 1615–1680.

Bermuda Wills. 13 volumes, 1648–1798.

Christ Church Records, 1668–1798, Devonshire Parish. Reel 45.
St. Anne's Church Records, Southampton 1619–1751. Reel 19.
St. John's Church Records, 1645–1722, Pembroke Parish. Reel 25.

In the United Kingdom

Bodleian Library, Oxford University, Oxford
Clarendon 102. The Case of the Bermudas, 1661.
Firth Manuscripts.
Rawlinson Manuscripts.

British Library, Manuscript Room, London
Add. 63,854. Letterbook of William Jessop, 1634–41. Transcript of Add. 10,615.
Egerton 2395. Papers Relating to English Colonies in America and the West Indies, 1627–1799.
Egerton 2643–2651. Barrington Manuscripts.
Harley 1238. Papers relating to the tobacco trade.
Sloane 758. Capt. N. Boteler Discourse Concerning Marine Affairs. His Journal on Providence.
Sloane 3662. Tracts on the East and West Indies.
Stowe 184. Historical Papers, Vol. I, 1628–1651.

Greater London Record Office, London
P92/SAV/512–554, 556–590. St. Saviour's Southwark, Vestry minutes.
P93/DUN/327. St. Dunstans, Southwark, vestry meeting minute book.
R563, R 578. Token books, St. Saviours, Southwark.

Mercers' Company Archives, Mercers' Hall, London
Colet Estate, Sherington Court Roll, 14 July 1635, Colet Box 5, roll 17.
   Box 29 Sherington Account Book.
Index to Company members 1619–1720.
Mercers' Company, Court Records 1619–1625, 1625–1631, 1631–1637.

Public Record Office
CO 1/ . 1574–. Colonial Office Records.
CO 30/1. Barbados Acts, 1649–1682.
CO 124/1, 2. Records of the Providence Island Company.
CO 278/2, 3. Records of Guyana, 1667–1674, microfilm.
E 157/20 1-e. London Port Register, 1634/5–1635.
E 179/ . Lay subsidies and ship money arrears.
E 190/41/4, 5; E 190/38/1. London Port books.
HCA 13/50, 52, 53, 54. Depositions given before the High Court of Admiralty, 1634–1638.
HCA 30/546, 1632–1639.
HCA 30/635. Book of Accompte for the Shippe called ye *Tristram and Jeane* of London wch came from Virginia 1637.
HCA 30/636. Records for the *Abraham*, 1637.
SP 16/298, 453. State Papers, Domestic, Charles I.

Minutes of the Council of Barbados, February 1654–December 1658. Two volumes. Typescript.

Miscellaneous Wills of the Prerogative Court of Canterbury (volumes titled Lee, Alchin, Berkeley, Essex, Laud, Coventry, Grey, Pile, Bowyer, Evelyn, Bunce, Goare, Foot, Exton, Pembroke).

Royal Commonwealth Society, London

N. Darnell Davis Papers. 15 boxes of papers relating to the West Indies.

Buckinghamshire Record Office, Aylesbury, Buckinghamshire

D/A/T/144/3; D/A/T/145. Olney Parish Register, Bishop's Transcripts.

D/A/T/157. Sherington Parish Register, Bishop's Transcripts.

D/A/V/2, 3. Archdeaconry of Buckingham, Visitation Book, 1633–34; 1635.

D/A/We, Wf. Wills.

D/X/398. Subsidy rolls.

PR 126/1/1. Lavendon Parish Register.

Essex Record Office, Chelmsford, Essex

D/ABA/5–7. Bishop of London Commissary Act Books.

D/ABV/1. Bishop of London Commissary Court, Visitations, 1633–1639.

D/ACA 50. Archdeaconry of Colchester Acts, 1634–1635.

D/ACV 5. Archdeaconry of Colchester Visitations, 1633.

D/ACW/ . Wills.

D/ALV 2. Bishop of London Consistory Court Visitations, 1634.

D/AEA 38–40. Archdeaconry of Essex Act Books.

D/DHt T531. Deed.

D/DMB M66–67. Great Bentley Manor, court rolls, 1617–1648.

D/DBM M257. Tendring Court books, 1627–1634.

D/DP M1203, M1204; M1210/1, 2. Bacon's Manor (Denge) court rolls, 1616–1648, 1664–1705.

DP 353. Tendring Parish Register.

Q/SR 274/12. Quarter Sessions, Typescript Calendar.

Q/SR 284–290. Essex Quarter Sessions, rolls.

T/A 400/1–5. Tillingham Manorial Records.

T/R 229/2. Denge Parish Register, transcript.

D/P 65/1/1. Great Baddow Parish Register.

Great Bentley Parish Register, transcript.

Great Bromley Parish Register, transcript.

Nazeing Parish Register, transcript.

Essex Record Office, Colchester, Essex

D/DHw T4. List of tenants (Tendring), 1629.

D/DU 40/2, 3, 4, 5, 12. Bromley Magna Court Rolls, 1610–1635.

D/DU 680/17. Manor of Shawes, Court Roll, 1613–1622.

D/DTs M27. Boxted Court Rolls, 1631–1647.

D/P 1171/8/1. Great Bentley Vestry Book.

Hertfordshire Record Office, Hertford, Hertfordshire
55AW36. Will of Walter Antrobus.
A25/2962. Account of estate of Thomas Lawrence.
ASA 22/1. Marriage Bonds and Allegations, 1611–1617.
ASA 7/29–30. Archdeaconry of St. Albans Act book, 1627/8–1633; 1633–1638.
Film 302. Great Amwell Parish Register.
Film 326. Ware Parish Records.
Film 650. Berkhamsted Parish Register.
Parish Records of St. Albans Abbey.

Kent Archives Office, Maidstone, Kent
P26/5/1. Biddenden Churchwarden's Accounts, 1594–1778.
TR 2203. Cranbrook Parish Register, transcript.
TR 1809/1. Biddenden Parish Register, transcript.
U1334T1. Biddenden deeds, 1626–1745.

St. Albans Public Library, St. Albans, Hertfordshire
Book of Enrollment #286.
Draft Minutes of the Borough Court, #289, 295, 296, 298.
Mayors Accounts, #157–165.
Mayors Court Book, 1586–1633.

Suffolk Record Office, Bury St. Edmunds, Suffolk
1531/7/1, 2. Lavenham assessment, 1635.
806/1/101. Lavenham terrier, 1633.
E 6/20/1, 4, 5. Lavenham Rectory Manor court rolls.
EE 501/2/3, 4, 5. Sudbury Borough Records.
HA 505/1/22. Lavenham Manor court rolls.
J 552/14. All Saints, Sudbury Parish Records.
J 562/59. Transcript of Lavenham Parish Records, marriages.
St. Mary's, Bury St. Edmunds, parish records.

Scottish Record Office, Edinburgh
GD 34/920–955. Hay of Haystoun Papers.

Index